# AIR CRASHES
## and
# MIRACLE LANDINGS

## 60 Narratives

**AIR CRASHES**
and
**MIRACLE LANDINGS**
Sixty Narratives

(How, When ... And Most Importantly Why)


by

**Christopher Bartlett**

**ISBN 978-0-9560723-2-0**

First Published April 12, 2010
Reprinted with Revisions and Updates September, 2012
by
OpenHatch Books, London, UK
***openhatchbooks.com***
***chrisbart.com***

Front cover photo
by
Florian Trojer (jetvisuals.com)
depicting a routine & safe flight departure
from Innsbruck Airport, Austria,
in accordance with published procedures

For
all those who died
and
all those who survived.

Lessons
were learnt
for the benefit
of us all.

## The Author

**Christopher Bartlett** initially trained as a mining engineer, a field where ensuring compliance with safety standards is of prime importance. His passion, however, has been flying, and notably air safety.

This was engendered as an Air Cadet during his youth and as a member of the British Interplanetary Society, as well as in the course of sessions on fighter simulators at the Air Ministry. He completed his two years' military service in the British Royal Air Force.

After taking a degree in Modern Chinese and Japanese at the School of Oriental and African Studies, London University, he became, amongst other things, a professional translator of Japanese scientific and technical material. This included Japanese rocket tests. He also wrote for magazines in the Far East.

His fluency and understanding of English, French, and Japanese enabled him to undertake research based on material published in its original format and note opinions and facts that were not widely publicized. In addition, his coincidental residence in countries when and where headline air crashes occurred has enabled him to add local color and extra details to a number of these accounts.

# CONTENTS

# Figures

Illustrations and diagrams are only included where needed for explanation.

To view images in color and detail, see

*DIAGRAMS & PHOTOS FOR KINDLE*
*READERS + LINKS FOR ALL READERS*
*on our website chrisbart.com*

# PREFACE

While covering the technical aspects of the various incidents described, and sometimes reading like a detective story, the book highlights the human factors, which relate not only to aviation but also to many other facets of our daily lives. Readers should find reassurance in the fact that many of the incidents occurred a long time ago and provided the lessons that have made flying so much safer today.

The intention was to explain not only how and why those accidents occurred, but also to increase the reader's interest in the underlying causes of accidents in general. While the book at times suggests possible causes not emphasized or cited in the official reports, hopefully sufficient facts have been included for the reader to draw his or her own conclusions, which of course may differ from those of the author.

In the haste to publish after some five years' research, and with the book continuously evolving (improving) after the initial proofreading, there were unfortunately grammatical and typographical errors in the first edition. We have therefore thoroughly proofread this updated version after adding inter alia an account of the Colgan Air disaster and the latest information regarding the loss of Air France AF447 with its many lessons for today's pilots lulled by automation. We have also revised some tongue-in-cheek remarks as well as comments suggesting some 'heroes' benefited from circumstances, which regrettably some readers misinterpreted to the extent of taking offense.

As it was not possible to consult all the individuals and organizations cited, the book may have unwittingly portrayed a few unfairly. That said, mention of a given airline, organization or individual may simply reflect their integrity and transparency.

Christopher Bartlett

# ACKNOWLEDGEMENTS

Many official reports, excellent articles, and books—not to mention films of varying accuracy—have contributed to this book's realization. Twenty thousand or more items available on the Internet provided background knowledge. In addition, I am sometimes citing from memory a detail or point made in now irretrievable coverage in the local media in the countries where the incidents occurred and I happened to be at the time.

Though it may seem ghoulish, reviewing Cockpit Voice Recorder (CVR) transcriptions included in official reports often seemed to give a real feel to what was happening in the cockpit, and a good idea of the cascading dilemmas facing the pilots.

I wasted much time, without coming to definitive conclusions, in some cases where official reports were contested as conspiratorial, as can happen when all parties—airline, manufacturer and investigating authority, and even victims—are from the same country. Once someone claims officials have tampered with evidence, have shredded it, and are lying to boot, there is no definitive answer. From a safety point of view, this may not matter overly as the conspirators, if any, know the truth, and stealthily, but eventually, take remedial measures.

In preparing the material, I was fortunate to come across *Air Disaster*[1] by the Australian, Macarthur Job, reviewing in several volumes the most notable jet-age airliner disasters up to 1994. Job succeeds in putting them in perspective with a wealth of technical and human detail. Those captivating volumes would be a good starting point for anyone wishing to read about a number of the pre-1995 accidents in much more detail than is possible here.

Similarly, *Disasters in The Air—The Truth about Mysterious Air Disasters*[2] by Jan Bartelski was of great value in making me look again at the assumptions that had generally been made regarding some notorious disasters, and notably the worst ever multi-aircraft disaster in which two 747 jumbos collided on the ground in fog at Tenerife in 1977.

Some of the episodes of the excellent TV series entitled *Air Crash Investigation*—also called '*MAYDAY*' in some countries—broadcast on the National Geographic Channel, yielded some useful new insights when the author was half-way through this book. Besides bringing events to life much as he has tried to do here, the very successful series has aroused the interest of many. The producers obviously devoted considerable effort, and not least money, to interviewing passengers in addition to aircrew, investigators, and experts.

At the other end of the spectrum, in that it is a textbook stuffed with concentrated information regarding all aspects of aviation safety, was

*Commercial Aviation Safety*[3] by Alexander T. Wells. Its depth of detail is such that it even mentions how cockpit noise affects pilots, and in so doing helps put other safety aspects in perspective.

*A Human Error Approach to Aviation Accident Analysis*[4] by Douglas A. Wiegmann and Scott A. Shappell was a valuable introduction to the academic work being done on accidents. Although purchased too late to be much help, I should mention *Aviation Disasters*[5] by David Gero, covering major civil airliner crashes since 1950. Much less discursive and opinionated than this book, it is a good tool for specialists wanting the cold bare facts concerning virtually every disaster.

There are a number of blogs covering commercial flying. They include *Patrick Smith's aviation blog* on salon.com; Just *about flying ...* formerly called *Ask Captain Lim* on askcaptainlim.com; and *Professional Pilots Network* on pprune.org. Besides providing much essential material, the official reports by air accident investigative bodies, such as the NTSB, AAIB, ATSB, BFU, and BEA, often made fascinating reading.

On a personal level, I would particularly like to pay tribute to the late John Hawkins for encouraging me in the early stages. His experience both as a metallurgist, and as Managing Director and Chairman of numerous companies in the *British Alcan Group*—developing high temperature alloys for aircraft including the supersonic Concorde—meant he was able to advise me about the evolution of these materials. He also informed me about some aviation incidents, which although in the public domain, did not make the headlines.

Others kindly read the manuscript and gave valuable advice. They include Keith Lakin, Adrian Wojcieh, James Denny, Mike Pegler, Gerald Burke, Jonathan Evans, Hélène Bartlett, Go Sugimoto, and the talented members of the *Three Pigeons* discussion group.

Finally, I would like to thank Ting Baker for rectifying proofreading mistakes in the first edition and in the updates.

---

[1] Air *Disaster (Vols. 1–4)*, Macarthur Job, Aerospace Publications Pty Ltd. (Feb 1995, June 1996, Oct 1998, and Sept 2001).

[2] *Disasters in The Air—The Truth about Mysterious Air Disasters*, Jan Bartelski, The Crowood Press Ltd. (15 Mar 2001).

[3] *Commercial Aviation Safety (4th Edition)*, Alexander T. Wells, McGraw Hill (Jan 2004).

[4] *A Human Error Approach to Aviation Accident Analysis*, Douglas A. Wiegmann and Scott A. Shappell, Ashgate Publishing Ltd., England (September 2003)

[5] *Aviation Disasters: The World's Major Civil Airliner Crashes since 1950*, David Gero (4th Edition).

# INTRODUCTION

Each of the fifteen narrative chapters covers a specific type of incident in chronological order. While indicating the evolution over time, this means the accounts of most significance and interest may well be nested within the chapter rather than found at the beginning.

Chapters 1–13 cover *regular accidents* (with regular having the sense it has in 'regular' coffee in US usage). By that, we mean accidents not due to military action, hijacks, or on-board explosives. This should not be confused with the specialist academic term *normal accident* used by Professor Charles B. Perrow, the well-known author of *Normal Accidents: Living with High Risk Technologies* (1984, rev. ed. 1999, Princeton), implying accidents are inherent in complex systems such as nuclear power stations (i.e. Chernobyl).

Chapter 14 covers accidents resulting from military decisions, while Chapter 15 looks at two cases where terrorists hijacked an aircraft in Algeria and four in the US with the intention of using them as flying bombs.

Chapter 16, the last chapter, is somewhat academic, drawing conclusions from the narratives and looking at future strategies for improving safety in aviation, such as ADS-B, the new air traffic control system based on GPS rather than fixed airways between radio beacons.

## Chapter 1: Loss of Power Over Water

Not so long ago, airliners flying long distances over water always had three, if not four, engines. Nowadays, the authorities allow airlines with good records to fly twin-engine aircraft on routes where the nearest diversion airfield can be as much as two or more hours' flying-time away.

Such flights are called ETOPS, standing for **E**xtended range **T**win-engine **OP**eration**S**. Airlines prefer ETOPS as they usually save money—two large engines being cheaper to buy and maintain than four smaller ones. ETOPS have become possible because well-maintained jet engines are today very powerful and, above all, reliable. Airbus had thought they had come up with a winner in the form of the four-engine A340 long-distance airliner only to see sales wither with the arrival of the cheaper-to-run Boeing 777 twinjet just when ETOPS had gained full acceptance.

Should an engine on one of the newer twin-engine airliners fail on takeoff, the pilots may well be better off, as regards reserve power and even handling, than if two engines failed on the same side on an older four-engine aircraft. However, if the fuel runs out, even the most reliable engine becomes a heap of useless metal.

The Hudson River 'miracle' ditching shown on the back cover of the printed version of this book has been included in this chapter because it shows that bringing a modern jet airliner safely down on water is feasible, given suitable conditions.

Also included is the remarkable feat whereby the pilot of an Airbus managed to glide a distance of some 80 miles and touch down safely on an island in the Azores after running out of fuel over the Atlantic.

## Chapter 2: Loss of Power Over Land

An airliner with its high landing speed and great mass almost invariably has to reach an airport or landing strip to effect a safe landing. Unlike loss of power over water where the aircraft is often at a very great height giving the pilots time to consider their options, loss of power over land may occur at any height but often near the ground where the pilots' options are very limited.

## Chapter 3: Runway Overruns

An aircraft can overrun the runway either on landing or on taking off. Normally there is a fair amount of clear ground beyond, so in most cases the consequences are not disastrous.

However, it may be another story if for some reason the aircraft veers off to the side and into an unforgiving building or is going so fast that it ends up even beyond the airport boundary. An overrun on landing may result from a combination of coming in too fast, touching down too far down the runway, on one that is too short, or on one contaminated by ice or standing water.

As many other types of accident decrease, landing overruns in bad weather are becoming one of the greatest dangers. Recent fatal accidents in Brazil and Thailand, and a close shave at Toronto for an Air France A340 demonstrate this.

In theory, an overrun on takeoff will only occur if the captain decides to abort the takeoff before the aircraft reaches the takeoff decision speed, $V_1$. After that, the aircraft should be able to take off safely even should an engine fail. Company regulations stipulate that once the aircraft attains takeoff decision speed ($V_1$) with no decision to abort, the takeoff must proceed—precisely to avoid the possibility of an overrun.

## Chapter 4: Mid-air Collisions & TCAS

A collision in the air between two aircraft is relatively rare, but is often fatal, as the industry slang 'aluminum shower' implies.

The situation regarding the air traffic controllers largely responsible for preventing those collisions is a difficult one.

On the one hand, they do not enjoy the prestige or sometimes very high salaries (plus little extras on the side) of the pilots; on the other hand, their task is very technical and demanding. One thing the pilots and controllers have in common is the ability to bring flight operations to an expensive halt by going on strike.

In some countries, the air traffic controllers have relentlessly wielded that power to the exasperation of authorities and travelers alike.

In 1981, US President Reagan took a stand by firing 11,000 controllers who had failed to return to work. Some 3,000 supervisors joined 2,000 nonstriking controllers and 900 military controllers in staffing airport towers. Before long, about 80 percent of flights were operating normally and airfreight remained virtually unaffected. In the end, the controllers were obliged to re-enroll on new terms.

In France where ATC strikes were endemic, the Government once tried to face them down but was less successful. Their attempt to use military controllers to keep the system going during a strike was short-lived as it was not long before two aircraft under military air traffic control collided near Nantes on France's Atlantic coast, forcing the Government to bring the civilian controllers back to work, with them saying, 'We said you could not manage without us!'

The chapter concludes with one of the saddest disasters ever, when an aircraft full of children collided with a cargo plane late at night between Switzerland and Germany. One of the fathers, who had lost his wife as well as his two children, subsequently stabbed the air traffic controller he thought responsible for their deaths.

## Chapter 5: Ground Collisions

Ground collisions can be very dangerous, and especially so on taking off when the (two) aircraft are likely to be heavily laden with fuel and moving fast. Indeed the worst-ever multi-aircraft disaster on Tenerife described in this chapter is a case in point.

An airliner fuselage is so thin—just about that of a credit card—that a fierce fuel-fed external fire may penetrate it in 90 seconds. That is therefore the time allotted in most regulations for evacuation.

Newly developed technologies, and even very simple ones, are reducing the risk of ground collisions, but they continue to represent a very significant risk.

The chapter includes a case where an aircraft operated by one of the best airlines mistakenly took off on an out-of-use runway and collided with construction equipment parked halfway down.

## Chapter 6: No Controllability

Only on rare occasions are pilots unable to control the aircraft because the control systems cease working for some cataclysmic reason. This is different from 'loss of control' where the controls are working but where say the aircraft stalls due to flying too slowly or with the wrong flap setting.

Since aircraft manufacturers design essential controls and control lines on the belt and braces principle with each one in duplicate if not triplicate, something major has to happen for them all to fail. Nevertheless, there are several examples in this chapter, ranging from incidents involving the DC-10 to the worst-ever single aircraft disaster where the failure of the rear bulkhead of a Japanese Boeing 747 blew off part of the tail, with the aircraft flying around drunkenly for thirty minutes before crashing into mountains.

The fear that an aircraft will become uncontrollable on being struck by a shoulder-launched surface-to-air missile fired by terrorists, has led the US authorities to carry out studies to see whether it would be possible to train pilots to fly the aircraft using engine power alone—something the DHL pilots of an Airbus cargo plane succeeded in doing at Baghdad.

## Chapter 7: Fire & Smoke

Fire evokes a very powerful primal fear, and pilots have good technical reasons to be extremely concerned at any sign of its outbreak. In the early days of flying, the engines ran on gasoline (petrol), which was much more inflammable than the kerosene (paraffin) used for jet engines today.

With hindsight, in many cases, such as the Swissair flight described here, making the earliest possible landing regardless of other considerations would have been the best option in the case of a suspected fire.

Yet, if aircrew shut down an engine on the mistaken assumption it is on fire, and the remaining engine(s) cannot keep the aircraft in the air, the outcome is almost certain to be disastrous. One such instance of hasty action is the British Midlands Boeing 737 crash at Kegworth in England, cited in virtually every commercial pilot's training as a classic example of what *not* to do.

The chapter concludes with the disaster that befell the most beautiful airliner ever—the supersonic Concorde.

## Chapter 8: Pilot Sick, Suicidal, or Inappropriate Response

With the airlines and the strict regulatory authorities ensuring aircrew undergo regular (often six monthly) health checks, pilots must feel their careers hang by a thread.

Though it is reassuring to know that with the more sophisticated tests we have nowadays, the likelihood of a pilot having a heart attack while flying is exceedingly small, it has happened as the account that begins this chapter shows. There is nevertheless the danger that pilots can suddenly fall ill, and airlines insist they eat different menus to avoid their risking simultaneous food poisoning.

There have been cases where pilots have inappropriately responded to a disengagement of the autopilot and in 'fighting to save the aircraft' have made it crash. The recent Colgan Air crash in the US is an example narrated here.

## Chapter 9: 'Fly-by-Wire'

*'If the idiots (i.e. the pilots) had kept their hands off the controls, it wouldn't have crashed,'* an Airbus executive reputedly said on learning about the crash of one of their fly-by-wire airliners.

The term *fly-by-wire* is confusing. Traditionally it meant replacing the direct mechanical or mechanical-hydraulic links between the cockpit controls and the movable flight control surfaces with indirect links actuated electrically and electronically.

Now the term also means computers, as opposed to the pilots, fly the aircraft—of course with the pilots telling them what they want to do.

Where Boeing and Airbus once greatly differed was to what extent the computer should be the final arbiter.

Airbus's computer would not let the pilots do things outside the flight envelope; whereas, Boeing's computer on the other hand tended to give the pilot more leeway. Boeing's argument was partly that in programming the computer to allow only what is definitely acceptable, one must exclude a gray area where a pilot might just get away with it—and save the aircraft.

While this chapter cites several early accidents involving the A320, the aircraft has become one of the most successful ever.

It also covers in detail the loss in 2009 of an Air France Airbus A330 en route from Rio de Janeiro to Paris, where it now seems an inappropriate response by the pilots rather than the fly-by-wire system was largely responsible. It is one the most important narratives in the book in that it demonstrates how automation has been so perfected with pilots 'outside the loop', that their ability to fly the aircraft using their cognitive and analytical skills has atrophied.

## Chapter 10: Metal Fatigue & Structural Failure

In the wake of the disasters that befell the world's first jetliner, the British de Havilland Comet, fuselage designs now avoid creating points where flexing and stress can concentrate.

Metal fatigue can be simply demonstrated by taking a thick copper wire, and repeatedly bending it back and forth about a particular point. It first bends relatively easily, but then suddenly becomes brittle and snaps.

Since the fuselage of an airliner inevitably expands and contracts according to the air pressure differential between the inside and outside every time it goes up and down, the number of flights (called cycles) rather than naked historical age is the critical factor in the aging of metal aircraft.

Thus, an aircraft flying one-hour short-haul routes will be much more vulnerable than one flying long-haul routes with flights lasting 10 hours or more.

## Chapter 11: Invisible Dangers—Turbulence

Pilots go out of their way to avoid storms not only for their passengers' comfort but also for the safety of the aircraft. However, for them to be visible on their radar they must contain raindrops or snow. Clear air turbulence is much less evident and can sometimes cause the aircraft to drop or rise alarmingly.

## Chapter 12: Controlled Flight into Terrain (CFIT)

The term Controlled Flight into Terrain (CFIT) describes what used to be a very frequent type accident, namely an aircraft under control inadvertently flying into the ground.

Fortunately, the incidence of such disasters dropped sharply with the introduction of the Ground Proximity Warning System (GPWS) that uses data from the radio altimeter system (giving the actual height of the aircraft above the ground) to warn the pilots if they are getting dangerously close to it or sinking too fast.

While saving many lives, GPWS had the drawback of not being able to warn pilots if they were flying into a cliff or steep mountainside lying straight ahead. The recently developed Enhanced Ground Proximity Warning System (EGPWS) is able to take into account the height of the terrain ahead even if it is rising steeply. It manages to do this by using GPS to determine the aircraft's precise location and accessing a database with the height of the terrain lying ahead.

## Chapter 13: Miscellaneous Accidents

This chapter examines how fatigue and old injuries may have impaired the judgment of Germany's World War I fighter ace, the Red Baron. It also analyzes the crash of an Airbus flying from Moscow to Hong Kong after the captain allowed his teenage son to sit in his seat.

In addition, it includes a unique case where a passenger with only rudimentary experience of piloting tried unsuccessfully to take the controls of a Boeing 737 after the pilots had fallen unconscious due to lack of oxygen as the autopilot took them up to their cruising height and then on for an hour to their destination.

## Chapter 14: Decisional Accidents—Military Action

The shooting down of an airliner by the military almost invariably involves a wide variety of players and factors, not to mention cover-ups and military hubris, making it difficult to narrate such events adequately, let alone as personally as for 'regular' accidents.

There have been three much-publicized cases where airliners have been brought down by military action. In the first two cases narrated here, Soviet fighters brought down a Korean Airlines aircraft that had strayed. In the third case, a US warship, the USS *Vincennes*, shot down an Iranian airliner on a designated civilian route.

With the military in the USA very likely now having been given the nod—under certain conditions—to shoot down an airliner if they *think* doing so might prevent a repeat of 9/11, this could lead the ill-intentioned to simulate such hijackings in the hope that one or more hapless airliners would be shot down accordingly.

## Chapter 15: Airliners Morph into Flying Bombs

As early as September 6, 1970, three airliners on their way to America were hijacked and made to land at a desert landing strip in Jordan called Dawson's Field.

With no ground facilities to keep the air-conditioning going and the Middle Eastern sun beating down on the fuselages, conditions inside for the passengers were almost unbearable. Adding to their misery were the inadequate toilet facilities—designed to work for half a day, not the several days they were confined there. In the end, the occupants were allowed off, and the three empty airliners were blown up.

Subsequently, extra precautions were taken and this meant fewer hijackings. However, the protocols for dealing with hijacks remained very much the same from then on until 9/11. The general idea was to play along with the hijackers in the hope that, with time, achieving an acceptable outcome without loss of life would be possible—which was usually the case.

Passengers never really considered the possibility that the hijackers might intend to use their fuel-laden aircraft as a flying bomb, even though seven years before 9/11, terrorists had hijacked an Air France airliner with the intention of crashing it on a Paris landmark, possibly the Eiffel Tower. The chapter begins with this Air France incident, which should have been a warning regarding 9/11.

Following that, the chapter describes the events of 9/11, but as there are many excellent accounts and movies covering them, the narrative concentrates on the timeline—timing was everything, and was notably the reason why the fourth group of hijackers failed in their mission.

## Chapter 16: Questions & Answers

This somewhat academic chapter briefly covers the nature of air crash investigations, the role of lawyers in the unfortunate blame game, and new analytical techniques for predicting accidents together with academic theories initially conceived in the context of the nuclear power industry.

Topics such as corruption, engineering ethics, whistle-blowing, cost-benefit—how much it is worth spending on safety measures to save a human life—emerging technologies, and even the location of the safest seat are also touched on.

## CHAPTER 1

# LOSS OF POWER OVER WATER

## THE AMELIA EARHART MYSTERY
## (Howland Island 1937)

### 'Gas is running low'

> One of the most talked about instances of an aircraft running out
> of fuel while flying over a vast ocean was that experienced by
> aviatrix Amelia Earhart in 1937.

Amelia Earhart achieved fame in 1928 as the first woman to fly across the
Atlantic, albeit as a passenger. She admitted that being a passenger, she was
little more than a sack of potatoes. However, the sack must have had grit
and courage, as it was a difficult and extremely dangerous thing to do at the
time.

Her fame increased when she became the second person to fly solo
across the Atlantic. Her 15-hour flight from Newfoundland to Ireland was
much shorter than Charles Lindberg's historic 33-hour flight in 1927 from
Long Island to Paris, but it was a considerable ordeal with icing problems
and leaking fuel splashing onto her face.

With the help of her husband, publisher G. P. Putnam, she had stepped
on a publicity treadmill involving a grueling lecture schedule, and a
constant need to find trailblazing feats to keep in the headlines and keep
the money coming in. In the summer of 1937, aged 40, and probably
somewhat jaded, she was going to embark on what should have been her
last major flying exploit—an eastwards round-the-world flight along the
equator in a Lockheed Electra twin-engine airliner fitted with extra fuel
tanks in place of the passenger seats.

She and Putnam were mortgaged to the hilt. A previous mishap when
taking off in the Electra from Honolulu on their initial attempt to make the
round-the-world trip in a westerly direction had added to their costs. On
their second attempt, the change in the trade winds forced them to make it
in an easterly direction.

Accompanying her on the trip in the key role of navigator was ex-
Pan Am navigator Fred Noonan. While reports that he was fired from the

airline for an underlying drink problem are disputed, he was an exceptionally capable navigator and an expert at celestial navigation.

Starting from Oakland in California, Earhart and Noonan flew to Miami and then on to Brazil before crossing the narrowest part of the Atlantic to Dakar. After crossing Africa, they flew on to Pakistan, Burma, Singapore, and Darwin in northern Australia. At times, Earhart was quite sick with dysentery, and she must have been quite exhausted when she arrived at Lae in Papua New Guinea after the short hop from Darwin. Lae was the departure point for the long trans-Pacific legs, first to tiny Howland Island and from there on to Hawaii.

Noonan was none too happy, and apparently went on a drinking spree at Lae after an argument with Amelia. When her husband in the States heard about it, he reportedly urged her to call off the venture. She was reluctant to do so as they had successfully flown 22,000 miles and only had 7,000 miles to go, and in her mind it seemed she had been more concerned about what would happen to her should she come down in an isolated spot in Africa than in the Pacific.

Whatever his condition, Noonan must have been quite daunted by the prospect of navigating over water with no landmarks to an island only 1.6 sq km in area rising only a foot or two above the sea.

Interestingly, it was the introduction of flying boats in the early thirties that enabled the US to take over a number of essentially uninhabited islands from the British, which it did so in the case of Howland only in 1935. Having jurisdiction at this convenient midway point between Lae and Hawaii in 1937, the US Government had prepared a landing strip on the island especially for her benefit. A US Coast Guard cutter was also ordered to stand by near the island to render assistance. Unfortunately, the published coordinates for Howland were out by some five miles.

For navigational reasons, Amelia and Noonan timed their departure from Lae so they would fly over land and various identifiable islands in daylight, and then fly overnight over the ocean to Howland, arriving there just after dawn. This meant that while over the ocean and far from land, Noonan would be able to check their position from the stars—provided the weather was not too cloudy.

Even after dawn with no stars to get a fix, Noonan would be able to establish his longitude (but not his latitude) by how far the sun was above the horizon for the time of day.

He would also be using dead reckoning, whereby one's position is calculated according to one's speed, direction of travel, and elapsed time. As one's actual speed and direction over the ground (as opposed to through the air) depends on the direction and speed of the wind, the method can introduce considerable errors over long distances.

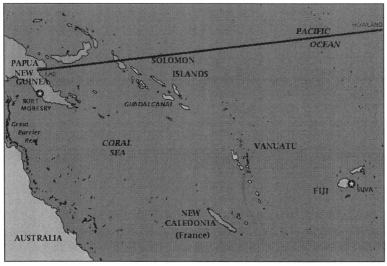

Figure 1  2,556-mile leg from Lae, Papua New Guinea, to Howland.

*See in color on our website chrisbart.com by clicking on*

*DIAGRAMS & PHOTOS FOR KINDLE*
*READERS + LINKS FOR ALL READERS*

Of course, for dead reckoning, correct identification of the waypoints is essential, and as mentioned below it seems Amelia and Noonan misidentified a ship for one that was meant to serve as a waypoint, partly due to inability to communicate by radio.

A classic way to compensate for the limitations of dead reckoning is to purposely aim for a point well to the left or right of one's destination and on completing the required distance make the 90° turn to the right or left to find it. Provided the offset is sufficient to allow for the navigational error, this avoids the risk of being almost right on one's destination and flying away from it.

Laden with maximum fuel for the 2,556-mile leg to Howland, the Electra labored into the air[1] at precisely 00:00 GMT (10 a.m. local time) on June 2, 1937. It seems that only the ground effect (air sandwiched between the wings and the ground acting as a cushion[2]) kept them in the air until they were able to raise the wheels to gain enough airspeed to climb away. When they were 4 h 18 min out, Earhart radioed an airport manager back at Lae that they were flying at 7,000 ft and 140 knots, which was ideal for the most efficient consumption of fuel. However, at 5 hours out, she had to climb to avoid a storm and in the process used up extra fuel, since unlike modern airliners fuel consumption was greater[3] at high altitudes.

Worse was to come. At her hourly call made when 7 hours out, she said that the headwind was 25 knots rather than the 12 knots she had

3

anticipated. If her effective speed was 12 knots slower than her expected ground speed of 140 – 12 = 128 knots, this headwind meant almost a 10% increase in the distance through the air. She seemed to have increased engine power to increase airspeed and optimize her ground distance covered per gallon, but there was certainly still a very significant fuel penalty due to the headwind.

Though she was able to call Lae for the first part of the trip there is no indication she was able to receive any message from Lae in return.

The US Government had placed a ship, the *Ontario*,[4] at the halfway point but it seems that though Earhart and Noonan saw a ship, it was another one 40 miles further north. This may have resulted in them thinking they were on the correct course when in fact they were heading to an area north of Howland Island. (A message she had wanted to send to the *Ontario* before leaving Lae regarding the radio signals the ship should emit had not reached it.)

As the aircraft got further from Lae and nearer Howland, the Coast Guard cutter *Itasca*, waiting just off the island, began to receive some messages but could not seem to contact the Electra.

Finally, at 7:42 a.m., 19½ hours after their departure from Lae, the *Itasca* received the following message from the Electra:

> *KHAQQ calling Itasca.*
>
> *We must be on you but cannot see you ... Gas is running low....*
>
> *Been unable to reach you by radio. We are flying at 1,000 feet.*

Indeed, the signal was so loud the radio operator expected to see them overhead. However, there was no sign of them. The transmission had not lasted long and the *Itasca* could not get a fix—some say because its direction finder was not working.

The *Itasca* emitted smoke, and had there been no cloud, the Electra could have flown higher and seen them from 50 miles.

An hour later, at 08:44, there was a message in which according to Doris L. Rich's biography,[5] 'Amelia's voice—shrill and breathless, her words tumbling over one another—came in.'

> *We are on the line of position 157–337.[6] Will repeat message ... We are running north and south.*

When nothing more was heard it became increasingly obvious that the Electra must have come down somewhere. The crew on board the *Itasca* searched the area where they thought they might have been but there was no sign of them, not even wreckage. The nearest land to Howland Island was 325 miles away, so if Earhart had indeed been as near the island as she thought she was, there was little chance of her having reached any other land. Some later alleged she had left their life raft behind to save weight.

On President Roosevelt's orders, a major search was launched, involving nine US Navy ships and 66 aircraft at a cost $4 million or more. They searched a vast area of the Pacific, including the various islands where some people suggested they might have come down. When the authorities finally called off the search after two weeks, the rumors began.

One rumor was that Earhart was a spy for the US Government. Hardly anyone believes this was so now. In the author's view, she would have been much better prepared especially as regards the use of the radio had she really been a spy. On the other hand, the generous assistance provided by the US Government before her disappearance and the $4 million spent afterwards no doubt had its military spin-offs.

In the course of the search, radio messages seeming to emanate from Earhart, some of which caused the US Navy to change the focus of their investigations, were received. While many were obviously hoaxes, they could not be certain that some were not genuine. Subsequently a woman's shoe was found on an island she might possibly have reached, only for it to be found not to be her size. Another claim was that the Japanese had captured the pair after a forced landing on one of the islands they controlled.

There are 50 or more books, any number of magazine and newspaper articles, TV documentaries, not to mention online forums covering her disappearance. The 2009 movie *Amelia* put some meat on the bones of her personal life and her affair with Gene Vidal. The dashing Gene Vidal was a West Point[7] quarterback, seventh medalist in the 1925 Olympic Games pentathlon, and a prominent figure in aviation. He also happened to be the father of the late Gore Vidal.

In an interview[8] with Robert Chalmers writing for the UK's *The Independent* newspaper, Gore Vidal mentioned that he once asked his father why he had not married Earhart. To which his father had replied, 'I have never really wanted to marry another boy.' Gore Vidal went on to say, 'And she was like a boy.' He then drew Chalmers' attention to a photo of her in a prominent place on a dresser, remarking, 'You see how one could see courage in those eyes,' and made it clear how much he admired her and even felt for her.

Searchers have spent tremendous sums trying to locate her aircraft on relatively nearby islands such as Nikumaroro, and under water near Howland. Recently more credence has been given to some of the radio messages received after her disappearance purporting to be from her. Though searchers are truly fascinated, there is a profit motive. Anyone who succeeds in finding the lost Electra could put the artifacts on show and write the definitive book on the subject of her disappearance.

Tom Crouch, senior curator of aeronautics at the National Air and Space Museum in Washington, who perhaps like others, feels he has devoted more than enough time to the case is quoted as saying, 'I'm convinced that the mystery is part of what keeps us interested. In part, we remember her because she's our favorite missing person.' One might push curator Crouch's argument further by saying that people even enjoy arguing about the clues, some of which may have been spun to show the parties, and notably officialdom, in a better light.

Furthermore, some dispute facts once taken as Gospel,[9] such as that navigator Noonan was a true alcoholic fired from Pan Am—it being pointed out that he seemed in good form in pictures of him helping Amelia into the aircraft at Lae. Even the idea that the Coast Guard cutter *Itasca* could have produced a meaningful column of smoke is disputed since doing so for any significant time would have compromised one of the vessel's boilers and any smoke would have quickly dissipated in the wind prevailing at the time.

That said, any reader hooked on the subject should note that local time at Howland is GMT +10.5 hours, and that this half hour step can be confusing when comparing times at other places such as Lae. What is somewhat unsettling is that the great strength of the transmission '*We must be on you but cannot see you ... Gas is running low....*'
gave the impression they were very close.

As mentioned, it even made the *Itasca*'s wireless operator think she might be right overhead and certainly indicated that Noonan had brought her quite close to the minuscule low-profile Howland Island (whose published coordinates were out by five miles). Furthermore, her final transmission at 8:44 a.m. was at Strength 5 (the maximum).

This signal strength and the later statement '*We are running north and south*' suggest that she was so determined to reach Howland that she kept trying to get there by going back and forth, rather than at some point continuing southwards on that line of position, which would very likely have taken them over other islands. Of course, if she waited too long, reaching any other island would be impossible.

Here and elsewhere, commentators have emphasized the general use of the already mentioned offset navigation technique whereby one aims to one side of one's destination. On reflection, there is a problem with this in the Earhart context. Firstly, when Amelia Earhart says at the outset, 'We must be on you but cannot see you....' it seems to imply they had flown directly to where they thought Howland was. The final message had been:

> We are on the line of position 157–337.[10] Will repeat message ...
> We are running north and south.

Noonan would have first determined the position of this line when the sun had risen some two hours earlier (see endnote reference to an Internet explanation of the significance of 157–337 degrees) and added to the extra time required so that the line would traverse Howland. If the unexpected headwinds had not delayed them, the dead reckoning element would have been much reduced.

What Earhart perhaps had not realized was that the chances of finding Howland visually in less than perfect weather would be slim. In fact, the weather was far from ideal and the only sure way of finding the island would have been by the radio direction finder. In addition, her lack of fuel might have tempted her to try to fly straight to Howland rather than safely to one side to avoid flying away from it. Everything thus depended on the ability to communicate by radio and the transmission of radio signals on frequencies that respective radio direction finders could pick up. Apparently, there was a lack of coordination between her and the Coast Guard prior to the flight. The Coast Guard later tried to portray her as a prima donna unwilling to listen to reason, leading some to interpret this to mean she was a spy unwilling to obey orders from the conventional military.

Though some of her contemporary women pilots were highly critical of her flying abilities, General Leigh Wade who had flown with her claimed she was a born flier 'with a delicate touch on the stick.' The movie clip [the real one, not the simulated *Amelia* movie one] showing how she managed the difficult takeoff from Lae with the aircraft so heavy with extra fuel that it could hardly get off the ground, seems to bear that out. Many a pilot would have pushed the nose up too far and stalled the aircraft. However, there was an early incident in her flying career where her judgment was in question in that she dropped down through cloud, coming out at the bottom, not realizing what would have happened had the cloud extended right to the ground. It also seemed that on her round-the-world venture her overriding fear was coming down in the jungle somewhere.

Anyway, she would have been very reluctant to give up as she and husband Putnam would be very unlikely to get their money back with a failed exploit. From a modern airline safety point of view, she at first seems to have been silly not to turn back to Lae when she found the climb to a higher altitude and the unexpected increase in headwind meant she would have little fuel in reserve even if she made a perfect course to Howland. However, going back to Lae would have involved going again over 9000 ft peaks on Bougainville Island in the Solomons (see Figure 1).

What is more, the takeoff from Lae, even though helped by the headwind that later caused her to use more fuel than expected, had been a touch-and-go affair, and she might not be so lucky a second time. Lack of high-octane aviation fuel on the island would mean waiting until further supplies arrived and paying for their shipment. Weather conditions might be even worse the next time, and there was no guarantee the US Navy would keep the *Itasca* on station there. Finally, she could not be sure the Electra could withstand another takeoff at 1.5 times its normal maximum takeoff weight.

On her other flights towards large landmasses, having ample reserves of fuel was not so critical—for instance on her trans-Atlantic solo flight she was said to have been hoping to emulate Charles Lindbergh's 1927 historic flight from New York's Long Island to Le Bourget Field in Paris, and yet ended up in Ireland, both large landmasses.

Her, some might say, forgotten navigator, the recently married Noonan, must also have had considerable courage to embark on the venture. What were he and Earhart arguing about on Lae? Were the fatigue and stress getting to her and making her disapprove of his conduct, or was he unhappy about preparations for the particularly difficult flight ahead? What is so tragic is that Noonan had her so close to Howland not only initially, but also when she made her final transmission. A modern air accident inquiry might say the direct causes of the tragedy, apart from the inherent risk, included:

1. **Failure to master the use of radio communication and particularly radio direction-finding technology (RDF), failure to ensure it was set up and tested properly, and failure to check the compatibility of radio communication and direction-finding equipment.**

2. **Failure to employ backup Morse code radio equipment (and associated direction-finding modes) perhaps on account of failure to master Morse code.**

Lack of funds probably meant the venture was not professionally managed, resulting in a lack of liaison between the parties regarding use of the radio equipment. Even had the *Itasca* been able to get an RDF fix, it would not have enabled them to give her the vector to reach Howland, as she was not receiving their transmissions.

On August 19, 2012, London's *Daily Telegraph* reported that a $2.2million mission, with sophisticated equipment and supported by the US Government, searching for wreckage of her aircraft on and around Nikumaroro atoll had been hampered by harsh underwater conditions, but had returned with video evidence showing an 'interesting debris field.'

---

[1] http://www.tighar.org/amelia_3.rm is a 30-second clip of the takeoff. It shows Earhart and Noonan apparently looking fit when boarding.
Also, see www.tighar.org.

[2] To describe the ground effect as simply a cushioning effect is an oversimplification as the aerodynamics are actually much more complicated.

[3] Amelia Earhart: The Mystery Solved, Elgen M. Long, Marie K. Long.

[4] http://www.thehistorynet.com/ahi/blearhart/index3.html.

[5] *Amelia Earhart*: A Biography, by Doris L. Rich.

[6] *Best explanation of significance of '157-337.'*
http://tighar.org/forum/FAQs/navigation.html

[7] US military academy

[8] Interview by Robert Chalmers, *The Independent*, Sunday, 25 May 2008.

[9] See http://www.tighar.org/forum/FAQs/Forumfaq.html

[10] For the best explanation of the significance of '157–337' see
http://tighar.org/forum/FAQs/navigation.html.

# BA 747 LOSES ALL POWER
# (Indian Ocean 1982)

## Mystery Phenomenon

> In 1982, a British Airways 747 encountered a strange almost mystical phenomenon high up in the lonely sky off Indonesia. With the aircrew not knowing why, all four engines flamed out (stopped), leaving the aircraft gliding through the night sky.
>
> *[British Airways Flight 9]*

Many of the passengers—and particularly those who had boarded in London and endured many stops and delays on what was then the world's longest scheduled flight, from London to New Zealand—were dozing off after the evening meal. Everything had been going smoothly on that almost final leg from Kuala Lumpur to Perth, Australia.

Then some two-and-a-half hours into the leg, passengers on the Boeing 747 started complaining that there were too many smokers. On seeing the haze at the back of the Economy Class cabin, the cabin crew wondered why so many were lighting up when they would normally be trying to get to sleep. As the smoke and acrid smell of burning increased, cabin staff surreptitiously went around ensuring a smoldering cigarette was not about to start a fire.

Meanwhile, profiting from a quiet moment on the flight deck, the captain had taken the opportunity to go to the toilet and stretch his legs. The first officer and flight engineer left in charge on the flight deck had the autopilot handling the aircraft and only needed to keep a look out and be ready for anything unexpected.

Having passed right over Indonesia's capital, Jakarta, the 747 was about to cross the mountains and head out over the Indian Ocean (though far from India!). Cruising at 37,000 ft, with bright stars overhead and little cloud below, the first officer and flight engineer began to see odd light effects ahead, which they later said were like St Elmo's fire—a phenomenon in which lightning dances around in the sky. Yet, their weather radar gave no indication of storm clouds.

Soon, with flashes of light and tiny balls of fire rushing at them and exploding on the windscreen, the crew's amazement switched to concern and the first officer called the captain who was relaxing just below.

Hurrying up the stairs, he too could hardly believe what he was seeing. No one could work out what it was—it seemed out of this world. High up in the sky, with no light pollution, anything producing some degree of light is immediately obvious, and a strange glow seemed to be enveloping the leading edge of the wings and the nacelles of the engines. Worse still, the engines themselves seemed to be illuminated from inside.

Passengers seated behind the engines were startled to see bright particles issuing from them. The rough running of the engines began to rouse the few passengers still asleep.

A pungent smell of smoke prompted the flight engineer to check for fire and consider shutting down the air-conditioning, even though he could not find any reason for it.

Two minutes after entering the zone where the strange phenomenon was occurring, the instruments indicated a pneumatic valve pressure problem for the No. 4 (outside right) engine, which afterwards surged and flamed out. A minute later, the No. 2 engine failed likewise, and failure of engines Nos. 1 and 3 soon followed. They had become a glider, with 247 passengers, including children and babies.

Though airliners do not make good gliders, their great cruising height—in this case 37,000 ft—means they usually have some time in which to restart the engines or select somewhere they might be able to land in the most unlikely event of the engines failing at cruising height. However, in their case their predicament was particularly serious in that the nearest diversion airport (Jakarta-Halim) had high mountains on its approach and it would be quite impossible to keep above the 11,500 ft minimum height needed to reach it safely.

Ditching a 747 in the sea in daytime when able to judge the height and direction of the swell would be difficult enough, but it was 10 p.m. and the chances of a successful ditching in the dark would be virtually zero. While any survivors might find the warm waters of Indian Ocean more hospitable than say the cold Atlantic, the likelihood of someone bleeding would mean it would not be long before the sharks came for a late supper.

The flight engineer made repeated attempts to restart the engines, much to the consternation of the passengers at the rear of the aircraft seeing burning fuel mixed with whatever had accumulated in the engines spewing out explosively each time.

With no power for cabin pressurization, the air pressure inside the aircraft was gradually dropping. After about five minutes it fell so much that the crew had to don their oxygen masks, not only because of their physical exertion but because they needed all their mental faculties and the human brain uses a surprising amount of oxygen.

It was only then that the first officer found his oxygen mask had been stowed incorrectly and was unusable, forcing them to drop down from 26,000 ft to 20,000 ft for his benefit. As they lost further valuable height and sank to 17,500 ft with the cabin pressure still falling, the passenger oxygen masks descended.

The situation seemed to be becoming more and more critical. Little did they know their imposed loss of height would finally be their salvation. Almost 12 minutes after losing all power, they found themselves nosing into normal air below the unnatural zone. Shortly afterwards, the first engine they had shut down, and the least subjected to whatever the cause was, sprang into life.

One engine alone would not provide enough power for them to climb, but would keep them aloft for much longer and give them some measure of control over their destiny. Subsequently, the other three engines also came back to life in quick succession.

Rather prematurely, they reported this reprieve to the tower controller at Jakarta, who told them to climb to 15,000 ft as the mountains between them and the airport were making them invisible to the Jakarta radar. In complying, they found themselves yet again in the abnormal zone, and one of the resurrected engines beginning to run so roughly that they had to shut it down. They lost no time in dropping down into the clear air again.

With careful nursing, the three other engines seemed to be sustaining their power. Thinking their tribulations were over, they approached the airport at Jakarta in high spirits only to find the windscreen had frosted over so much that everything was a blur.

They even had to request that the tower decrease the intensity of the runway lights because of the glare. Fortunately, each windscreen panel had a narrow strip of clear glass down each outboard side, allowing them to see just enough to land safely. The captain performed well, making a very good landing with help from the first officer reading out the heights.

One passenger was violently sick due to mental stress as they came in— in the case described on page 15 where Captain Piché managed to glide 80 miles to safety, his passengers were vomiting beside the runway after their emergency evacuation following their precipitous landing, so it is surprising there were not more passengers who were sick.

The 747's landing at Jakarta had in the end been normal, but in view of the doubtful state of the engines they asked to be towed to the terminal— with the passengers thanking God and above all the crew, personified by the captain, for their deliverance.

The odds against all *four* engines of an aircraft failing for reasons other than fuel depletion or contamination with water or ice crystals, are so great that it is (or was) thought to be virtually impossible. However, the aircrew had trained for such an eventuality and performed very competently, as did the cabin crew.

Soon they learned that what they had encountered had been ash from a volcano, which explained why being forced to lose height due to the first officer's faulty oxygen mask had been such a blessing. Had they spent longer in the ash-laden environment it is conceivable that the engines would have silted up too much to be relit. Some would argue the aircrew should have put on their oxygen masks earlier and thereby solved the problem with the first officer's mask before being obliged to descend. However, not doing so happened to work to their advantage.

The authorities closed the skies around the volcano (Mt. Galunggung) to aircraft for a week. Just four days after they were reopened, a Singapore Airlines 747 encountered conditions similar to those that had caught the BA crew by surprise. Forewarned, the SIA crew took evasive action, but even so, had to divert to Jakarta-Halim as three of their engines had overheated.

There was an almost identical incident in 1989, when a KLM flight from Amsterdam to Anchorage in Alaska encountered an ash cloud from Mt. Redoubt and all four engines flamed out due to compressor stalls[1]. As in the BA case, the pilots were able to restart them on exiting the plume of ash. The situation was not as critical as the BA one since the aircraft was better placed with respect to the airport—the BA aircraft had a range of high mountains between it and the airport—and the cloud of ash was not so extensive.

In a Commendation Ceremony for both the aircrew and cabin crew, BA was happy to bathe in the reflected glory. The captain in question, Captain Eric Moody, subsequently became, and still is, a TV pundit on aviation matters, and a much sought-after after-dinner speaker.

In a deftly written review of the TV documentary entitled *All Engines Failed,* the UK's *Daily Mail* said, Moody *'displayed the stiff-upper-lip spirit that built an empire'* when he uttered the words that are every air passenger's worst nightmare, *'Ladies and gentlemen, this is your captain speaking. We have a small problem. All four engines have stopped. We are doing our damnedest to get it under control. I trust you are not in too much distress.'*

The crisis resolved itself thanks to difficulties with the first officer's oxygen mask forcing Moody to bring the aircraft down to uncontaminated air where the engines could restart before silting up completely. To be fair, the captain's calm demeanor and brave words must not only have reassured the passengers, but have helped the crew perform optimally in the circumstances.

---

[1] The term Compressor Stall (in an engine) is somewhat confusing as it has no connection with the normal use of stall (aerodynamic stall) where the airspeed is so slow that the wing ceases to provide lift.
Situation produced by the abnormal flow of air through turbine or jet engine caused by a number of factors including ingestion of birds and Side Slipping. Sometimes results in loud bangs.

Often no damage to engine, but sometimes engine will flame out, be irretrievably damaged, or catch fire. Some stalls affecting entire engine referred to as compressor surges. Though somewhat frightening for passengers, usually not serious.

# HIJACKED ETHIOPIAN 767 DITCHES (Comoros 1996)

### Within Sight of Bathers—Video Seen Around the World

> The media frequently compare this ditching of a hijacked Ethiopian airliner with the 'miraculous' Hudson River ditching described later in this chapter. They often fail to point out that the Ethiopian pilot was fighting off a hijacker and only had limited control of the aircraft due to insufficient electrical power.
>
> *[Ethiopian Airlines Flight 961]*

In 1996, an Ethiopian Airlines Boeing 767 was seized by three hijackers who thought that the range quoted in the in-flight magazine meant it could fly all the way to Australia, when in fact the pilots had only loaded enough fuel for the leg in question—a quarter of the distance.

They would not believe this was not possible and insisted on going on. In an impossible situation, the captain tried to keep within sight of the African coast, but the hijackers noticed this. Pretending he was complying and going out towards the open sea, the captain, Leul Abate, flew towards the Comoros Islands. The fuel was running out when they neared them, but this did not prevent the hijackers remonstrating with the pilots and preventing them from landing at the main airport.

Finally, with no fuel left and no engine power, they had to ditch in the sea just off a beach. The left wing and its engine touched the water first, and as a result, the aircraft started to spin leftwards and broke up. Of the 175 crew and passengers, only 48 survived. Premature inflation[1] of lifejackets despite a warning not to do so was the cause of a number of the fatalities.

*See photo on our website chrisbart.com
by clicking on*

*DIAGRAMS & PHOTOS FOR KINDLE
READERS + LINKS FOR ALL READERS*

Aircraft should stay afloat for quite a while provided they do not break up. Even with a fair amount of fuel on board, they will not sink like a stone since the fuel (kerosene) is less dense than water and provides some buoyancy, and if the fuel has run out the tanks will be full of air. That said, the high stalling speed of modern jetliners makes a successful ditching very tricky. Having the flaps fully extended in the extreme downwards position to give more lift and a lower landing speed as on land may not be desirable

13

as the resistance generated when they hit the water at speed risks tearing the wings off.

Letting the landing gear down[2] to reduce the speed is not an option either, since the aircraft would topple forwards and cartwheel the moment it broke the surface of the water. On the other hand, the engines are designed to break off when striking an obstacle, and would normally do so, except that in the Ethiopian ditching, the aircraft struck the water while banking, thus causing it to spin round rather than slowing with both engines breaking off.[3]

The situation Captain Leul Abate faced was much more difficult than the one Captain Sully faced on ditching in the Hudson River.

1. **Abate was coming down in the sea with a certain swell.**

2. **He was fighting off one of the hijackers.**

3. **Having run out of fuel, he did not have the auxiliary power unit (APU) to generate electrical power, and only had minimal power for the most basic instruments and controls generated by the RAT.[4] As a result, the aircraft was difficult to control anyway, and an untoward bank caused by interference by the hijackers could not be easily corrected.**

However, the Ethiopian pilot did succeed in bringing the aircraft down by a beach with tourists (hence the video that can be found on the Internet) from which rescue attempts could be made.

---

[1] Besides their bulk making it more difficult for people to get out, prematurely inflated lifejackets can cause the wearer to float upwards if the cabin fills with water resulting in their being trapped against the ceiling (or the floor if the aircraft is upside-down).

[2] The undercarriage can be allowed to fall down through gravity if there is no hydraulic power to operate it. However, many accounts report that reluctant pilots are to do this if there is any chance of having to ditch as it is impossible to retract it thereafter.

[3] Unlike the flaps, which have to withstand strong forces pushing them backwards, the main purpose of the engine mountings is to withstand the thrust of the engines pushing forwards, and they are designed to break off backwards if they hit a solid object—water being like a brick wall when struck at speed.

[4] RAT (Ram Air Turbine). In the absence of electrical power from the engines or from the Auxiliary Power Unit (APU), a turbine is extended from the fuselage and generates some electricity by wind milling. This is only enough to keep the most basic controls operating and not enough for the sophisticated computer controls that make flying the modern airliner precisely so easy.

# 80-MILE ATLANTIC GLIDE
# (Azores 2001)

### 'Pilot Hailed as a Hero Becomes a Zero'

> Switching to today's ETOPS[1] era, with twin-engine aircraft allowed to fly far from possible landing places, we have an instance where an airliner ran out of fuel over the Atlantic 80 miles from the nearest landing place: a US military airfield on an island in the Azores.
>
> Reaching it was one thing; adjusting height and speed so as not to overshoot or undershoot was another.
>
> *[Air Transat Flight 236]*

A paper used the glib Hero-to-Zero headline[2] to describe 48-year-old French-Canadian Captain Robert Piché's temporary fall from grace after gaining instant fame for the handling of his ultra-modern Airbus A330 that had run out of fuel mid-Atlantic.

The nearest possible landing place was a US air force base on an island in the Portuguese Azores 80 miles away. Carefully nursing his aircraft, he managed to glide there and come in at 400 mph rather than risk falling out of the sky by attempting an extra circuit to lose more height and speed.

With no air brakes or flaps, and only the landing gear to slow him, Piché raised the nose to decrease the sink rate and increase forward resistance. Hitting hard near the threshold, he burst[3] eight tires and skidded to a halt almost three quarters of the way down the runway. Waiting fire services quickly ensured the sparks resulting from friction between exposed metal wheel rims and the runway did not start a fire, which was unlikely in view of the empty un-ruptured fuel tanks.

All on board evacuated in less than 90 seconds thanks to the excellent work of the cabin crew, whom some passengers later accused of panicking as they were shouting so loudly—the airline retorted that they had to shout to ensure everyone heard them. Only 12 of the passengers sustained injuries in the course of the evacuation, and those were minor. Some were vomiting beside the runway after the tension of the long glide.

On Piché's return to Canada people showered praise on him, but to one journalist he obliquely replied, 'I don't consider myself a hero, Sir. I could have done without this.' This probably rightly conveyed his sentiment of just having done his job and having been lucky, but could also have intimated his fear that details of his prison sentence in the US for allegedly smuggling marijuana in a light plane in his younger days would leak out.

Before readers jump to conclusions regarding his suitability to be a captain, they should note that in applying for a job with the airline, he did not hide that fact. Indeed, in an interview quite some time after his great feat, he claimed the experience of facing death several times as the only French-speaking inmate in an American jail was what had given him the fortitude to make the successful landing even after enduring the stress of the long glide.

Investigations subsequently showed the cause of the incident was faulty maintenance by the airline.

However, there remained the question as to whether Piché and his first officer aggravated the situation by poor judgment? Were they largely responsible for their own misfortune? Alternatively, had the sophisticated computer systems and displays on the aircraft been at fault?

The Canadian authorities' imposition of a $250,000 fine on Air Transat and the reduction of their ETOPS rating to a maximum diversion time of only 90 minutes attest to the seriousness of the maintenance lapses. They discovered that on finding metal filings in the oil, engineers had temporarily installed the only replacement engine Rolls-Royce they had available on site for loan in such situations—one that happened to be a slightly older version and one not equipped with a fuel pump. With no pump, they decided to use the one fitted to their own newer engine that they were removing, despite the concern expressed by one member of the team.

The airliner had crossed the Atlantic thirteen times since the change to the older model engine without anyone realizing that using parts designed for the newer engine on the older version would allow the fuel line to chafe. On that fourteenth crossing, the fuel line ruptured and broke. The fuel kept pouring out of the wing and even though Captain Piché asked a crewmember to check, they were unable to see it in the darkness.

The inquiry's findings were as follows:

1. **Main cause was irresponsible maintenance.**

2. **Piché and his first officer had possibly aggravated the fuel leak situation by wrong decisions regarding the transfer of fuel between tanks.**

Having reviewed the aircraft's computer systems and displays, Airbus took measures to make pilots aware of abnormal fuel consumption even without doing the calculations themselves. They revised the manual to even further stress the need to avoid transferring fuel where any suspicion of a fuel leak existed. Rolls-Royce was the subject of some criticism for putting Air Transat in a difficult situation by not providing the pump with the engine.

## The Pilots' Performance

Being able to glide so far was due not only to good calculation of the optimum glide slope and avoiding over controlling, but also due to the aerodynamics of the A330, and the great height at which they were initially flying.

Perhaps the key to this success was the way Piché eased the aircraft along and risked coming in too fast rather than losing more height by circling—as it was suggested the first officer wanted to do—and the possibility of stalling away from the runway.

Some commentators have remarked that the aircraft would have toppled over the cliff at the far end of the runway and into the sea had Piché not landed so adroitly. In fact, the 'cliff' is an optical illusion when looking along the runway towards the end, as the ground merely slopes downwards beyond the runway giving the impression that it is a sheer drop to the sea. Even had the aircraft been about to go over the so-called cliff, all would not have been lost, as Lajes is a military field with arresting chains at either end of the runway. Controllers can raise these if an aircraft (with possibly a weapons payload?) looks as though it will overrun.

Had there been enough electrical power to keep the flight recorders functioning, investigators would have been able to learn more about the glide and final control inputs. With the batteries drained in the course of the long glide, the Ram Air Turbine[4] (RAT) was providing essential power for instruments and controls. However, electricity for the flight recorders was not considered essential at the time, though the NTSB now say it should be maintained in all circumstances.[5]

Piché with his charming unconventional personality became a hero, especially in Canada, with hundreds of people wanting to interview him. He was asked to open various events, almost like royalty. He had a biography written about him, and spent some time on sick leave, apparently with alcohol problems brought about by the unwanted roller coaster ride of fame and shame. He then gave up drinking entirely and returned to work as a pilot at the airline.

It is a very human story, made more dramatic by the perception that the landing was on a remote island, which consequently must have poor facilities. As mentioned above, this was not the case. Piché was the first to admit that luck played a part. The weather was almost perfect unlike the day before and the day after. Air Traffic Control (ATC) had by chance allotted him a route 60 miles further south than usual, thus putting him just within gliding range of the Azores when the fuel ran out.

Other pilots have successfully made dead-stick landings, and most of them, including Piché, deserve praise. The question is to what extent was Piché responsible for his own misfortune?

## Culture of the Airline

The culture of the airline surely played a part. When the fuel imbalance became serious enough to be worrying, it seemed the pilots hesitated to divert immediately as they were wondering what the airline would say if they landed in the Azores with full tanks. Pilots working for a major carrier might not be under such pressure—as their precautionary error on the side of safety would only be a mere blip compared with the airline's vast scenario of operations.

For Air Transat, the cost of the diversion and schedule disruption would have been of concern, but the fear of losing their ETOPS classification through too many diversions for mechanical reasons would have worried them even more. As already mentioned, a regulation designed to ensure safety sometimes has the opposite result.

## Lawyers

If the pilot actually saves the aircraft and its occupants, some passengers— egged on by lawyers—are prone to exploit the situation. For instance, when a Boeing 777 crash-landed miraculously just inside London Heathrow's perimeter fence with everyone evacuating virtually unharmed (see page 52), the passengers were full of praise. However, after the elapse of some days, some began to talk of compensation, leading the airline to treat them with kid gloves, with the Chief Executive calling them personally on the phone to show his concern for their well-being.

In this Azores incident, a lawyer immediately contacted the airline (Air Transat) to arrange a deal, whereby Air Transat would pay out a once-only sum, rumored to be $10,000 per passenger, in compensation. Apparently, some 100 passengers signed up for that. Another law firm was soon establishing a class action lawsuit.

## Conclusion

Piché's was a remarkable feat meriting its inclusion in our list of miracle landings in Chapter 16.

---

[1] Explanations of technical terms, such as ETOPS, can be found in *THE FLYING DICTIONARY,* Christopher Bartlett, OpenHatch Books.

[2] University of Utah uses this phrase in study project literature.

[3] A number of accounts give the impression the tires burst because of the force of the impact. Actually, they burst because the anti-locking system was not functioning and with the wheels locked by the brakes, the tires just skidded over the runway without rotating.

[4] The Ram Air Turbine (RAT) is a 'windmill' that drops down to generate emergency power for key instruments.

[5] The NTSB has stressed the need to ensure CVRs and FDRs have the required electrical power in all circumstances—for instance when a Swissair airliner lost electrical power in a fire, the recorders stopped working and investigators had great difficulty in determining subsequent events.

# US AIRWAYS FLIGHT 1549
# (Hudson River 2009)

### Sully the Saint

> Just as we were saying how difficult it is to ditch an airliner successfully in the sea, there has been the widely publicized case of an Airbus suffering a bird strike on taking off from New York's La Guardia Airport and ditching in the nearby Hudson River with no fatalities. See photo on back cover of the printed edition.
>
> *[US Airways Flight 1549]*

No commercial airline pilot has been quite as sanctified[1] as 58-year-old Captain Chesley B. Sullenberger III (nicknamed Sully) who ditched his Airbus A320 in New York's Hudson River without a single loss of life, except for some hapless birds. The fact that he seemed so unpretentious made his elevation to sainthood even more palatable. One could not imagine a nicer hero.

There is in no denying that he did a great job, not only bringing the aircraft down safely, but also ensuring that everyone had evacuated. However, one might ask to what extent did the fact that he could ditch in optimum conditions with publicity assured in midtown New York with photographers on hand play a part in making it such a celebrated case.

### Cactus 1549

'Cactus' is the call sign air traffic controllers use for US Airways. This seems bizarre until one realizes that Cactus was the call sign used by American West Airlines (AWE) with which US Airways had merged, and which indeed flies to many locations where cacti do grow in the wild. The merged airline also keeps the American West identification code: 'AWE.' The name 'US Airways' was retained for the public, allegedly because it sounded more prestigious, and doing so had the advantage of keeping both parties to the merger happy.

After lifting off from La Guardia's[2] Runway 4 at 3:25 p.m. on January 15, 2009, Cactus 1549 (US Airways Flight 1549) was handed over to 'Departure' (control) with clearance to climb to 5,000 ft.

Including the two pilots and three cabin crew, there were 155 people on board the Airbus 320. It was a beautiful day, but rather cold.

### Exchanges with Air Traffic Control (ATC)

To simplify the following transcriptions of exchanges between the aircraft and ATC, we refer to US Airways flights as 'Cactus' rather than 'AWE,' and use 'Departure,' when in fact it is *'New York TRACOM[3] La Guardia Departure.'*

'Departure' was the controller handling flights from climb out (i.e. after they had taken off) to the time they reached approximately 18,000 ft, and were then handed over to the 'ATC Center' (in this case New York Center) covering the upper skies for the whole area.

After two or three routine exchanges between Departure and Cactus 1549, Departure gave instructions to turn left, as a first step on the two-hour flight to Charlottesville, but not so far left that its track would encroach on traffic out of New Jersey (airport).

Departure (3:27:32 p.m.):

> *Cactus 1549, turn left heading two seven zero.*

There was no confirmation from the aircraft. Then, four seconds later, with a slight error in the call sign indicative of the gravity of the situation:

Cactus 1549 (3:27:36 p.m.):

> *Ah, this is Cactus 1539 (sic) ... hit birds, we lost thrust in both engines. We're turning back toward La Guardia.*

Departure:

> *Okay. Yea. You need to return to La Guardia ... Turn left, heading of, uh, Two two zero.*

Cactus 1549:

> *Two two zero.*

Departure called the La Guardia tower, telling them to stop all departures; that the aircraft in trouble was actually Cactus 1549; and that they had lost all engines. The tower (local controller) found this difficult to grasp, perhaps because the simultaneous loss of all engines is almost unheard of.

Departure clarified:

> *... Cactus 1549 has lost thrust in both engines.*

Tower:

> *Got it.*

Departure to Cactus 1549:

> *Cactus 1549, if we can get it to you, do you want to try to land runway 13?*

Runway 13, perpendicular to the one from which Sully had just taken off, had the advantage that aligning with it would be quicker and involve less turning—in a turn the sink rate increases.

Cactus 1549:

> *We're unable. We may end up in the Hudson.*

Departure:

> *All right Cactus 1549, it's going to be left traffic to runway 31.*

Cactus 1549:

> *Unable.*

Departure:

> *Okay, what do you need to land?*

Departure:

> *Cactus 1549, Runway 4 is available if you want to make left traffic to Runway 4.*

Cactus 1549:

> *I am not sure if we can make any runway. Oh, what's over to our right? Anything in New Jersey, maybe Teterboro?*

(Departure called Teterboro[4] airport and told them that La Guardia Departure had an 'emergency inbound' … and asked if their Runway 1 would be okay. Approval was given.)

...............................................................

In parallel, there was an exchange at Teterboro between their Area Supervisor and Operations, which included the supervisor saying:

> *Yeah, he's going to land here 'cause he's, he's, he's* [sic] *falling down right now. He's coming in, he's going to land.*

(Later)

> *Why would he land here by the Lincoln Tunnel? Why didn't he land at La Guardia or Newark?*

...............................................................

Departure to Cactus 1549:

> *Cactus 1529, turn right two eight zero, you can land Runway 1 at Teterboro.*

Cactus 1549:

> *We can't do it.*

Departure:

*Okay. Which runway would you like at Teterboro?*

Cactus 1549 (3:29:28 p.m. and last transmission):

*We're going in the Hudson.*

Departure:

*I'm sorry, say again Cactus.*

Departure quickly dealt with another aircraft before saying:

*Cactus, ah, Cactus 1549, radar contact is lost you also got Newark airport off your 2 o'clock and about 7 miles.*

Having overheard the earlier exchange, the pilot of Eagle 4718 called Departure:

*Eagle 4718, I don't know, I think he said he was going in the Hudson.*

On the outside chance that it might be useful, Departure transmitted information about the runway available at Newark, seven miles away from the Cactus 1549's presumed position—no longer visible on the radar, possibly due to the high buildings.

**Events in the Air**

Just before Captain Chesley B. Sullenberger III reported the bird strike and announced his intention to return to La Guardia, the Airbus had been climbing through 3,200 ft under takeoff power with everything quite normal.

The flock of birds appeared from almost nowhere. The first officer flying the aircraft at the time saw them first. Sully saw them just as they were about to hit and later said he wanted to duck. They struck the windscreen and other parts of the aircraft with unusually loud thuds, as they were so large. A passenger in first class later said he saw a 'gray shape' shoot past his window and go into the engine, and that he knew it had done so because of the colossal 'bam.'

The engines powered down, with another passenger later saying they 'sounded like a spin dryer with a tennis shoes rolling around in it.[5]

Sully took over control from his first officer, Jeffrey Skiles, with the words 'my aircraft,' and he, or the A320's computer, or both, pushed the nose down so the aircraft would not stall.

Interviewed later on the CBS *60 Minutes* program, Sully said:

*It was the worst sickening, pit of the stomach, falling through the floor feeling I've ever felt in my life.*

*The physiological reaction I had of this was strong and I had to force myself to use my training and to force calm on the situation.*

As detailed in the transcription above, Sully informed Air Traffic Control (ATC) of the situation and indicated his intention to turn back to La Guardia.

The heading (two two zero) the controller had given him would bring him round for an approach to Runway 13—perpendicular to the one from which they had just taken off.

After he and the controller had considered other runway options, Sully said he was not sure they could make any runway and asked if there was anywhere in New Jersey such as Teterboro on the other side of the Hudson River.

The controller confirmed that Teterboro's Runway 1 was available, but Sully realized that he could not be certain of being able to reach it, especially as it would involve a sharp turn to line up with the runway that would result in even more loss of height. He might come down in a built-up area with loss of life on the ground as well as in the aircraft.

His only option was to ditch in the Hudson River as he had anticipated earlier on. He therefore continued his turn to the left until he was flying along the left bank of the wide river.

He skirted the George Washington (suspension) Bridge with its 604 ft (184 m) twin towers. Manhattan's Central Park was ahead on the left.

With the first officer Skiles vainly trying to restart an engine using a checklist conceived for dual engine failure at cruising height (around 35,000 ft), Sully brought the aircraft over the river itself.

He made the single announcement for the benefit of the cabin crew as well as the passengers:

*This is the captain—brace for impact!*

The aircraft was at 500 ft, and the time between the captain's announcement and the actual impact seemed inordinately long, perhaps because the great height of the buildings in Manhattan gave passengers the impression they were lower than they really were. In addition, the A320 was leveling out and losing speed so it was not travelling too fast on hitting the water.

The flight attendants were following their training, shouting 'BRACE! ... BRACE! ... Heads down! ... Stay down!' in unison at intervals. One flight attendant later mentioned her concern that some passengers were raising their heads to look out of the windows. This was understandable as some 90 seconds elapsed from the captain saying, 'Brace for impact' and the actual collision.

Not realizing they were landing (ditching) on water, some passengers were worried that they might do a 9/11, that is to say fly straight into a building and end up inside a ball of fire.

Lest we forget the short timeframe, Sully only had about three minutes from the time the engines failed to the time they would inevitably come down, either under control with the possibility of survival if a suitable spot could be found, or out of control following a stall with very little hope of but a few surviving.

## The 'Impact'

Sully had been able to restart the Auxiliary Power Unit (APU) to generate electricity, while in addition the Ram Air Turbine (RAT) had apparently deployed automatically. This meant he had more than adequate power to run his cockpit displays and control systems. For the Airbus A320, the manufacturer recommends Flaps 3 and a minimum approach airspeed of 150 knots, with 11 degrees of pitch at touchdown. It seems that Sully got the touchdown speed right, all the time being careful not to let it fall so low that a disastrous stall would result, though the inquiry said that the fact that he had switched on the APU meant that the computer automatically tipped the nose down when he let the speed fall too low earlier on.

He had the wings level at touchdown. The fact that some panels at the bottom of the rear fuselage were damaged enough to let water in and only one engine sheared off suggests to the author that a slightly less steep angle might have been better, but that is really quibbling.

What is certain is that the bottom of the fuselage at the rear struck the water first and sufficiently hard to damage to some panels. In consequence, the experience of those on board differed considerably, with the female flight attendant at the rear possibly getting the worst of it, and the pilots at the front getting the best of it. Apparently, the two pilots were surprised at how 'smooth' their touchdown had been.

On coming to a halt, the aircraft had slewed around no doubt because *only one* engine had sheared off. (Aircraft engines slung under the wings are attached in such a way that they will break off under an extreme rearwards force such as in the case of hitting an object when crash-landing or the water when ditching. This prevents the wing(s) being ripped off.)

## Events on the Ground (on the Water)

After a few moments of 'surprise' at how well it had appeared to have gone (at the front end of the aircraft), the two pilots knew that only half the battle had been won. All depended now not only on getting everyone out safely but also on their being picked up before the cold water (36°F/2°C) of the Hudson River took its toll. Pictures of the passengers standing on the wings so happy to be still alive give the impression the evacuation was something of a picnic. This was far from the truth, particularly for the passengers and the flight attendant at the very rear of the aircraft.

As mentioned, the impact with the water had damaged fuselage panels at the rear. Water was seeping in from there and from a rear door that a 'panicking passenger' had opened contrary to the instructions of the female flight attendant, who then tried to shut it without success. People at the back had to clamber over seatbacks to escape the influx of water, not knowing whether the situation might suddenly worsen. As they moved forward towards relative safety, the flight attendant who had been at the rear realized for the first time that she might survive.

The first officer had been using a ditching checklist written on the assumption that the decision to ditch would be made at a great height with plenty of time to prepare. This meant that he did not get as far as the line where it said, 'Press the ditching button' (at 2,000 ft), which would have closed various vents and the like. As a result, more water than otherwise would have been the case was coming in. Even so, this did not mean the aircraft would immediately sink completely. Kerosene (the fuel) is lighter than water and would have provided some buoyancy, as would empty space in the fuel tanks, which would not have been full, as the flight was not expected to be long.

Sully had brought the aircraft down between two ferry terminals and help was soon on its way. Before leaving the aircraft, he had walked up and down twice to make sure no one remained. He then stepped out and told rescuers to 'save' people on the wings first as he knew the life rafts could stay afloat almost indefinitely. A helicopter arrived on the scene, but pulled back so that its downdraught would not blow people off the wings, and a 'frogman' in a wetsuit had to jump off from a much greater height than usual to help a woman in difficulties in the water.

Finally, the rescuers were able to save everyone, with only two people suffering somewhat serious injuries, one of whom was the flight attendant who had been at the rear and who had not noticed the gash in her leg—extending down to the muscle—until rescued. It was an almost unbelievably fortunate outcome.

## Conclusion

Following the fairy tale ending, many in the media and a number of 'experts' were saying Sully had succeeded in doing something unique—ditching a large modern jet airliner without a single fatality—without pointing out that modern jet engines are so reliable that hardly any pilots are required to attempt it. His relatively low height meant he had only three minutes to play with and very limited options. However, he had the advantages of:

1. **Enough electrical power for the instruments, controls, and computers, thanks to his prescience in restarting the auxiliary power unit (APU).**

2. **The proximity of a ditching site situated between two ferry terminals with small maneuverable ferries plying between them.**

3. **Smooth water and no strong gusting crosswind.**

4. **A long stretch of river meaning that, apart from the desirability of coming to a halt between the ferry terminals, the actual touchdown point was not critical.**

Investigators have said that Sully's restarting the APU (something not on the checklist) was a determining factor as regards the favorable outcome. The electrical power it provided enabled him to maneuver the aircraft optimally using the computers, which, as already mentioned, pushed the nose down when he was at one point flying too slowly and possibly risked stalling.

Lack of time also meant the captain could not explain to the passengers that they were coming down on water. If he had, they would perhaps have been putting on lifejackets and not adopting the brace position, and worse still have inflated them prematurely, thus impeding evacuation.

Sully performed admirably, using his skill and other qualities—including gliding technique—honed over his long and varied career. However, he deserves much praise for his judgment in deciding to ditch in the Hudson rather than attempt to make it to La Guardia or Teterboro. Those on board were fortunate that such an ideal—water temperature apart—ditching site was at hand.

While many passengers personally thanked Sully for saving their lives, some as usual explored the possibility of suing the airline for their suffering. It would be interesting to know whether the 'panicking passenger' who opened the rear door and put people at risk when told not to do so by the flight attendant was amongst their number.

Modest to the end, Sully said when interviewed on a TV chat show to promote his book, that the reason he was the focus for so much adulation is that we are all looking for, and hoping to find, a hero. As said at the beginning of this narrative, it would be difficult to find a nicer or indeed kinder one.

---

[1] Term used by Robert Kolker in the *New York Magazine* in a long feature entitled *My Aircraft* to describe the treatment accorded Captain Chesley B. Sullenberger III (nicknamed Sully) following his feat. The piece also goes into interesting detail as to how, in general, the social and financial standing of pilots has changed from that of gods just below astronauts to that of drivers just above bus drivers.

[2] Nearer the city center than JFK, and with shorter runways, La Guardia was the logical airport for the two-hour flight to Charlottesville in North Carolina that the Airbus was about to make.

[3] Aircraft are handled by the 'tower' (local controller/LC) at takeoff. Once aloft, they are soon handed over to Terminal Radar Approach Control (TRACOM), which controls flights up to a height of 18,000 ft and a range of say 50 miles. Very often TRACOM is called Approach or Departure (control). Here we are talking about 'New York TRACOM La Guardia Departure.

When an emergency occurs, it has been found to be preferable that the aircraft is not be obliged to switch from frequency to frequency, and so in this case Departure (control) remained responsible. Hence, we use the term 'Departure' even though it may seem illogical when the aircraft is trying to land.

[4] Teterboro was actually New York's first airport, but is now a 'relief' airport handling smaller craft, including aircraft used by the US Federal Reserve.

[5] *The Miracle of the Hudson Plane Crash*, Channel 4 (UK), February 19, 2009.

# CHAPTER 2

# LOSS OF POWER OVER LAND

## CONSCIENTIOUS CREW FORGET FUEL REMAINING (Portland 1978)

### Classic Case Heralded CRM (Crew Resource Management)

> An absurd United Airlines DC-8 accident prompted the introduction of CRM, which initially stood for Cockpit Resource Management, but now allegedly stands for Crew Resource Management to reflect the role of crew working in other parts of the aircraft.
>
> *[United Airlines Flight 173]*

On December 28, 1978, a United Airlines McDonnell Douglas DC-8 with flight number 173 was approaching Portland Airport in Oregon, USA. The 189 people on board included the captain, the first officer, a flight engineer, a deadheading[1] captain two weeks from retirement, and four cabin attendants. There were six infants. The ETA was 17:15 and everything was so far on schedule.

On leaving the gate at the previous stopover at Denver there had been enough fuel for the 2 hr 26 min leg to Portland, with an additional 45-minute fuel reserve to meet FAA requirements and a further approximately 20-minute fuel reserve to meet company contingency requirements. Portland Approach Control had given them clearance to make a straight-in landing on Runway 28, so they should have been landing with their fuel reserve of just over an hour intact.

As they descended through 6,000 ft with the runway in sight, the first officer, who was the pilot flying (PF), requested 15 degrees of flap and the lowering of the landing gear. The captain extended the flaps to 15 degrees, and initiated the lowering of the landing gear, which to his surprise dropped down with an unusual thump and more quickly than usual. The captain later said the first officer had noticed a simultaneous yaw to the right. The jolt was even more noticeable to the flight attendants and passengers further back in the aircraft. More disconcertingly, one of the landing gear indicator lights failed to show green, presenting the crew with the possibility that the right-hand landing gear assembly was not properly down and locked.

Unaware of any such problem, Portland Approach told them to switch to the Portland Tower frequency for the actual landing. UA173 declined, saying they had a 'gear[2] problem' and wanted to stay with Approach, maintaining a height of 5,000 ft and a speed of 170 knots.

[According to AVweb.com, one of the approach controllers in question said as recently as 1998/9, that the controller gave the captain the option of holding at 6,000 ft over the Laker outer compass locator until he sorted out the problem. From there he could have made a dead-stick landing at any time onto either runway, but instead opted to orbit 20 miles or so southeast of the airport.]

Approach agreed to this request to orbit, telling them to turn left onto a heading of 200 degrees that would take them away from the airport and out of the path of any other incoming aircraft.

Portland Approach (17:14:43):

> *United one seventy three heavy, turn left heading, one zero zero*
> *and I'll just orbit you out there 'til you get your problem right.*

With UA173 being orbited by the controller, the crew went through all the landing gear checks in their manual. The mechanical (as opposed to electrical) indicators seemed to show the main landing gear was down and locked, and according to company regulations, they could have landed at any time at the captain's discretion. In such situations, it is usual for the aircraft to fly past the control tower to get a visual check from the ground, but on a dark winter evening, this was perhaps not a valid option.

As exhibited throughout the incident, the captain showed great concern regarding the situation in the passenger cabin, and called the senior flight attendant to the flight deck for a briefing.

At 17:38, somewhat belatedly—the possible checks should not have taken so long to complete—they contacted the company's San Francisco Maintenance Control Centre and explained the situation.

However, San Francisco could not think of anything further the crew could usefully do, and in view of the confirmation given by the mechanical indicators were wondering when the captain would proceed with his inevitable landing. After explaining the situation, the captain told them he had 7,000 lb of fuel on board and expected to hold for 15 or 20 minutes, adding that he intended to have the flight attendants prepare for an emergency landing.

At 17:44:03, San Francisco Maintenance Control sought to confirm his intentions.

> *Okay, United one seventy-three.... You estimate that you'll make a*
> *landing about five minutes past the hour. Is that okay?*

Captain:

> Yeah, that's [a] good ball park. I'm not gonna hurry the girls. We got about a hundred sixty five people on board and we ... want to ... take our time and get everybody ready, and then we'll go. It's clear as a bell and no problem.

The captain briefed the senior flight attendant about getting ready for the emergency landing and possible evacuation, but did not give her a deadline or suggest any state of urgency. (He later said he assumed it would take 10 or 15 minutes, and that final preparations could be carried out as they came in to land.)

At that time, all three aircrew were fully aware of the fuel situation as at 17:46:52 the flight engineer replied to the first officer that they had 5,000 lb of fuel left. Not only did the first officer acknowledge this, he immediately asked the captain:

> What's the fuel show now?

The captain replied:

> Five.

The first officer duly repeated:

> Five.

Further confirmation that there was only about 5,000 lb of fuel left was given by the fact that the inboard fuel pump lamps start to blink, as they are meant to do if the fuel level falls below 5,000 lb. At that point, the aircraft was about 13 nm south of the airport and heading *away* from it on a west-southwest heading.

With not much time before the fuel would run out, they yet again discussed the status of the landing gear, before being interrupted by a course change and advisory from Approach control.

[17:50:20] Captain to flight engineer:

> Give us a current card on weight. Figure about another fifteen minutes.

Flight engineer:

> Fifteen minutes?

Captain:

> Yeah, give us three or four thousand pounds on top of zero fuel weight.

Flight engineer:

> Not enough. Fifteen minutes is gonna ... really run us low on fuel here.

29

The two pilots then busied themselves with preparations for landing, while the flight engineer replied to questions from the company representative at Portland about the fuel load on landing and the number of passengers. Finally, the flight engineer asked the captain whether he could inform the company representative that they would be landing at 'Five after.' The captain said, 'Yeah.'

At 17:55:04, the flight engineer reported completion of the approach descent check. When the first officer at 17:56:53 asked about how much fuel he had, the flight engineer replied that 4,000 lb remain, namely 1,000 lb in each tank.

The captain then sent the flight engineer to the passenger cabin '*to kinda see how things are going*.' In his absence, he and the first officer discussed the importance of giving the flight attendants time to prepare, what cockpit procedures would be required in the event of an emergency evacuation, and finally whether the brake anti-skid devices would be working.

At 18:01:12, Portland Approach put them on another orbit.

*United 173 heavy turn left, Heading one niner five.*

By complying with those instructions to orbit instead of requesting immediate clearance to proceed with the landing in accordance with the initial timetable, the first officer—with the captain's apparent acquiescence—sealed the fate of the aircraft.

At 18:01:34, the flight engineer returned to the flight deck with the news that everything would be ready in another two or three minutes. He and the captain briefly discussed the mood and state of the passengers.

[18:02:22] Flight engineer:

*We got about three on the fuel and that's it.*

Captain:

*Okay. On touchdown, if the gear folds or something really jumps the track, get those boost pumps off so that … you might even get the valves open.*

At 18:02:44, Approach Control, no doubt surprised that the whole affair was taking so long, asked to be appraised of the situation, and was told by the first officer that they still had an indication of a landing gear abnormality; they expected to land in about five minutes; and would need emergency services standing by.

At 18:03:14 with the aircraft about eight nm south of the airport and heading away from it, Portland Approach told them to advise when they would like to begin their approach, to which the captain replied:

*They've about finished in the cabin. I'd guess about another three, four, five minutes.*

As is customary for a possible emergency landing, Portland Approach asked for a final confirmation as to the number of persons on board and the amount of fuel remaining.

The flight crew spent the next 2½ minutes discussing technical matters. They wondered whether the horn that warns pilots if they are landing without the landing gear locked down would not be an indication of its true status. They also wondered whether the tripping of the landing gear circuit breakers might mean the spoilers and anti-skid brakes would not deploy automatically.

The senior flight attendant came back to the flight deck to report that she thought they were ready, with the aircraft by then about 17 nm south of the airport and still heading away from it. After talking to her for about half a minute, and going into detail about whether able-bodied people were by the exits and noting the fact that the off-duty captain would be in the first row of coach behind the galley, the captain said to her:

> Okay. We're going to go in now. We should be landing in about five minutes.

It was 18:06:40 and they were 19 nautical miles south-southwest of the airport, and still heading away from it.

Before the flight attendant could answer, the flight engineer or the first officer interjected.

> I think you lost number four Buddy, you...

Whereupon the flight attendant said, 'Okay, I'll make the five-minute announcement. I'll go, I'm sitting down now.'

First Officer to flight engineer:

> Better get some cross feeds open there or something!

Flight engineer:

> Okay!

The flight attendant said 'All righty' as she started to make her way back to the passenger cabins.

At 18:06:46 the first officer twice told the captain they were going to lose an engine. The captain twice replied, 'Why?' to which the first officer twice replied 'Fuel.' They both told the flight engineer to open the cross feeds and there seemed to be some confusion as to how much fuel they had.

At 18:07:06 the first officer declared the engine had flamed out.

At 18:07:12, almost an hour after declining their initial clearance to make a landing approach, the captain finally asked for it again. The controller accordingly gave him an initial heading vector of 010 degrees, which they turned to so they were again 19 nm south-southwest of the airport.

Flight engineer (18:07:27):

> *We're going to lose number three in a minute too.*

The crew tried to see if they could keep the engines going by opening cross feeds.

Approach (18:10:47):

> *18 flying miles from the field.*

Approach (18:12:43):

> *12 flying miles from the field.*

The flight engineer declared they had just lost two engines, '*One and two.*'

Approach (18:13:29):

> *8 or 9 flying miles from the field.*

Captain (18:13:38):

> *They're all going. We can't make Troutdale (a nearer general aviation airport).*

First officer (18:13:43):

> *We can't make anything!*

The captain then told him to declare a Mayday. The first officer did so, ending his transmission to the tower with the words:

> *We're going down. We're not going to be able to reach the airport.*

The captain later said that in the minute or so he could remain in the air there were few options, and no good ones. Congestion due to rush-hour traffic would make landing on the highway along the bank of the Columbia River a disastrous proposition and icy water in the fast moving river itself would certainly result in many fatalities even should he be successful in ditching there in the darkness. He therefore opted to bring the aircraft down in a wooded area with no visible lights about six nautical miles east-southeast of the airport.

His skill no doubt helped keep casualties to a minimum. Initial impacts were with trees, before the aircraft destroyed two fortunately unoccupied homes. Just before the aircraft came to a halt some 500 meters from the point of initial impact with the first tree, the vertical stabilizer on the tail snagged some high-tension electric transmission lines, and this encounter no doubt helped bring the aircraft to a final halt. The outbreak of fire, so much feared by the crew, did not occur—there was no fuel left. A tree penetrating the fuselage near the flight engineer's position caused some fatalities back from there.

Remarkably 'only' eight passengers and two crew (the flight engineer and the senior flight attendant, who was said to have saved lives by preparing so well for the possible emergency evacuation), were killed. A further 21 passengers and 2 crewmembers incurred serious injuries. Out of the 189 persons on board, 158 escaped relatively unscathed.

The passengers did not receive any warning from the aircrew that the aircraft was coming down and initially thought they were landing at the airport. After they started striking the trees a flight attendant shouted out, 'Hold your ankles!'

## The Inquiry

The inquiry revealed that a fault due to corrosion in part of the landing gear mechanism had caused one set of wheels to freefall down into place rather than sink down gently. The temporary imbalance in drag (one set of wheels came down earlier than the other) had produced the yaw noticed by the first officer. Furthermore, in the process of dropping down into place, the gear had damaged the micro switches used to show whether the gear was fully down and locked. In fact, the aircraft could have landed safely at any time.

The inquiry concluded that the crew, having become so absorbed in trying to solve the landing gear problem and thinking about the possible consequences, failed properly to consider the fuel consumption rate. However, they did note that when asked about the fuel they would have if they landed as planned (at five-past the hour), the flight engineer had said, 'Fifteen minutes is gonna ... really run us low on fuel here!'

For the hour they were orbiting, the captain was considering every eventuality, even the mental state of the passengers, in detail. He even sought to arrange for the San Francisco Maintenance Office to handle certain procedures to avoid the risk of bad local publicity. At one point, the off-duty about-to-retire captain—who subsequently returned to the passenger cabin to better help with a possible evacuation—suggested the flight crew put on their jackets so as to be more recognizable and to expose less bare flesh in the event of fire.

Much of what the captain did and thought about was very commendable, but one has to wonder whether the drip-drip effect of spending so much time thinking about what might happen in the unlikely worst possible scenario did not affect the crewmembers' grasp of the overall situation.

## Cockpit Resource Management (CRM)

The incident revealed the need for formal policies and programs to ensure aircrew function well as a team, with each having defined complementary duties rather than everyone focusing on a single matter. United Airlines took the experience to heart and became the first to initiate such a program, using some of the techniques already used by business and management consultants. As mentioned at the beginning of this chapter, they called this Cockpit Resource Management (CRM), now changed to Crew Resource

Management, to reflect the important role of others, such as cabin crew and even ground staff such as maintenance staff.

In presenting the NTSB report in conjunction with a posting in January 1997 saying 'the survivors had held a reunion at which the captain received a standing ovation,' AVweb commented, 'We let our readers judge for themselves whether the captain was a "hero" or a "heel".'

---

[1] Deadheading is an aviation term used to refer to crew who are traveling without charge on the flight to take up duties elsewhere on the network, or who are returning from such duties. Sometimes referred to as 'positioning.'

[2] US pilots usually use the term 'landing gear' for undercarriage.

# GLIDING EXPERIENCE SAVES THE DAY
# (Gimli, Canada 1983)
## Metric Conversion Mix-up

Considering there are relatively few instances of aircraft, such as Piché's, gliding long distances to a safe landing, it is surprising that a Canada-registered aircraft had also featured in a gliding incident 18 years before. That time it was over water. This time it was over land.

*[Air Canada Flight 143]*

In July 1983, Captain Bob Pearson and First Officer Quintal, like Piché, also became instant heroes when their sophisticated Air Canada Boeing 767 ran out of fuel despite their flight management computer (FMC) indicating they still had enough fuel for several hours' flying.

They had set off with their fuel gauges not working and the FMC was calculating the amount of fuel in the tanks by deducting the amount consumed by the engines from the amount measured by dipsticks on departure. Thus, the amount indicated by the FMC depended on correctly knowing the amount of fuel initially in the tanks.

The Boeing 767 was merrily flying along with the FMC showing the theoretical amount of fuel remaining. Regardless of whatever the FMC said, they should have had no need to worry as the dipstick checks at Montreal and then Ottawa had shown they had ample fuel for the 3,574 km leg to to Edmonton, and would still have the required reserves!

Just over halfway, with the readout from the FMC indicating several tons of fuel left, a beeping sound drew the relaxing pilots' attention to low pressure in one of the two fuel pumps[1] feeding the left engine. Soon afterwards, the instruments indicated low pressure in the other pump. Like Piché, Captain Pearson's first thought had been of a possible computer error or sensor fault. However, the aircraft was virtually new, and for two pumps or their pressure sensors to fail was troubling enough for Pearson to decide to divert to the nearest appropriate airport, which was Winnipeg. Still at 41,000 ft, they throttled back the engines to begin descent into Winnipeg, some 120 nm away.

Shortly afterwards the displays warned of a similar low fuel pump pressure situation for both pumps feeding the engine on the opposite side. For so many pumps to be affected simultaneously was a sure sign of a fuel problem, and their fears were confirmed when a few minutes later the number one engine flamed out, followed three minutes later by the number two engine. Normally, the fuel measurement system would have given a warning once the fuel level fell to 2 tons, giving them more than adequate time (over land) to make an emergency landing under power.

They were by then down to 25,000 ft with still 65 nm to go to Winnipeg. As in the case of Piché's aircraft, a small RAT (ram air turbine) had dropped down from the underside of the aircraft to provide just enough power for essential flying controls. The once sophisticated screens were blank, and all they had was the artificial horizon, airspeed indicator, altimeter and a magnetic compass that was difficult to read because, unlike the usual gyrocompass, it was not very steady.

With no vertical speed indicator,[2] judging the optimum glide path was exceedingly difficult, and amid his other tasks, the first officer had to get the Winnipeg controller to constantly give the distance remaining to Winnipeg and try to work it out from tables.

With them down to 10,000 ft and descending to 9,500 ft, the distance remaining was 45 nm. They were losing height faster than expected and at that rate all hope of making Winnipeg had gone. The situation was desperate.

Just as the captain was about to ask Winnipeg for anything nearer, the first officer suggested they try Gimli Air Force Base where he had been temporarily stationed during his military service. He knew it had two runways of sufficient length. Reassuringly, air traffic control informed them Gimli was only 12 nm from their location.

As air traffic control guided him towards Gimli, the captain learnt that though it was no longer an operational military base, light aircraft were using the right-hand runway. However, the controller could not guarantee the runway would be clear.

They did not want to lose too much height before being sure they could identify the Gimli base. When the first officer did sight it, they were much too high, posing the problem of how to lose both height and speed in the distance that remained without the help of flaps or air brakes.

By a lucky coincidence, Captain Pearson happened to be an experienced glider pilot. By a series of difficult sideslips and yaws that only a glider pilot could manage,[3] he brought the speed and height down to a reasonable degree, and with the runway ahead, told the first officer to lower the landing gear.

In the dusk, they could only see one clearly defined whitish runway ahead, and assumed incorrectly it must be the (actually darker) right-hand one on which they planned to land, which they could not see because of its darker color. Thus, they were unknowingly lining up with the disused left-hand runway, which that weekend was being used as a racing car circuit with a strip down the middle and the cars going down one side and up the other.

The first officer duly selected landing gear down but nothing happened. Frantically, he searched in the manual to see how to let the wheels fall just by gravity but could not find the explanation—actually (and logically) in the hydraulics section—because the index failed to mention it. He then tried the alternative gear extension switch and with a sigh of relief heard the wheels drop down. To his consternation, there was no green light to confirm the nose wheel had locked.

Coming in 50 knots faster than normal, the captain made a perfect landing on the wrong runway only to find there were people, including children, on it. Luckily, the last race of the day had just finished and all were congregated at the far end. The captain applied the brakes as hard as possible and as the aircraft slowed, the unlocked nose wheel assembly collapsed to produce a shower of sparks. The failure of the front wheel was a blessing in disguise as it helped stop the aircraft just short of a group of very surprised adults and children.

With the collapse of the nose wheel assembly, the aircraft had tilted forward with the tail high up in the air, making the chutes at the rear too steep to use safely. However, with relatively few passengers on board, all were able to exit easily and safely from the front. Again, with no fuel, there was little likelihood of a major fire, and fire extinguishers from the race organizers ensured smoke coming from the front did not develop into a fire.

As usual, a series of failures and misunderstandings was responsible for this ridiculous near disaster. Taking away any one of them would have prevented what could have been a terrible disaster.

## Multiple Causes:

There are so many little factors that not every reader will want to read this next part in detail:

### 1. Non-compliance with Minimum Equipment List (MEL)

For safety reasons, essential systems in aircraft are in duplicate, triplicate and sometimes quadruplicate. In addition, some items are not 'safety critical' in the sense that they do not significantly affect safety. Therefore, for every aircraft, there is a MEL showing what systems or items must be working. The pilots run through this list before every flight, and check their aircraft meets minimum requirements before setting out, even though the maintenance personnel will have themselves verified this before handing over.

Sometimes there may be a 'special-case MEL' with conditions attached to it. For instance, when maintenance staff in Tokyo recently found a faulty engine on a 747 that could not be easily (or cheaply) repaired there, the airline (British Airways) decided to have it repaired in London. They were able to fly the aircraft back to London on three engines on the condition that there were no passengers and they had an extra pilot who would have to come from London to assist. A three-engine 'ferry flight' must have a specially trained captain—as improper application of asymmetric power can be disastrous.

Many of the provisions in the MEL are obvious and apply to similar aircraft, but others are specific to a particular aircraft type. When a new aircraft is developed, the aircraft manufacturer issues a MEL, which the airline and manufacturer update. The newly developed and sophisticated Boeing 767 (with screens replacing many traditional dials) was a completely new aircraft for Air Canada so the MEL was not definitive. With so many revisions, pilots often had to check with Maintenance management to be sure what was permissible.

When Pearson arrived at Montreal Airport with First Officer Quintal, they met the incoming captain, Captain Weir, and naturally discussed the condition of the aircraft. Weir said there was a problem with the fuel gauges, and went on to mention the fact that they had (once) blanked out. Weir himself had misunderstood the technician in Edmonton, who had said they had blanked out coming in from Toronto several weeks earlier—Weir thought he meant that they had blanked on the flight that had just come in from Toronto. Anyway, Captain Pearson believed the aircraft he was to take over had come in with all the fuel gauges blanked out and that it would be reasonable to carry on, especially as the new part was waiting in Edmonton (their destination).

It would have been difficult for Pearson to refuse to fly an aircraft that he thought other captains had deemed acceptable—and especially so when Maintenance had confirmed that complying with the MEL did not pose a problem. In fact, the other captains had flown the aircraft with the fuel gauges working with input from just one processor channel, which satisfied the MEL, provided ground staff carried out a dipstick check as well. Maintenance was wrong to say departing with none of the fuel gauges working complied with the MEL.

## 2. The Technical Fault

Much earlier, the technician in Edmonton had found that the entire fuel gauge system blanked out when one of the digital processor channels failed.

Failure of one element in a two-channel fuel indication system should not have crippled the entire system. However, poor design (not by Boeing) meant there was not enough power when one side failed and this accounted for the whole system going blank from time to time because of a fickle connection in the right-hand channel.[4]

Any car owner knows how difficult it is to find an intermittent fault, as it is never there when you are looking for it. It can also lure the user into a sense of false security as things may revert to normal for a long time, only for a failure to occur when there is a temperature or pressure change or when there is turbulence. This is why the faulty part in Pearson's aircraft was not repaired earlier.

### 3. Misunderstandings—Language

The *qualified* technician in Edmonton found he could get the fuel gauges to work by isolating the defective processor channel. He therefore switched off that channel and agreed with Maintenance that the aircraft could fly like that while waiting for the spare part—provided a dipstick check was carried out. He left a note on the tripped circuit breaker saying the channel was inoperative. In the maintenance log, he wrote:

SERVICE CHK—FOUND FUEL QTY IND BLANK—FUEL QTY #2 C/B PULLED & TAGGED—FUEL DIP REQD PRIOR TO DEP. SEE MEL.

As Stanley Stewart says in his excellent account in *Emergency* (published by Airlife), the technician was referring to the fuel indicators going blank during the check, but that would not be clear from the text. Of course, the technician's 'SEE MEL' supposedly but not obviously restated the need to have a dipstick check as well as one processor channel working.

### 4. Too Many Cooks

Had no one else stuck their oar in, all would have been well, at least as regards keeping the fuel gauges functioning. Unfortunately, while waiting to dipstick the tanks after refueling in Montreal a *lesser qualified* technician had noticed the pulled circuit breaker with the tag saying 'Not Operational.' Though not properly qualified to test the system, he tried resetting the breaker thus making the fuel gauges go blank. Before he had time to re-pull the breaker and see if that made the gauges work, he was called away to check the tanks using a dipstick. He forgot about it, but did remember to put a note in the log

FUEL QTY IND U/S. SUSPECT PROCESSOR UNIT AT FAULT. NIL STOCK.

He then signed out the maintenance log as satisfactory.

### 5. Metric Conversion Error

When dealing with fuel volumes—such as when refueling or using a dipstick to check the amount of fuel in a tank—the unit used is the liter. However, weight is what the pilots want to know, as it is so important when flying. For instance, the 'V' takeoff speeds vary according to the gross weight of the aircraft (BOW[5] + passengers + cargo + fuel).

Up to that time, the unit used to express weight at the airline had been pounds. Like many countries other than the US, Canada was changing over to the metric system, and the 767 was the first aircraft type in the Air Canada fleet to have the fuel weight expressed in kilograms rather than pounds.

Everyone dealing with that 767 knew the weight of the fuel had to be expressed in kilograms, but in converting liters to kilograms they *all* used (or copied) the wrong conversion factor. Any kid educated at school in the metric system would have known that one liter of water weighs one kilogram, and little stretch of imagination would be required to know that with kerosene being slightly lighter than water, one would have to use a conversion factor of less than 1.0 (actually 0.8). Instead, they used the conversion factor for converting liters to pounds, which is 1.77. As a result, they only had some 10 tonnes (metric tons) of fuel in the tanks and imagined they had 22, and that was the figure programmed into the FMC.

On checking the calculations, Captain Pearson failed to notice the use of the wrong conversion factor.

## Conclusion

This incident was the result of many errors and failures. As Professor Reason[6] says, with the best will in the world, it is impossible to prevent all errors, and the important thing is finding ways to cope with them.

Failure to follow the MEL and the bad design of the overall fuel processor system that allowed failure of one part to cripple the entire system would seem to be key errors. Badly relayed information and cryptic technical logs also played a significant part.

It is a pity no one questioned whether the result was reasonable when converting liters to kilograms. However, that would depend on familiarity with liters and kilograms.

---

[1] For safety reasons always at least two.

[2] A very useful instrument showing rate of descent (or ascent) in feet per minute.

[3] Tricky, as airspeed indicators are not accurate when the aircraft is side slipping.

[4] Investigators later found a wire connecting a coil for the right channel had been cold-soldered and not tinned beforehand. Cold soldering tends to produce fickle electrical connections and sparking.

[5] BOW or Basic Operating Weight is the weight of the aircraft with its crew, which is a constant value.

[6] Professor Reason is a famous academic specializing in safety. See Index.

# AVIANCA FLIGHT 52 MISSES LAST CHANCE (New York 1990)

### Deferential First Officer Fails to Use the 'E'-Word

> The survivors and relatives of those who died when Avianca Flight 52 ran out of fuel while attempting to land at New York's JFK airport were incensed when reminded the official inquiry attributed the accident almost entirely to the first officer's failure to use the term *emergency* in his radio transmissions to air traffic control.
>
> However, the courts subsequently made the FAA, as the controllers' employer, liable for 40% of the $200,000,000 awarded as compensation.
>
> *[Avianca Flight 52]*

The lights in the passenger cabin of the Columbian Avianca Boeing 707 flickered as the fuel supply to the engines became erratic. With so little fuel left, no measure (such as avoiding an angle of attack that would make the fuel slosh to the sides of the tanks) other than coming down on a runway or flat open space could save them. However, JFK airport was 15 miles away, and the hilly ground of the affluent residential district of Cove Neck on Long Island lay ahead.

A few seconds later, the engines fell silent leaving only the rustle of the wind against the fuselage—soon to be drowned out by the screams and exclamations of the passengers realizing they might be facing their Maker.

How, in what one would imagine to be one of the most sophisticated Air Traffic Control (ATC) zones in the world could the pilots and passengers of Avianca Flight 52 find themselves in such a predicament?

It was due to what, with hindsight, was a whole series of missed opportunities to avoid the possibility of a disaster.

The first of these was not diverting to their alternate, Boston, when on approaching the New York control zone an hour and a half earlier controllers had informed them their wait in the holding pattern would be **at least** 45 minutes. The pilots possibly thought the controller was being careful and that the wait would not be very much longer. In fact, they had to hold for 77 minutes.

Then, as the aircraft was subsequently handed over from one controller to another, the *first officer* who was handling radio communications used phrases such as 'We're running out of fuel.' He evidently thought this clearly indicated their fuel predicament, but he failed to convey the true situation to the controllers, who had perhaps 50 aircraft in the sky, all in a sense

41

running out of fuel and all wanting priority. If they started to let aircraft that had not declared an *emergency* jump the queue, a traffic jam would develop over the airport, perhaps compromising the safety of other aircraft also low on fuel.

Another factor explaining the controllers' apparent lack of probing into Avianca 52's status was that with the aircraft being handed over successively from controller to controller, none had the time to build up a detailed picture. Aircraft have to be pigeonholed in the controller's mind, and this is particularly so at busy times—it is either a normal flight or it is an emergency.

When, after 77 minutes, Flight 52 was allowed to exit the holding pattern (after the crew being asked how much longer they could hold), they were passed on to the Approach Controller, who—unaware of their predicament—greeted them as follows.

Approach (21:03:11):

> *Avianca zero five two heavy, New York Approach good evening. Fly*
> *heading zero six zero.*

After acknowledging this, the Avianca flight crew, consisting of the captain, first officer, and flight engineer, agreed on the need, when less than 1,000 lb of fuel remains in any tank, to avoid doing anything such as raising the nose too much or accelerating violently, that might cause it to slosh to one side leaving the outlet uncovered.

As the controllers bought them in and gave them course changes, the first officer and flight engineer surmised they were being 'accommodated' and that they (the controllers) were aware of their situation. At no point did they tell the approach controller they were low on fuel, no doubt assuming that the previous controller had informed him of that fact. Apart from the controller telling them to make their speed 160 knots if practical, there is nothing of note from the controller, before he hands them over to the tower controller, who greets them:

Tower (21:15:23):

> *Avianca zero five two heavy, Kennedy Tower, runway two two left.*
> *You're number three following seven two seven traffic on a, ah,*
> *niner mile final.*

The tower, finding the more modern aircraft following behind was in danger of catching up with the old Boeing 707, asked Avianca 52 for their airspeed (140 knots) and asked them to increase it by 10 knots, impatiently telling them, 'Increase! Increase!' Avianca 52's captain, who was flying the aircraft, seemed to be having some difficulty hearing these exchanges and what the first officer and flight engineer were saying.

They proceeded with the standard pre-landing checks and the lowering of the landing gear. Duly cleared to land, they asked for a wind check and were told it was 190 degrees at 20 knots. (Actually, the wind speed at their location was apparently of the order of 60 knots, with the difference between that and the 20 knots given to them for the airport representing considerable wind shear.)

The tower, still concerned about the separation from the TWA aircraft behind them, asked for their airspeed again, and on being told it was one-four-five, asked the TWA aircraft behind if they could match it.

The TWA pilot said:

*Okay, we'll do our best.*

The Avianca flight was all set for landing, but sank a little below the glide slope. The tower, increasingly concerned about the separation asked the TWA craft to reduce its final airspeed, if feasible. With the TWA crew saying they could not go slower, the tower asked Avianca 52 to increase theirs by 10 knots, but finding they were getting too close, ordered the TWA heavy to turn off left and maintain 2,000 ft.

The tower then informed American Airlines Flight 40 they had become number two in the landing sequence, behind a 707 (Avianca 52).

It was then, with everything seemingly fine for the landing, that Avianca 52 encountered wind shear 2.5 nm from the runway. The aircraft sank, with the *Whoop, Whoop. PULL UP* from the Ground Proximity Warning System (GPWS) warning the crew they were in danger of hitting the ground. To recover, the captain pushed the throttles forward, thus using up much of the remaining fuel. After sinking to the dangerously low height of 200 ft two miles from the runway, the aircraft finally pulled out of its descent.

Captain:

*Where is the runway?*

The GPWS repeated, *Whoop, Whoop, PULL UP* three more times.

Captain:

*The runway! Where is it?*

The automatic *Glide slope!* warning sounds twice.

First officer:

*I don't see it! I don't see it!*

The captain ordered the raising of the landing gear as they aborted the landing.

The glide slope warning sounded twice again, presumably because they were by then *above* it.

The first officer then informed the tower they were executing a missed approach.

It is very likely that the pilots failed to see the runway in the poor visual conditions due to the nose-up attitude of the aircraft at the critical moment as they recovered from the perilous sink rate brought about by the wind shear.

The tower told them to climb and maintain 2,000 ft, and subsequently asked them to confirm they were making a left turn (according to the standard missed landing procedure) just as the TWA craft had done just before.

The captain then specifically told the first officer to tell the controllers it was an '*Emergency.*'

Instead, the first officer simply confirmed to the controller they were executing the left turn as instructed, adding that they were running out of fuel:

> *That's right, to one eight zero on the heading—and—ah, we'll try once again. We're running out of fuel.*

The tower simply said '*Okay,*' and gave the next aircraft, American Airlines Flight 40, clearance to land, adding that a DC-9 had reported wind shear, with a gain and loss of 10 knots, from 700 ft down to the surface.

The Avianca captain *again* told his first officer to tell the tower it was an emergency, adding:

> *Did you tell him?*

The first officer said:

> *Yes Sir. I already advised him.*

This was not strictly true, as the first officer had not used the term *emergency*. In addition, as pointed out by the NTSB investigators, the flight engineer had failed to remind the pilots that to all intents and purposes that would represent their one and only chance to land. This fact should have been also made clear to approach control and the tower, lest they order a go-around such as the one they had ordered the TWA aircraft to execute for lack of separation.

Also, even without using the term *emergency*, it is difficult to understand why, in the even more desperate situation following the missed approach, the first officer failed to inform the tower they had under ten minutes of fuel left. Some commentators have suggested it was because they were unable to work out a precise figure!

Whether it would have been possible to free up either of JFK's very long 31L or 31R runways and get the Avianca flight far out enough to line up and come in with sufficient fuel remaining is open to question. Performing flying club antics with an airliner would have been difficult enough even in good visibility.

Thus not realizing the severity of the situation, the tower controller who was about to hand over to a colleague at the end of his shift simply handed them over to the approach controller.

The captain told the first officer to tell approach they didn't have fuel, but the first officer, after automatically acknowledging the order to climb and maintain 3,000 ft, reverted to saying '*We are running out of fuel, Sir.*' The controller replied, '*Okay,*' and gave them a new heading.

Again, the captain asked the first officer if he had advised ATC they didn't have fuel. He confirmed that he had, adding optimistically, '*and he's going to get us back.*'

The approach controller then gave instructions to two other aircraft. After giving Avianca 52 a new heading, he showed his concern as follows:

Approach control (21:26:35):

> *And Avianca zero five two heavy, ah, I'm going to bring you fifteen miles northeast, and then bring you back onto the approach. Is that fine with you and your fuel?*

First officer (21:26:43):

> *I guess so, tha (sic) you very much.*

The captain asked what the controller said, but before the first officer could tell him, the flight engineer bizarrely said:

'*The guy is angry.*'

Approach control continued to give instructions both to them and to other aircraft as if things were normal. At one point, on being asked to climb, they replied in the negative saying they were running out of fuel. Approach replied '*Okay,*' and gave a slightly different heading.

[The controller, knowing they did not have much fuel, evidently wanted to avoid them creeping up on the aircraft in front and having to go around again.]

Approach control (21:31:01):

> *Okay; and you're number two for the approach. I just have to give you enough room so you can make it without, ah, having to come out again.*

The first officer acknowledged. To which the controller replied:

> *Thank you, Sir.*

This was hardly the sign of an angry controller, unless said sarcastically and presumably the controller would be too busy for such niceties. The controller then dealt with a couple of other aircraft before giving Avianca 52 a 30-degree change of heading to the left to bring them nearer the heading for the outer marker.

*[CVR anomaly—hiccup due to fluctuating power supply, no doubt corresponding to flickering of cabin lights (21:32:38).]*

Flight engineer (21:32:39):

> *Flame out! Flame out on engine number 4.*

Captain (21:32:49):

> *Show me the runway.*

First officer to controller (21:32:49):

> *Avianca zero five two. We just, ah, lost two engines and, ah, we need priority, please.*

The controller then gave them a new heading to intercept the localizer more quickly.

21:32:56:

> *[Sound of engine(s?) spooling down]*

The captain and first officer then talked about setting the ILS (instrument landing system). The captain said:

> *Set the ILS, let's see.*

Approach control (21:33:04):

> *Avianca zero five two heavy, you're one five miles from the outer marker; maintain two thousand until established on the localizer. Cleared for ILS two-two left.*

Avianca 52 acknowledged this.

Captain (21:33:22):

> *Did you select the ILS?*

First officer (21:33:22):

> *It is ready on two.*

21:33.24

*[End of CVR recording—in view of the CVR hiccups when the power supply fluctuated, it is evident that there was no battery backup, and the end of the recording did not correspond with the impact with the ground.]*

The flight data recorder provided no evidence because someone had rendered it inoperable by taping back the foil inside. However, examination of the engines at the crash site immediately revealed they had not been rotating under power when the aircraft struck the ground.

Surviving passengers and the only surviving crewmember—the leading flight attendant—were able to describe the last moments. Radar records gave useful information about heights and tracks.

According to a witness on the ground, the aircraft dropped silently out of the sky. Without evidence from the flight data recorder, ascertaining the precise sink rate and forward speed prior to impact was impossible.

From the distribution of the debris and the injuries to passengers it was possible to deduce that the forward speed on impact had not been so great—although shattered, most parts relatively speaking were in the right places, with the wings sticking out from the fuselage in the normal place and not lying somewhere else.

The aircraft had apparently belly flopped into a gully, hitting the odd tree and slithering up the higher far side. The fuselage had snapped in at least two places, with one break right behind the flight deck, so that the nose, with the flight crew inside, flipped over the brow to land near a house.

Lack of fuel meant there was no fire, but the great g-forces of the impact meant all 85 survivors were injured in some way. Of the 158 persons on board 73 died. Most deaths were due to head and upper body injuries, and three doctors involved in the treatment of the injured wrote a paper analyzing the injuries, suggesting it might provide valuable lessons regarding better constraints for passengers.[1] Cost-benefit considerations meant that not all suggestions would be implemented.

As regards passenger survival, this accident was somewhat atypical in that the aircraft had completely empty tanks, and getting out before succumbing to the effects of smoke inhalation was not the key to survival.

As usual, a whole series of factors was responsible for the disaster:

1. Lack of assertiveness on the part of the first officer, perhaps explained in part by an inferiority complex when dealing with the 'superior' American controllers—at one point the flight engineer even remarked that the controller sounded angry!

2. Hoping for the optimum scenario—though the controller at the outset might have done better to suggest a more probable hold time rather than saying '*at least* 45 minutes.'

3. The 'creeping up' of events, in that they remained on hold for so long that the option of diverting to their alternate, Boston, was lost—this could be classed as indecision.

4. The first officer handling the radio communications did not even once use the word 'emergency,' though told to do so by the captain.

5. Neither did he inform the tower that their attempt to land was in fact their one and only chance, in which case the controller could have tried to talk them down until they could see the runway using radar.

**6. Finally, there was a fatal dose of bad luck in that just as they were coming down towards the runway expecting everything to be finally all right, they had to raise the nose to regain height lost due to the wind shear, and probably thereby failed to pick out the runway in the murk.**

ATC was under great pressure having to cope with so many aircraft holding in the difficult weather conditions, having to order some to go around because of lack of separation. Had this not been so, the controllers might have felt able to devote time to exploring what the first officer really meant when he repeatedly told them (but to different controllers) that the aircraft was running out of fuel. Something that would have been true to a greater or lesser extent for many of the aircraft they were handling at the time.

---

[1] J Trauma. Feb 1993; 34(2):282-4. *Analysis of injuries following the crash of Avianca Flight 52*, Dulchavsky., Geller E.R., Iorio D.A., Department of Surgery, Division of Trauma, State University of New York, Stony Brook.

# CHARTS DID NOT SHOW BUILT-UP AREAS
# (London 2004)

This incident involving London's Heathrow showed that air traffic controllers should keep aircraft with engines failing for one reason or another away from cities, even if that means exposing their occupants to greater danger.

*[Evergreen International Cargo]*

An excellent article by Ben Webster in the *London Times*, dated January 13, 2006, had the following headline

*STRICKEN JUMBO WAS ALLOWED*
*TO FLY OVER CENTRE OF LONDON*

The subtitle was:

*With One Engine Down, and Three Failing*
*the 747 Flew over Thousands of Homes*

The article related how in April 2004, an American-owned Evergreen International cargo plane, en route from Ramstein in Germany to New York and not expecting to come anywhere near London, found itself in minor trouble off Southend-on-Sea at England's southeast tip.

At a cruising height of 36,000 ft, one engine flamed out, and could not be restarted despite repeated attempts by the flight engineer. Not able to maintain that height with one engine out, they were obliged to descend anyway, and came down to 21,000 ft, at which point the captain found the other three engines were losing power. The pilots contacted the company's maintenance base by radio, but the engineers could not suggest a solution. In consequence, the captain declared an 'emergency,' and asked for clearance to land at London's Heathrow airport, perhaps not quite realizing it was almost on the opposite side of a sprawling metropolis.

Having been given the necessary clearance, the captain set the configuration for gliding, on the principle that too much height and too much speed was better than not having enough to get to the airport. Passing over Croydon in the southwest suburbs of London, the female first officer told the controller:

*We're just not sure we're gonna get enough power to land.*

Like Captain Piché in the Azores, they were in the awkward situation of having played it safe and thereby being too high on approach but with not enough margin to go around. Using good airmanship, for which he later

49

received compliments, the captain was able to get rid of the excess height and speed by a number of snake-like maneuvers and sideslips, and land successfully. Had visibility been bad, he might well have not succeeded.

Maintenance engineers were unable to find the cause of the problem, and the aircraft was permitted to continue on its way after extensive tests to ensure the engines were working properly.

Investigators found out the pilots did not have charts for England, and thus did not know there were other major airports that could be reached without passing over densely populated areas. London's Heathrow, with its long runways, must have seemed the safer bet to the pilots when they pushed the button marked 'Nearest' to see the nearest airports with their distance and the length of their runways displayed on their console.

The UK Air Accident Investigation Bureau (AAIB) criticized Evergreen for not ensuring a full set of charts was on board, but was more critical of the air traffic controllers who at least were aware of where London and its conurbation was! The AAIB wondered whether the controllers had struck the right balance between the interest of the four people on board and those of the people on the ground. They said the controllers lacked clear guidance about the advisability of allowing aircraft in difficulty to fly over congested areas.

To be fair to the controllers, their initial appraisal of the situation was that the aircraft had 'lost' one engine. The Boeing 747 can fly safely on three engines, and British Airways, the biggest user of Heathrow, sometimes has its 747s come in for maintenance with only three engines working.

On one occasion, the author's BA flight from Tokyo to London was cancelled because of trouble with an engine. He learnt that the aircraft would be flown without passengers 6,000 miles back to London over Russia on three engines. Presumably, repairs would be easier and cheaper at the airline's home base at Heathrow. Crews specially trained to cope with the asymmetric thrust on takeoff normally perform such flights.

In a highly publicized case, a BA 747 had trouble with an engine after taking off with passengers from Los Angeles and attempted continue to London's Heathrow on three engines. However, with only three engines, they had to fly at a lower altitude where fuel consumption was higher, and this coupled with an unfavorable headwind meant they had to land prematurely at Manchester (UK) so that they could maintain the necessary fuel reserves, thus not exposing the passengers to any particular risk, just inconvenience.

The FAA, however, was not pleased and decided to fine the airline, claiming that while it might have been unreasonable to fly around jettisoning enough fuel to return to Los Angeles, they should have stopped en route in the US once sufficient fuel had been used up to land safely. It raised questions of sovereignty as US and UK regulations differed on the matter.

Thus, if the Heathrow controllers refused to allow 747s to land there with only three working engines, it would inconvenience BA, as well as others. In the Evergreen International incident just described, it was only later that it became apparent that the situation flight was going to be serious.

As one of the world's busiest airports, Heathrow is something of a special case in that the flight paths for landing on its two parallel runways usually entail flying over the city. Because of the prevailing wind from the west, and because aircraft have to line up and stabilize their approach—unlike taking off when they can peel off—more than 600 flights a day may pass over London. For a short while following the 9/11 World Trade Center attacks, aircraft were not allowed to fly over central London, but the measures were abandoned after a couple of weeks or so. In terms of flight paths, London would seem to be very vulnerable to a 9/11-type attack.

The sight of airliners flying in and out of Reagan Washington National airport located near the Pentagon and three miles from the White House is somewhat surprising. However, the aircraft operating in and out of that airport belong to domestic carriers and extra precautions are taken.

At least until recently, general aviation (private) aircraft have not been allowed to use Reagan Washington National airport—much to the chagrin of legislators and lobbyists who were often beneficiaries. Where the occasional exception was made, special checks were required before takeoff (at the airport or at the one from which the aircraft was departing) and an air marshal had to be on board in addition to specially approved pilots.

Hijacked and 'suspicious' aircraft straying over the White House are perhaps now liable to be shot down. Doing the same thing to aircraft flying over the center of London would not be such a simple choice in view of greater potential casualties on the ground. Even so, the British authorities envisage having anti-aircraft missile sites near the 2012 Olympic Games venue. They hope they will act as a deterrent and the difficult launch decision will not be necessary. Of course, they may really be thinking in terms of shooting down a tiny private plane rather than a giant airliner laden with fuel.

To conclude, regulatory bodies and air traffic controllers have to give more weight to protecting people on the ground, and in consequence may face some fateful decisions.

# BA 777 STAGGERS INTO HEATHROW
# (London 2008)

For a freak reason that took UK investigators many months to establish, the engines of a British Airways Boeing 777 failed to provide thrust just at the moment the pilots wanted them to spool up to allow them to reach the runway when coming into London's Heathrow. Fortunately, by reducing flap to decrease drag they just got over the perimeter fence and crashed down short of the runway with no loss of life.

The media hailed the captain as a hero, but an unjustified whispering campaign at the airline that he had frozen at the controls led to him resigning in disgust only to find no other serious airline would employ him. Finally, after publication of a book about the affair by the captain and his wife, the airline took him back.

*[British Airways Flight 38]*

After a long flight from Beijing which only differed from many others in that the aircraft flew through some exceptionally cold air early on during the route, the British Airways Boeing 777 was coming in quite normally to land at London's Heathrow's Runway 27L. As is normal after what is virtually a long steady glide under the new arrangement to save fuel, a little extra thrust was required at the last minute to prevent the aircraft losing too much airspeed and sinking below the glide path.

To the pilots' dismay, this was not forthcoming, and it looked as if the aircraft was destined to 'touchdown' just before reaching the airport. The first officer was flying the aircraft at the time, and although normally the captain takes over in a crisis; the captain let him continue—an apparently sensible decision as the first officer had the feel of the aircraft and there was so little time left. The captain reduced the amount of flap to 25%, thus reducing the drag and allowing the aircraft to fly further. The aircraft staggered over the perimeter fence and came down heavily on the grass just beyond—some 1,000 ft short of the paved runway.

The right main landing gear broke off, while the force of the impact forced the landing gear on the left into the wing. The first officer managed to keep the aircraft in a straight line and thus prevent it from cartwheeling. After skidding across the grass, it ended up just at the beginning of the runway paving. Despite an escape of fuel due to the pilots' failure to switch off the fuel supply to the engines correctly, there was no fire and no fatalities. The 136 passengers and 16 crewmembers evacuated the aircraft via the chutes with one passenger suffering a broken leg. The airline and no doubt its insurers soon deemed the aircraft not worth repairing and classed it as a 'write-off.'

According to initial media reports, many passengers considered it a non-event with some only thinking it had been a hard landing. Most were more concerned about their insensitive treatment on reaching the terminal.

Yet some days later with the arrival of lawyers on the scene, some passengers were talking of the great 'distress' they had suffered as justification for suing the airline. This in turn led to the CEO of BA personally contacting passengers to head off legal action by showing special personal concern. In this context, one might mention that some at BA think some Business and First Class passengers regard the airline as a 'soft touch' in that they greatly exaggerate their suffering when things go wrong in order to obtain free flights and/or upgrades. Passengers in Economy are not treated so benignly by the airline.

The UK's Air Accident Investigation Board (AAIB) concluded that ice in the fuel was the probable cause and recommended modifications to the fuel supply system on 777s fitted with Rolls-Royce engines. While it was not possible at that time to find cast iron proof that ice in the fuel was the cause, concern increased, as there had been another case where an engine of a 777 flying in cold conditions had temporarily lost power.

The NTSB, the US equivalent to the AAIB, was more forceful in its recommendations, which were announced at the same time as those issued by the AAIB. This put the UK investigators on the back foot, a stance that some circles in the UK regarded as 'bad form.' The NTSB maintained that interim precautionary measures, such as coming down to warmer air rather than staying high up, could expose aircraft to greater risk than usual.

### Conspiracy Theory

As mentioned elsewhere, when people from the same country as the airline and the manufacturer of the aircraft or engines in question investigate an accident someone will say there has been a cover-up. Even in this case, people claiming to have 'contacts airside at Heathrow' were alleging the aircraft had run out of fuel. As evacuating passengers could smell the leaking fuel one can easily discount this, but it does show how easily misinformation can be spread.

### Cause Finally Proven

The UK investigators looked at every possible reason for the engines not responding, but failed to find anything wrong with the computers or the programming. Indeed, the valves supplying fuel to engines had opened fully in response to the demand for more thrust. The quality of the fuel itself was checked and found to be above average. It was from South Korea, and had been shipped to a Chinese port and sent directly by pipeline to Beijing

Airport. Investigators found some object/debris in the fuel tanks, no doubt left there at the time of manufacture.

The investigators concluded that ice must have been the cause, but despite numerous attempts over many months to reproduce the situation in tests they were unable to replicate a situation where ice formed on the inside of the fuel pipes and broke off to block the fuel-lubricating oil heat exchanger. They compared the flight in question with thousands of other flights, and found that although the weather over Russia had been exceptionally cold, the pilots had constantly checked that the temperature of the fuel never fell to the level where it would become waxy. There was only one case where a Rolls-Royce engine on a 777 had behaved similarly. However, that had happened to a Delta aircraft at cruising height and only involved a single engine and had resolved itself when the pilot throttled back before reapplying power—something the BA pilots could not have done in their predicament.

Finally, investigators noted again that the aircraft had flown so precisely for hours on auto throttle that there had never been a demand for a surge in power. The simple conclusion was that this allowed ice to build up inside the fuel pipe and remain there until the sudden demand for power prior to landing. They noted that this had been true in the case of the Delta 777 too.

Replicating the situation in tests, they found ice built up on the inside the pipes and when a sudden demand for high power was invoked the ice broke off in such quantities that the heat exchanger was blocked. The cause had been proven conclusively, much to the relief of the many users of the Boeing 777.

The problem only pertained to 777s fitted with Rolls-Royce engines because the tubes in their heat exchangers carrying the fuel through the hot oil protruded a few millimeters from the part carrying the oil and could not melt large quantities of ice deposited on them when cold fuel was flowing. Incidentally, the pilot of the Delta 777 unblocked the exchanger by throttling back and giving the ice time to melt. The temporary solution was to power up the engines from time to time to prevent the build-up of ice inside the pipes. The long-term solution was to redesign the heat exchanger.

## Sour Aftertaste

As mentioned at the beginning of this narrative, an unjustified whispering campaign at the airline that Captain Burkill had frozen at the controls finally led to him resigning in disgust only to find no other serious airline would employ him. Even though faultless, any pilot involved in a serious incident can have difficulty finding employment elsewhere, and in Captain Burkill's case the rumors did not help. Falling on relatively hard times, he wrote a book, *Thirty Seconds to Impact*, about the affair and its aftermath in conjunction with his wife.

Finally, British Airways reinstated him.

# CHAPTER 3
# RUNWAY OVERRUNS

## 100-MPH QANTAS OVERRUN
## (Bangkok 1999)
### 'Safest Airline' had Blind Spot—Standing Water

> Australia's Qantas airline mostly flies long-haul routes to the world's major airports where there is relatively little risk.
>
> Operating many fewer flights than say America's American Airlines or United Airlines, it is easy as an aviation official has said to see how, with luck, Qantas might never have suffered a 'hull loss,' while the two US airlines might not have been so lucky.
>
> In the following incident, Qantas came close to blotting its copybook, and indeed only avoided doing so by carrying out the most expensive repairs ever made to a civilian aircraft.
>
> *[Qantas Flight 001]*

Looking out from the 28th-floor balcony of a tower apartment on the bank of Bangkok's Chao Phraya River, the author watched a cascade of torrential rain of an intensity he had never before witnessed. He wondered how pilots of incoming aircraft could cope with it.

As if in answer to that question, the next day's *Bangkok Post* had a few lines, saying a Qantas 747 had been involved in some trouble at the airport, with no injuries. The incident was termed a mere mishap. However, when more details became available, perhaps through disaffected Qantas staff, the 'mishap' became headline news in Thailand.

Apparently, the jumbo was still traveling at 100 mph (160 km/h) when it ran onto the grass at the end of the paved runway overrun area after coming in to land. The *Bangkok Post* was later to comment, '*It was a miracle a fire leading to many deaths had not occurred*,' adding that the landing had also been a 'fiasco,' in that, as explained later, some systems on the aircraft 'assumed' it was about to take off, which for a brief moment it was.

The Thai authorities were miffed to discover Qantas staff had removed the Quick Access Data Recorder but finally asked the highly respected Australian Transport Safety Bureau (ATSB) to investigate the incident. After all, in the absence of significant injuries, and with damage limited to Australian property, the Thais preferred to take a back seat.

This was a fortunate decision as the final 186-page ATSB report[1] into the incident is an exceptionally complete and lucid document by any standards. For the technically minded, it is like a detective story in that there is enough basic information for the reader to draw his or her own conclusions regarding what might or might not have happened, had this or that parameter been different. Academics at England's Bath University have now based some of their crew/machine interaction research on this report.

Based largely on facts derived from the ATSB report, this is what apparently happened. (Anyone fascinated by the affair should read the engrossing full report.)

## How the Events Unfolded

Qantas 1, a Boeing 747 flight from Sydney to London with an intermediate stop at Bangkok, first nosed into the exceptionally heavy rain at a height of 200 ft, and with just 850 meters to go before crossing the threshold of the slightly shorter of Bangkok Airport's two parallel runways. The aircrew, consisting of the captain, first officer, who was the pilot actually piloting the aircraft (PF), and second officer, were aware they would encounter difficult conditions since the storms over the airport had long been visible on their weather radar. Now, at 'late final,' the usually crisp white runway lights were only visible to the PF for brief moments after each pass of the windscreen wiper blades.

Another Qantas aircraft, call sign Qantas 15, had been about three minutes ahead of them in the landing sequence, but had decided to go-around because of poor visibility. The crew of Qantas 1 were still on the approach control frequency and were not aware of this.

Therefore, when they moved to the tower frequency and were informed that a Thai Airbus had landed ahead of them and 'braking was good,' they thought the interval was the usual three minutes when in fact it had become six. This is a long time in a tropical storm. Had the tower told them their colleagues just ahead had abandoned their landing, their mindset might well have been different—there would have been less pressure to land.

As Qantas 1 descended in the downpour to 140 ft, the captain became concerned that while the aircraft had speeded up it had not descended sufficiently fast, and said to the first officer:

*You are getting high now!*

Shortly afterwards came the automatic voice warning that they were at *100 ft.*

The captain said:

*You happy?*

The first officer replied:

*Ah, yes.*

According to the ATSB report, the first officer later stated that he felt he was getting near his personal limits by this time, but was happy to continue with the approach, as the captain appeared to be happy. He maintained that he had the feel of the aircraft and it made more sense for him to continue rather than hand over control at that point. The second officer also reported that he was comfortable with continuing the approach at that stage. (The first officer had decided to carry out the approach manually, rather than use the autopilot, in order to 'keep his hand in').

On crossing the runway threshold,[2] they were 32 ft *above* the ideal height, almost 15 knots *above* the target speed, and 19 knots *above* the reference speed $V_{REF}$. These excesses were just within company limits. At the same time, the distorting effect of the rivulets of water on the windscreen would certainly have made it difficult for the first officer to judge distances correctly.

The *50 ft* altitude warning sounded, and the nose went up slightly resulting in the aircraft prematurely beginning its flare,[3] and prompting the captain to say:

*Get it down! Get it down! Come on, you're starting your flare.*

Acknowledging this, the first officer began to retard the engine thrust levers in preparation for touchdown. The rate of descent that had already dropped to approximately *5 ft/sec*, slowed even further due to the flare.

The first officer later reported that although the reduced visibility made it difficult to judge the landing flare, they were already in it and thought it best to pursue it and allow the aircraft to settle onto the runway. He believed that they had more than enough runway remaining for them to stop.

The *30 ft* warning marking the height they would normally have begun their flare sounded, with the longer than usual interval between the 50 ft and 30 ft calls indicating a slower than normal descent. The captain, no doubt getting concerned about the delayed touchdown, increased the auto-brake setting to '4' without advising the other crewmembers, as it did not materially affect the touchdown.

> *With only 10 ft left before the dangling main wheels would first touch the runway, the captain ordered a 'go-around.' He felt the aircraft was 'floating' and he could not see the far end of the runway. In addition, he was not happy with the speed, which again was within company limits, but at the upper limit of what he personally was prepared to accept.*

Instead of using the Take-Off Go-Around (TOGA) switch that would have reconfigured the aircraft automatically for takeoff, the first officer initiated the go-around by pushing the engine thrust levers forward. This is quite common practice as the automatic TOGA go-around controlled by the aircraft's computers can be a little alarming to the passengers, as it is very abrupt and indelicate on the assumption that it may be an emergency such as the presence of another aircraft on the runway.

Anyway, the first officer reacted very quickly so it did not make much difference, except that a manual go-around is easier to cancel.

With the engines needing some eight or so seconds to spool up from idle, the aircraft's main wheels would inevitably brush the runway before the aircraft could regain enough speed for positive lift.

Just then, when it seemed they were rightly going to forgo the landing in the name of safety, a let up in the rain allowed the captain to see right to the far end of the runway. Reassured, he cancelled the go-around by putting his hand over that of the first officer resting on the throttles to pull them back to idle. For a moment, the first officer was unsure who was flying the aircraft. Worse, one lever slipped from his grasp and remained forward in the 'takeoff thrust' position.

The 747's systems interpreted the fact that one lever remained forward as an intention to take off and disarmed both the automatic braking and automatic deployment of the spoilers. (Spoilers are flat panels hinged at the front set on top of the wings, which flick up to 'spoil' the flow of air over the wing. This not only produces an air braking effect but also pushes the aircraft down thus improving the grip of the tires on the runway.)

Having to pull the 'recalcitrant' lever back to join the others in the idle position possibly made the first officer forget to apply *reverse* thrust.

Braking manually as hard as they could, the two pilots at the controls were shocked to find the usually exceptionally effective carbon brakes were hardly slowing the aircraft at all. This was particularly troubling, as having landed so far down the runway in the first place, and furthermore having for a moment one engine thrusting them forwards with the spoilers and wheel brakes in consequence not performing as usual, meant even more of the remaining runway had been used up. With the tires aquaplaning on the layer of water on what little runway remained, they ran onto the short overrun area and onto the grass at an incredible 100 mph.

Fortunately, the heavy rain that had initially been their undoing ultimately proved their salvation, for the rain-sodden ground allowed the huge wheels to sink deeply into it with the result that the aircraft finally came to rest some 240 yards (220 m) further on, without encountering any serious obstacle on the way. People walking around the site the next day must have smiled on seeing the word 'LONGREACH' that Qantas emblazon on the nose of its 747s. No one thought to paint it out as airlines sometimes paint out their logos on the tailfins of burnt out aircraft that have crashed.

The rain and wet ground may indeed have saved them a second time by quickly dousing any nascent fires.

With the aircraft having come to a stop, the captain, immediately reviewed the situation, made more difficult by the fact that wires for communicating with the cabin crew, as well as those for the PA (public address) system, had been severed as they pass close to the crushed nose-wheel section. Receiving information piecemeal by messenger, he waited some 20 minutes and the arrival of rescue vehicles before ordering the evacuation.

The ATSB board of inquiry thought this delay in evacuation had been unwise, as the captain could not have been sure fire would not break out. In addition, the batteries supplying power for the emergency lighting system were on the verge of giving out, as the designers did not anticipate emergency evacuations taking so long. If fire had subsequently occurred, an evacuation without even emergency lighting would have been a nightmare.

In the event, waiting for transport avoided injuries and the danger that the captain later mentioned of having considered passengers being struck by aircraft when tempted to 'walk over the adjacent busy runway towards the brightly lit terminal.'

On board, there had been 3 aircrew, 16 cabin crew and 391 passengers. None sustained significant physical injury.

Despite the soft ground, the aircraft itself sustained a considerable amount of damage and stress—as evidenced by the $75,000,000 *initial* estimate for the cost of repairs.

### Verdict—Not What You Might Expect

From the above account, one might immediately assume that the flight crew was responsible for the near disaster, and even culpable.

Instead, the ATSB, relying very much on Professor Reason's 'Swiss Cheese' accident model and his other work in drawing its conclusions:

> Found that Qantas had not properly prepared their Boeing 747-400 pilots for landing on 'contaminated' [i.e. water-covered or icy runways]; and, partly to reduce costs, had introduced a new, 'less conservative' (= more risky) standard landing procedure, without proper consideration.

The ATSB report noted:

> With the introduction of the more powerful carbon brakes Qantas had changed their standard landing procedure to Flaps 25.[4] Idle/Reverse Thrust rather than the previous more conservative Flaps 30, Full-Reverse Thrust.

Flaps are extensions to the leading edge and trailing edge of the wings that configure the wing to give more lift especially at low speed when taking off or landing. 'Reverse thrust' simply means that cowlings on the engines move so that the thrust from the engine pushes the plane backwards rather than forwards. Before the introduction of the better-performing carbon brakes, passengers would almost invariably hear this engine roar just after landing. '*idle*-reverse' in itself does little to slow the aircraft, but does mean the transition to '*full*-reverse' can be accomplished quickly.]

Qantas made this change in landing procedure for financial reasons and, to some extent, noise abatement reasons.

They could save money because carbon brakes wear less if applied continuously rather than on-and-off. In addition, with a flap angle of 25°, there is less wear on the flap mechanism. It would also reduce maintenance costs for the thrust reverser mechanism. However, extra wear on the tires would negate some of these gains.

Comparison in the ATSB report with five other major airlines flying routes in Asia and worldwide—unnamed due to reasons of commercial confidentiality—showed the others to be more conservative:

1. **Many stressed the need to be more wary of storms and the need to use flaps 30/full-reverse thrust in heavy-rain situations.**

2. **The other airlines had more experience than Qantas of flying into difficult airports.**

Some Qantas pilots believed the more conservative Flaps 30 also made it easier to land precisely at the desired point—Qantas 1 landed well beyond the ideal touchdown point.

Anyway, the crew of Qantas 1 did not discuss the Flaps 30/full-reverse option even though their weather radar had revealed the storms over the airport when they were far away with plenty of time.

The ATSB report said this was probably because with the introduction of the new standard, landings were hardly ever made with Flaps 30 and they were unlikely to try something with which they were unfamiliar.

According to reference data supplied by Boeing, the aircraft *could not have stopped in time* on the contaminated runway using the standard Qantas Flaps 25 idle-reverse landing procedure. This remained true even if it had landed at the ideal touchdown point 400 yards (366 m) from the threshold. However, it *could* have stopped if had they used full-reverse thrust in addition—and everything else had been ideal—that is to say, no cancelled go-around, etc.

The whole incident could have been avoided had the captain not dismissed the first officer's earlier suggestion that they hold off to the south until the weather improved, saying it was only a shower. Their aircraft was not the only one trying to come in, so it was just matter of opinion, bearing in mind that conditions can suddenly change in that part of the world.

The ATSB report cited the following adverse factors in the reverse order of their occurrence.

Paragraphs in square parentheses are the author's comments.

**1. Reverse thrust**

Had they not in the turmoil forgotten to engage reverse thrust, even in the idling mode as specified in their standard landing instructions, there would have been a slight deceleration effect rather than the slight acceleration produced by idle-forward. Many Qantas pilots said they had occasionally forgotten to engage reverse thrust when something distracted them. Normally, this would not have serious implications and therefore would not be uppermost in their minds. Of course, full reverse rather than idle reverse thrust would have been better.

**2. Non-verbal cancellation of the go-around**

The captain, perhaps because it was a habit developed in the course of his frequent work training pilots, cancelled the go-around merely by putting his hand over that of the first officer to pull back the engine thrust levers. It was unlucky one lever remained forward with the consequences already mentioned, and as said, the first officer for a moment wondered who was flying the aircraft. Theoretically, this direct action by the captain would have averted the delay between his issuing the command (to cancel the go-around) and its execution.

**3. Cancellation of go-around**

Pilots generally do not consider canceling a go-around to be good practice as it can lead to confusion and other problems, as was indeed the case here. However, put yourself in the captain's place. There he was—so he thought—finally safely on the ground after a difficult landing. In the atrocious weather conditions, a second landing might be even trickier with not much reserve of fuel for a third attempt. Moreover, both he and the first officer were convinced there was more than enough runway to stop, which there would have been, had it not been for the standing water on the runway.

Ordering and subsequently canceling the go-around meant more runway was 'used up' due to the engines beginning to power up—not to mention one engine continuing to pull because of the 'lost' thrust lever, that in turn made the aircraft 'think' it was taking off, which prevented immediate deployment of the spoilers and application of the brakes on touchdown.

### 4. Landing too far down the runway

The first officer came in somewhat fast and too high, and initiated the flare early, consequently touching down far along the runway. He attributed this partly to the heavy rain.

[One point not stressed by the investigators was that the depth of the water at the beginning of the runway where aircraft normally land (and where the Airbus six minutes ahead found braking had been 'good') was doubtless less deep than at the other end because landing aircraft would have splashed it away. If he had touched down earlier, braking might have been sufficient to reduce the speed enough to prevent aquaplaning on reaching that presumably deeper water.]

### 5. No prior decision to use safer Flaps 30 with full reverse thrust

The crew's experience of trouble-free landings in heavy rain in places such as Bangkok and Singapore may have made them overlook the possible severity of some patches of rain in Thailand.

### 6. Qantas had abandoned use of windscreen water-repellent

Qantas had abandoned the use of water-repellent on Boeing 747s, deactivating the systems several years before for financial reasons and ostensibly to protect the environment—water repellents consist of fluorocarbons that cause depletion of the ozone layer.

[It is perhaps true as some Qantas pilots maintain that water-repellents do not *in general* make much difference. Again, the author's experience of driving in Thailand showed that in torrential downpours they make an incredible difference to visibility through the windscreen even well after the wiper blades have passed. Thus, merely the use of water-repellent could have greatly changed the scenario: the first officer might not have landed so far down the runway; and the captain might have been able to see the far end of the runway early on and not have ordered the go-around in the first place.]

### 7. Second officer's wife

The ATSB report discounts the presence of the second officer's wife in the cockpit as an adverse factor in the incident.

[Could concern for his spouse have led to a moment's inattention causing the second officer to miss noting the first officer had not applied (idle)-reverse?]

**8. Autopilot not used**

The first officer flew the aircraft manually to get more hands-on practice.

[Computers generally fly aircraft more accurately than humans can. Furthermore, the diffractive effect of the layer of water on the windscreen would have made it difficult for the first officer to judge the distance correctly.

The aircraft would surely have come in at the slower correct speed, and touched down near the optimum point on the runway, had the first officer flying the aircraft (PF) opted to use the automatic pilot.

This would have given an extra 636 meters, not to mention the already stated fact that the beginning of the runway might well have had less water on it—partly because aircraft landing there would have dispersed it. One cannot fault the first officer for deciding to fly the aircraft manually, and had it not been for the standing water, his landing would have been just about acceptable.]

## Conclusion

Qantas, in the inquiry's view, seemed to have erred in not training pilots suitably for coping with contaminated runways. Though Boeing said the aircraft could not have stopped in time with the given configuration, even had everything apart from the aquaplaning been perfect, in the author's opinion the overrun would only have been slight, and most airports have some spare space at the end of their runways for such eventualities. It was the combination of so many other negatives that made this a potential disaster, which would have been the case had the soggy ground not slowed the aircraft. Had there been solid obstacles earlier in the path of the aircraft as it hurtled off the runway, any one of these factors could have meant the difference between life and death for hundreds of people.

In response, Qantas have introduced changes in their training and management to avoid such an incident happening again. As usual, other airlines will have learnt from this mishap at no cost to themselves.

In May 2000, after being repaired in China, that same aircraft had to turn back on a flight out of Hong Kong because of generator problems. According to *The Sydney Morning Herald*, a Qantas engineer—who did not wish to be named—had told them he and his colleagues had predicted such electrical problems 'because of the quality of workmanship in China.' One should note, however, that *The Sydney Morning Herald* said Qantas' Chief Executive, Mr. James Strong,[5] denied that Qantas had had the aircraft repaired rather than scrapped, just so Qantas could maintain its claim that it had never had a hull loss. According to Mr. Strong, the $100,000,000[6] cost of the repairs only represented 40% of the cost of the aircraft. However, there is no mention in this of the scrap value, as parts could surely have been re-used.

In addition, there were probably considerable additional costs in terms of the Qantas management time required to oversee the repair project in China. People who have flown in the repaired aircraft have noted how the front looks newer than the back.

**Personnel Changes at Qantas**

Very often airlines and organizations wait quite some time before officially announcing personnel changes after an accident. To bolster its position, the airline will initially express full confidence in those involved, only to let them go later, as was the case for the Singapore Airlines pilots involved in the takeoff from the disused runway at Taipei (see page 86), where two of the three were later dismissed. Did the same apply at Qantas after the incident just described?

One wonders, because on May 30, 2003, *The Australian* featured the startling headline, 'Qantas Safety Tsar's Reign Ends.' According to the article, Ken Lewis (the 'Tsar' in question) had 'left the job after 23 years as head of safety and almost four decades at the airline.'

It added that he would continue to advise senior management until leaving the airline.

The paper emphasized that he was highly respected throughout the industry 'having qualified as a meteorologist, worked as a flight attendant, as a ground simulator instructor and navigation instructor, and is a qualified air safety instructor.' He had held positions on international safety bodies and was at the time President of the Australian Society of Air Safety Investigators.

Though he was certainly a good man—incidentally more problems seem to have occurred since his replacement!—one wonders whether his qualifications would have given him the mindset and weight to influence senior Qantas management (including the bean counters) in the manner the investigators thought necessary in this particular case.

The article in *The Australian* also mentioned that the airline was replacing its chief pilot and returning him to line flying. Possibly the moves were prompted by the fact that the airline was under investigation regarding another incident, in which a 737 landing in rainy conditions veered off the runway for a while at Darwin after a heavy touchdown just beyond the normal runway threshold. Again, no one was injured, but there was some damage to the tires and flaps.

However, in January 13, 2008 *The Sydney Morning Herald* in an article about the slide in Qantas' share value and Merrill Lynch's sell recommendation said the carrier, a week previously, had suffered 'arguably the biggest dent to its once enviable safety reputation in decades' after one of its Boeing 747s lost electrical power on approach to Bangkok. It was referring to a Boeing 747-400 London–Bangkok flight that lost electrical power from all four engine-driven electrical generators 15 minutes out of Bangkok and had to rely on back-up power to land there.

Battery power would only have lasted for about an hour and had the aircraft been a long way from an airport and in bad weather, the situation could have been precarious. Unlike many twin-engine aircraft, the four-engine 747 is not fitted with a RAT—a Ram Air Turbine to generate emergency electric power while gliding.

Investigators found the loss of electrical power had been caused by water entering the electrical equipment bay through cracks in the drip shield above it. Checks found similar cracks in the shields of other 747-400s in the Qantas fleet, and all were repaired. Whether or not there is any direct connection is not certain to the author, but a court case was to proceed regarding a Qantas 'engineer' with allegedly fake qualifications who had worked on that model of aircraft.

Airlines do go through periods where one problem after another crops up and often end up better as a result. Citing these incidents at Qantas is merely to remind passengers that they should be wary of safest airline claims based on raw accident statistics that do not take into account the nature of the routes flown. On the other hand, if they are flying those intrinsically safer routes there will generally be less risk than on the average flight, whatever the carrier.

## A380 Rolls-Royce Engine Incident—Crew Performed Admirably

In recent years, Qantas have had incidents where the crews handled the difficult situations exceptionally well. In one such case, a Rolls-Royce engine on an A380 Airbus out of Singapore shattered with fan blades damaging part of the wing and severing several control wires. The crew very competently brought the giant aircraft back to Singapore despite the computer indicating over 100 problems.

Though the superjumbo Airbus A380 also came out of the incident honorably by showing that it could still fly despite very significant damage, the same could not be said for Rolls-Royce, as the engine failure was due not to a maintenance failure but to their piping design error resulting in a fire that softened metal supporting the fan disc.

Rolls-Royce paid £62m to Qantas to compensate for the grounding[7] of its A380 fleet, but the total cost to the engine maker in terms of reputation and replacing many other engines used on A380s operated by Qantas, Singapore Airlines and Germany's Lufthansa must have been considerable.

---

[1] http://www.atsb.gov.au/aviation/acci/ojh/summary_a.cfm
[2] The threshold is the beginning of the runway proper.
According to the Qantas flight manual, the ideal landing point is 1000 to 1500 ft (305-458 m) beyond the threshold. This gives a safety margin to avert the danger of

landing short of the runway.

[3] The landing flare (usually performed at a height of about 30 ft) consists of raising the aircraft nose to produce (1) *extra lift* to break the descent and (2) *extra drag* to slow the aircraft so it subsequently sinks onto the runway. It is rather like a big bird landing, except that birds can lower their 'flaps' and do a flare dramatically at the very last instant, which aircraft, at least with present technology, cannot.

[4] Flap settings are UP (no flap), 5, 10, 15, 20, 25 and 30. Originally, these merely indicated the angle of the flap at the trailing edge, but now they represent the configuration of a combination of elements.

[5] Mr Strong was one of those considered for the post of Chief Executive of British Airways. Finally, the job went to a New Zealander, Roderick I. Eddington.

[6] It is difficult to come by hard facts regarding the precise sum, and what associated costs are included, etc. What is clear is that it was a considerable sum and that the CEO seemed to have decided on repairs even before an accurate estimate could be made. Incidentally, comments about this include a comical photo that *purports* to show the right-hand slide from the upper deck resting on top of a tree.

[7] The Roll-Royce engines on the Qantas A380s were more susceptible to failure than those used by Singapore Airlines and Lufthansa because Qantas flights from Los Angeles had to take off at maximum rated thrust in order to carry the fuel required for the very long flight from there to Sydney. Though the engine failure occurred on a flight taking off from Singapore, the engine in question had been used on many takeoffs from LA in the course of which the piping had been weakened more than usual.

# AIR FRANCE A340 GUTTED BY FIRE
# (Toronto 2005)
## All Evacuate—Many with their Carry-on Baggage

> A more recent overrun in heavy rain by an Air France A340 at Toronto differed from that of the Qantas 747 at Bangkok mainly in that even though it was traveling 20 knots slower than the Qantas craft on reaching the end of the runway, there was little clear ground beyond. In addition, the ground that remained was not soft enough to have a braking effect.
>
> The aircraft caught fire, yet surprisingly all on board survived. Some of the similarities with the Bangkok 'mishap' are striking.
>
> *[Air France Flight 358]*

Just as with the Qantas 747 at Bangkok, the Airbus A340 from Paris was being flown manually as it came in to land in a storm at Toronto's Lester B. Pearson International Airport. This meant that when the throttles were pushed forward to compensate for a sudden switch to a tail component to the wind, they stayed forward longer than they would have been the case under auto-throttle, which in turn contributed to the aircraft passing over the runway threshold at 70–80 ft, some 40 ft higher than usual.

The rain and poor visibility then made it difficult to bring the aircraft down quickly and as a result, it touched down more than two-fifths of the way down the 9,000 ft (2,743 m) runway at 143 knots (274 km/h) IAS (indicated airspeed), with only 5,250 ft (1,600 m) of runway left. The spoilers duly deployed after 3 seconds and maximum manual breaking was applied. Yet idle reverse thrust was only selected 12.8 seconds after touchdown (at IAS 118 km/h with only 670 m of runway remaining), and full reverse only after 16.4 seconds. This delay can be attributed to the pilot flying (PF) concentrating on keeping the aircraft on the runway in the relatively strong cross wind, and the fact that attention was not drawn to the failure to apply reverse-thrust as the pilot not flying (PNF) was not making the customary announcements confirming deployment of the spoilers and thrust reversers.

Unable to stop in time, the aircraft departed the runway at 86 knots corrected *ground* speed, passing over a grassy area, and then a road before ending up in a minor ravine. Most of the damage to the aircraft occurred in the ravine.

With fire breaking out, an emergency evacuation was ordered.

Ignoring instructions from the cabin crew not to do so, almost half the passengers retrieved their carry-on baggage. One man even blocked an aisle as he busied himself rearranging items in his case. Ignoring angry comments from passengers standing behind him and orders from the flight attendant to leave his baggage and go to the emergency exit, he persisted, obliging the attendant to redirect passengers through the middle bank of seats to the other side of the aircraft to gain access to the only available emergency exit in the aft cabin.

Of the 309 people on board, 12 (2 crew and 10 passengers) suffered serious injuries, nine of which were incurred at the time of impact, and three in the course of the evacuation.

The two members of the cabin crew incurred their serious injuries at the time of impact, but were still able to perform their duties. Passengers with serious impact injuries were nevertheless able to walk.

At the time, the airport was on 'Red Alert' because of rain and lightning, and some have argued that the control tower should not have permitted the landing, with others saying the decision was up to the captain who had sufficient fuel to divert.

Considering that everyone survived, and that investigators did not have to recover wreckage from inaccessible places such as the bottom of an ocean, the inquiry took an inordinate length of time to publish its conclusions. Strong representations made by the parties and notably the airline were said to be the reason for this delay.

The free-lance French aviation writer François Hénin has said the accident was essentially due to a failed approach—the aircraft came in too high and landed too far down the runway—and a lack of communication between the pilots. Interestingly, he points out how adroitly Air France had drawn people's attention away from the fact that there had nearly been a fatal disaster with the airline seeming at fault. They had done this by flooding the French media with accounts of the truly remarkable job the Air France cabin crew had done in getting people out in time—when their performance had merely been okay.

Hénin cites this poor landing as an example of laxness (lack of *rigueur*) at the airline.

# CHAPTER 4

# MID-AIR COLLISIONS & TCAS

## TWO JAL AIRCRAFT IN NEAR MISS
## (Japan 2001)

### Police Treat Pilot as Criminal

> TCAS or Traffic Alert & Collision Avoidance Systems are fitted in various versions to all airliners to alert pilots of the presence of other aircraft in their vicinity, warn them of any danger of collision, and as a last resort with the situation becoming dangerous *ordering* them what to do to avoid a collision. The computers in the two aircraft communicate with each other so they do not both move in the same direction as people meeting head on in the street tend to do. Disobeying TCAS not only means risking people's lives, it can even lead to criminal prosecution as the following case in Japan shows.
>
> *[Japan Airlines Flight 907 and Japan Airlines Flight 958]*

In terms of the number of lives lost, Japan Airlines holds the record for the worst-ever crash involving a single aircraft. The airline also almost managed to claim the record for the worst-ever mid-air collision, when two of the airline's aircraft were involved in a near miss. Had they collided the death toll could have been as high as 677.

These 'records' however really only reflect the fact that Japan has some airliners configured to carry a large number of passengers not requiring excessive amounts of room on relatively short-haul routes.

Not so long ago, the airline went through a patch where it was subject to

warnings from the Japanese aviation authorities regarding safety.

The near miss in question involved the following aircraft:

**Flight number JL907**, Japan Airlines Boeing 747, with 427 people on board had just climbed out of Tokyo's domestic Haneda Airport bound for Okinawa to the south, and was seeking permission to finalize its climb to 39,000 ft. On board, the flight attendants were just starting to serve drinks.

**Flight number JL958**, a Japan Airlines DC-10, with 250 people on board, was coming in from Pusan in South Korea to land at Tokyo's Narita International Airport to the northeast of Haneda Airport.

At 15:46, a trainee controller (under supervision) duly authorized JL907 to climb to 39,000 ft (Flight Level 390[1]). Two minutes later, the nearby DC-10 crew reported they were at 37,000 ft (Flight Level 370), meaning their paths would cross in the vertical plane, which of course would not matter if they maintained separation in the horizontal plane.

However, six minutes later the trainee controller discovered they were on courses that could result in a collision. In probably a panicky reaction to the aural warning of the potential conflict, the controller, who had intended to tell JL958 (the DC-10) to descend, mistakenly told JL907 (the Boeing 747) to do so.

The TCAS in the descending Boeing 747 gave an aural conflict resolution advisory to climb. Notwithstanding the fact that TCAS resolution advisories are mandatory, the 747 captain continued his descent in accordance with the erroneous ATC instruction.

Meanwhile, the DC-10 that had continued when the controller attached the wrong flight number to the order to descend initiated a descent in accordance with instructions from its onboard TCAS. (When the trainee controller noticed the DC-10 was continuing to fly level he ordered it to turn right but apparently this message did not get though.) The supervisor had tried to order the 747 to climb, but in vain as he said 'JAL 957', which applied to neither—he meant JL907.

Seeing the two aircraft were about to collide head-on, the JAL 747 captain forced his aircraft into a steep dive and succeeded in missing the DC-10 by 345–550 ft (105–165 m) laterally and 65–200 ft (20–60 m) vertically.

Drinks trolleys on his aircraft hit the ceiling and one boy was thrown four seat rows. On the JAL 747 five passengers and two crewmembers sustained serious injuries, while about 100 crew and passengers sustained minor ones, mostly limited to bruising. No one was injured on the DC-10, which continued on to Narita as scheduled, while JL907 returned to Haneda Airport.

To the consternation of many in aviation circles, the Japanese police treated the Boeing cockpit like a crime scene. The captain, who probably thought he had done well to save the aircraft by putting his aircraft into a steeper dive, must have been surprised to find he was going to be put on trial with prosecutors demanding a custodial sentence though they subsequently relented. Prosecutors pursued the air traffic controllers, with at one time 100 civil service demonstrators protesting outside a court in their favor. Various trials and appeals concerning the air traffic controllers have continued year after year, with one even in 2008.

TCAS has been very successful in preventing mid-air collisions, and as usual, it is surprising the pilots, who originally thought it would be a 'nuisance,' delayed its introduction for so long. The system can even be useful for warning pilots, taking off in fog or rain, of the presence of an aircraft that may be waiting to enter or entering the runway halfway down.

There are now improved versions of TCAS able to handle separation in the horizontal plane and tell aircraft to go left or right as well as up or down. Ideally, it should include a program to prevent an aircraft being ordered to fly into the ground should an incident happen low down. However, some projects designed to incorporate this have been cancelled because of cost.

The next generation (NextGen) air traffic control system using ADS-B (see *The Flying Dictionary*) should make conflicts even less likely and facilitate their resolution.

Incidentally, the Las Vegas Hilton Hotel allegedly installed a TCAS-based system to enable it to switch off its lasers when an aircraft was in the vicinity. Perhaps this allowed the owners to escape the temporary ban on lasers within a 20-mile radius of Las Vegas airports imposed by the FDA in 1996 following reports of pilots being temporarily 'blinded' by them.

---

[1] To avoid collisions, air traffic controllers tell aircraft to fly at Flight Levels, which are usually in thousands of feet, but measured in hundreds of feet. Therefore, FL350 is 35,000 ft. However, as this division by 100 when dealing in thousands can be confusing, we give the actual height in feet.

# DHL CARGO 757 & TU-154 COLLIDE
# (Lake Constance 2002)

### Distraught Father Stabs Air Traffic Controller

An air traffic controller, alone at his desk in the middle of the night, with his phones not working and his conflict alert warning system not fully functioning, only became aware of a potential collision situation at the last moment.

He issued instructions to ensure the two aircraft did not collide. The pilot in one aircraft obeyed him despite the onboard collision avoidance system (TCAS) ordering him to do the opposite; the pilot of the other was meanwhile very properly obeying the TCAS Consequently, the two aircraft turned towards each other, just as people coming face to face in the street tend to do.

*[Bashkirian Airlines Flight 2937 and DHL Flight 611]*

After keeping a low profile during an extended period of medical leave in his home country following the terrible incident, the air traffic controller, Danish-born Peter Nielsen, had returned to assume 'other' duties at Skyguide, the Swiss air traffic control company. One evening, a middle-aged stranger came to his suburban residence near Zurich Airport, Switzerland, and after a brief exchange of words in German at the front door proceeded to stab Nielsen to death in full view of his wife.

A senior police officer soon dismissed the notion that it had been a hit man, saying:

*Hit men don't get emotional and they don't use a knife.*

Soon it was realized that the middle-aged man must have been the father of one or more of the many children killed 623 days earlier in a mid-air collision over Lake Constance, lying between Switzerland and Germany, and touched at its foot by Austria. Many could sympathize but not condone.

The terrible collision had occurred at 35,400 ft in a virtually empty sky at 23:35 local time on July 1, 2002, and had been between a Tupolev-154 airliner with 69 people, including 52 children, on board and a DHL cargo plane with just two pilots. Everyone on the two aircraft lost their lives. Among the dead were the wife, son, and daughter of 48-year old Viktor Kaloyev. Those who knew Kaloyev said he had been implacably distraught since losing everything he had to live for, and indeed, it was he who had been responsible for Nielsen's demise.

A court subsequently sent Kaloyev to a psychiatric hospital. However, was his act of vengeance misplaced? Was he right to focus on the air traffic controller?

As is usual in an air accident, a whole series of unfortunate events and failures, on their own of little consequence, led to the midair collision for which Viktor Kaloyev held Nielsen responsible.

Five and a half minutes before the eventual collision, Nielsen had authorized the DHL cargo aircraft flying north to climb to 36,000 ft to save fuel. Meanwhile the TU-154 was flying in a westerly direction at the same altitude, meaning they were at right angles.

Their speeds and relative positions were such that they might collide or rather risked a 'lack of separation.' Air traffic controller Nielsen would usually have realized this quite soon.

The scenario evolved as follows:

1. With his companion taking a rest (as allowed by company regulations) outside the control room, Nielsen was handling all the air traffic in the Zurich area, and had to watch over two screens and slide his chair between them. This would not have been too difficult if traffic had been virtually nil as usual at that time of night, or if he had been able to devote all his time to controlling the air traffic rather than on working the public phone lines (see below).

2. In addition, in the (roughly) five minutes prior to the collision he had been responsible for four aircraft on one frequency and a fifth on another. Then, moments before the collision, a sixth aircraft had called in.

3. The air traffic control system was in 'fallback mode' for servicing, which meant aircraft needed to be further apart than usual. In addition, the 'short-term' conflict alert system, which would have warned Nielsen of an impending collision, was not working. It would have given an audible warning and shown the echoes of the aircraft in red. It seems Nielsen was not aware that this was not functioning.

4. Management had allowed engineers to switch off the special phone system so they could perform overnight maintenance. Though based on quite an old analogue system, it used dedicated lines to link the neighboring control centers, enabling the automatic rerouting of calls if one line failed, and included a 'priority ringing system' so a controller could tell if a call was especially urgent, as in the case in question.

5. Using unfamiliar public phone lines, Nielsen had wasted considerable time just before the collision contacting a nearby German airport to hand over a delayed incoming Airbus. Worse still, the phone outage meant a controller 100 miles away in the German Karlsruhe Center could not get through to warn him of the danger, despite 11 desperate attempts.[1]

6. The DHL aircraft obeyed the TCAS, but TU-154 obeyed Nielsen. Both aircraft were equipped with Traffic Alert and Collision Avoidance Systems (TCAS), which warn pilots of nearby traffic and tells them what to do to avoid a collision should one seem imminent. To avoid aircraft turning into each other, the computers in the two aircraft decide which way they should go, for instance telling one to go CLIMB and the other to DESCEND, as in this case.

7. Nielsen had also noted the potential danger of collision—and about 44 seconds before the impact—told the TU-154 to descend immediately as there was 'crossing traffic.' The DHL 757 continued to implement the TCAS instructions to descend, but the TU-154, after seeming to have hesitated, obeyed Nielsen instead and likewise descended.

8. Twenty-two seconds before impact, the TCAS in the DHL 757, sensing the increasing danger, ordered the DHL to increase (its rate of) descent.

9. Eight seconds before impact, the TCAS ordered the TU-154 to further increase (its rate of) climb, not taking into account it was doing the opposite.

10. From paint marks and scratches on the debris, the investigators established that the two aircraft collided as shown in Figure 2  The DHL 757 almost entirely passes under the TU-154.; and that it was the tailfin (vertical stabilizer) of the DHL 757 that first hit the TU-154 fuselage just in front of the wings.

For the occupants of the TU-154, including the many children, death was surely relatively quick. That was not true for the DHL pilots, as their aircraft subsequently flew on relatively intact for some distance and crashed 8 km away from the location of the debris from the TU-154, which had broken up in the air. The DHL cockpit voice recorder features the voices of the pilots even after the impact between the two aircraft.

In view of the above, it is difficult to blame Nielsen, who nevertheless had found the shock and sense of responsibility difficult to bear. His fellow controllers were shocked too.

Figure 2  The DHL 757 almost entirely passes under the TU-154.[2]
Courtesy German Federal Bureau of Aircraft Accident Investigation – BFU

When interviewed by a German magazine two weeks after the accident Nielsen expressed his sorrow, but said he was part of a system and networks with many interrelated features ... (even though) as an air traffic controller he was responsible for ensuring accidents didn't happen.

The presence of an extra captain of very great seniority in the jump seat of the TU-154 would seem to have been the critical factor as regards the failure to obey the TCAS instructions, in that he apparently stopped the first officer doing so, which partly explains the apparent hesitation just mentioned.

The senior captain in the jump seat may have acted thus because he was from the 'old school' and had considerable experience of flying in the Soviet Union where TCAS is little used and obeying the air traffic controller would be the norm and built into his psyche. Be that as it may, psychologically speaking, once having just started taking evasive action by going one way it is not easy to immediately re-adjust one's thoughts and switch to the opposite halfway through.

That said, one must be very unlucky to collide with another aircraft at 11:35 at night when there should be much available space in the sky. One must be even unluckier to collide at right angles where the horizontal separating effect of any variation in relative speeds is maximal. Some people partly blame the Swiss Air Force for appropriating so much space for itself that commercial airliners are 'funneled'[3] through the rather limited space over Lake Constance.

Though there is a lot of empty sky at night, cargo aircraft, by the very nature of their tasks, often do fly at night. They are especially vulnerable to collisions because radar systems are taken out of service then for maintenance and everyone tends to be less alert, not only because it is

nighttime, but also because there is usually not enough action to keep people on their toes.

Sadly, had Nielsen been really incompetent or careless and had not finally noticed the potential conflict (lack of separation), the accident would probably never have happened. All one can say is that he was largely a victim of circumstances with so much equipment either in fallback mode for servicing or unavailable as in the case of the telephones. Regulations and manning levels should not have made it possible for him to be left to cope with everything on his own in such circumstances.

Professor Ladkin cites an academic study of this incident with special regard to the use of TCAS.[4]

Once again, this is an example of an accident in which the presence on the flight deck of a very senior man was a negative factor.

Newer versions of TCAS are intelligent enough to reverse their commands should they find that one of the aircraft is not complying, as happened in this sad case, which anyway has made pilots all over the world more aware of the obligation to comply.

---

[1] Skyguide are now introducing a new phone system, improving the back-up phones, and providing controllers with mobile phones as a third line of defense.

[2] From the German investigators' report.

[3] See 'Funneling (Navigational Paradox)'in *THE FLYING DICTIONARY.*

[4] Computer Related Incidents with Commercial Aircraft. July 1, 2002.
http://www.rvs.uni-ielefeld.de/publications/compendium/
incidents_and_accidents/Ueberlingen2002.html

# CHAPTER 5

# GROUND COLLISIONS

## KLM 747 ENCOUNTERS PAN AM 747 ON TAKEOFF (Tenerife 1977)

### Worst-Ever Multi-aircraft Disaster

> This, the worst-ever multi-aircraft disaster, was similar to so many other disasters in that it involved a whole list of factors and strokes of bad luck, and as is usual would not have happened had any one of them been absent.
>
> *[KLM Flight 4805 and Pan Am Flight 1736]*

One Sunday afternoon in March 1977, a terrorist bomb and the possibility of another had made the authorities temporarily close Las Palmas Airport in the Spanish Canary Islands. Most of the incoming flights were diverted to Los Rodeos, a less important airport on the nearby island of Tenerife, turning that relative backwater into a hive of activity. Aircraft languishing there waiting for Las Palmas to reopen were blocking key taxiways, including the normal route for taxiing to the far end of the runway for takeoff.

Though it had a good long runway, the airport's ground handling facilities were not designed for aircraft as large as the Boeing 747. As a result, a Dutch KLM 747 and a Pan American 747 parked on the apron were taking up so much of the available space that the Pan Am 747 would not be able to squeeze past the KLM to get out. They were both waiting to resume their journey to Las Palmas.

The KLM 747 had just come from Amsterdam, a four-hour journey, with a group consisting mostly of young Dutch tourists. The 248 people on board included 48 children, 3 babies, 2 pilots, a flight engineer, and 11 cabin crew.

The Pan Am 747 had come from Los Angeles with a stop in New York for refueling and a change of crew before the 8-hour transatlantic flight to what should have been Las Palmas where the mostly elderly passengers were to join a cruise liner. The 396 people on board included the 2 pilots, a flight engineer, and 2 company employees in the cockpit jump seats. The 747, 'Clipper Victor,' was said to have a dent in its nose—made from a champagne bottle when it had made the inaugural commercial Boeing 747 flight from New York to London on January 21, 1970! It was one of the first 'jumbos.'

The KLM 747 also supposedly had some fame associated with it, in that a photo of its captain, Dutchman Captain van Zanten, was being used in KLM's advertising material, including that in the in-flight magazine the passengers must have been perusing during the long delay. Much has been made of this publicity photo, with suggestions that van Zanten was a self-important stuck up prig—a captain-of-the-Titanic-like figure—as maintained by the Spanish side. The author, as surely were many others, was seduced by this simplistic portrayal until he found *Disasters in the Air* by Jan Bartelski, a pilot with KLM, who had held important posts with the International Federation of Airline Pilots Associations (IFALPA).

Bartelski's role at IFALPA, where admittedly defending the interests of pilots would be paramount, seems to be reflected in his very 'pro-pilot' approach to accidents, but many of the points he makes cannot be lightly dismissed. His 30 years at KLM do give him some inside knowledge.

According to Bartelski, van Zanten was rather a serious and introverted man, and the only reason for the publicity department using his photo was likely to have been his availability for photo sessions. As a training captain, van Zanten was usually freely available at the home base—other captains would be either away flying aircraft or resting at home. Indeed, the photo of van Zanten included in Bartelski's book gives the impression of a rather accommodating person.

Again, he says van Zanten was not as senior as suggested. It is well known that, because of the inheritance from powerful unions, much at the major airlines depends on seniority (rather than ability—provided the pilots of course can pass the necessary tests). As KLM had promoted van Zanten out-of-turn to the rank of captain when the captain in charge of 747 training retired, the Dutch Pilots' Union insisted he only fly routes when no other captain was available. This limited his amount of 'line experience' even more than normal for a training captain.

First Officer Meurs, also a captain, seconded Captain van Zanten. Though very experienced on other aircraft, Meurs had only flown 95 hours on the 747, having shortly before converted to the aircraft under the instruction and authority of Captain van Zanten himself. This supposedly made Meurs particularly deferential towards his captain. However, Meurs was an outspoken and extrovert type, and van Zanten had followed his advice at several points while proceeding to the end of the runway for takeoff. Assisting them was the Flight Engineer Schreuder.

In charge of the Pan Am 747 was Captain Victor Grubbs, a 57-year old with over 21,000 hours of piloting experience. First Officer Bragg and Flight Engineer Warns were with him on the flight deck, together with two company employees in the jump seats.

The waiting dragged on all through the afternoon with the KLM crew becoming increasingly worried that their permitted flying time would expire. If it did, they would have to stay overnight at Los Rodeos or Las Palmas and fly back to Amsterdam the following day—upsetting their private plans for that day. In addition, in the peak season and with the local KLM representatives already overwhelmed, it would be virtually impossible to find overnight accommodation for the passengers.

A number of potential accidents due to fatigue had made the Dutch authorities establish strict legal limits for hours of duty, removing the discretion the captains previously had had in this regard. The regulations were so complex that captains often had to ask the airline's operations center for a ruling to cover themselves. Contacting their HQ by high-frequency radio, the KLM crew were relieved to have a ruling that they would be okay provided they got away before a certain time later that evening.

Finally, with news that Las Palmas Airport had reopened, other aircraft began to take off for that airport, which made Captain van Zanten realize that refueling delays at Las Palmas might jeopardize their chances of getting off from there before their permitted flying hours were up. He therefore opted to refuel at Los Rodeos instead with enough fuel to continue on to Amsterdam from Las Palmas.

The Pan Am crew found they could not taxi to the runway with the huge KLM jet blocking their path. After the long wait for flights to Las Palmas to be authorized, they were not at all happy to be told by the KLM crew—with no hint of apology—that refueling would take some 35 minutes. On hearing that, the Pan Am first officer and engineer actually got out and paced the ground to see whether there just might be room for them to squeeze by. Visibility was falling, so that when refueling had finally finished and the two aircraft could leave the apron for takeoff, visibility was down to 300 meters.

Los Rodeos Airport, at an altitude of some 2,000 ft, is subject to cloud, rather than typical lowland fog. However, it can be quite worrying as visibility can be very poor at moments, and improve or worsen suddenly.

With the taxiways parallel to the runway leading to the holding point for takeoff blocked by parked aircraft, the air traffic controller told the two aircraft to enter the runway at the end they were at and back-taxi up it. The KLM 747 in the lead was to proceed right to the far end; perform a U-turn; and wait for permission to take off. The Pan Am 747 was told to follow the KLM 747 but turn off at the third taxiway on the left, in order to be out of the way and give the KLM a clear runway to take off.

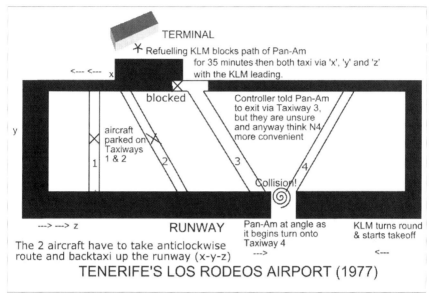

TERMINAL
✗ Refuelling KLM blocks path of Pan-Am
for 35 minutes then both taxi via 'x', 'y' and 'z'
with the KLM leading.

blocked

Controller told Pan-Am
to exit via Taxiway 3,
but they are unsure
and anyway think N4
more convenient

aircraft
parked on
Taxiways
1 & 2

Collision!

RUNWAY

Pan-Am at angle as
it begins turn onto
Taxiway 4
--->

KLM turns round
& starts takeoff
<---

The 2 aircraft have to take anticlockwise
route and backtaxi up the runway (x-y-z)

TENERIFE'S LOS RODEOS AIRPORT (1977)

Figure 3  Normal clockwise route blocked by parked a/c.
[Schematic—not to scale]

As Los Rodeos was merely a diversion airport for emergencies, the Pan Am crew only had a small-scale plan showing the layout. What is more, the taxiways did not have signs identifying them and, looking at their plan, the obvious exit to take seemed to be the fourth taxiway since it turned off at a comfortable 45° with a similar easy turn at the end taking them to the end of the runway for takeoff. The third exit would require two difficult 135° turns and initially would take them back towards the terminal. Not sure whether the controller had said the first or third exit, they had asked him to repeat his instructions. The controller had done this, saying, *'Third taxiway, One, Two, Three; Third.'*

On reaching the third taxiway, the Pan Am crew was loath to take it in view of those awkward 135° turns, not to mention the additional distance involved, and proceeded slowly onwards to the fourth turn-off. Anyway, the controller had told them to report when they left the runway, and it would be inconceivable that he would give the KLM 747 permission to take off before confirming they were clear.

Some commentators have suggested the controller asked the Pan Am to make the awkward 135° maneuver because he had little experience of handling aircraft as large as the 747. However, as the Dutch investigators subsequently showed, this 135° turn was by no means impossible. Oddly, no one seems to have suggested that, consciously or out of habit, the controller might have been trying to keep the two aircraft well separated in the fog. Had the Pan Am 747 been instructed to take the fourth and last turn-off and missed it in the poor visibility, they would have come face-to-face with the KLM 747 with hardly any room to maneuver at best. As aircraft cannot go backwards on their own, a tractor might have been required to separate them, and this would have meant closing the runway and further delays for all the other waiting aircraft.

On reaching the end of the runway, van Zanten duly made the tight 180° U-turn to face back down the runway ready for takeoff—directly facing the Pan Am 747 trundling towards him. The poor visibility meant the aircraft were out of sight of each other, and out of sight of the control tower.

Van Zanten spooled up the engines a little and allowed his giant aircraft to inch forward a little—according to the Dutch comments made later, this application of a small degree of power was a normal maneuver to check the functioning of the engines, and not an indication he was about to initiate the takeoff. Whatever its significance, First Officer Meurs said:

> Wait a minute; we don't have an ATC clearance.

Van Zanten replied:

> No, I know that. Go ahead and ask.

He then applied the brakes fully. Meurs then called the control tower, saying:

> KLM4805 is now ready for takeoff—we're waiting for our ATC clearance.

The tower replied:

> KL4805. You are cleared to the Papa beacon. Climb to and maintain Flight Level 90. Right turn after takeoff. Proceed with heading 040 until intercepting the 325 radial from Las Palmas VOR.

Van Zanten apparently assumed this meant they were also cleared for takeoff, and as Meurs began confirming the ATC clearance by reading it back to the controller, he released the brakes and this time advanced the throttles to give high but not maximum takeoff power.

With Meurs occupied with confirming the ATC clearance, van Zanten then said to Flight Engineer Schreuder:

> Let's go! ... Check the thrust.

The first officer, though preoccupied with reading back the ATC clearance to the tower, added a phrase that *could* have saved them. However, it failed to do so because he used a Dutch idiom that in English had a different sense:

> Roger, Sir, we are cleared to the Papa beacon, Flight Level 90 until intercepting the 325. We're now at takeoff.

Meurs, using the Dutch idiom, meant they were actually taking off, and indeed, when the two words *at takeoff* left his mouth, the aircraft had already been gaining speed for six seconds. The controller—as anyone used to speaking English—naturally assumed *at takeoff* meant the KLM 747 was at the takeoff position at the end of the runway, awaiting clearance to proceed.

In a run-of-the-mill fashion, the controller then said:

*Okay. Standby for takeoff. I will call you.*

However, the crew of the Pan Am 747, feeling vulnerable and fearful that the 'impatient KLM 747' might take off at any moment, had interrupted the tower's reply with the frantic words:

*We are still taxiing down the runway!*

The *simultaneous* radio transmissions produced a radio squeal called a heterodyne, with the result that the KLM 747 only heard the single word 'Okay' from the controller, and neither the rest of the controller's sentence nor the words from the Pan Am 747 regarding the fact they were still taxiing down the runway.

However, the tower did hear the Pan Am transmission, and thinking the KLM 747 was still holding, replied:

*Roger Pan Am 1736, report runway clear.*

Pan Am:

*Okay—will report when clear.*

Controller:

*Thanks!*

This exchange, taking place when the KLM jet had already been accelerating for 20 seconds, was being followed by KLM Flight Engineer Schreuder—but not by the two pilots who were concentrating on the takeoff in the fog.

Schreuder expressed his concern to his colleagues somewhat hesitantly in Dutch, with words to the effect:

*Did he not clear the runway then?*

Not understanding what he meant, van Zanten said:

*What did you say?*

The flight engineer clarified his question:

*Did he not clear the runway—that Pan American?*

Van Zanten and Meurs very affirmatively reply:

*Yes, he did.*

Having expressed his doubts deferentially as a question rather than as a strong positive statement that the Pan Am 747 was possibly still on the runway, the flight engineer was caught off-foot, and merely repeated the questioning statement.

Captain Grubbs in the Pan Am 747, not knowing that Dutch-speaker Meurs had meant they were actually taking off when he had said, 'We are at takeoff,' nevertheless sensed van Zanten was extremely anxious to get away and might take off at any minute. Addressing his crew, he exclaimed:

*Let's get the f\*\*k out of here!*

The others agreed, commenting sarcastically about van Zanten keeping them waiting for so long (while refueling), and then developing a sudden urge to get away.

Only seconds later, the crew of the Pan Am 747 sighted the first glimmer of the KLM 747's landing lights piercing the fog, some 580 meters away. Those lights grew brighter and brighter, as Captain Grubbs pushed his throttles fully open to try to pull out of the way. He did not stand a chance of succeeding in the eight seconds that remained before the inevitable impact since his engines needed five of those seconds just to spool up enough to *begin* accelerating the massive jumbo with its considerable inertia.

Grubbs and his colleagues could only pray that van Zanten would manage to get off the ground in time to pass over them. One of them even muttered:

*Get off! Get off!*

It was only as his KLM 747 attained the takeoff decision speed, $V_1$, of about 140 knots, that Captain Van Zanten in turn saw the Pan Am 747, which by then was less than 500 meters ahead of him. Even though he had not quite reached rotation speed, $V_R$, he yanked the control column so far back that the rear underside of his aircraft made a long gouge in the concrete runway.

Lifting off at that slow speed with the added burden of the 55,500 liters of fuel he had cannily just loaded was never going to be easy. Even so, his aircraft heaved itself up enough for the nose wheel to pass over the Pan Am craft.

All to no avail, as the No 4 engine pod suspended below the right wing struck the Pan Am 747's humped back just behind the flight deck, crushing the first class upper passenger cabin behind the pilots and ripping off the flight deck roof. When the first officer almost instinctively reached up for the engine fuel shut-off levers he found nothing there!

Though van Zanten had placed his aircraft in a sharp nose-up attitude, its trajectory at that slow speed and great weight was virtually horizontal. In consequence, the massive main landing gear wheel bogies dangling well below the nose wheel were bound to slam into the roof of the Pan Am's main cabin and crumple it as they rolled over it. Again, that sharp nose-up attitude meant the tail section of the KLM was lower still, so that it in turn sliced neatly between the double tracks of carnage created by the landing gear bogies.

With fire breaking out in both aircraft, the KLM 747 continued its trajectory for a second or two before crashing down onto the runway with engines and other pieces falling off. Having slithered to a halt some 450 meters from the point of collision, its fuel tanks exploded, engulfing the fuselage in fire. None of the 248 people inside even managed to open a door or emergency exit, let alone jump out.

As already mentioned, passengers usually have a 90-second time frame to escape when an aircraft on the ground is seriously on fire. In the case of the Pan Am 747, there was only a minute. In the main cabin where many of the passengers were quite elderly, those still alive on the side opposite the one receiving the full impact of the KLM's main wheels had their escape hampered by debris, and few managed to get to the exits.

Helped by the collapse of the floor of the 'upper deck first class' cabin behind the flight deck, the three aircrew and the two company staff with them in the jump seats were able to escape with those in the 'lower deck first class' section below. Those in the upper deck cabin that had received the direct impact of the KLM's right engine pod did not stand a chance.

A number of the Pan Am passengers had to jump to the ground from a considerable height, sustaining further injury. In fact, nine out of the seventy people who did get out alive subsequently died from their injuries, making the final death toll for that aircraft alone 335.

Adding 335 to the 248 dead in the KLM 747, the total death toll was to be 583, making it the worst ever aircraft accident, if one excludes 9/11 where, in terms of occupants of the four aircraft, less than half that number were killed—and that was not really an accident.

## Conclusion

Though a whole series of factors led to the disaster, it is tragic that one piece of bad luck, namely the simultaneous transmissions making both—except for the controller's *Okay*—inaudible to those on the KLM flight deck, plus the misuse of English at the last moment meant the normal final safety defenses were breached.

While it has been generally assumed that using the phrase 'We are at takeoff' to mean 'We are taking off' was quite usual for a Dutchman speaking English, could the reality have been more complex? It is possible that the first officer, who was quite used to speaking English, had regressed psychologically and reverted to Dutch idiom under the stress engendered by having to read back the airways clearance while the impatient captain was initiating a tense takeoff in fog.

The fact that the KLM aircraft had declined (on the grounds of being too busy) to receive that airways clearance earlier meant that Captain van Zanten was preoccupied with handling the aircraft and the first officer was preoccupied with reading back the clearance. Thus, van Zanten was effectively carrying out a tricky takeoff in fog with assistance from the flight engineer rather than the first officer.

Rather than van Zanten causing the disaster by being domineering, one could say the flight engineer was not assertive enough when he so obliquely and so tentatively suggested the Pan Am 747 might not have cleared the runway. Certainly, van Zanten was impatient in not waiting for the first officer to finish reading back his airways clearance to the tower.

The Pan Am crew might have made more of the fact in their exchanges with the controller that they were wondering whether they were taking the appropriate exit. However, they did twice indicate they were still on the runway. Perhaps they began to think better of what they had done and that is why the captain said, *'Let's get the f\*\*k out of here!'*

The Dutch investigators said the air traffic controller could have performed better, and that the sound of a football match broadcast in the background suggested he might have been distracted from his tasks. Had there not been a football match playing on a radio in the control tower, and had it not been a critical stage in the match, it is possible the control tower would have made an intermediate check of the Pan Am 747's progress.

Another factor in the disaster may have been the fact that the controllers had been having a hard day dealing with the many diverted flights and things were finally easing up, which is just the time accidents tend to happen, as people are a little less sharp once the pressure is off. According to Bartelski, the Spanish authorities very likely sought to protect their controllers by only providing investigators with a poor copy of the control tower recording tape, which could not be synchronized with the cockpit voice recorder (CVR) tapes in the two aircraft.

One point made by Bartelski and not generally known is that following the Tenerife accident, all KLM pilots were made to undergo strict practical hearing tests in addition to the usual audio graph tests, and as a result, two older captains had their licenses withdrawn. Because of medical confidentiality, Bartelski says there is no direct evidence that a hearing deficit should be considered as a likely contributory factor. However, he points out that *if* van Zanten had such a deficit, he would have been more likely to miss the word *report* in that possibly life-saving transmission from the tower to the Pan Am 747:

**Roger Pan Am 1736, report runway clear.**

# SIA 747 TAKES OFF ON DISUSED RUNWAY (Taipei 2000)

### Wish Fulfillment—You See What You Expect to See

> Singapore Airlines (SIA) has one of the best reputations in the industry—with a young fleet and flight attendants who see their often short career at the airline as a good qualification for marriage. In fact, being accepted as a female flight attendant at the airline is very difficult, so great is the demand.
>
> The news of the 'absurd' disaster at Taipei in Taiwan in which one of their aircraft took off in atrocious weather on a disused runway with construction equipment parked in the middle came as a great shock.
>
> *[Singapore Airlines Flight 006]*

An English edition of the Japanese *Yomiuri* newspaper had the following paragraph:

> *In what is probably a world first, the operators of Tokyo's Narita airport have decided to use paint and nets to camouflage part of the new 2,180-meter runway to keep aircraft from accidentally landing on an unused section. The camouflage is designed to make the superfluous section of the runway look like grass.*

Why should Tokyo's International Airport go to so much trouble and expense when all they had to do was to use the traditional 'X' (no entry) signs to denote that section of runway was out of use? According to officials at the airport, one reason was an incident in 2000, when a Japan Air System jet accidentally landed at the Haneda domestic airport on a new but unused runway despite it having those Xs.

Another reason may have been the death trap at Taiwan's Taipei Airport into which a Singapore Airlines Boeing 747 was lured on the stormy night of October 31, 2000.

That night, one of the worst typhoons that Taiwan was to experience in recent years—dozens of people were killed—was on its way, and already bringing torrential rain and gusty winds. If SIA trans-Pacific flight SQ006 bound for Los Angeles did not get off quickly, company regulations might forbid it from doing so on account of the increasing crosswind component.

Canceling the departure would mean waiting until the crew had had their mandatory rest, and leaving the next day.

> *That said, the captain did not seem to be overly hurrying things along in order to get away before conditions deteriorated further.*

*He apparently told the catering people, who were having trouble loading the victuals due to the terrible weather, to 'slow down and take their time.' He did, however, take extra precautions, one of which—or as some might say, both of which—were to prove fatal.*

Firstly, he decided to handle the takeoff himself instead of letting the first officer do it as had been planned.[1] This meant he would be preoccupied concentrating on the physical handling of the aircraft rather than on the overall situation.

Secondly, and this was certainly the most fatal decision, instead of choosing Runway 06 on the southern side of the terminal building, which SIA invariably used in view of its proximity to their boarding gate, he opted to use the 'safer' Runway 05L to the north. This slightly longer runway should have given a greater margin of safety in the wet and slippery conditions and had the advantage of being a Class II weather rating.

While the captain and first officer had quite often flown out of Taipei, they had not used Runway 05L on the northern side for two or three years. The layout they were used to using to the south was much simpler, consisting of just a taxiway and a runway parallel to it, instead of a taxiway, a minor runway, and the major runway, as on the north.

To reach the main 12,008-ft Runway 05L, they would have to taxi past the end of the shorter 05R, which had just been taken out of service (with that end used as a supplemental taxiway), and the middle-to-far end used to park construction equipment, including concrete blocks.

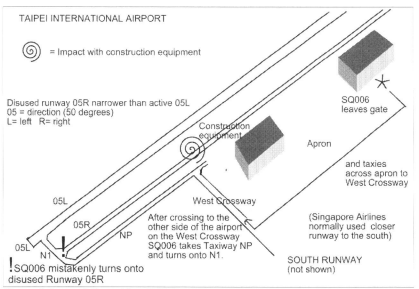

Figure 4  Route followed by SQ006.

Despite the rain and slippery conditions, the SIA 747 negotiated the taxiways to the other side of the airport and made the 90-degree right turn to enter taxiway N1, which would first take them past the end of the disused Runway 05R and then on to the wide active Runway 05L quite a bit further on.

The trap into which they were to fall into was a perfect line of closely spaced green taxi lights leading in a neat curve to (the disused) Runway 05R. In the heavy rain, these were very inviting, especially to pilots who were used to Singapore, which has a system whereby controllers turn taxiing lights on and off to show the pilot where to go, so all he or she has to do is to *follow the green*. On the other hand, at Taipei the green taxiway lights leading straight ahead that they should have followed to take them to the operating runway were few-and-far-between with one not working at all and another quite dim.

Of course, had visibility been better, the crew of SQ006 would have been able to pick out the bright lights of the operating runway straight ahead. Indeed, the pilot of a cargo plane belonging to another company that took off eight days after the SQ disaster, but in not quite such poor visibility, said he too had been tempted to follow the bright green lights leading to the disused runway. He had not done so because in the better conditions the bright lights of the operating runway ahead were visible straight ahead.

As every motorist knows, distances seem much greater when moving very slowly in poor visibility, and the crew perhaps thought they had come a fair distance when they mistakenly followed those beckoning green lights and lined up for takeoff from the disused runway. All three pilots assumed it was the runway.

There was a delay of about a minute before they started their takeoff roll, during which it seems they were assiduously calculating the crosswind component of the head wind to make sure they were not breaking any company rules. Had they not been so preoccupied with the letter of the law, they might have thought it odd the centre lights were green and not white as they should be on an operating runway. It seems—though not 100% provable—that there were no runway edge lights. The captain was '80% sure' he saw the runway edge lights; the first officer said he did not see any lights other than the centre lights. The disused runway was 15 meters narrower than it should have been, but perhaps the very absence of runway edge lights made this less obvious. Lights shining on raindrops might have given the impression they were difficult-to-see edge lights.

On an operating runway, there would normally, but not necessarily, also have been the bright touchdown lights indicating where aircraft should land.

Something the crew did notice and that could have saved the situation was the failure of their Para-Visual Display (PVD) to activate (to un-shutter) on turning onto the 'runway.' The equipment sounds complicated, but is merely an instrument with a horizontal rod somewhat like the sign outside a barbershop. A computer senses deviation from the runway centerline and indicates this to the pilots by varying the speed and direction of rotation of the striped rod, producing the optical illusion that the lines are moving to the left or right. This instrument can be helpful for keeping on the runway centerline when visibility is extremely low, even down to 50 meters.

Though this helpful piece of equipment was not working, the pilots did not worry any more about it when they found on lining up that visibility was not bad enough for them to need it.

After rechecking that the crosswind did not exceed authorized limits, they commenced their takeoff roll. The aircraft gathered pace normally, but four seconds after reaching the takeoff decision speed, $V_1$, of 142 knots, the captain uttered an expletive and the two words:

*Something there!*

He tried to lift off, but with an aircraft full of fuel it was too late. Instants later, the aircraft's nose wheel hit the first concrete block.

Then as the huge fuel-laden aircraft was trying to rise, contractors' equipment, including two excavators and a bulldozer, ripped into its hull like an iceberg into the *Titanic*, by which time the speed had reached 158 knots. The 747 fell back, crashed into more construction equipment and concrete blocks, and broke its back. With fire spreading from the left wing, it exploded and ended up (perhaps fortunately) in three pieces.

Some of the passengers and crew were able to scramble out of the breaks in the fuselage and certain exits. Some exits were unusable due to raging fires outside, while the powerful wind made it difficult to open others—some have suggested the Asian flight attendants were not strong enough. In cases where exits could be opened, the escape chutes often did not deploy properly with one blowing back into the aircraft and pinning down a flight attendant, others flapping around and some catching fire.

Nevertheless, the survival rate was 54%. Of the 179 (159 passengers and 20 crewmembers) on board, 96 survived, and 83 died. Most of the survivors were injured in some way, but as in many terrible disasters, some, 16 in all, escaped unscathed. The pilots were among the survivors and someone saw one of them assisting a flight attendant who had lost a leg.

This was a big shock for SIA, an airline highly respected throughout the industry for the expertise of its management and its efficiency, not to mention the elegance of its cabin staff. Except for a crash involving its subsidiary, SilkAir, where there were suspicions that the pilot crashed the aircraft on purpose in a kind of suicide, this was their first fatal crash in their 28-year history.

SIA were also famous for having one of the youngest fleets at a time when British Airways was still flying some 27-year-old Boeing 747s.[2]

Many motorists have taken a wrong turning on badly signposted roads in heavy rain, but how could highly trained pilots do such a thing? The captain had 11,235 hours of flight time.

After some bad PR due to their Los Angeles office prematurely reporting no casualties to news organizations phoning from around the world, SIA won plaudits, at least locally, by admitting responsibility, with the Chief Executive Cheong Choong Kong saying at a press conference in Singapore after returning from Taipei:

> They are our pilots. It was our aircraft. The aircraft should not be on that runway. We accept full responsibility.

In addition, the airline offered to pay $400,000 to the families of those killed, and to compensate generously the survivors for their expenses and so on.

## Points Related to this Disaster

A feature of the Boeing 747 that many must have noticed is that the pilots are very high up off the ground, rather like the drivers of some SUVs looking down on others from their lofty perch. The reason for this was that the design for the 747 was originally based on one for a military freighter (the C5A) that could be loaded from both front and rear with large items such as vehicles. Boeing had been competing with Lockheed and McDonnell Douglas. Boeing lost the contract to Lockheed perhaps because of cost, but was unfazed and immediately started work on the 747, which ultimately was to revolutionize long-distance air travel. The then head of Boeing had in fact gambled on the success of the 747 as an ideal aircraft for long-haul air travel in a new mass market

This height off the ground may have made the task of those SIA pilots seeing the markings on the ground even more difficult. Interestingly, the Airbus 380 design for a true double-deck super-jumbo has the cockpit set lower down.

It was quite clear that the taxiing lights at Taipei's international airport left much to be desired. The airport did not have ground radar enabling controllers to see the location of aircraft in bad visibility, but Taipei airport is not alone in this regard, and its absence was not contrary to international regulations.

When the Taiwan authorities finally produced their 508-page report into the disaster, it raised so many points that it was difficult to see the wood for the trees. In addition, many of these points seemed to lay the blame on the SIA pilots rather than the airport. The Taiwanese allowed the Singapore side to participate in the investigative phase, but not in the analysis phase. The Singapore side was unhappy about that and produced a 'Commentary' rebutting many of Taiwanese side's conclusions, just as the Dutch had done many years earlier for the Tenerife disaster.

The Singapore view was that it was a 'systems failure' with many factors involved. The Taiwanese view was that while the airport may have had its shortcomings, the pilots should have, and would have, realized they were on the wrong runway, if they had taken more care and paid more attention. In addition, according to them, SIA had not trained the captain in poor visibility taxiing, and so on and so forth.

In some respects, it is paradoxical that the crew may have made the mistake because they were being extra cautious checking and rechecking the crosswind component to make sure they were allowed to take off under company regulations. Unfortunately, their checklist did not include checking repeatedly, and by all possible means, that they were on the correct runway. One could say, that they should have been trained to consider whether failure of the Para-Visual Display (PVD) to activate (to un-shutter) on turning onto the 'runway' should be seen as reason to think they might not be on the active runway, but probably most airlines would have failed to think of that.

One point that might seem strange to some was the Taiwanese Chinese investigators asking the pilots whether they had any 'cultural problems' regarding their relationship with other crewmembers. This really alluded to the crew being partly Malaysian and partly Chinese.

SIA later dismissed the captain and first officer, after having overtly given all three pilots full support during the course of the inquiry. However, they did not dismiss the third officer whose facile explanation as to why the Para-Visual Display was not working may have meant loss of a chance to realize they were not on an active runway. Some say this accident was a classic case of 'scenario fulfillment,' in that people see what they expect to see.

One would have thought an accident like this would be unlikely to recur, as pilots would surely be extra careful following this event. This was not to be so. Sadly, it was a pre-dawn takeoff from the wrong runway by a Comair commuter jet at Lexington on August 27, 2006 that would mark the end of the 'safest ever period in US commercial aviation history.'

---

[1] Had the captain himself not been handling the aircraft and concentrating on turning in slippery conditions, he might have been more aware of his location.

[2] BA thought that its reputation for excellent maintenance would enable it to sell these geriatrics at a good price, until one was found to have a wing spar almost eaten through by corrosion. The second hand value of BA's older aircraft plummeted accordingly. According to a British newspaper that had considerable difficulty obtaining the information, BA repaired the aircraft and allocated it to a Caribbean route, which they would not name.

# FRENCH AIRLINER CLIPS UK FREIGHTER
# (Paris CDG 2000)
## Some Air Traffic Control Exchanges in French

In the Linate accident, the pilots of the straying Cessna might have recognized their error had the controller not spoken in Italian to the other light aircraft waiting for them to pass.

Communications with commercial airliners should normally be in English, and one would expect this to be particularly true at a major international airport such as Paris' Charles de Gaulle. Shortly before the accident described below, Air France's safety department had recommended its pilots consistently use English in the interest of safety. Not only did some pilots oppose this; politicians and the press said it threatened the role of the French language in the world.

*[Air Liberté and Air Van Freighter]*

It was 02:50, and with very little traffic, the controllers at Paris' Charles de Gaulle Airport were not using the southern control tower. In addition to the usual cargo flights, there was the unusual problem of coping with some 20,000 Spanish football fans returning to Spain after watching the Valencia/Real Madrid match in Paris.

Speaking in *French*, a controller cleared an Air Liberté MD-80 charter flight carrying 150 of those fans for takeoff from the far end of Runway 27.

Speaking in *English*, another controller told the English crew of a Shorts 330 'Sky Van' cargo plane to hold before entering the second section (3,300 ft further down) of that same runway, since the small twin-turboprop cargo plane did not need as much runway as the airliner to take off.

The controller had told the crew of the Air Van that they would be Number 2. The cockpit voice recorder (CVR) of the cargo plane showed that its English captain was wondering who Number 1 was and whether it was the Boeing 737 that had just landed. No doubt thinking that was the case, he moved onto the runway just as the MD-83 (on Section 1 of the runway) was gathering speed on its takeoff run.

In 33 seconds, the MD-83 attained $V_1$, and was just about to reach rotation speed, $V_R$, when its captain saw the cargo plane nosing onto the runway. With only five seconds remaining before certain impact, he proceeded to abort his takeoff—something virtually never done after attaining takeoff decision speed, $V_1$. However, it was fortunate that he did, as a third of his left wing was shorn off as it struck the nose of the Sky Van, killing its first officer[1] and seriously injuring its captain. Fortunately, with plenty of runway left at such a large airport, the MD-83's crew were able to bring their damaged aircraft to a halt without any loss of life.

The subsequent inquiry mentioned poor coordination between the controllers, and that the rainy conditions, light pollution (caused by floodlights, and 10 vehicles with rotating lights involved in construction work near the threshold) made observation more difficult for the controllers. In addition, the MD-83 had delayed its takeoff because of an auto throttle problem, and this made the situational development different from what the controllers had anticipated.

This was perhaps one of those dangerous half-way situations, where conditions were not good enough to see perfectly, but not bad enough to use all means—including ground radar—to check what was happening.

In addition, it would have been a quiet time with everyone rather relaxed. Interestingly, psychologists note an inverted 'U-curve' for the effect of stress:

1. **No stress, people are not switched on.**

2. **Medium amount of stress, they are at their best.**

3. **Too much stress, their interactive skills diminish.**

Even so, the key finding of the inquiry seemed to be that *if* communication between the French aircraft and the control tower had been in English, the crew of the cargo plane would have known the MD-83 was about to take off and would not have entered the runway.

Readers will note that the narratives in this chapter have a number of common threads.

---

[1] Traditionally, the captain sits on the left and the first officer (copilot) on the right. This is because holding patterns at airports usually involved left-hand turns and this permitted the captain to see where they were going by looking out of his side window.

# SAS MD-87 ENCOUNTERS CESSNA ON TAKEOFF (Milan 2001)

## Air Traffic Controllers Sentenced to Prison

> Poor indications on the ground featured in a disastrous accident at Milan's Linate Airport in which a passenger jet collided with a small Cessna crossing its path during takeoff.
>
> Yet again, the collision occurred just as the departing aircraft was about to lift off.
>
> Use of Italian instead of English to communicate with another general aviation aircraft meant that the pilots of the Cessna were less aware of what was going on than they might have been.
>
> *[Scandinavian Airlines Flight 686 & Cessna Citation CJ2]*

According to some accounts, 27 minutes elapsed before the air traffic controllers at Milan's second airport, Linate, realized the two aircraft they had 'lost' had collided at the airport itself.

Two and a half years later, the April 17, 2004 edition of London's *The Independent* newspaper carried the following report from its Rome correspondent Peter Popham:

> *A court in Milan convicted four airport officials of manslaughter and negligence yesterday after Italy's worst aircraft disaster, in which 118 people died when a Danish airliner and a Cessna executive jet collided on the runway at Milan's Linate airport in October 2001....*
>
> *... All passengers and crew in both planes died, as well as four baggage handlers when the Swedish plane ploughed into a baggage handling building.*
>
> *The judges found all four defendants guilty and handed down stiff sentences of between six-and-a-half and eight years. Seven more defendants have yet to be sentenced.*
>
> *As the verdicts were read out, the wife of one man killed in the accident screamed from the gallery, 'On your knees. On your knees, assassins!'*

Of course, there were to be appeals and one wonders how much time the defendants actually spent in prison. The court sentenced the air traffic controller to eight years even though the prosecutors had only asked for three years, perhaps because of the banter in the control tower, where the controllers joked that the bangs they were hearing sounded like their shift leader's head being banged against the control tower windows. Yet, one must feel some sympathy for the controllers in that respect. Their job is very stressful, and like surgeons, they no doubt make jokes of dubious taste to relieve the tension.

Apart from Japan, where the police feel they should find someone criminally culpable in any accident, it is rare for those thought to be responsible for an air accident to face prison sentences, and even more rare for the accused to include senior managers and officials. This shows the shambles at Milan's Linate Airport. However, though the situation at Linate was extreme, many of the faults, such as poor taxiway markings and careless use of language, also applied to the two terrible accidents already described in this chapter.

Milan's Linate Airport is prone to early morning fog, and at the time of the accident, there was no operating ground radar system. The old system had broken down and the new and much better system bought from Norway some four years earlier had not been set up due to administrative delays.

After the accident, the so-called administrative and technical problems quickly evaporated and the system was set up in a couple of months. Part of the delay had been due to the inability to decide whether the airport or air traffic control should be responsible for setting it up.

The brand new—only 28 airframe hours and 20 cycles—twinjet Cessna Citation with its two German pilots and two passengers[1] had landed early that morning in fog with its pilots not qualified to land in such poor visibility. The Cessna had come to a stop just beyond the taxiway leading off to the left to the general aviation apron to the west.

However, as there was hardly any traffic at the time, the air traffic controllers allowed it to do a U-turn on the runway, and back-taxi to exit, this time on the right, to the general aviation apron to the west. This enabled them to avoid taking a circuitous route via the commercial airliner apron situated to the northeast.

When ready to set off for their next destination, Le Bourget (Paris), visibility was still too bad for the pilots to take off with their pilot's license ratings. However, it was not against the rules for them to taxi in the hope that visibility would improve by the time they were to take off. (In fact, none of the controllers had checked their qualifications regarding poor visibility flying.)

Contrary to international convention, the numbering of the taxiways at Linate was not consistent. They should have been numbered in a clockwise direction. R6 should have been R5, and R5 further round the clock to the north should have been R6.

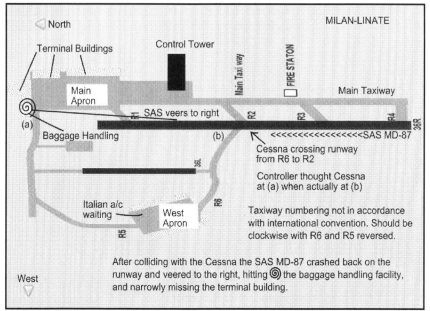

Figure 5  The Cessna should have taxied north via R5 not via R6.

(Based on ANSV document)

The Cessna pilots duly parked on the West Apron after arriving directly from the runway.

However, when it was time for them to leave the West Apron for departure, the airport was busy, so the ground controller instructed them to taxi *north* via taxiway R5 and call him back when they reached the stop bar to the main runway extension[2] (just before point (a)).

Ground control:

> *DVX taxi north via Romeo five QNH1013...call me back at the stop bar at the main runway extension.*

DVX:

> *Roger via Romeo five and 1013 and call you back before reaching main runway.*

The controller did not pick up on the fact that the callback omitted the word 'north,' but possibly for him the word was only to make his instruction clearer—for him the pilot had correctly repeated the key information, *R5*. Some investigators have suggested the German pilot missed the word 'north,' as it is very short when spoken in English by an Italian.

Seven seconds later, the ground controller gave a similar authorization to taxi *via R5* to another light aircraft parked on the West Apron north of where the Cessna had been. However, the controller gave his instructions in Italian and told them to wait until the German Cessna had passed by before moving off. The German pilots in the Cessna could not follow this exchange in Italian.

After a while, the controller checked with that second light aircraft, asking them whether they were duly proceeding along taxiway R5. They replied they were still waiting for the Cessna to pass. Their pilot then asked (in Italian) whether the controller knew where the German was. The controller replied that the Cessna was on the main apron, and added:

> *I should say you can go.*

Frustrated by the unnecessary wait, the Italian pilot replied:

> *I should say so! We move.*

If this exchange had been in English, it might have given the Cessna pilots another hint they were on the wrong track.

The Cessna, erroneously proceeding southeast along taxiway R6, instead of north via R5, came to a spot a little before the runway marked S4, and informed the controller they were 'Approaching the runway... S4.' The controller might have misheard[3] and anyway *S4* did not have any significance for him, as it was not on any of his plans of the airport.[4] The controller told them to:

> *Continue your taxi on main apron. Follow the 'A' line.*

The Cessna read back the instruction correctly:

> *Roger, continue taxi in apron, 'A' line....*

The controller replied:

> *This is correct. Please call me back entering main taxiway....*

About that time, the controller told an aircraft actually on the main apron to call back on entering the main taxiway.

The Cessna pilot could have been in no doubt that he was going to cross a (the) runway, but he had the green center lights continuing past the stop bar lights, and could have been under the impression that he should cross the runway as quickly as possible.

Having taken the same route in the opposite direction when landing, he should have known he was not at the northern runway extension, but possibly in the path of an aircraft taking off or landing.

The Cessna moved forward towards the runway and began to cross, unaware that a SAS MD-87 airliner waiting to start its takeoff roll, had received its takeoff clearance and was already moving forward. They were unaware of this fact as the takeoff clearance had been (as is normal) on the tower frequency, which the taxiing Cessna pilots would not be using.

The point where the Cessna was traversing the runway proper was 1½ kilometers from the point where the SAS aircraft had started its takeoff roll just 37 seconds earlier. Consequently, the SAS MD-87 was traveling at about 146 knots and well into its rotation when it encountered the Cessna directly in its path.

The nose landing gear lifted off two seconds before the impact, and though the main landing gear was still touching the ground, the weight was coming off the main wheels with their shock absorbers extending. (The lift-off of the nose wheel had automatically sent a signal to the SAS home base in Copenhagen indicating that the flight had duly taken off!)

A fraction of a second before impact, there was a distinct nose-up elevator input and crew exclamation on the MD-87, so they could only have seen the tiny Cessna at the very last moment. Following the collision, the crew of the MD-87 advanced the throttles further, but the extra power was not forthcoming as the right-hand No. 2 engine at the rear had fallen off and the only remaining engine was failing, no doubt due to ingestion of debris.

Nevertheless, the MD-87 continued its climb to a height of 10½ meters (35 feet) before plunging down onto the runway 8.5 seconds after separating from the Cessna. Not only did the MD-87 not have enough thrust from the remaining engine to climb away, the loss of the heavy rear-mounted No. 2 engine meant the center of gravity had moved too far forward for the aircraft to fly. Realizing the hopelessness of the situation, the pilots pulled back the throttle levers.

Having vainly accelerated to a speed of 166 knots, the MD-87 fell down on the runway, with the right-hand main wheels missing, and failing hydraulic pressure. This meant that the aircraft tipped to the right and the right wingtip struck the ground causing the aircraft to slew around. The crew applied reverse thrust to the remaining left-hand engine, but with the engine so close inboard (unlike wing-mounted engines that are further out) the directional correction it provided was limited.

Lack of hydraulic pressure meant the brakes were ineffective. Veering slightly to the right, the SAS MD-87 was still traveling at 139 knots when it slammed into the baggage handling building located 460 meters beyond the end of the runway and not far to the right of the runway axis.

Just six seconds had elapsed from the moment the MD-87 fell back on the runway and its collision with the building. Four baggage handlers in the building, and all 104 passengers and 6 crew on the airliner were killed.

The situation for the two pilots and two passengers in the frail Cessna was hopeless from the start, and all were either immediately killed by the impact or in a minute or so by the fire and smoke. All told, the total death toll was 118. Had it not been for the fine airmanship of the MD-87 crew in trying to straighten out the trajectory, it could have been even worse with the aircraft veering further to the right and striking the passenger terminal rather than the baggage handling facility.

As mentioned at the beginning of this section, the failures of the controllers and those running the airport were so many and so glaring that they were held criminally responsible. However, did the investigators fully consider the possible fatigue of the Cessna pilots?

The official report only said they presumed the Cessna pilots duty time had started at 04:30 local time. One supposes they worked this out from the time it would have taken the pilots to fly to Linate from Cologne.

One of the German pilots was 64, and the other 36. There is no knowing what they were doing before they picked up the aircraft for the middle-of-the-night departure from Cologne, but it is quite likely they would have been pretty tired by the time they asked for clearance to taxi at 06:05 at Linate. That was the moment they made the fatal mistake of not noticing the air traffic controller had said they should go *north* and call him back when they reached the stop bar at the main runway 'extension.'

What the controller quite meant by *runway extension*, meaning an imaginary line continuing on beyond it to taxiway N5, may not have been clear. Since the Cessna pilots did not confirm the word *north,* they possibly had not noted it. It is quite possible that after their brief break, one (or both) German pilots was not fully alert. Without evidence from a cockpit voice recorder, it is difficult to be sure of the exact situation—they could have been distracted by the passengers' presence.

Nevertheless, how the Cessna managed to take taxiway R6 instead of R5 is something of a mystery, unless one assumes that the pilot looking at the plan of the airport was not concentrating because of tiredness or some other reason. It was confusing, if not looking at the plan, to have taxiway R5 above R6 in the clockwise direction. In addition, as they had followed that route on coming off the runway on their arrival, that route might have seemed more logical as it was only about a third of the distance. There is a slight parallel with the crew of the Pan Am 747 at Tenerife in that their taking the 45° taxiway rather than the difficult 135° taxiway leading back towards the terminal would seem more logical and be much shorter.

The Cessna pilots only had one chance to determine what number taxiway they were on, and that was where the yellow lines on the apron forked, with the yellow line for taxiway R5 forking to the left (and north) and the yellow line for taxiway 'R6' forking to the right. The nearest taxiway light in the wrong direction (R6) was only 80 meters away, while that for R5 was 350 meters away, thus perhaps luring them in the wrong direction just as with the Singapore Airlines pilots at Taipei. However, if the Cessna pilots and the Singapore Airlines pilots had been looking at the plan of the airport they surely would have seen their error.

Once the Cessna pilots had made the mistake—for whatever reason— there was no further indication along the whole length of the taxiway indicating its number. Whatever the truth, the controller had pigeonholed them in his mind as being on R5 and nothing they said apart from the meaningless (to him) statement that they were at 'S4' indicated otherwise. Even if they missed the stop bar on taxiway R5 at the runway *extension*, the controller would assume they could not come to much harm, as any aircraft taking off would be well into the air by then.

Both at Linate and Tenerife, the aircraft taking off were almost airborne. Had distances and loads been only a little different, the carnage might have been much less, if not completely averted. To a lesser extent, the same might be said to apply to the Singapore Airlines disaster at Taipei.

---

[1] A Cessna sales manager and a prospective customer.

[2] The controller meant a theoretical line extending from the end of the runway, not that the runway went physically as far as that. However, charts showing the layout of the taxiways and runways did not mention that spot in those terms.

[3] The German pilot did use the term 'Sierra 4' so it could not have been so unclear.

[4] The marking 'S4' had been painted on that taxiway many years before when it was thought extra parking spaces might be needed for airliners. However, the project was terminated when the flights were transferred to Milan's other airport. Serving no purpose, it was not mentioned on airport plans.

## CHAPTER 6
# NO CONTROLLABILITY

### DC-10 CARGO DOOR OPENS INFLIGHT
### (Windsor/Detroit 1972)
**Cabin Floor Reinforced for Piano**

> Two years before the disastrous crash near Paris of a Turkish DC-10, an almost identical scenario had taken place when a DC-10 was climbing out of Detroit.
>
> However, in the Detroit case, reinforcement of the passenger cabin floor (to support a piano for an inaugural flight) meant it did not buckle downwards as much under the sudden pressure difference when the hatch of the cargo hold underneath failed.
>
> *[American Airlines Flight 96]*

On June 12, 1972, an American Airlines DC-10 bearing Flight Number 96 took off from Detroit for Buffalo with only 56 passengers. Normally, there would have been no need to open up the rear cargo hold with so little baggage to load—also they would not want to shift the center of gravity too far back. However, the manifest included a coffin and perhaps out of consideration for the baggage handlers at Buffalo, the decision was taken to load it into the rear hold situated under the floor of the aft passenger cabin.

Though the points of departure and the destination were both in the US, the route was almost entirely over Canada as the frontier came southwards to follow the center of Lake Erie. With the first officer at the controls and flying on autopilot over the Canadian side of the Lake, they were near Windsor, Ontario[1] and coming up to 12,000 ft on their routine climb to 23,000 ft, when the pilots heard a bang from behind and felt the impact of a rush of air on their faces. The flight deck door sprang open and a lot of dust started flying around. An explosive decompression had obviously occurred.

Back in the passenger cabins, the rush of air was propelling papers and other loose items rearwards, with the situation being worst right at the rear where two flight attendants in seats by the rear doors were for a moment sucked downwards towards the floor buckling into the cargo hold below. The flight attendant on the left could actually peer into the cargo hold and see the gaping black hole where the door had once been.

Unaware of this, the pilots' immediate thought was that something had struck them, but whatever the cause of the decompression, they first had to determine what controllability they had:

1. **The rudder pedals were jammed against the stops at the 'full left turn' position.**

2. **All three throttles had sprung back to their 'idle' stops.**

3. **Engines (1) and (3) mounted on the wings seemed to be okay, and despite having begun to spool down due to the movement of the throttles, responded when these were pushed forwards. Engine No. 2 in the tail was no longer functioning and its throttle was anyway immovable.**

4. **The vital (apart from the rudder) control surfaces in the tail, namely the elevators, were barely working and felt very heavy.**

5. **Despite the rudder pedals being jammed at full left, the aircraft was yawing to the right.**

6. **However, by increasing the power on the right engine, reducing that on the left engine and applying a fair amount of left aileron it was possible to get the aircraft to fly straight.**

Subsequently, by adjusting engine power and varying the amount of aileron, the pilots found they were able to steer the aircraft very roughly where they wanted to go, with an inevitable time lag between the input and the response due to the engines needing time to spool up and down.

The DC-10 is notable for having the engines mounted under the wings and very low slung, with this compensated for by having the engine in the tail very high up and at a slight angle. This 'leverage' (mechanical moment) allowed the pilots to raise or lower the nose by juggling engine power. However, without the compensatory engine high up in the tail, there was the danger of pushing the nose up too far, and not being able to push it down. The pilots had to be very wary and proactive—if they got into too sharp a dive they might not be able to pull out of it, or in trying to do so might not be able to push the nose down afterwards and end up stalling.

By making a long shallow approach, the captain managed to bring the aircraft down onto Detroit's 10,500 ft (3,200 m) long, 200 ft (60 m) wide runway at just 30 knots over the normal approach speed and even managed a 'flare' by having both pilots heaving back on the leaden elevator controls at the last moment.

The touchdown was a good one in the circumstances, but once on the runway, application of left aileron could not prevent their trajectory veering to the right because of the rudder sticking out to the right. As they left the runway, the first officer, realizing they would be in trouble before the reverse thrust and brakes could slow them enough, increased reverse thrust on the left engine beyond the normal limit and at the same time disengaged reverse thrust on the right-hand engine by pushing the throttle lever forward. This succeeded in countering their deviation, and it was not long before their airspeed had dropped enough for the protruding rudder to have little effect so that the nose-wheel steering—always wanting to veer left under the command of the jammed rudder pedals—came into play, bringing the aircraft back to the runway. They ended up half-on and half-off the runway, and some 500 meters from the end.

The captain had not jettisoned fuel because of uncertainty regarding the extent of the damage to the rear of the aircraft. Even had he opted to do so, the fuel dumping limitation (already mentioned) on the DC-10 would not have allowed him to drain the tanks enough to prevent fire in a crash-landing.

The few occupants were able to evacuate in less than a minute, making it a lucky outcome for all concerned. Proficient handling of the stricken aircraft by the crew had saved the day, but why had the incident happened in the first place, and why did the apparent failure of a cargo hold door have such consequences?

The simple answers are:

1. The door locking mechanism was badly designed.

2. The floor did not have vents in it to allow air to pass through it without it buckling first.

3. The control lines for the rudder, elevators, and rear engine were attached to the underside of that floor.

A fascinating and troubling book, *THE DC-10 CASE: A Study in Applied Ethics, Technology, and Society*[2] describes the 'scandal' and human factors that had resulted in an inherently dangerous aircraft, and allowed it to continue as such, leading ultimately to the loss of a DC-10 that happened to be virtually full on taking off from Paris. Here we use background information from that book, without the space to do it justice, though some of the ethical points are touched on in the final chapter.

### The Door Latching Mechanism

Recovery of the cargo hold door from a field under the flight path meant the investigators had all the elements required to determine the immediate cause of the near disaster. The hinges and interfaces between the door and the fuselage were all in good condition, and the investigators quickly concluded the C-latches must have opened for some reason.

As their name implies, the C-latches affixed to the bottom of the door are shaped like the letter 'C,' and in theory swivel round when the door is locked so as to encircle a very solid crossbar (spool) on e doorjamb, so that the greater the force trying to prize the door open the firmer it should hold. This supposes proper engagement of the C-latches in the first place.

Unfortunately, 'give' in the various levers and components of the locking mechanism and poor design meant those doors on DC-10s could appear to be properly locked when in fact the C-latches were not properly 'home.' This was partly because the original design had envisaged using hydraulic power to operate the primary (non-manual) locking system and this was subsequently changed to electric on the demand of the airlines on grounds of economy (cost and weight) grounds. Hydraulic operation is generally much more 'positive.'

## McDonnell Douglas

McDonnell Douglas, the DC-10's manufacturer, had had numerous complaints from airlines about the door in question. The problem with the aft cargo hold door—as were a number of other problems with the DC-10— was said to be due to the frenetic pace at which the aircraft was brought into production, with Lockheed's very similar TriStar in direct competition, and the Boeing 747 lurking in the background.

Although, the competing Lockheed TriStar L1011 was an excellent aircraft, McDonnell Douglas had the advantage that US airlines were so used to buying its aircraft that they were likely to choose them out of habit and inertia. This did not prevent the airlines playing off the two companies against each other, with the result that prices became so low that neither aircraft would ever be a big money-spinner, unlike the Boeing 747, which was in a category above.

In addition, delays in developing the power plant for the TriStar had almost led to the demise of the UK engine manufacturer Rolls-Royce, which had to be bailed out by the British Government, and in turn meant that Lockheed got off to such a delayed start that sales never took off. Despite offering inducements (bribes)[3] to sell the aircraft abroad, total sales only came to some 250 units compared with the 500 needed for the project to break even. This ultimately led to the great Lockheed, famous for such great airliners as the beautiful Constellation, withdrawing completely from the civilian airliner market.

Inducements paid in Japan in the expectation that All Nippon Airways (ANA) would purchase the Tristar led to the resignation and subsequent trial of Japanese Prime Minister, Tanaka Kakuei.

In parallel, a very senior manager at Hong Kong's Cathay Pacific Airways had to resign in disgrace for accepting inducements, albeit on a much smaller scale. Ironically, the two did their respective airlines a favor by stopping them from jumping on the dangerous DC-10 bandwagon before its problems were resolved. The DC-10 that crashed outside Paris as described in the next narrative with the loss of all on board had originally been destined for ANA.

Like the fatal *Put on Your Manager's Hat* decision to launch the Challenger Space Shuttle, many engineering ethics courses cite as classic examples for study the decisions subcontractors made concerning the DC-10 cargo hold door when engineers were fully aware of the problems.

## The Subcontractors

The contractor for McDonnell Douglas was Convair, and six weeks after the Detroit/Windsor incident in 1972, Convair's Director of Product Engineering, Daniel Applegate, submitted a memo to his superiors officially delineating problems with the cargo hold door that had become apparent as early as August 1969. These had been confirmed in a ground test the following year. According to some reports, those tests also revealed what could happen to the passenger cabin floor.

Following the discovery of the problems by its engineers, Convair's management was halfhearted in pursuing the matter with McDonnell Douglas for fear that under the terms of their contract they might have to pay the cost of the modifications. McDonnell Douglas's management was in turn fearful about the effects any delay might have on their sales. Undoubtedly, the best option would have been to redesign the whole thing, but as such systems have to go through a lengthy approval process with the FAA, it was too late to start over and they therefore fiddled with an 'approved' design as modifications would only be minor and quickly certified. (Another instance where regulations meant to ensure safety have the opposite effect.)

The opening of a cargo hold door at altitude is always a serious matter, as the slipstream usually wrenches it off. If it were a front cargo hold door, it could damage the control surfaces on the wings or disable the engines under the wings,[4] or, if at the rear, damage the horizontal stabilizer and elevator on the tail as happened in the Detroit/Windsor case.

What manufacturers did not properly consider at the time was the disastrous knock-on effects of such a decompression. Not only would the passengers risk being sucked out or struck by flying objects, they would also be subjected to the physiological effects of explosive decompression. The downwards buckling of the passenger cabin floor under the pressure differential could also damage the vital control links and hydraulic lines leading to the tail, generally attached to its underside. This in turn could make the aircraft uncontrollable.

Within three weeks of the Detroit/Windsor scare, the NTSB made two urgent recommendations:

> 1. **Modification of the DC-10 door locking mechanism so it would be physically impossible to bring the vent-flap locking handle to its stowed position without the C-latch locking pins being fully engaged.**

**2. Vents (holes) should be incorporated in cabin floors to considerably relieve sudden pressure differentials such as those caused by the opening of a cargo hold door in flight.**

## The Gentleman's Agreement

The NTSB could only advise. It was up to the FAA to make these two modifications mandatory.

Just when the FAA was about to issue an Airworthiness Directive (AD) making interim and long-term solutions mandatory for all US operators of the DC-10 (which foreign operators would have followed), discussions between the FAA Administrator and the president of the Douglas Division of McDonnell Douglas led to the senior FAA technical staff being overruled.

Douglas and the FAA were no doubt being subjected to screams from US airlines not wanting to take their aircraft out of service in the peak summer season.

So finally, the FAA did not issue that Airworthiness Directive.

Instead, McDonnell Douglas almost immediately issued 'recommendations,' and in particular the installation of a 'lock-mechanism viewing window.'

This 'gentleman's agreement' between the FAA administrator and McDonnell Douglas' Douglas Division president sufficed to prevent a repeat accident *in the US*.

However, for foreign airlines without the expertise and qualified staff widely available in the US, this was *not true*. Admittedly, the terrible disaster that was ultimately to befall a newer DC-10 was partly due to McDonnell Douglas itself supplying the aircraft with even its own recommended modifications not having been carried out.

---

[1] In books and documents the incident is often simply referred to as the 'Windsor incident.'

[2] *THE DC-10 CASE: A Study in Applied Ethics, Technology, and Society.* Edited by John H. Fielder and Douglas Birsch, State University of New York Press.

[3] Perhaps because Lockheed were desperate their inducements were possibly particularly blatant. It is usually the agents on a commission who are the ones who pay the inducements, which of course do not have to be in cash.

[4] See 'Business Passengers ejected from 747 (Honolulu, 1989).'

# PACKED DC-10 CRASHES MINUS 6 PASSENGERS (Paris 1974)

### Fatal Repeat

> This disastrous DC-10 crash outside Paris was a rerun of the Detroit/Windsor incident except as regards the strength of the rear cabin floor.
>
> Compounding the great missed opportunity to make essential improvements after that incident was that even the more limited improvements recommended by McDonnell Douglas were not made on an aircraft supplied long afterwards—the work was 'inexplicably' signed off by three of their own engineers as having been done.
>
> *[Turkish Airlines Flight 981]*

Demand that day for seats between Paris and London was particularly high as one of the two main airlines serving the route, British European Airways (BEA), was on strike. This was part of a negotiation tactic to get a better deal for its staff in its merger with British Overseas Airways (BOAC) to form what is now British Airways (BA). There was some friction, as BOAC people appeared to see themselves 'above' those at BEA, who were apparently paid less to fly less exotic routes. Fans returning to England from a rugby match in Paris the previous day were putting added pressure on the few available seats.

Hence, when a Turkish Airlines DC-10 arrived en route for London, stranded travelers clamored for seats, and as a result, it unusually departed for London with most seats filled.

Taking off in an easterly direction from Orly Airport situated to the south of Paris, it skirted the city and continued some 25 miles, before turning north towards England, with everything seeming routine.

The Detroit/Windsor incident repeated itself just as the almost full-to-capacity wide-bodied DC-10, likewise climbing to cruising height, came abreast of the northern limits of Paris' suburbs at a height of some 9,000 ft and a speed of 300 knots.

However, this time the floor had not been reinforced, and so opened up much more. Six hapless—or perhaps fortunate passengers—were sucked downwards, and disappeared through the chasm in the floor and out of the failed door to subsequently hit the ground still strapped-in in the two rows of their three-abreast seats.

Coinciding with an emergency transmission from the aircraft, French air traffic controllers saw the 981 flight number transmitted by the DC-10's transponder disappear from the secondary radar. However, the primary radar, which works by bouncing a radio wave off an aircraft showed the 'echo' separating into two blips—a large one and a much smaller one.

The large one veered northwestwards, before disappearing after a minute, while the weaker one (the six passengers in their seats no doubt held together by the broken-off rail used to attach the seats to the floor) remained stationary before disappearing after a couple of minutes or so.

The large blip (the aircraft itself) had come down in Ermonville Forest, some *13 miles* northwest of the point where the decompression had occurred.

## The Crash Site

The high sink rate and forward speed meant the trees could not cushion the terrible impact. Air crash sites are usually horrible, but this one was particularly so. The absence of a conflagration meant the scattered distribution of body parts was immediately obvious.

In *Air Disaster (Vol. 1)*, Macarthur Job describes how Police Captain Lanier, who was one of the first to arrive, described the terrible scene and saw two separated hands, a man's and a woman's, clasped together. In such circumstances, there was no hope of any survivors.

## The Pilots

What had been the situation on the flight deck in those final minutes? Could the pilots have saved the aircraft? Indeed, it seems they had finally found a way to at least to bring the aircraft out of its fatal plunge, but did not have enough height left.

The buckling of the floor had, as in the Detroit incident but to a greater degree, damaged or severed the triplicate hydraulic lines serving the tail and the control cables both for the tail flight control surfaces and rear engine.

From the cockpit voice recorder (CVR) and the flight data recorder (FDR), investigators ascertained that pressurization-warning klaxons sounded in the cockpit when the cargo door blew out and that the crew thought there had been a failure of the fuselage. Not that it made any difference in this case. Apparently, the situation developed as follows.

Going into a 20-degree dive, the DC-10's airspeed increased alarmingly, and despite the engines being throttled back, the overspeed alarm sounded. With not quite a minute having elapsed since the nightmare had started, the captain astutely decided their only hope was to ignore the aural overspeed warnings and go for even more speed. Pushing the throttles forward, at the same time he said, '*Speed!*'

Whether it was the speed itself or rather the nose-raising torque of the two viable engines slung so low below the wings, or a combination of both, the aircraft gradually began to level out, with the rate of descent decreasing so much that the g-forces would have forced the pilots and passengers hard down into their seats.

They were almost level when they struck the trees of Ermonville Forest at 430 knots! Had they had a greater height margin, the story could have been different with the captain's call for 'speed' allowing them to fight on.

All 339 people remaining on board died in the subsequent crash. Perhaps because the captain had cut the engines just before impact, there was no major outbreak of fire.

As the high-speed impact had so traumatized the bodies, it was evident that this absence of major fire would not have made much difference to the occupants. However, the relative lack of smoke and fire did make it surprisingly difficult to locate the exact site of the crash in the relatively vast forest. The total death toll, including the six passengers ejected earlier, came to 345.

## Comparison

With so little means of control—just the engines—the situation facing the Turkish pilots was more akin to that faced by those of the Sioux City DC-10 rather than those at Detroit. However, it differed in that the Sioux City aircraft became uncontrollable at the great height of 37,000 ft and not at 9,000 ft. Besides, it did not start to dive on its own. This gave the Sioux City pilots more than ample time to decide what action to take, whereas in the Paris case, only 72 seconds elapsed between the decompression and impact with the ground, and only 10 seconds between the initiation of the almost successful addition of power to bring the aircraft out of its dive and that impact. Had the Paris pilots been able to recover in time, would they have been able or lucky enough to replicate the Sioux City feat?

At first, with the aircraft having disintegrated into tiny pieces, as had the passengers, the investigation looked as if it would be difficult. Post mortems of the relatively intact passengers ejected right at the beginning in their seats, provided valuable evidence, and notably that it was not due to a bomb as had first been feared. Furthermore, recovery of the cargo door with its mechanism virtually intact as in the Detroit/Windsor case was a great help.

The investigators found:

1. **Firstly, the stiffening of the linkage from the flap handle had not been done as proscribed in Service Bulletin 52-37. Some modifications had been made, but an item not up to aeronautic quality had been used and in fact, these had made the door even more vulnerable to improper locking than the one on the Detroit DC-10.**

2. **The micro switch system for indicating (on the flight deck) whether the door was locked was not adjusted optimally.**

3. **The door did have the proscribed window for checking whether the latches had gone home. However, the cargo handler responsible for closing the door was not qualified or told to perform that check, which was normally done by a Paris-based Turkish Airlines engineer (who was on holiday) or in his absence by the flight engineer (who failed to do so).**

The 'gentleman's agreement' mentioned above between the head of the FAA and the President of the Douglas Division of McDonnell Douglas had meant the radical measures recommended by the NTSB after Detroit were not made mandatory.

However, the scandalous aspect was that even the 'half-measures' proposed by McDonnell Douglas' Service Bulletin to airlines had not been carried out by themselves on an aircraft ordered and delivered long afterwards. (Eventually, it transpired that three engineers at Douglas or its subcontractor had signed-off the work as having been completed.)

The airline and the manufacturer paid out some of the highest compensation ever for an air disaster without admitting culpability. Had the disaster occurred in the US, the damages would have been far higher.

Though it is clear the main problem was one of engineering ethics, there were as usual multiple factors—not least the fact that the flight engineer did not do a visual check through the observation window prior to departure from Paris.

The FAA hurriedly made the measures recommended by the NTSB after the Detroit incident mandatory. These included having vents in cabin floors to relieve extreme pressure differentials. Passengers are safer now thanks to that.

# TEXTBOOK SPEED SEALS DC-10 FATE
# (Chicago 1979)

**Would not have Flipped at Slightly Higher Speed**

> The photo of the DC-10 banking at 90 degrees with one engine missing told all. An engine had fallen off the wing, but that should not have prevented it from flying. Lack of an 'unnecessary' safety feature allowed the slats on that wing to retract.
>
> In contrast to Lockheed, it seemed MacDonnell Douglas was loath to incorporate 'unnecessary' safety features.
>
> Failure to include a slat-locking mechanism led to the accident below.
>
> *[American Airlines Flight 191]*

Just as the American Airlines AA191 afternoon flight taking off from Chicago for Los Angeles was rotating at a $V_R$ of 145 knots, the *rear* support of the pylon holding the No. 1 (left) engine failed.

The powerful takeoff thrust then pushed the engine assembly forwards and upwards as it pivoted on the *front* support, which in turn fractured. Finally, the engine with the pylon still attached passed over the top of the wing, and because of its weight and the low airspeed tumbled to the ground without damaging the DC-10's high-up tail assembly.

The wing minus its engine dipped for a moment, but then came up again as the pilot used the ailerons to climb out at 159 knots—6 knots above the safe climb-out speed ($V_2$), which was the minimum allowed.

Despite the separation of the engine, there was every indication they would be able to return safely to the airport, and the controller observing the takeoff from the tower asked the pilots if they wanted to come back, and if so on which runway.

According to the flight data recorder (FDR), the aircraft then accelerated to reach a maximum speed of 172 knots 9 seconds after becoming airborne. At 140 ft agl, and still climbing, the pilot apparently let the airspeed fall back in accordance with the airline's engine failure procedure. On reaching a height of about 325 ft agl, with the airspeed dropping back to the recommended 159 knots, it had been initially and with no problem when they climbed out, the left wing from which the engine had fallen inexplicably began to drop.

The aircraft yawed to the left and was soon side slipping in a 90-degree bank with the wings perpendicular to the ground as shown in the photo on the next page.

 (Courtesy NTSB)

Figure 6  Left wing stalls
(because slats on that wing retracted when the engine fell off.)

See in color on chrisbart.com by clicking on
*DIAGRAMS & PHOTOS FOR KINDLE*
*READERS + LINKS FOR ALL READERS*

The final reading obtainable from the data recorder three seconds prior to the left wingtip hitting the ground showed 112 degrees bank and a nose-down attitude of 21 degrees. The aircraft then flipped over and exploded, and a large fireball, fed by the large amount fuel, engulfed the debris.

'Would-be' rescuers said the crash scene was a horrible sight with no body intact and even those remains charred beyond recognition.

All 271 people on board were killed together with two bystanders making it the worst air disaster up to then in US history. It could have been worse as the aircraft came down just short of a large caravan park, and fuel storage tanks further on.

For the 100 or so investigators sent to the scene, there were two main questions:

1. **Why had the pilots lost control when the aircraft should have been able to fly in that configuration at that airspeed?**

2. **Why had the engine and pylon fallen off in the first place?**

## Change of Configuration Stall

The outer leading edge slats on the left wing had for some reason retracted, and this had led to a *change of configuration stall*, that is a stall where an alteration to the position of the flaps and/or leading edge slats means the aircraft can no longer fly at the given airspeed.

Paradoxically, had the captain not followed the rule book to the letter, and reduced speed on the loss of the engine, he would have been above the stalling speed for that configuration and the ailerons would have been sufficient to compensate for the discrepancy in lift due to the retracted outer slats on the left wing. Someone said he could have flown all the way to Los Angeles. The rule (later modified) had been made to protect the other engines, which automatically spool up to maximum or above maximum rated power when an engine fails on climbing out on takeoff to compensate for the loss of power. The pilots are told they should level out and decrease the power on the remaining engines, which the pilots of the DC-10 duly did.

However, as in so many crashes, there were other unfortunate factors. Firstly, on twisting upwards and passing over the wing the engine assembly had severed a cable passing just inside the damaged leading edge of the wing that should have transmitted the information that the slats had retracted to the pilots.

Secondly, the stick shaker (stall warning system) did not activate and the instruments were not working properly because the electric circuit had been locked out. Also, with the inner slats still deployed there would have been virtually no buffeting that the pilots could sense. That electrical system could have been unlocked by the pilots but they were too busy, and for the engineer to do so he would have had to turn his seat around and unbuckle himself, which was hardly possible in the time available.

Not knowing what was happening, and with no time, the pilots could not have been expected to realize where the route to salvation lay. Also, the dissymmetry in lift and resultant banking meant that the minimum control speed ($V_{MC}$) as well as the stalling speed would rise so quickly that even getting the wings level would quickly become hopeless. Pilots given the full background were able to save the aircraft in the simulator, but those not so briefed reacted as the actual pilots had and crashed.

## DC-10 Design

The DC-10, unlike many other aircraft, did not have a mechanical locking device to keep the slats from retracting under external force in the event of a failure. However, in most cases of failure, the hydraulic fluid trapped by a valve would prevent that happening.

Anyway, even if the slats did retract, the ample power available from the engines would immediately give them sufficient speed to both avoid a stall and have controllability via the ailerons. The possibility of an engine failure coupled with an undesired slat retraction was considered improbable.

However, in the case in question, the separation of the engine and pylon damaged the hydraulic lines and caused the slats to retract. Some maintain McDonnell Douglas was taking risks by having so many vulnerable lines just behind the leading edge of the wings.

## DC-10 Maintenance and Forewarnings

Reviews of eyewitness reports and examination of the wreckage indicated that the pylon's rear bulkhead flange had been cracked beforehand. In view of the considerable safety margin built in, this could hardly have happened during normal operations and must have happened during maintenance. Indeed, the pylon (together with the engine) had been removed and replaced two months earlier to substitute the bearings. Investigators found a large number of deviations in the maintenance work at a number of airlines. For instance, maintenance workers on finding certain bolts difficult to remove would remove them in a different order from that specified, thereby placing excess stress on certain ones.

The FAA grounded all US-registered DC-10s subject to a check of the rear flanges in question. Four American Airlines aircraft and two Continental Airlines aircraft had cracks there. Continental had found their cracks in the rear flanges in the course of maintenance and replaced them! Other airlines had not experienced that problem.

## Forklifts

The reason soon became obvious. The two airlines had devised what they thought was a super efficient way to remove the engine and pylon simultaneously using a forklift, disregarding the McDonnell Douglas maintenance manual that said they should be removed individually.

The DC-10s engines are cantilevered far in front of the wing, which means a considerable mechanical moment (levering) is imposed if the engine is lifted more than a certain extent, and that can put tremendous stress on the rear flange. In addition, vibrations from the forklift can be transmitted to it. The accident was partly attributed to poor communication between the parties, namely Continental, the FAA, the manufacturer and the airlines, regarding the earlier problems at Continental.

## Final Remarks

This disaster led to three Airworthiness Directives and an almost unheard of 38-day grounding of the fleet, whereas the DC-10 scenario at Windsor Ontario where a cargo door blew off and the floor buckled downwards with no deaths had resulted in none! (Unfortunately, that scenario was to be repeated with 345 deaths.)

The damage to McDonnell Douglas' reputation in the eyes of the public was so great that many orders for the DC-10 were cancelled. The company subsequently dropped behind the competition after failing to develop any more radically new airliners, and was finally taken over by Boeing.

Yet, the modifications and changes in maintenance procedures introduced following this disaster, coupled with those made in the light of earlier ones, mean the DC-10 is now statistically one of the safest aircraft, and pilots who fly it seem to appreciate its qualities.

# JL123, WORST SINGLE AIRCRAFT DISASTER (Japan 1985)

### Rear Bulkhead Fails, Tailfin Blown Off, then Hydraulics Fail

> This disaster in Japan where a Boeing 747 staggered drunkenly around the sky for half an hour with passengers writing 'last wishes' on their boarding passes must have been a terrifying experience, as well as being the worst single-aircraft crash ever.
>
> *[Japan Airlines Flight 123]*

*Off-duty flight attendant, Yumi Ochiai,[1] felt her hair lift off her neck, and a momentary sense of weightlessness as the staggering 747, with its 524 terrified occupants, began its final downwards plunge, shaving trees on one desolate mountain ridge, and ending up on another.*

*Her pelvis broken, and trapped between seats in the remains of the broken-off tail section, she was fitfully aware of the cries of young children, but their cries had faded as the severe injuries, shock and cold of the night took their toll. One young boy who was not to survive indicated his determination to be strong, exclaiming, 'I am a man!'*

The Boeing 747 SR (Short Range)—a jumbo specially adapted and reinforced to carry as many as 550 passengers on domestic short-haul routes in Japan—was the early evening shuttle from Tokyo's domestic Haneda airport to Osaka, Japan's second largest city 400 kilometers away to the south.

The flight was being flown by First Officer Yutaka Sasaki, 39, an experienced pilot training for promotion to captain. In the right-hand seat acting as copilot was Captain Masami Takahama, 49, a JAL instructor with more than 12,400 hours experience. Hiroshi Fukuda was the flight engineer.

Unusually, the occupants were mostly women and children, for it was the Obon August holiday period when the Japanese go back to their hometowns to visit family graves and see relations. The aircraft was virtually full, and most of the passengers were clad in only the lightest of clothes in anticipation of a clammy mid-summer evening. As in a number of flights that have ended in disaster, the flight number was easy to remember, 'JL123.'

Haneda, situated at the edge of Tokyo Bay and very close to the center of the city, had served as Tokyo's international airport until the construction of Narita Airport in the face of fierce opposition some 50 miles (80 km)

115

away. With little need for noise-abatement over the sea, JL123's climb out of Haneda was a simple affair. Ten or so minutes after takeoff, the busy pilots were able to relax. Everything seemed normal.

The first indication the Tokyo controller had that everything was not so came without any forewarning at 7.25 p.m.—13 minutes after takeoff and just as JL123 was leveling out at its cruising altitude—when the echo for the aircraft on his radar screen switched to 7700, the *emergency* code.

Shortly afterwards came the following disjointed call from the aircraft:

> *Tokyo. Japan Air 123. Request immediate... ah... trouble. Request return back to Haneda... descend and maintain Flight Level 220.*

JL123 then asked for the vector (course) back to Oshima Island, the waypoint on the easiest oversea route back to Haneda. The controller gave the crew permission to descend and indicated the appropriate course, but instead of turning 177° to go back on its tracks, JL123 merely made a very slow right turn of some 40°. Surprised by this non-compliance, the Tokyo controller repeated his instructions.

JL123 still did not comply, and with the aircraft heading for dangerous mountains, Japan Airlines operations center called them on the company frequency, without extracting more information except that the crew thought a rear cabin door (R5) was broken and that they were going to descend.

Watched by the air traffic controllers in Tokyo, the 747 meandered in an area of treacherous mountains not far from Japan's famous Mount Fuji. The pilots kept repeating they were *out of control*, while at the same time requesting directions back to Haneda. Periodically losing considerable height and partially regaining it, the aircraft, at one point, made a tight 360° turn.

Finally, after some 30 minutes, the echo on the screens showed JL123 rapidly losing altitude, before sinking out of radar view. The controllers vainly hoped the 747 had merely gone into a valley, but getting no reply on the radio, they finally accepted that it must have crashed.

A US transport aircraft taking off from the US Air Force Yokota airbase thirty-five miles away reported seeing fire in the midst of the mountains 'that was very likely to be the crashed aircraft.'

It is not easy to be sure who saw what and when. The author read a report that five minutes after the crash the Japanese Air Self-Defense Force had scrambled two F4 Phantom fighters to investigate, and that 20 minutes later, they were able to report the presence of fires and the general location as '*299° and 35.5 miles from Yokota US airbase's TACAN.*'[2]

Certainly, Yokota airbase in the outer west-northwest suburbs of Tokyo was relatively near, and it has been said recently, perhaps in connection with the excellent TV series *Air Crash Investigations* that a helicopter from

Yokota reached the site 20 minutes after the crash, but was called back so that the Japanese 'Self-Defense Forces' could take over. (The US military have a privileged, but sensitive, presence in Japan, and scrupulously avoid making any comments that could in any way cause friction, and so it is not easy to check these things out.)

Macarthur Job's *Air Disaster (Vol. 2)* also mentions a Japanese helicopter reaching the site and reporting the wreckage was scattered on a 45-degree slope with fires and virtually no likelihood of any survivors, and that in view of the darkness, rain and steepness of the terrain landing there would be impossible.

Subsequently, other helicopter crews, working from maps, gave many erroneous locations. In such terrain, without GPS and with one peak looking very much like another, one had to know the area and have reasonable visibility to get the location right. It was becoming pitch dark. Officials, by their very nature, were wondering whether the crash had occurred in Gunma Prefecture or Nagano Prefecture. Which police force would be responsible?

At the time, Japan did not have a civil emergency unit[3] to deal with such events. Also, lingering antagonism between the police and fire department (which had at one time had been a single organization) meant, according to some, that the police did not immediately call in the more suitable fire department helicopters. Furthermore, use was not made of US forces with their considerable experience of plucking downed pilots at night from the mountains of Vietnam, perhaps because of 'face' or the fact that no one wanted to take the responsibility if things went wrong.

In addition, one has to remember no one was expecting there to be survivors. Perhaps we are wiser nowadays with experience showing that at least some of those on board can survive the most horrendous crashes. Adding to the confusion was the absence of high officials away on the Obon National Holiday—the holiday those passengers had been looking forward to enjoying.

To complicate matters, the crash site was in a particularly inaccessible place. No roads came anywhere near, and it was dark. Finally, at 05:37 the *following* morning, a Nagano Prefecture police helicopter reported that the fuselage was scattered in an area some 700 meters east of the prefectural frontier and was all in Gunma Prefecture. With the site pinpointed, the main 'rescue' teams could set off on what they expected would be a body-recovery rather than rescue mission. The earlier reports regarding the fires and the sighting of wreckage scattered over a wide area implied there was little chance anyone could have survived.

Because of the steep tree-covered slopes at the crash site, the authorities had determined that helicopters could not land close to the site even in daylight. To make matters worse, the weather then closed in.

At 08:49, the process of lowering 73 paratroopers by rope from giant helicopters hovering over the site began. They were to be the first people on the scene, nearly *14 hours* after the crash. Just as the first paratroopers to descend were confirming by radio at 09.25 that there were no signs of survivors, two members of the Nagano Prefecture rescue team descended at a point 1½ miles (2.3 km) away. Subsequently, at 10:15, the neighboring Gunma Prefecture police team arrived on foot after scaling the mountains.

### Survivors—12-year-old Schoolgirl Symbolizes Disaster

At 10:54, and almost *16 hours* after the crash, a firefighter from Ueno Village and a member of the Nagano Prefecture police rescue team unexpectedly found a survivor trapped in the broken-off part of the rear cabin that had slid some way down the ridge from the main crash area. She was the off-duty JAL flight attendant who had heard the cries of the dying children. Next, they found a mother and her eight-year-old daughter under nearby wreckage. All had fractures.

Most surprising of all was the discovery of 12-year-old Keiko Kawakami in the wreckage of the tail section with hardly an injury other than a slightly injured arm. Reports that rescuers found her wedged in a tree may be mistaken, as there is a photo of that wreckage with arrows showing the spots where she and the other three of the four survivors were found.

She said she found herself in the wreckage with her mother dead, and her father saying he could not help, as he could not move. When he died, she consoled her sister, who was to die too, saying their grandmother would look after them.

A photo taken from the ground showing Keiko being clasped around the waist by a paratrooper in combat gear as the two of them are being winched up into a giant helicopter came to symbolize the disaster. For years, weekly magazines used this appealing image on commuter train posters to advertise any issue with purported new facts about the crash, or failing that with anything showing Japan Airlines in a bad light.

Hopes of further survivors engendered by this good news soon evaporated. Others had survived the impact and some of them almost surely could have been saved had help come earlier.

What had really happened to the passengers in those 30 minutes leading to the final plunge onto the mountain ridge? What was behind what to this day remains the worst-ever crash involving a single aircraft?

### The Passengers

The flight data recorder and descriptions by the rescued off-duty flight attendant, Yumi Ochiai, reveal how terrifying the 30-minute roller-coaster ordeal preceding the crash must have been. The aircraft would yaw, pitch and roll, with each cycle taking about a minute-and-a-half. In addition, there would be the vacillating scream of the engines as the pilots tried to steady the aircraft vertically and horizontally, and attempted to nudge it in the direction they wanted. A number of the adults scribbled last words to loved ones on the back of their boarding passes or other scraps of paper.

## The Flight Crew

Thanks to the cockpit voice recorder (CVR) the situation in the cockpit is well known as there are both the crew's conversations between themselves and their exchanges with the air traffic controller—a couple of times the captain tells his colleagues to ignore the air traffic controller and concentrate on keeping the aircraft in the air rather than on ATC.

Although the pilots are speaking in Japanese, there are easily identifiable words from the captain, such as *Flap up! ... Power! ... Power!*

Finally, at the end of the half hour, one clearly hears the verbal warnings from the aircraft's Ground Proximity Warning System (GPWS) making a whooping sound immediately followed by the words: 'PULL UP!' repeated five times over a period of nine seconds. Perhaps the most distressing part is that there follows the sound of one impact, followed a second later by another, as the aircraft bounced from one ridge to another. Then silence.

For the crew it had been a desperate struggle, as the only way they could maneuver the aircraft appeared to be by varying the relative thrust of the engines. At one point, they made, as mentioned, a tight 360° turn.

Tokyo ATC was calling them, and the nearer American Yokota Air Base was doing likewise. Though the Tokyo controller had suggested Nagoya Airport to the south, they seemed intent on going back to Haneda. Perhaps they were more familiar with it, perhaps because it was 'home,' and perhaps because it was at the (sea) water's edge and they could ditch the aircraft in the water if their approach failed and they did not come a cropper on the unforgiving sea wall on its perimeter.

The crew knew they had no hydraulic pressure to control the aircraft's control surfaces, but did not know why. This in itself was surprising to them as aircraft manufacturers design these key hydraulic systems with built-in redundancy on the 'belt and braces' principle, in that if one fails one of the others will take over. The systems were in triplicate. In addition, they did not know why the aircraft was so unstable. It was yawing (veering violently from side to side), rolling (one wing tipping down one moment, the other wing the next), and pitching (nose down one moment, nose up the next). Indeed, it was misbehaving in all three axes with a phugoid motion. This porpoise-like pitching and to some extent the rolling could be explained by the lack of hydraulics to control the ailerons and elevators, but why was the yawing so considerable—little did they realize that most of the tail plane had been lost.

However, in trying to go back to Haneda instead of going to Nagaoya where they could at least have ditched in the sea en route should they not be able to reach it, they ended up going over the mountainous terrain near Mount Fuji.

When, over the mountains, they repeatedly tried to turn towards Haneda, the aircraft seemed to want to go the other way. Finally, when the speed dropped sufficiently, the first engineer (perhaps on his own initiative) lowered the landing gear. This had the effect of stabilizing the aircraft somewhat, but had the disadvantage of making the aircraft lose height and at the same time made it more difficult to steer away from the mountains. The pilots tried lowering the flaps, but this made things worse, so they retracted them just before the crash. (They were able to lower the landing gear and maneuver the flaps by using a backup electrical system.)

They probably were doomed from the moment the incident started thirty minutes earlier. Knowing what we now know, one can say that it was a great feat of airmanship even to stay aloft for so long. In addition, Japan is not a good country to be in such a predicament, for it consists mostly of steep volcanic mountains. What little flat ground exists is put to use. Had the aircraft managed to escape from the high peaks near Mount Fuji to make its way directly to Haneda, it could have crashed on built-up areas with even greater loss of life. Housing in Japan is often frail and closely packed and the aircraft could have cut a long swathe through suburban housing.

## The Cause

No one could understand what had happened, and rumors were rife and some continue to be so. Had it been hit by a missile? On the other hand, was it a bomb? Was it a meteorite?

Then some solid information began to come in. People on the ground had seen the 747 staggering through the evening sky, and an amateur photographer even had a blurry photo of it—*without its vertical tailfin.*

A Japanese naval vessel then recovered a large portion of the tail from the sea in the area where the pilot had first declared the emergency some 30 minutes before the crash. Subsequently, searchers recovered other pieces in that area.

Never had there been a structural failure like this on a Boeing 747. The aircraft was relatively old, but there were 747s twice as old still flying safely. However, as Japan Airlines employed the aircraft on short domestic routes with many takeoffs and landings, it did have a large number of flight cycles, and it was thought likely that the accident might be linked to that.

A flight cycle is one takeoff and landing, and is significant because each time an aircraft climbs into the sky, the pressurized air in the cabin makes the fuselage stretch a little, so everything moves and warps slightly. When the aircraft descends, the opposite happens. Metals do not 'like' constant flexing beyond a certain elastic limit. A phenomenon called 'fatigue failure' occurs where the metal becomes brittle and fails. Anyone who has tried to

120

break a thick copper wire has experienced the phenomenon: one bends it one way and then the opposite several times, it suddenly becomes brittle and breaks.

After the world's first passenger jet (Comet) disasters due to metal fatigue in the late 1950s, manufacturers had been very careful to avoid areas of stress concentration. Thus, it was unlikely Boeing had made such a design mistake. Nevertheless, it was very worrying for the company, as the safety of the entire fleet of 747s might be questioned and lead to enormous financial loss. A number of countries immediately ordered their airlines to carry out checks on the tail section.

Boeing sent telexes to all users with information about the maximum number of cycles other 747s had flown without structural trouble. The maximum number of flight cycles for any 747 was 22,970 cycles, which was somewhat more than for the crashed aircraft's 18,830. Thus, though JL123's number of cycles was relatively high, it was not deemed excessive.

Investigators began to direct their attentions towards the rear pressure-bulkhead, which though made of quite thin material is a kind of 'plug' keeping the pressurized air in the cabins from escaping through the rear of the aircraft. However, Boeing had designed it to last at least 20 years, and the crashed aircraft was only 11 years old. The bulkhead could have failed because of corrosion—indeed another type of aircraft flying out of London had crashed due to corrosion of the rear pressure bulkhead 14 years previously—but there was no sign of corrosion on the JAL bulkhead.

Then one of Boeing's investigators discovered a small piece of the rear pressure bulkhead with repairs made using a splice and rivets—with merely a single row of rivets. How could there only be a single row of rivets when Boeing, for the very fatigue failure reason mentioned above, always mandated that there be a double row of rivets to prevent concentrated stress leading to fatigue cracking?

Records showed the aircraft had suffered a tail strike seven years earlier on landing at Osaka Airport with its nose too high in the air, and had been out of service for three months for repairs. Boeing immediately thought they were off the hook as was assumed Japan Airlines had been responsible for the incorrect repairs. Then to their consternation, they discovered the repairs had been carried out under the supervision of, and according to instructions from, their own engineers sent over from the States!

There followed a period of buck-passing. Japan Airlines said Boeing was responsible for the crash due to the faulty repairs; Boeing said it was Japan Airlines' fault for not having detected the crack. One of Boeing's arguments was that as the Japanese are chronic smokers there must have been visible signs of tar on the edges of the developing crack on the far side (from the cabin). Japan Airlines countered by saying it was in a visually inaccessible place and anyway no one would expect to see anything wrong at such a spot in the absence of signs of corrosion, say from water from the toilets or galley. These fatigue cracks can take years to develop and might have been virtually invisible anyway early on.

Allegedly, Japan Airlines accepted 20% of the blame on the grounds that for an extended period up to the disaster, whistling had been heard at the back of the aircraft in question and no one had checked it out. (A number of websites say this, but as they use identical wording, they must be copying one another, making it difficult to find the original source.)

## Boeing

Finally, both companies realized their slanging match was mutually damaging and decided to compromise. After all, Japan Airlines was a major Boeing customer and falling out with them could in the long-term cost much more than the immediate costs. Another point was that the accident happened in Japan where there is not the lawyer-compensation culture found in the USA, and the sums to pay out were not as great as they might have been. After arranging for some free modifications to existing 747s worldwide to ensure that failure, however unlikely, of another rear bulkhead, would not result in catastrophic consequential damage, Boeing finally came out of the affair relatively unscathed.

## Japan Airlines

The same was not true for the Japan Airlines. No one could prove it was entirely their fault, but the Japanese press turned on them like a lynch mob. This was partly due to the haughty attitude the featherbedded airline had shown over the years. The media hounded them relentlessly, picking up on every possible fault. It took years for them to recover, and perhaps, domestically, they never quite have.

A mentally ill pilot trying to commit suicide three years earlier by purposely crashing on landing at Tokyo's domestic Haneda Airport did not help the airline's case. In that incident, the first officer had struggled with the captain unsuccessfully, and the aircraft crashed into the sea just before the Haneda runway, with 24 killed and 141 injured. Following that incident, passengers and colleagues would nervously scan the faces of JAL pilots to see if there were any signs of mental trouble. Even the slightest tick or mannerism was liable to raise suspicion!

In Japan, it is always felt that someone should take the blame, and demonstrate his or her contrition. In the case of the 747 disaster, the police treated the crash site as a crime scene and only let the investigators 'borrow' the debris.

The main purpose of air accident investigations in the West is to determine the cause so a similar thing does not occur again, but, even in the US, there is an increasing tendency to obfuscate since the potential legal liability can be so costly. However, where the impartiality of the accident investigators might later be questioned, as in the case of the Airbus crash at a tiny air show in France, there is something to be said for judicial authorities ensuring the flight recorders are not tampered with—assuming the judicial authorities can be trusted.

In the following months, someone at JAL did commit suicide, leading the press to conclude he was the man responsible for the bad repairs or for not finding the crack in the pressure bulkhead. In fact, the suicide had nothing to do with the crash.

Yet, if someone at JAL *had* felt personally responsible, that individual might well have committed suicide, bearing in mind the case around then where passengers who had had omelet for breakfast on a JAL flight staggered off the aircraft at Tokyo with serious food poisoning. A young JAL cook at the Anchorage stopover with an infected hand had handled the 'mix,' which had presumably been left standing uncooked. No one died, but he committed suicide nevertheless. Most safety experts would now say it was a systems or management failure, for the airline should have ensured the 'youngster' had gloves and or had been kept off work, and so on.

## Conclusion

The conclusions were that to prevent such accidents one should:

1. **Find ways to avoid and detect such maintenance or repair mistakes through better management (oversight) and improved checks.**

2. **Ensure one failure does not result in collateral damage that could endanger the aircraft.**

The author has heard it suggested that had Japan Airlines carried out maintenance less assiduously, and left holes and weak parts in the fuselage behind the bulkhead, the air would have been able to escape through those without blowing off the tailfin!

## Was Depressurization so Rapid?

Recently, a retired JAL pilot, Hideo Fujita, wrote a book entitled *Kakusareta Shougen* (Hidden Testimony) doubting that sudden depressurization ever occurred, and that the cause of the accident must lie elsewhere. His reasons for doubting that the decompression was as sudden as claimed were:

1. **The pilots were able to continue physically demanding movements without donning their oxygen masks for some time even though the aircraft was at 21,000 ft where the air is thin.**

2. **The rescued off-duty flight attendant had heard a 'bang' above her, not behind her, and had seen no papers flying around in any direction—which one would have expected had the air been rushing out of a big hole. [In the author's opinion, the panels of the tailfin could have been blown off without the immediate exodus of a large volume of air.]**

3. **Shortly after the crash, Japan Airlines said the rescued off-duty flight attendant had said she had seen air coming out of the floor vents, when in fact she could not have seen them from her seat and had anyway never heard of the term.**

Whatever the truth, it is certain that the official cause of the crash being faulty repairs by individuals was very convenient for Boeing and even JAL. The Japanese police were not able to get their hands on the US 'individuals' and prosecutors were not intent on pursuing the matter.

Nothing was ever really made of the fact that more people could certainly have been saved had help come earlier. The report from a helicopter arriving early above the crash scene, that there were surely no survivors was a factor. The Americans, who were probably the best placed to help in view of their experience in extracting downed pilots from the Vietnamese jungle, were kept away. Whether it was a question of 'face' or because no one wanted to stick their neck out and order an operation that could easily have led to casualties on the US side is difficult to judge. The US military presence in Japan is such a delicate issue that no one on the US side would want to comment. Judging by the appreciation shown for the help given by the US forces in connection with the recent earthquake and tsunami, attitudes may have changed radically.

One has to remember the slopes were too steep (and tree-covered) for helicopters to land even in daylight and that most of the potential survivors would have been in the tail section that had broken off and slipped down the steep slope to end up quite some distance from the main site. They would have been difficult to find in the dark, notwithstanding the cries and moans mentioned by off-duty flight attendant Ochiai.

Another footnote to the JL123 disaster is that for the Japanese families, the proper handling and fullest possible recovery of the bodies and all their parts was of the utmost importance. Senior people from the airline attended every funeral, and staff continue to visit the crash site on every anniversary. The impact on the airline's daily operations must have been considerable.

In Japan, whenever a calamity happens, and especially to Japanese traveling or working abroad, the company or travel agency set up an 'HQ' with the staff waiting by the phones all night for the latest news—and for visits by TV crews. Many colleagues come in to the office though there is little of use they can do, but their very presence shows sympathy with the dead and their families.

---

[1] While in hospital Yumi Ochiai also mentioned hearing the sound of helicopter rotors and seeing lights, which could have been those of the US helicopter ordered back or those of the first Japanese helicopter.

[2] TACAN (Tactical Air Navigation) is a more accurate military version of the VOR beacon for giving bearings. It is not so useful now that there is GPS.

[3] One has now been set up at the old US air base, at Tachikawa situated just outside Tokyo.

# UNCONTROLLABLE DC-10'S MIRACLE LANDING (Sioux City 1989)

### Controlling DC-10 by Engine Power Alone

> There is one very famous case where, by juggling engine power alone, pilots were able to land an 'uncontrollable' DC-10 with many of the occupants surviving.
>
> No one was able to replicate this miracle landing in the simulator, and many wondered to what extent good luck had played a part.
>
> *[United Airlines Flight 232]*

United Airlines Flight UA232 from Denver to Philadelphia with a stopover in Chicago was more than halfway through its first leg. On board the three-engine DC-10 were the two pilots, Captain Haines, aged 57, First Officer Records, aged 48, and the flight engineer, Second Officer Dvorak, aged 51, 8 cabin attendants and 285 passengers. It was mid-afternoon, and they were flying in almost perfect weather at the economical height of 37,000 ft and at their designated cruising speed.

Just as they were effecting a slight change of heading, the aircraft juddered and passengers heard a thud at the rear. The instruments indicated something had happened to the No. 2 engine (mounted in the tail), and that it was spooling down. It would have to be shut down in accordance with the engine shutdown checklist, which should be no big problem as it was the center engine and the aircraft could fly easily on two engines, and especially if the thrust on each side was equal.

While losing one engine was not much reason for concern, of much more concern was the fall in pressure and loss of fluid in *all three hydraulic systems*. First Officer Records informed the captain that the aircraft was no longer responding to the controls and, on taking, over the captain was able to confirm the desperate situation for himself.

Even by deploying the Ram Air Turbine (RAT) to power the emergency generator to supply the backup hydraulic pump it proved impossible to restore hydraulic pressure. The aircraft was descending slowly with a gentle rolling and pitching motion.

Minneapolis Center proposed they divert to Des Moines International Airport, which though 100 nm away had the advantage of wide, long runways. However, the controller suggested they try Sioux City as they were already heading in that direction. The DC-10 pilots agreed this was the best option.

With some difficulty, they had established direct contact with the company's maintenance department in San Francisco, but no one could come up with any helpful suggestions. Meanwhile, Captain Fitch,[1] a 46-year-old off-duty company DC-10 check and training captain who had been sitting in the First Class passenger cabin, made his presence known and offered his services, which were to prove invaluable as events unfolded.

After asking Captain Fitch to go back to the cabin and check on the damage, Captain Haynes gave Fitch the task of working the throttles—a key task as it was the only way they could maneuver the aircraft and it was a full-time task. This would leave Haynes and First Officer Records free to deal with the other tasks and hopefully find a solution with the help of the airline's experts.

To find links to videos of Fitch describing his actions
 go to the chrisbart.com website and click on

*DIAGRAMS & PHOTOS FOR KINDLE
READERS + LINKS FOR ALL READERS*

The situation was very similar to that of the Japan Airlines 747 just described, in that the DC-10 had what is called a phugoid motion, like a sine wave. That is to say, on pitching downwards it would progressively gain speed until at a certain point it would pitch upwards and progressively lose speed until at a certain point it would pitch downwards for the whole cycle to be repeated. The problem was that after each cycle, the aircraft ended up lower, and it would not be long before they struck the ground.

Experimenting with a throttle lever in each hand, Fitch did achieve some measure of control, and finally, by being proactive, and anticipating the phugoid motion was largely able to iron out the highs and lows. The fact that the aircraft had an inherent tendency to yaw to the right and pitch downwards with the right wing tending to drop made his task even more difficult, as he had to solve the two problems simultaneously.

However, one feature that made the DC-10 easier to control is that with the center engine high up at the tail, the two engines under the wing are very low slung so that when power is applied the nose is levered upwards.
Realizing the situation could deteriorate at any moment, Fitch told Captain Haynes they needed to get down as soon as possible. Haynes concurred and asked the first officer to give him the V speeds for a no-slats no-flaps landing—they would be able to lower the landing gear using the backup method. The 'clean' (i.e. no slats, no flaps) maneuvering speed would be 200 knots. Furthermore, the speed would have to be above that for Fitch to be able to control the aircraft.

They had dumped fuel, but 15 tons remained as the DC-10 has an automatic dump shut-off valve to ensure that dumping cannot reduce the amount of fuel below that level.

The Sioux Gateway Airport[2] controller told them one runway was closed, but they could land on either of the other two active runways. Haynes intended to go for Runway 31, which was the longest and widest.

However, as they got nearer, Haynes realized that as they could only manage to make right turns and just about manage to fly straight ahead, they could not turn left to line up for an approach to Runway 31. He asked for, and obtained, permission to go for the 'closed' Runway 22 that by then lay straight ahead. The controller reassured them by saying there would be no trouble with the wind and that the presence of a field at the far end would make up for its shorter length.

## The Touchdown and Aircrew Performance

They had no micro-control—that is to say no means to make last-minute adjustments such as for the crosswind component, and their speed and rate of descent were extreme to say the least.

Compared with maneuvering by means of control surfaces (i.e. ailerons, elevators and rudder), which take effect almost immediately, control inputs via the throttles only take effect with a delay of 20 seconds or even more depending on what is required. For example, to get into the desired position for touchdown would necessitate preplanned inputs performed some 40 seconds beforehand. If something unforeseen occurred, there would be insufficient time to make a correction.

Compared with the normal landing speed for a DC-10 of 140 knots, they were doing 215 knots and accelerating. Worse still, their rate of descent was 1,850 ft per minute and increasing compared with a normal touchdown rate of descent of no more than 200 to 300 ft per minute. Besides adding an extra 10 knots to their landing speed, the quartering tail wind was causing them to drift away from the runway centerline.

By dexterity and/or good luck, Captains Fitch and Haynes had brought them in almost exactly as intended. An amateur video—the professional photographers had been expecting the aircraft to come in on the main runway—of the event gives the impression that it is going to be a perfect, routine landing.

Captain Haynes[3] has said this video was very deceptive. Though it appeared to show them steady at 300 ft, they were actually losing control and did not have sufficient height to regain control, which they were losing because the reduction in speed meant the aircraft was commencing 'a down phugoid' and reasserting its tendency to bank to the right.

Haynes has also said, Captain Fitch who was at the throttles added power to correct that bank, but that unexpectedly[4] the left engine spooled up faster than the right making the situation only worse. The bank

127

increased to 20 degrees, at which point the right wingtip hit the ground just short of the runway and to the left of the centerline with the nose pointing somewhat downwards.

The starboard landing gear came down just left of the runway, with the engine on that side striking the ground also to the left of the runway almost at the same time. Accounts then differ.

*According to most news reports,* the right wing sheared off and the aircraft flipped on its back, slid down the runway, and then off to the right of the runway over a total distance of almost a kilometer.

*According to Captain Haynes* the aircraft did not cartwheel as many news reports maintained, but slid sideways on the (intact) left landing gear and the stub of the right wing for 2,000 ft. Finally, the left wing came up, and because there was no weight in the tail (as it had broken off), the aircraft flipped over and bounced.

Haynes said that with all the smoke and fire, no one can quite remember what happened then. However, fortunately for them, and but not so for the occupants of the first class cabin, the cockpit broke off.

Examination of the wreckage showed the fuselage had broken into five pieces:

1. **The cockpit where all four occupants survived.**

2. **The first class cabin just behind the cockpit where apparently no one survived.**

3. **Almost ¾ of the economy class cabin from the front galley behind first class right back to the trailing edge of the wings, where almost ¾ survived, albeit with injuries.**

4. **A short section comprising six rows of seats from the trailing edge of the wings to just before the tail section, where only one person survived with injuries.**

5. **The tail section behind that with just two rows of seats in which seven people surprisingly survived.**

Incredibly, 185 people out of 296 survived, making a death toll of 111. That so many survived was to some extent due to the sterling efforts of the cabin crew and their rigorous training in a simulator that made a crash-landing and fire seem real.

Even so, their contribution would have probably been in vain—supposing they were even still alive—had not the high rate of descent and the 215 + 10 knots ground speed been absorbed in some manner. This is a prime example of the fact mentioned in this book's preface that the more horrendous-looking crashes *can* be the most survivable due to the fracturing and crumpling absorbing the shock.

Unlike the Staines 'heart-attack crash' near London's Heathrow, where the aircraft belly-flopped with the landing gear up and the wings level and ended up virtually intact, but with everyone dead or dying, the DC-10's right wing and right landing gear and right engine struck first and progressively absorbed the downwards momentum as they crumpled and sheared off. Then the 3,000 ft skid decelerated the aircraft even more, before the breaking up of the fuselage (into the five pieces) absorbed almost all of what speed remained.

The official report into the accident mentions that the crop of high corn where the main part of the fuselage ended up upside down hampered rescue efforts by firefighters, and recommended that having agricultural crops in proximity to runways should be reconsidered. Thinking of how the rain sodden ground helped slow Qantas 1 on its 100 mph overrun at Bangkok, one cannot help wondering whether the high corn helped slow the aircraft.

Looking at the feat from a piloting perspective, the main lesson does seem to be the importance of Cockpit Resource Management (CRM), though according to Captain Haynes, it was first called Cockpit Leadership Management. Each person performed his allotted task, and 'ideas were thrown around.'

With hindsight, one idea, which could/should have come to mind, was that the pilots could have transferred fuel from the tanks in the right wing to those on the other side to correct the tendency to bank to the right. Haynes admitted in his presentation at NASA's Dryden Flight Research Center that people would be likely to think of that nowadays, but they did not think of it then, perhaps because they were too pre-occupied with immediate problems. One wonders why people back at Maintenance and Operations did not think of that either. One problem was that people on the ground took some time to grasp fully what was happening, as the situation was so unbelievable.

Certainly, the retention of so much fuel because of the DC-10's fuel dumping restriction was unfortunate—another example of a measure deemed to increase safety doing the opposite.

## The Mechanical Causes

The underlying cause of the incident was failure of the engine's fan blade disk due to a casting fault that had remained undetected for 17 years. Though the engine had a protective girdle, this was designed to arrest the loss of a single blade flying out prior to the engine being shut down (or spooling down on its own), not for failure of the disk retaining the whole set of blades.

The accident led to much more stringent checks during the manufacture of engine components and during maintenance. In recent years, the need to ensure engines are reliable enough for ETOPS has spurred progress in checking such components.

The accident also prompted action to find ways of maintaining some measure of control even in the event of such a multiple hydraulic failure.

An interesting point later made by Captain Haynes when giving a talk at NASA's Dryden facility was that modern computers could be made to adapt to flying an aircraft by juggling engine power alone—the pilot would then move the controls in the normal way and the computer would hopefully do the rest! The aircraft would have to be designed accordingly, and whether this would be worthwhile to save perhaps one aircraft every ten years was in his opinion a matter for reflection—the funds might be more effectively spent preventing such an eventuality in the first place.

Actually, NASA's Dryden facility did initiate such a project but did not pursue it. However, according to *Flight International*, the US Department of Homeland Security (DHS)—realizing the increasing danger from Man-Portable Air Defense Systems[5] (MANPADS)—was reactivating the project, calling it Propulsion Controlled Aircraft Recovery (PCAR).

However, instead of using computer technology, the aim was to provide guidelines to help line pilots control crippled aircraft with just the throttles and without special computer assistance. Apart from some extra training, the program would not involve extra costs, as it would need neither extra software nor hardware. Tests are being carried out on simulators, with the Boeing 757 first, and a United Airlines Airbus 320 or another Boeing next.

Apart from being famous as an exceptional feat of piloting, the Sioux City 'miracle landing' was captured on video and is often shown in documentaries, such as the *Horizon* aviation safety documentary on British TV, to prove that many survive crashes one would think are cannot be survived.

---

[1] Dennis Fitch died of brain cancer on May 7, 2012, aged 69. Many obituaries said how much he was admired as a person and portrayed him as the hero of the Sioux City DC-10 landing.

[2] Sioux City Gateway Airport with some might think the unfortunate three-letter code SUX.

[3] Slide show presentation by Captain Haynes at the NASA Ames Research Center, Dryden Flight Research Facility, Edwards, California (1991)

[4] Just before the touchdown, the first officer is telling Fitch to apply left throttle—there seems to be some inconsistency.

[5] Usually in the form of shoulder-launched missiles.

# DHL AIRBUS MANEUVERED BY ENGINE POWER (Baghdad 2003)

## Controlling Airbus by Engine Power Alone

> Outside Homeland Security circles, not much attention has been paid to the feat whereby the three-man crew of a European Air Transport/DHL Airbus A300B4 freighter brought their aircraft safely back to Baghdad Airport by juggling engine power alone after it had been struck by a SAM (surface-to-air missile).
>
> French journalists allowed to accompany the group launching the two missiles—one missed—had photos and even a six-minute video of the event.
>
> *[DHL Cargo Flight Bagdad]*

Some superior surface-to-air missiles (SAMs) possessed by insurgents in Iraq had a maximum range of 4.5 km at heights up to about 10,000 ft. Aircraft coming into Baghdad would keep well above that ceiling and descend spirally at the last minute with degrees of bank impossible to practice in simulators set with the conventional parameters. However, departure from Baghdad was more risky for workhorse aircraft unable to climb quickly (as opposed to fighters).

As a result, the DHL Airbus freighter that took off from Baghdad at mid-morning on November 22, 2003 was only climbing through 8,000 ft at 09:15 when one of the two Russian-made SAM-14s fired from the ground struck it near the left wingtip.

The crew, consisting of two Belgians, Captain Eric Gennotte and First Officer Steeve Michielsen, and Scottish Flight Engineer Mario Rofail, felt a judder, followed shortly by an alarm indicating trouble with the hydraulics. The flight engineer saw that two of the three independent systems showed zero pressure and a complete loss of fluid. Before the crew could go through the steps required for flying with just one hydraulic system operable, the pressure in the third and only remaining system had dropped to zero. The instruments also seemed to indicate the fuel in the outboard left wing fuel tank had disappeared.

Like the 'uncontrollable' JAL 747 and the Sioux City DC-10, their only hope lay in varying the engine thrust to direct the aircraft, except that compared to the JAL 747, they still had the complete vertical stabilizer (tailfin) to steady them horizontally. Even so, the aircraft yawed to the left and the left wing began to sink with the nose dropping. However, by adjusting the relative thrusts of the engines—more power on the left, less on the right—it was possible to correct this before the craft entered into a sideslip and spin from which it would have been impossible to recover without the help of the rudder and ailerons.

On limping back towards the airport, the tower erroneously informed them that the left engine was on fire. From their position on the flight deck, and with no cabin crew (and no windows since it was a freighter), the crew were unable to see the extensive damage to the left wing. They had some measure of control, but—concerned about the alleged engine fire—did not dare spend time experimenting like the pilots of the Sioux City DC-10 had been able to do. Even so, they finally had to abort their first landing attempt.

On their second attempt, some 16 minutes after the missile strike, they were aiming for Runway 33 Right, but luckily as it turned out, touched down on 33 Left, the runway parallel to it. 'Touched' down is something of a misnomer, as they came down hard with a sink rate of some 2,000 ft/min instead of the usual maximum of 300 ft/min, and an airspeed of roughly 215 knots instead of the usual 140 knots or so. They were lucky as they veered off to the left, and, with no hydraulics to operate the steering, were unable to correct their course. Had they been on the right-hand runway as they intended they would have collided with the fire station!

With no brakes, no spoilers and no flaps, they only had reverse thrust to slow the fast-moving aircraft. Once off the runway, a 600-meter run through the sand with its sparse grass helped bring it to a halt at a razor wire (barbed wire) barrier. The crew was able to evacuate safely down a second chute after finding the first damaged by the razor wire.

## Conclusions

The September 12, 2006 edition of the UK's *Flight International* headlined *'The NASA and the US Department of Homeland Security's Project' to see whether it might be very cost-effective and possible to teach line pilots 'throttles-only' techniques for controlling aircraft in view of the increasing concern about the MANPADS risk.'*

The article quoted an interview the magazine had with the stricken A300's flight engineer, Mario Rofail, a year after the DHL Baghdad incident. Rofail observed, *'Situations like this are unique every time. You cannot train for them.'* While agreeing regarding the uniqueness, the magazine did think some instant guidelines could be invaluable since:

> The task is difficult and delicate. Every change of power when handling an aircraft using 'throttles only control' produces non-intuitive secondary and tertiary effects that cannot be countered with trim, stick or rudder, and the desired reaction to power changes is slow to develop. The only speed band available for controlled flight may be within a few knots of the airspeed for which the aircraft was trimmed when the hydraulics drained from the horizontal stabilizer actuators.

CHAPTER 7

# FIRE & SMOKE

## FIRE IN VARIG 707 TOILET ON APPROACH TO ORLY (Paris 1973)

### Dense Smoke in Cockpit Forced Pilots to Land Short

> With the high cost of aircraft, and passengers' (and the crews') lives so valuable, it is surprising that simple safety features such as smoke detectors in the toilets were not in use at the time of this accident and only made mandatory in the US after an in-flight fire in the area of a washroom ten years later.
>
> *[Varig Flight 820]*

Friends and relatives of passengers on the Brazilian Varig flight from Rio de Janeiro about to land at Paris' Orly Airport were impatiently watching the arrivals board. They could not understand the delay as it was well past the past the 'expected' time still being indicated.

These were old-style mechanical boards, where the letters and numbers flip over until they arrive at the right one. When those for their flight finally stopped, those expecting to see 'Landed' saw just the two words 'Contact Company.'

This was somewhat different from what happened when an Air France A330 plunged into the sea in 2009 on exactly the same route. Even though the aircraft had been 'lost' many hours before its scheduled arrival in Paris, the signboards used the much kinder term 'Delayed.'

In 1973, surprise changed to alarm as the assembled greeters began to grasp that something terribly wrong must have happened. Only later did they learn that a fire had broken out in one of the aircraft's aft toilets on the final approach to the airport.

Informed by the pilots of their situation, Air Traffic Control (ATC) had duly authorized the captain of Varig Flight 820, Gilberto Araujo da Silva,[1] to make a quick straight-in landing. Despite being able to breathe thanks to their full-face oxygen masks, the pilots opted to crash-land 5 km short of the runway, as the smoke was so dense they could not even see their instruments and had to stick their heads out of the cockpit windows to see where they were going.

Ten occupants—all crew members—managed to escape. Fire crews, arriving some six to seven minutes later, were only able to rescue four unconscious occupants, just one of whom subsequently survived. In all, 7 crew and 116 passengers died. Most of the deaths were by inhalation of carbon monoxide and other toxic products resulting from the fire. For some passengers it would have been like a prison gas chamber, since hydrogen cyanide was one of the gases given off by the smoldering plastics.

This accident led to the overdue installation of smoke detectors in aircraft toilets, a review of air supply to flight decks, and a review of the plastics used in cabin interiors.

Surprisingly, it was not this event, outside the US, that made the FAA mandate that aircraft lavatories be equipped with smoke detectors and automatic fire extinguishers, but the 1983 Cincinnati Air Canada Flight 797 in-flight fire in the US ten years later. The FAA then also mandated that within five years jetliners be retrofitted with fire-blocking layers on seat cushions and floor lighting to lead passengers to exits in dense smoke.

In the case of Air Canada 797, the DC-9 was flying at 33,000 ft from Dallas to Toronto when a fire developed in the area of a rear toilet. Before long, the cabin began to fill with thick black smoke as the aircraft made an emergency descent. As in the Varig case just described, the smoke was so dense the pilots had difficulty seeing their instruments. In their case, they did manage to effect a landing at the Cincinnati Airport, but shortly after the doors and emergency exits had been opened, a flash fire swept through the cabin before everyone had had time to escape, with the result half of the 46 people on board died.

Possibly, the Varig incident awakened the authorities to the obvious need for fire-detectors in aircraft toilets, while the Cincinnati incident confirmed it. Sometimes it needs an accident in the US to make Congress press for action—though it is not certain whether that was true in this case.

---

[1] Gilberto Araujo da Silva, was flying a Varig Cargo Boeing 707 that was lost on January 30, 1979 over the Pacific Ocean.

# TRISTAR DELAYS EVACUATION
# (Riyadh 1980)
### All Die when Home and Dry

---

This example 'highlights'—to use an unfortunate word—the danger of failing to evacuate a burning aircraft as soon as possible. While some passengers are likely to sustain minor injuries when going down the emergency chutes, it is better than *risking* dying from smoke inhalation and/or the actual fire inside the aircraft.

In this case, not only was cockpit resource management (CRM) poor or rather non-existent, the second officer was dyslexic, and had been thumbing through the flight manual repeating, 'No problem, No problem.'

*[Saudia Flight 163]*

---

The Saudi Arabian Airlines L1011 TriStar had come in to Riyadh from Pakistan's commercial city, Karachi. At about 10 p.m. it lifted off for Saudi Arabia's own center of commerce, Jeddah. On board were 287 passengers, 11 cabin crew, and 3 aircrew. For such a short domestic hop, there would be relatively little fuel on board and no need to jettison it if an emergency landing became necessary.

It had a Saudi captain, a Saudi first officer with very limited experience of the L1011, and an American second officer who reputedly had been a captain at the airline but on being found to be dyslexic had been allowed to stay on as a flight engineer. One would have thought being dyslexic would be a greater handicap for an engineer than a pilot.

While climbing through 15,000 ft to their cruising height, the flight crew heard an alarm. A warning light indicated the presence of smoke in the rear cargo hold, C-3. This first indication of possible trouble occurred just seven minutes after takeoff.

The crew then spent some four minutes verifying the alert with the second officer thumbing through the flight manual to find the procedure to follow. This delay added eight minutes to the time it would take to get back to Riyadh since they would have to double back. They had reached 22,000 ft when the captain decided to return to do just that. Two minutes later the wisdom of his decision was confirmed by the presence of smoke to the rear of the passenger cabin.

Perhaps because the first officer had little experience of the L1011, the captain did not delegate tasks. He not only flew the aircraft himself but also performed the other tasks such as communications with the cabin crew and the airport. He was undoubtedly overstretched, but managed to touch down

135

normally on the runway, despite having shut down the rear engine due to a jammed throttle lever—the fire had burnt through the cables.

Unbelievably, once on the ground, the captain did not try to stop the aircraft as quickly as possible, but let it trundle down the runway for 2 minutes 40 seconds! Even more unbelievably, the crew left the engines running for a further 3 minutes 15 seconds after that, thus holding off the rescuers, who then found their unfamiliarity with the exits meant they could not gain access for a *further* 23 minutes

The sequence of events was as follows. Slight discrepancies in the timings are due to them being derived from different sources.

## In the air

| Lapsed time | Local time | |
|---|---|---|
| | 22.08.00 | Takeoff from Riyadh |
| 00.00.00 | 22.14.54 | C-3 cargo hold smoke alarm |
| 00.05.06 | 22.20.00 | Return initiated |
| 00.07.06 | 22.22.00 | Smoke at rear of cabin, passengers panicking |
| 00.10.32 | 22.25.26 | #2 throttle jams/fire already in cabin |
| 00.12.46 | 22.27.40 | Captain tells all to stay seated. Passengers 'fighting' in aisles |
| | Final approach | Captain tells crew *not* to Evacuate |
| 00.21.30 | 22.36.24 | Touchdown |

## On the ground

| Lapsed time | Local time | |
|---|---|---|
| 00.00.00 | 22.36.24 | Touchdown |
| 00.02.40 | 22.39.04 | Continues down runway for 2 min 40 seconds |
| 00.05.55 | 22.42.18 | Engines cut |
| 00.28.38 | 23.05.00 | Rescuers finally succeed in opening door 2R |
| 00.31.30 | 23.08.00 | Fire engulfs interior–no doubt due to ingress of oxygen |

136

By the time the rescuers gained access, the 301 occupants were long dead. The influx of oxygen caused the fire to burn even more intensely with the result the aircraft ended up with its upper half mostly burnt away.

The captain had specifically instructed his colleagues on the flight deck *not* to evacuate. So confident was he that evacuation would be unnecessary, he did not even tell the cabin crew to get ready just in case. There was a final transmission after the aircraft had stopped that an evacuation was about to take place. No one opened, or managed to open, a single exit.

Another theory was that the doors could not be opened because the air pressure inside the cabin was higher than outside.[1]

Whatever the judgmental mistakes and failures of coordination on the part of the aircrew, a better form of heat and acoustic insulation above the cargo hold might have prevented the fire propagating so rapidly. Indeed, Lockheed subsequently replaced it with high-strength glass laminate.

Then there is the question of how the fire started. Interviews recorded for a 1999 BBC Panorama TV program called *Die by Wire* suggest the fire might have been caused by the Kapton insulation used for the electric wiring.

### Comments by Investigators and Others

Review of the CVR showed a serious breakdown in crew co-ordination almost from the first sign of trouble.

1. **The captain failed to delegate responsibility to the other crewmembers, who included an American flight engineer in addition to the first officer, deciding to fly the aircraft and try to assess and remedy the problem as well.**

2. **The first officer had very limited experience on the L1011 and did not try to assist the captain in flying the aircraft or monitoring communications or systems.**

3. **The second officer, who was thought to be dyslexic, spent nearly all of his time searching through the aircraft's operations manual, the whole time repeating to himself, '*No problem.*'**

The airline modified the procedures for coping with such emergencies and stepped up their training for evacuations. In addition, they made sure the C-3 baggage areas were sealed off.

It seems incredible that with conditions bad enough for passengers to be panicking and 'fighting in the aisles,' the captain did not bring the aircraft to the most immediate stop possible, and evacuate. The pilots were furthest from the fire.

One possibility is that with the captain doing everything himself, he did not realize the seriousness of the fire, especially as the fire warnings ceased. However, they had ceased as the fire had destroyed the sensors!

Was this an instance where using video cameras to give pilots an indication of the situation in the passenger cabins could have been helpful?

## Michael Busby

In the course of reviewing and updating parts of this book, we have come across an account[2] of what happened at the Riyadh airport by Michael Busby, an expat, who says he was watching from his villa nearby.

He claims the reason the captain of the L1011 went the full length of the runway, leaving far behind the emergency vehicles standing by halfway down, and then moved off onto a taxiway, was that the Saudi King's 747 was about to take off, and was already taxiing. According to Busby, whenever the King's aircraft was in motion, the protocol was that all other aircraft should stop. Any Saudi not complying would be given a severe prison sentence. Foreign aircrew would be summarily dismissed.

Though it would explain a lot, it is difficult to believe that such a fact, if true, would not have surfaced before, or been given more prominence when Busby suggested it. One could understand companies such as Lockheed, hoping perhaps for major contracts in Saudi Arabia, not wanting to go down that avenue.

Busby notes that the passengers were mostly poor pilgrims renowned for bringing their stoves with their liquid fuel with them. Whether or not that had any bearing on the fire itself or its propagation, their families would not have been in a position to pursue the matter.

## A Salutary Lesson?

Elsewhere in this book, we have mentioned how litigious passengers can be after having had to evacuate an aircraft via the emergency chutes when no fire eventually breaks out. Looking at this terrible tragedy, they should perhaps ask themselves whether they really would prefer that the crew allow them to stay on board when in doubt.

---

[1] Plug doors cannot be opened if the pressure inside is significantly higher than outside and is why passengers should not panic when they see a frightened passenger trying to do so at 35,000 ft.

The L1011 had a system to relieve the pressure on the ground but apparently, this was not used, perhaps because of damage in the fire. Later extra measures were taken to prevent such an eventuality at all airlines.

[2] http://www.scribd.com/doc/38040625/Death-of-An-Airplane-The-Appalling-Truth-About-Saudia-Airlines-Flight-163 Dated 2010

# 737 STOPS WITH FIRE UPWIND (Manchester, UK 1985)

### Breeze Blows Flames onto Aircraft

> As firefighters well know, fire is a capricious enemy, in that how it evolves very often depends on something else that is fickle and difficult to predict—the *wind*.
>
> A simple matter of how the aircraft stops with respect to the wind, albeit so slight a wind as to be insignificant from a flying point of view, can determine whether passengers live or die.
>
> A courtesy maneuver to leave the runway clear for other aircraft doubtless increased the number of fatalities in the case we now describe.
>
> *[British Airtours Flight 28M]*

The first production Boeing 737, 'short to medium range' airliner, was delivered to Lufthansa in 1968 and after a slow start became the most prolific airliner in the Western world.

British Airtours, a subsidiary of British Airways, was using one for a routine charter flight from Manchester in England to Corfu in Greece on August 22, 1985.

Virtually full, with 131 passengers and 6 crewmembers, the 737 was already engaged in its takeoff run with the first officer as the handling pilot, when there was a loud thump or thud. Assuming it was a tire blow out, the captain ordered, 'STOP,' and at the same time pulled back the throttles and engaged reverse thrust. After having attained a maximum speed of 126 knots, the aircraft began to slow, with the captain checking that the spoilers had deployed.

Again thinking it must have been a tire blow out, the Captain Peter Terrington told First Officer Brian Love not to 'hammer the brakes,' in order to limit the damage to the landing gear, and anyway there was plenty of runway left as the decision to abort the takeoff had been taken well before $V_1$. The first officer, who had been applying maximum braking, duly eased up on them.

As the groundspeed fell to 85 knots some 9 seconds after the 'thud,' the captain called the tower to inform them that they were abandoning the takeoff. Almost immediately, there was a fire warning for the left-hand engine. The tower then confirmed there was a 'lot of fire,' and that the fire appliances were on their way.

With the speed of the aircraft below 50 knots, the captain queried the tower as to whether an evacuation seemed necessary. The controller replied, 'I would do via the starboard side.'

This was merely 20 seconds after the thud and 25 seconds before the aircraft came to a final stop. Some 6 seconds later and 14 seconds before the aircraft eventually stopped, the captain turned the aircraft to the right so it could exit the runway via 'link Delta.' Then, before the aircraft came to a complete halt, he told the cabin crew to evacuate from the starboard side.

However, pooled fuel on the ground was burning, and flames were already lapping the rear fuselage. When the rear right-hand door was opened no one was able to escape from there because of the flames; and worse still, flames soon penetrated the cabin. What had at first seemed to be a minor incident was quickly turning into a disaster.

Because of difficulty in opening other emergency doors and for reasons such as obstructions, 2 crewmembers and 53 passengers died; 15 passengers sustained serious injuries; and 63 passengers and 1 firefighter had minor or no injuries.

Training material for US firefighters even cites the disaster in stressing the danger hydrogen cyanide (HCN) given off by burning plastics represents:

> The (Kegworth) fire killed 54 people of whom 47 had possibly lethal cyanide levels while only 11 had possibly fatal levels of carbon monoxide.[1]

The painstaking studies of the disaster led the investigators to make 31 recommendations—many of which were at the time deemed too expensive or not worthwhile on a cost-benefit basis. (At the time, the cost of a single passenger fatality was not the US$2.5 million it is in the US today.)

The 31 recommendations included the need to bring aircraft to a stop in such a way that the wind helps rather than hinders, and modifications of the air-conditioning system to prevent the spread of fumes and flashover fires. Allegedly, a passenger sitting next to an emergency exit was incapable of opening it, thus delaying exit from there for one crucial minute.

The underlying cause of the fire was improper cold fusion welding of a defective casing in the left engine. This was in part due to poor collaboration and poor exchange of information between the engine manufacturer (Pratt & Whitney) and British Airways.

A journalist/expert writing an article on 'air crash survival' used this incident to demonstrate that escaping alive from such situations depends largely on a person's single-mindedness and 'will' to survive. Hesitating to act in the few seconds available can be a death sentence.

---

[1] There is a discrepancy of one in the total number of fatalities, perhaps because one victim died later. Other figures 'don't add up' because a victim could die from both causes.

# 737 PILOTS SHUT DOWN WRONG ENGINE (Kegworth, UK 1989)

### Classic Case Cited in Pilot Training

> The disaster described below was at one time the most often cited by pilot-training schools as an example of the dangers of precipitous action.
>
> *[British Midland Flight 92]*

Pilots around the world were incredulous; some even thought Boeing might have connected the instruments the wrong way round. If not, how could experienced pilots make such a mistake—confusing right with left? In addition, the pilots had believed there was a fire, when there was no fire.

The early evening British Midlands Airways 737 flight from London to Northern Ireland was at 28,300 ft, and climbing under rated power towards its cruising height of 35,000 ft. Then, 13 minutes following takeoff, there was a loud bang, followed by a thumping noise and vibration. Passengers in the rear of the aircraft were disturbed to see flashes issuing from the tailpipe of the No. 1 engine on the left—very apparent in the wintry darkness. Smoke or something like it then started coming in through the air-conditioning.

Pilots can observe events in front of them, but not nearly so easily see what is happening to the aircraft and engines behind them. There are plans to install mini TV cameras everywhere, both for technical reasons and as an anti-terrorist measure, but for the moment the pilots have to rely on their instruments in the first instance, and perhaps later on reports from cabin crew and passengers. The pilots felt the shudder and vibration, and heard the noise. The captain later said he smelt and saw smoke coming in through the air-conditioning; the first officer just noticed the smell of burning.

The captain immediately disengaged the autopilot and took over control according to standard procedure. He then asked the first officer which engine was giving trouble.

The first officer replied:

> *It's the lef ... It's the right one.*

To which the captain replied:

> *Okay, throttle it back.*

The captain, later said he *thought* the smoke was coming in from the passenger cabin, and based on his erroneous knowledge of the way the air-conditioning on that model of the 737 was designed, concluded the smoke

141

must be coming from the right-hand engine. In fact, he could not have been sure where the 'smoke' was coming from.

Whatever the facts, this meant the first officer was confirming what the captain already thought. The captain gave his order to throttle back the right engine 19 seconds after the onset of the vibrations, so we are talking about a short time frame and little time for reflection or study of the instruments.

When questioned later, the first officer could not say which instrument indication made him conclude it was the right engine. From the exact words of the first officer, it would seem that the F/O was not sure, but felt obliged to give an answer. Could he have subconsciously sensed the answer the captain expected? Otherwise, why would he switch from *'lef...'* to *'right'*?

With the auto throttle disengaged, the first officer duly throttled back the right engine. One or two seconds later, the vibrations seemed to decrease, seemingly confirming that the right engine had been the one producing the vibrations. Actually, the vibrations coming from the left engine decreased because it was no longer operating at full rated-power as the auto-throttle was disengaged when the captain took over control manually.

The captain's and first officer's preoccupation with communications with ATC (Air Traffic Control) and contacting the company retarded the envisaged complete shutdown of the right engine, as the pilots were required complete the checklist procedure together. In fact, the shutdown procedure was not initiated until 2 minutes 7 seconds after the initial major vibration. During that time, the vibration indicator showed no abnormal vibration for the right engine, which was not true for the left engine, where the vibration remained high, but not as high as initially. Indeed, just before the shutdown, the first officer had remarked:

*Seems we have stabilized. We've still got the smoke.*

By adding the remark about the smoke, was he trying to hedge his bets with the captain? Whatever the case it must have lessened the impact of the statement that they seemed to have stabilized. To be fair, after the shutdown of the right engine, the captain did try to review with the first officer what they had done and what symptoms they had seen, saying:

*Now what indications did we actually get. (It's) just rapid vibrations in the aeroplane—smoke...*

Unfortunately, communications from ATC cut short this review. (One of the conclusions of the subsequent inquiry recommended that ATC should not overload pilots in emergencies.)

They were diverting to the airline's home base, East Midlands Airport, which happened to be nearby. However, the airport's proximity meant they had no time to reassess the situation, or even monitor the functioning of the left-hand engine over an extended period of level flight. The fact that ATC told them to change frequencies only served to increase their already high workload.

They increased power on their one-and-only engine[1] as they leveled out for a moment and made a turn to line up with the runway, and descended through 3,000 ft, 13 miles from the runway. Descending with gradually increasing flap, they put the landing gear down at 2,000 ft agl, and continued in with finally 15 degrees flap. Then at 900 ft with only 2.4 miles to go to touchdown (on the runway), the thrust provided by their remaining engine suddenly fell away.

The captain called for the first officer to restart the No. 2 engine but they were going much too slowly for a windmill start, and the failing No. 1 engine could not provide the pressure required to restart the good engine. The flight manual did have details of how to relight using the auxiliary power unit (APU), but this explanation only applied to the No. 1 engine.

Given time and a very good knowledge of the system, a pilot might be able to work out a way to restart the No. 2 using the APU. This would involve switching off the air-conditioning and other procedures, and even if the first officer had been able to accomplish this, he could not have brought the engine up to speed in time to save the aircraft. Thus, the fact that the manual lacked such an explanation did not make any difference to the outcome.

Some 17 seconds after the loss of power from the No. 1 engine, its fire warning system activated. However, at that juncture, lack of airspeed and height, not fire, was the captain's principal concern. Switching on the PA, he warned the passengers and cabin crew of the imminent contact with the ground by repeating the words:

*Prepare for crash-landing!*

The captain hardly needed the aural Ground Proximity Warning System (GPWS) to tell him they were below the glide slope as he raised the nose in a vain attempt at least to get over the main M1 freeway (motorway), which unfortunately lay transversely in a cutting along the airport perimeter. With the stick shaker[2] indicating they were about to stall, and their airspeed was down to only 115 knots, the aircraft grazed the top of the hill lying just before the cutting. With all lift virtually gone, it lopped off the tops of the trees on the nearside face of the cutting, and plunged onwards and downwards so that the nose struck the foot of the incline on the far side face.

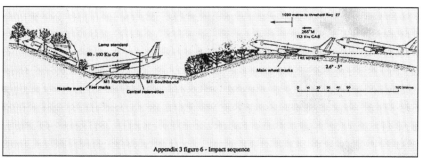

Figure 7  Kegworth impact sequence.

(Courtesy UK AAIB)

Taking into account the downwards component of the trajectory, the encounter with the roughly 30-degree upwards slope of the opposite face was equivalent to encountering an obstacle sloping at some 50 degrees head-on—at a ground speed of 80–100 knots.

Though the aircraft did slither some way up the far side of the cutting, the deceleration, both vertically and horizontally, was many times more than for a crash-landing on level terrain.

Indeed, the stresses imposed were so great that the rear section broke off and ended up lying upside-down on top of the fuselage.

Partly because the central fuel tank was empty for such a short journey and partly thanks to the rapid arrival of the airport fire services, there was no major fire. In total, 47 passengers perished, 67 passengers and 7 crewmembers were seriously injured, and 4 passengers and 1 crewmember had slight or no injuries.

Though considered the classic case of what not to do, there were a number of contributory factors to what came to be called the 'Kegworth Air Disaster' in view of its proximity to the village of that name. These include the following:

### 1. False positive

Professor Peter Ladkin[3] says this is the only case he is aware of where a false positive features in an air accident. That is to say, the mistaken corrective action (shutting down the good engine) seemed to be solving the problem, thus making the pilots think they had done the right thing. This is unlike in medicine, where the long period of time over which recovery or improvement of the patient for any unrelated reason can be attributed to action by the doctor or surgeon means such false positives are well known.[4]

The cessation of the vibrations was one thing, but to confirm things by saying that the smoke disappeared when the pilots shut down the No. 2 engine was with hindsight rather dubious thinking, since smoke would not normally disappear immediately.

## 2. Engine Instrument System (EIS) difficult to read

Before the introduction of two-man flight crews, the primary instruments showing the *performance* of the engines were in front of the pilots and the secondary instruments indicating the *condition* of the engines, such as oil temperature and pressure, and vibration were in front of the flight engineer. However, with the sidelining of the flight engineer, these secondary instruments had to be in front of the pilots.

In the earlier version of the aircraft, the B737-300, this was done by having traditional cockpit dials with mechanical hands as in traditional clocks, there being two panels side by side, one with the main flying instruments and the other showing the condition of the engines (oil pressure, vibration and so on). These earlier ones with needles were easy to read, and in particular comparing the angle of the needles made comparison of the relative status of the engines easier as the dials would be side by side.

However, as anything mechanical is liable to go wrong and anyway requires costly maintenance, LEDs[5] were used instead of the mechanical hands. However, instead of redesigning the panels to take full advantage of the virtues of an electronic display, the designers wanted to maintain the same general layout as before so pilots could switch from one model of the aircraft to another without (expensive) recertification.

In reality, LEDs could not simulate the previous clock-like hands because those available at that time could not be bunched up at the center of the dials to look like a continuous line. Instead, the designers placed three rather pathetic-looking LEDs at intervals around the perimeter of the dials.

These could still be read by pilots with their good eyesight when looking for a particular reading, but made comparison and noticing anything unusual more difficult. In addition, Boeing had reduced the size of the secondary engine display relative to that for the primary display instruments.

The captain and first officer had very little experience (23/53 hours respectively) on the 737-400 version, and the airline did not yet have a simulator where they could have practiced using the new Engine Information System (EIS) with its diodes. In addition, the captain said his considerable experience with other aircraft had led him to distrust vibration readings in general and he did not include them in his usual scan of the instruments. His conversion training had not included instruction that technical improvements meant that spurious vibration readings were very unlikely.

Interestingly, this layout for the 737 instruments seems to have been retained almost to the present day, except that the three diodes have been replaced by large easily seen brightly lit squares.

### 3. Training and checklists

In the training of the BMA 737 pilots, the need to think or check things out before taking precipitous action was stressed, but as already mentioned there had not been training on a flight simulator with the new hybrid EIS display. There was a checklist for what to do in case of vibration from the engines and one for what to do when smoke occurred, but not one for when they occurred simultaneously.

At the time, pilots at BMA had not been made fully aware that there was no need to shut down engines completely because of vibration. Nor that engine fans that are vibrating or out of true could have their fan tips touching the rubber seals on the periphery and that this could produce smoke and a smell of burning, but did not mean the engine was on fire.

Thus, as the investigators said, the situation was outside the pilots' experience and training.

### 4. Workload and stress—fear of fire

In many emergencies, airlines usually insist that captains take control. Captains also tend to take control in difficult situations when it is not quite an emergency. Doing something physical makes the captain feel he is coping, and incidentally relieves stress.

The trouble with this scenario is that the captain is concentrating on the mundane task of flying the aircraft, or, as in the case of SQ006 at Taipei, maneuvering it over the slippery taxiway in bad visibility and heavy rain.

Instead of taking over, the BMA captain might have done better to let the autopilot stay engaged for a while. The Flight Data Recorder (FDR) revealed that when he disengaged the autopilot, the aircraft yawed 16 degrees to the left—a sign that the left engine was producing less power than the one on the right—but he did not seem to notice it, as he did nothing to correct it.

The fact that the first officer reported to ATC early on that they had an 'emergency situation like an engine fire' shows they were concerned about fire even though up to then none of the engine fire alarms had triggered.

It is an interesting psychological point that a smell can instantly transport one mentally to a certain place, and the shaking of the aircraft followed by the smell of burning may have caused the pilots to react more instinctively and precipitously than they would have done in the event of a fire-warning light coming on. Anyway, a fire warning would have immediately indicated which engine had the problem.

The official report made the additional point that having another pilot take over the handling of the aircraft (as PF—pilot flying) meant monitoring of the instruments was less consistent than it might have been.

Up until the onset of the vibration, the first officer had been flying the aircraft and would have been concentrating on the main instruments, not the engine vibration indicator—it being the role of the PNF (pilot non-flying, in this case the captain who did not believe in scanning vibration readings) to do the general monitoring. With the captain having suddenly taken over, the first officer was immediately asked which engine was giving the trouble, and gave an opinion without later being able to say what instrument readings give him that opinion.

The captain must have thought the first officer had good reason to say it was the right engine that was giving trouble—and this only confirmed his own opinion based on how he believed the air-conditioning system worked.

### 5. Unfortunate timing

It is almost impossible for pilots to do anything to save the situation when trouble occurs when there is insufficient height and speed at certain critical moments, such as just before landing. They did not have the height or speed to restart the good engine, and not enough height to choose a flat place to land. Had the airport been further away they would have had a better chance to discover problems with the No. 1 engine when still high enough to restart the other engine.

### 6. Passengers & three members of the cabin crew were aware the left engine had the problem

Passengers at the rear who had seen the 'sparks' from the left engine when the initial trouble occurred were somewhat perplexed when the captain said he had shut down the right engine, but did not inform the cabin crew because the captain sounded supremely confident.

The three members of the cabin crew who had also seen the sparks apparently did not notice the captain saying the right engine had been shut down—they knew the purpose of the announcement was to reassure the passengers and were no doubt extremely busy with their own duties getting ready for the unexpected landing.

A retired British Airways flight attendant has suggested to the author that the failure to pick up on the captain's 'mistake' might have come about because cabin staff themselves often get confused about left and right as they face backwards when addressing the passengers.

Just after shutdown of the No. 2 engine, the captain called the Flight Service Manager (FSM) to the flight deck to tell him to clear things for landing, and at the same time asked him about the smoke.

*Did you get smoke in the cabin back there?*

And got the reply:

*We did. Yes.*

This perhaps only confirmed the captain's mistaken view that the right-hand engine must have been at fault.

The FSM departed but returned a minute later to say the passengers were panicky, and it was only then that the captain announced to the passengers that a little trouble with the right engine had produced some smoke but it would be OK, as they had shut it down, and would be landing about ten minutes thereafter.

## Cause of the Engine Problem

Subsequent studies showed a vibration harmonic at certain speeds of rotation caused the fan blades to rub against the rubber seals on the periphery, producing the burning smell, and causing one blade to break. The manufacturer rectified the harmonic problem and allowed extra space between the blades and the seals to give a greater safety margin should such vibration re-occur.

## Other Similar Incidents

Before these modifications, other 737s with the same engine—including a BMA 737—had similar engine problems when climbing at maximum rated power. Benefiting from the lessons learnt from the previous incident, the crews immediately studied the vibration indicator and made sure they shut down the correct engine before landing safely. After those incidents, pilots safely used a lower power rating until the manufacturer modified the engines as described above.

This was not an in-flight fire at all. Though the first officer had cited the possibility of an engine fire, the instruments did not give a fire warning until the No. 1 engine failed just prior to the crash. As so often when pilots have been partially responsible for a crash, the airline first defended them, and then 'let them go.'

## Rearward-facing Seats?

The high number of fatalities and injuries in what was a crash at relatively low speed led the authorities to examine the safety aspects of the seating, the strength of the flooring, and the locking of the overhead lockers. Some asked whether rear-facing seating might have offered greater protection. At first sight, rear-facing seating as in most British Royal Air Force Transport aircraft would seem to offer greater protection. The comprehensive official report said rear-facing seating could impose too great a stress on cabin flooring. In addition, the report said other arguments raised against rearward-facing seats were:

1. They could be less effective in accidents in which the main deceleration force is not along the longitudinal axis of the aircraft.

2. They could expose occupants to the risk of injury from loose objects in an accident.

3. Great improvements had been made in the design and construction of forward-facing seats.

**4. They may not be suitable for use in modern jet transports with their high climb-out angles and that they could be 'psychologically less attractive to passengers.'**

## Passenger Revolt

Interestingly, a recent event shows passengers are not completely powerless. As a Phuket Air 747 was taking off for London's Gatwick Airport after making a refueling stop at Sharjah International Airport (UAE) in April 2005, a male passenger in a window seat shouted out that fuel was pouring from the wing down onto an engine pod.

Screaming passengers, fearing they would suffer a similar fate to that of the Concorde passengers at Paris, stood up and refused to sit down, and subsequently claimed they forced the pilot to abort the takeoff. Saying they had rectified the problem, and that the tanks had merely been overfilled anyway, the pilot made another attempt three hours later, but passengers again noticed a fuel leakage, and the aircraft was temporarily grounded. It was allowed to leave later, with some passengers refusing to board and booked on alternative flights.

After various problems were discovered with its aircraft, Phuket Air lost the right to fly to England, though one of their 747s remained sequestered for a while on the tarmac at London's Gatwick Airport because of unpaid bills.

This is a case where the passengers *did* make their observations known to the crew.

---

[1] With the increase in power, the FDR then began showing maximum vibration for the operating engine, but the pilots did not notice it.

[2] To warn pilots that they are about to stall—flying too slowly to stay in the air—the joystick or control is made to shake.

[3] Well-known safety expert and author of many articles.

[4] Doctors knowingly or unknowingly exploited this in the case of tonsillectomies so often carried out at the age where children are gaining natural immunity and would get fewer infections anyway. Some doctors call the operation a 'pecuniectomy'—a money-making procedure.

[5] LEDs are light emitting diodes—a type of indicator lamp used in all sorts of equipment because they consume little current and do not burn out.

# TWA-800, CENTER FUEL TANK EXPLODES (JFK-Outbound 1996)

### Hunt for Lost Suitcase Causes Delay under Sun

> A cluster of three catastrophic accidents to aircraft departing New York's JFK Airport fed conspiracy theories, and in particular with regard possible US military activity.
>
> *Concerning the Fall of TWA 800, Swissair 111 and EgyptAir 990* by Didier de Fontaine[1] debunks the claims of one proponent of such conspiracy theories. Yet, these have many legs like centipedes.
>
> *[Trans World Airlines Flight 800]*

The approach to the investigation was somewhat peculiar because having an aircraft blow up on its own with no other aircraft that could have collided with it seemed to indicate something suspicious and hence the FBI played a prominent role from the start—taking over parts of the investigation for a while. Finally, the NTSB concluded it was due to an explosion in the central fuel tank, but could not find conclusive evidence regarding what initiated it.

Seven years after the disaster, technicians were readying many pieces of the reconstructed jumbo jet, which were to go to George Washington University in Ashburn, for training air safety investigators. The NTSB had spent four years collecting these pieces and putting together a 27-meter (90-ft) section of the aircraft. Salvaging them from the sea had been a difficult task in itself.

The aircraft for Trans World Airlines (TWA) Flight TW800 to Paris had arrived at New York's JFK International Airport from Athens at 16:31 on July 17, 1996. After cleaning and servicing it was due to depart for Paris at 19:00 but because of a delay, caused mainly by a search for a missing item of luggage, did not depart until 20:03. The air conditioners were not needed when cleaners and mechanics started servicing the aircraft, but the extra hour's wait at the end and the hot conditions meant they were working hard for about 2½ hours prior to departure and pumping out a great amount of heat. The fuel in the center wing fuel tank would normally have absorbed some of this heat, but as that was virtually empty as little fuel was required for the relatively short hop across the Atlantic to Paris, the temperature of that tank would have risen significantly.

At 20:18, the aircraft was cleared for takeoff. The climb out from JFK over the sea proceeded as usual. Then passing under the control of the Boston Air Route Control Center, it received various instructions regarding its flight level. Up until then, the only thing of note was the captain saying:

*Look at that crazy fuel flow indicator there on number four ... see that?*

One minute later, Boston Center told them to climb from Flight Level 130 to Flight Level 150. As they were complying, there was loud sound after which the CVR stopped working (20:31:12). The aircraft had broken up with the pieces falling into the sea.

With many aircraft in the general area, Boston center received a number of reports from pilots about witnessing an explosion, with the most detailed being that of the captain of an Eastwind Airlines Boeing 737:

*Saw an explosion out here ... ahead of us here ... about 16,000 feet (4,900 m) or something like that, it just went down into the water.*

As the debris had fallen into the sea in a busy area a few miles off the coast, it was only a matter of minutes before people in all sorts of craft, both military and civil, were on the scene. As feared, there were no survivors, making the death toll 230.

There was much suspicion that the aircraft had been blown up by a terrorist bomb, shot down by a US missile or even some secret 'ray gun' under test. A respected CIA agent (now deceased) said that on reviewing the radar tracks, he immediately thought the shooting down by a US missile was a possibility—there is nothing sinister in this as 'accidents' do happen.

Perhaps no other air crash has received the attention this one has, especially as regards 'conspiracy theories.' Numerous books have been written, and even to explain the detailed work undertaken by the NTSB over some four years would take up too much space here. For any reader wanting more details, a good start would be the piece in Wikipedia with much detail and references to the various sources.

Much of the NTSB's work involved disproving that such and such, say a missile or bomb, could have been the cause. They concluded that an explosion of the center fuel tank was the cause, and that though the equipment in the tank for measuring fuel level used voltages that were too low to cause ignition, a short circuit in wiring outside *might* have led to an overvoltage in wires to that equipment.

The NTSB was not enamored with the concept of only relying on avoiding ignition sources in the fuel tank in the early 747-100 as the sole means of protection and thought having the air conditioning dissipating so much excess heat into the tank was undesirable. One has to wonder whether the heating of the tank while looking for the suitcase was a factor.

---

[1] Didier de Fontaine was debunking the theories of Elaine Scarry, Professor of Aesthetics and Value Theory in the English Department at Harvard University published in the *New York Review of Books* (NYRB).

# HAZMAT VALUJET
# (Everglades, Florida 1996)
### O₂ Generators in Airtight Cargo Hold

> While great attention is paid to what passengers bring onto the aircraft, this is not always true for cargo.
>
> The following case received much publicity, in great measure because passengers' voices on the CVR recordings spelt out their predicament as the metal-melting fire took hold.
>
> *[ValueJet Flight 592]*

The Everglades subtropical National Park in Southern Florida is said to be the only place in the world where alligators and crocodiles cohabit. Much of it consists of swamp interspersed with strips of shallow water filled with vegetation, with mud at the bottom. A worse place for recovering the bodies and debris from an air crash would be difficult to find. Not only were the hot and humid working conditions particularly difficult for people working in protective suits, the evidence and body parts were difficult to locate in the ooze. The only good news for the investigators was that the shockwave, while attracting the alligators, had scared away the poisonous snakes.

ValuJet Flight 592, a DC-9 with 105 passengers, 3 cabin crew and 2 pilots, had just taken off in the early afternoon from Miami International Airport for Atlanta, and climbed through 10,000 ft, when the pilots heard a strange sound. No sooner had they concluded it was from an electrical bus than other electrical problems manifested themselves. Shortly afterwards, shouts of 'FIRE, FIRE'—presumably from the passenger cabin—could be heard on the CVR.

The 35-year-old female captain of the DC-9, Candalyn Kubeck, did not declare a Mayday, but radioed the Miami International Airport controller saying an immediate return to Miami was required. The controller, not grasping the situation, twice gushed on with the instructions for the routine handover to Miami Center (Control). Once her words had sunk in, he lost no time giving her a heading and a height (7,000 ft) to return to Miami, and asked for the nature of the problem. Kubeck told him it was smoke, in the cabin and in the cockpit.

Shortly afterwards, she asked if there was an airport even nearer, but continued to be vectored to Miami, perhaps because there was not deemed to be one suitable. Anyway, it became academic, as radio communication with the aircraft was then lost.

Captain Kubeck had 2,000+ hours experience on the aircraft type, and 9,000 flying hours in total. Neither her ability, nor that of her first officer, Richard Hazen, a 52-year-old ex-Air Force pilot, could have made any difference to the subsequent outcome—an event sometimes referred to as the 'ValuJet situation' where an extremely fierce fire in a vulnerable part of the aircraft is only detected a few seconds before the aircraft becomes uncontrollable.

In this case, *only forty-nine seconds* had elapsed from the first hint of trouble to the moment someone opened the flight deck door and said:

*Okay, we need oxygen; we can't get oxygen back there.*

The following extract from the CVR, with some standard acknowledgements omitted for brevity, gives a good idea of how the situation evolved.

| Elapsed time | Local time | |
|---|---|---|
| -6:54 | 14:04:09 | Takeoff from Miami (V$_R$) |
| 0:00 | 14:10:03 | Strange noise heard in cockpit: probably that of tire bursting in the hold. |
| 0:04 | 14:10:07 | Captain: *What's that?* |
| 0:05 | 14:10:08 | First officer: *I don't know.* |
| 0:09 | 14:10:12 | Captain: *?? bout to lose a [electrical] 'bus'* [1] |
| 0:12 | 14:10:15 | First officer: *We got some electrical problem.* |
| 0:14 | 14:10:17 | First officer: *Yeah. That battery charger's kicking in. We gotta ...* |
| 0:17 | 14:10:20 | Captain: *We're losing everything.* |
| 0:18 | 14:10:21 | Departure control gives frequency for handover to Miami Center. |
| 0:19 | 14:10:22 | Captain: *We need to go back to Miami.* |
| 0:20 | 14:10:23 | Shouts from passenger cabin. |
| 0:22 | 14:10:25 | Female voices shout: *Fire ... Fire ... Fire ... Fire ...* |
| 0:24 | 14:10:27 | *WE'RE ON FIRE!* (repeated) |
| 0:26 | 14:10:29 | Departure control repeats instructions for handover to Center. |
| 0:29 | 14:10:32 | R/T First officer to departure: 592 needs immediate return to Miami. |
| 0:32 | 14:10:35 | Departure control: *...Roger, turn left heading 270, descend and maintain 7,000.* |

| | | |
|---|---|---|
| 0:38 | 14:10:41 | Departure control asks what kind of problem they are having and is informed it is smoke in the cockpit and cabin. |
| 0:49 | 14:10:52 | Sound of cockpit door moving. |
| 0:55 | 14:10:58 | 3rd cockpit microphone: *Okay, we need oxygen, we can't get oxygen back there.* |
| 1:04 | 14:11:07 | Departure control: *... When able, turn left heading 250, descend and maintain 5,000.* (592 acknowledges) |
| 1:09 | 14:11:12 | 3rd cockpit microphone: *Completely on fire.* |
| 1:11 | 14:11:14 | Shouting from passenger cabin subsides—perhaps because occupants are overcome by smoke. |
| 1:18 | 14:11:21 | Loud sound like rushing air—cockpit window opened? |
| 1:35 | 14:11:38 | R/T first officer to departure control: *... 592, we need the closest airport available.* |
| 1:39 | 14:11:42 | Departure control does not propose another airport; says 'they' (Miami) will be standing by and 592 can plan for Runway 12.... |
| | 14:11:45 | 1 min 12 sec interruption to CVR. |
| | 14:12:48 | [CVR stops recording] |
| 2:54 | 14:12:57 | [CVR restarts] Loud sound of rushing air? |
| 2:55 | 14:12:58 | Departure controller tells 592 to contact Miami approach, correctly telling them to remain on his frequency. |
| 3:08 | 14:13:11 | CVR recording interrupted for unknown period. |
| | 14:xx:xx | CVR restarts for a moment. Apart from a radio transmission from an unknown source, one can only briefly hear the loud sound of rushing air. Recording ends. |
| | 14:13:34 | Total loss of control is evident from the trajectory of the aircraft. (Pilot incapacitation/aircraft uncontrollable.) |
| | 14:13:42 | Impact with ground (radar data). |

For the passenger cabin to be completely on fire after 1 min 9 sec elapsed time and not just filling with smoke shows just how quickly the situation had got out of hand.

In fact, after fusing and melting the electrical cables, the fire was eating away at the steel control cables needed to maneuver the aircraft. The aircraft then keeled over, plunged downwards, seemed to try to right itself for a moment, perhaps due to action by the pilots or autopilot, and then continued nose-downwards into the swamp below.

The force of the impact was such that both the aircraft and passengers ended up as a dispersed collection of difficult-to-recover pieces. All 110 people on board would have died instantly on impact, if they had not already succumbed due to the fire and noxious smoke.

With a stroke of luck—a searcher stepped on it—the flight data recorder (FDR) was soon found, and with the cockpit voice recorder (CVR) was retrieved from the ooze of the swamp. Together with the evidence from the Miami ATC recordings, they confirmed that fire had brought about the crash. In addition, the debris showed the fire had been limited to the forward cargo hold and the area immediately above, thus making the usual painstaking piecing together of the entire mud-encrusted aircraft irrelevant.

For a fire in a hold to set the cabin above on fire, it had to have penetrated the cabin floor. In fact, some of the aluminum used in the construction of the passengers' seats was found to have melted, showing the temperature even there must have reached 1,200°F (650°C) before the aircraft cooled down on hitting the watery swamp.

Investigators later established that the temperature in that hold could have reached 3,000°F (1,600°C). Not only had these high temperatures deformed and melted the floor separating the cargo hold from the passenger cabin, but they had first fused the electrical cables (the first anomaly the pilots noticed) and then the steel cables essential for controlling the aircraft. This would have made it impossible for the pilots to pull the aircraft out of its precipitous dive into the swamp—assuming they were still able to function.

Oddly, the hold in question was a 'D-Class' hold and virtually airtight, so that any fire ignited there would normally soon consume the available oxygen and die down, and in the absence of a fire-extinguishing system would only smolder, at least until someone opens the hatch, which would be on the ground. This led to the following two questions:

**1. What had ignited the fire?**

**2. Where had oxygen come from?**

As study of the cargo manifest soon revealed it must have been the five boxes of discarded oxygen generators loaded there. There were also three tires, at least two of which were mounted on wheels and hence liable to burst violently if overheated in a fire.

These oxygen generators came from three second-hand MD-80 aircraft that were being modified and checked out at Miami by SabreTech, a large contractor responsible for ValuJet's line and heavy maintenance. ValuJet had purchased these aircraft to upgrade and improve its fleet.

Oxygen generators supply oxygen to passengers should the cabin depressurize. These consist of canisters placed *at intervals* in the fascia above passengers that produce oxygen by an exothermic (heat-producing) chemical reaction triggered by a spring-loaded firing pin striking an explosive percussion cap. A lanyard pulls out the retaining pin when emergency oxygen is required.

On firing to provide oxygen, the temperature of the canister shell can reach 475–500°F (246–260°C), but this heat soon dissipates if the canisters are placed individually with clearance for air around them. However, having dozens of them piled together in a cardboard box and surrounded by bubble wrap with nowhere for the heat to go other than into neighboring canisters could produce a chain reaction should one fire accidentally.

The canisters loaded into that hold should have been fitted with safety caps to prevent such accidental firing. Furthermore, the ramp agent present in the cargo hold as the boxes were loaded heard a 'clink' and objects moving around inside one of the boxes, which were stowed on top of the tires with no restraints to ensure they stayed in place. Possibly that box could have fallen off.

### Probable Cause

The National Transportation Safety Board (NTSB) determined that the probable causes of the accident, which resulted from a fire in the airplane's D-Class cargo compartment initiated by the actuation of one or more oxygen generators being improperly carried as cargo, were:

1. **The failure of SabreTech to properly prepare, package, and identify unexpended chemical oxygen generators before presenting them to ValuJet for carriage.**

2. **The failure of ValuJet to properly oversee its contract maintenance program to ensure compliance with maintenance, maintenance training, and hazardous materials requirements and practices.**

3. **The failure of the Federal Aviation Administration (FAA) to require smoke detection and fire suppression systems in D-Class cargo compartments.**

Contributing to the accident was:

1. **The failure of the FAA to adequately monitor ValuJet's heavy maintenance programs and responsibilities, including ValuJet's oversight of its contractors, and SabreTech's repair station certificate.**

2. **The failure of the FAA to respond adequately to prior chemical oxygen generator fires with programs to address the potential hazards.**

3. **ValuJet's failure to ensure that both ValuJet and contract maintenance facility employees were aware of the carrier's 'no-carry' hazardous materials policy and had received appropriate hazardous materials training.**

Incidentally, those horrifying words on the CVR so shocked the US Congress as well as the public that criticism of the FAA became especially harsh.

Had the FAA made the installation of fire-detectors and fire-suppressant systems mandatory for such D-Class cargo holds, the pilots might well have been able to bring the aircraft back before things got out of hand. An interesting point was that the maintenance workers doing 12-hour shifts *were* concerned about the safety aspect, but their focus was on the safety of the MD-80s they were working on!

William Langewiesch has covered this organizational accident in detail in the March 1998 edition of the *Atlantic Monthly*, referring to the work on the prevention of such accidents carried out by academics. Incidentally, he adds that some academics claim the extra safety features incorporated into systems can in themselves lead to accidents as in the Chernobyl case, and here in the ValuJet case.

In a submission to a newsgroup,[2] in answer to a question from a reader of the *Atlantic Monthly* article taking up this point, Mary Shafer says:

> *She studied the question of emergency oxygen for passengers in cases of cabin depressurization and could find no case where it had saved a life other than for individuals having breathing difficulties or heart attacks.*

That is not to say there are no cases, but one might argue that having emergency drop down oxygen masks may have on occasion prolonged the agony of passengers in doomed aircraft?

---

[1] Fundamental electric power distributor. (See note for Swissair on-board fire.)

[2] Newsgroups: sci.aeronautics.airliners. Date: 06 Jan 2000 01:26:07. From: Mary Shafer shafer@rigel.dfrc.nasa.gov
Subject: Re: Cabin Depressurization

# SWISSAIR-111 ONBOARD FIRE
# (JFK-Outbound 1998)

### Was the Flight Entertainment System Responsible?

> In this second disaster to befall an aircraft departing JFK, investigators suspected, but could not prove, the wiring of the entertainment system had been responsible for starting a fire in the cockpit wiring.
>
> Investigators recommended that aircrew be made aware of the need to land as quickly as possible in the case of potentially serious onboard fires. Any delay incurred due to the desire to dump fuel is liable to close the narrow window of opportunity to save the aircraft.
>
> *[Swissair Flight SR111]*

Swissair Flight SR111 had taken off from New York's JFK Airport en route for Geneva at 18:17 with 215 passengers and 14 crewmembers. The aircraft was a McDonnell Douglas MD-11, a tri-jet that had evolved from the DC-10, with the addition of much automation to dispense with the need for a flight engineer. A more logical name might have been the DC-11, but one can understand the manufacturer's hesitation to suggest it was a DC-10+. Actually, the famous 'DC' designation stood simply for the rather unglamorous sounding 'Douglas Commercial' and 'MD' fitted the company name similarly.

Following the great circle route to Western Europe skirting Canada's Eastern seaboard, the MD-11 was some 66 nm from Halifax and at 33,000 ft, when the crew alerted Monckton Center that a serious situation was developing but not one that could be classed as an emergency. They did this by using the words 'Pan, Pan, Pan' instead of 'Mayday, Mayday, Mayday.'

*Swissair 111 heavy is declaring Pan ... Pan ... Pan.*

*We have smoke in the cockpit, request deviate immediate right turn to a convenient place, I guess Boston.*

As Boston was then 300 nm away, and Halifax International Airport only 66 nm away, the controller asked whether they would prefer to go to Halifax to which SR111 agreed, and began descending from 33,000 ft.

The controller agrees about Halifax and informed them that the active runway was 06, and went on to ask whether they wanted a vector for it.

SR111 answered in the affirmative, and was told to turn left onto the north-northeast course of 30 degrees.

The controller informed them they had 30 miles to go to the runway threshold, at which SR111 surprisingly demurred, saying:

*We need more than 30 miles ....*

The controller instructed them to turn left... to lose some altitude, and SR111 confirmed they were turning left.

SR111 called the controller, saying:

*We must dump some fuel. We may do that in this area during descent.*

The controller said, 'Okay,' whereupon SR111 told him they could turn left or right toward the south to dump fuel.

The controller told them to make what was in effect a U-turn to the left and to inform him when they were ready to dump. They duly made the U-turn.

Just as they were about to find themselves over the sea where the controller would expect them to announce they were ready to dump, they informed the controller that it was an emergency, saying:

*We are declaring an emergency at time zero one two four... we are starting vent now.*
*We have to land immediately.*

Confirming their clearance to commence dumping fuel on that track the controller asked to be informed when the fuel dump was completed.

He called again, repeating his authorization to dump.

Some six minutes after that the aircraft struck the water after having made a 360-degree turn.

All 229 persons on board lost their lives.

How did the situation deteriorate so quickly?

On the other hand, was it more serious than thought right from the beginning?

**The Final Report**

The 352-page final report of the Canadian Transport Safety Bureau can be found via their website: http://tsb.gc.ca/.

It has much general technical information about wiring, highly automated aircraft systems, and measures to prevent and deal with onboard fires. Anyone especially interested in this accident should consult the report directly. To sum it up rather inadequately, it made the following points:

1. Aircraft manufacturers, regulators, operators, and pilots do not normally consider smoke or fumes issuing from the air-conditioning system to represent a serious and immediate emergency requiring an immediate landing.
For example, in the British Midland accident when the pilots shut down the wrong engine, the 'smoke' exiting the air-conditioning came from the engine fan blades rubbing the rubber seals and did not represent a fire at all.

2. The Swissair crew initially thought it was something affecting the air-conditioning and went through the checklist for that, and reasonably did not think it was a dire emergency—hence use of 'Pan...Pan...Pan' rather than 'Mayday.'

3. The fire started in an inaccessible place in the cockpit where there was wiring and involved wiring for the entertainment system. Instead of being connected to a bus dedicated to passenger facilities, the entertainment system (which used a considerable amount of power) was connected to a main bus. Finally, when the pilots eventually realized the problem must be electrical in nature, various instruments and equipment were already failing, and they had to fly manually.

4. Contrary to early reports, the pilots could not have reached Halifax, even had they opted to come straight in from the moment they declared Pan Pan Pan.

5. Though there was a sign of arcing of the cable for the in-flight entertainment system cable in the area where the fire started, there was no proof that it was this that actually started the fire.

The following recommendations were made:

*We recommend that the Safety Regulation Group re-iterates its advice to airlines that the priority in certain emergencies, such as in-flight fires, is to land, rather than to seek to dump fuel in order to avoid an overweight landing. It should ensure through its inspections that airlines are passing on that information to aircrews.*

*Furthermore, we recommend that air traffic controllers be given similar advice, so that they are able to respond appropriately to such emergencies.*

# SUPERSONIC CONCORDE
# (Paris CDG 2000)

**Five-star Airliner Crashes on Two-star Hotel**

---

Concorde was the most glamorous and most beautiful airliner ever built. It stirred the hearts of the public in France and the UK—who had paid out so much in taxes to support it, and its wealthy passengers.

At the end of its life, much of it was 'old technology'—with production having ceased, there was no incentive to make costly improvements, even to the tires.

With so few flights, it fell statistically from one of the safest aircraft to one of the most dangerous when disaster befell.

*[Air France Flight 4590]*

---

## Concorde's History

The world's first supersonic airliner, the Concorde 001, rolled onto the tarmac in 1967, but according to CNN it took two more years of testing and fine-tuning of the powerful engines before it made its maiden flight over France on March 2, 1969. The original plan was for a production run of 300, but in the end, the production run was limited to just 14. Air France cannibalized one of those for spare parts in 1982, and another crashed, leaving five for Air France and seven for British Airways when the two airlines withdrew it from service in 2003.

These days, the authorities would never certify such a noisy bird, so Concorde was surviving on the certificates issued in the 1970s. Even then, the US would not approve inland flights, so its regular scheduled flights to the US were mostly to the East Coast and New York in particular. Some said it was sour grapes at being beaten to the post on the part of the US.

When Concorde finally entered airline service it was a Pyrrhic victory for its makers, or rather the two nations of taxpayers who provided such generous funding. Key countries on major overland routes refused to allow it to pass over their territories. For timesaving reasons it was essential to fly overland as the aircraft did not have the range to fly the long routes over the Pacific Ocean. Finally, the fuel-guzzling Concorde had the misfortune to come on the scene just as fuel prices were skyrocketing.

As a result, the majestic Concorde mainly benefited the rich and famous, though many found First Class on a conventional aircraft to be preferable to the cramped seating on Concorde. Some celebrities, such as the British TV personality David Frost, were virtually commuting between London and

161

New York. Not so well known, is the good use courier companies such as DHL put it to in delivering documents and financial instruments for major companies where time really was money. Even so, not enough demand existed to employ fully even that tiny fleet.

Air France had more difficulty filling seats than British Airways who actually made a healthy profit[1] out of it. Not only was this because more top business people and celebrities fly to London, but also partly because London is nearer than Paris to New York and Washington—quite significant with an aircraft operating near the limit of its operating range. Air France in particular used charter flights and excursions to help fill those seats

## The Fatal Flight

Indeed, the flight that was to last only a minute or two before ending in disaster just after taking off from Paris' Charles de Gaulle Airport in July 2000 was just such a charter flight. It carried elderly Germans to New York to join a luxury Caribbean cruise.

Concorde spooled up its engines to take off with its long beak[2] tipped 5 degrees downwards, and pointing just in front of another Air France aircraft that had brought the French President and his wife back from an official visit to Japan. Though so slim and elegant, the Concorde was almost certainly overweight, with fuel representing just over half her total weight.

The captain *thought* they had an all up weight (AUW) of 185,100 kg, placing them, he said, at the aircraft's structural limit. He did not know this was an underestimate[3] and did not include 19 items of baggage loaded at the last minute. Finally, it is likely that the unburned fuel in the rear tank and the 19 extra items of luggage had moved the centre of gravity too far aft.

Much to the surprise of the Bureau d'Enquêtes et d'Analyses (BEA—the French Air Accident Investigation Bureau), the announcement by the control tower of an 8-knot tailwind did not elicit any comment from any of the aircrew. At the very least, the captain should have considered taking off against the wind. Although a wind of 8 knots may not seem much, the difference between a headwind and a tailwind is double, making a difference of 16 knots. Because of limitations on the maximum speed for the tires, a tail wind of 8 knots would have meant they were much too heavy.

An article in the British Sunday newspaper, *The Observer*, written by David Rose shortly after the crash with comments by veteran Concorde pilot John Hutchinson, said they could no doubt have 'got away' with being overweight had other things not gone wrong.

The crew had decided 150 knots should be $V_1$, the speed at which they would be committed to continuing the takeoff, and 183 knots should be $V_R$, the speed at which they would rotate and expect to soar into the sky.

A supersonic delta-wing aircraft like Concorde differs from other aircraft in that the wings do not provide any real lift before rotation. In consequence, the tires continue to bear the entire weight of the aircraft throughout the takeoff run. This in turn means they are particularly vulnerable just before rotation as there is not only the weight of the aircraft to consider but also the tremendous centrifugal forces acting on their treads due to the wheels' high rate of rotation. In addition, at high speeds, sharp objects on the runway are far more likely to cut into them.

Shortly after Concorde had reached $V_1$, the right-hand tire on the left-hand main landing gear ran over a curved strip of metal that had just fallen off a DC-10 that had taken off shortly before. Curved like a loop, the titanium strip was lying sideways up, with its concave side facing the oncoming tire, thus ensuring the tire would trap it rather than roll it over and bend it flat. The tough metal sliced into the tire, causing the tire to break up under the enormous centrifugal forces. Later, investigators found a 10 lb (4.5 kg) piece of rubber from the tire on the runway near that point.

After complex studies the BEA investigators concluded the lump of rubber had forcefully struck the underside of the wing, pushing it and the fuel tank so rapidly inwards that it induced a shock wave in the fuel of such intensity that the virtually *full* tank ruptured elsewhere—a phenomenon that had never been seen before in a passenger aircraft. Had the piece of rubber just pierced the tank, as in a previous instance in Washington in 1979, the damage to the tank would doubtless have been less.

From the amount of fuel on the runway and other evidence, it is estimated that kerosene was pouring out from under the wing at a rate of 60 kg/sec. In the Washington incident mentioned above, the fuel did not catch fire and the aircraft was able to take off and return safely. Perhaps because of the much greater amount of fuel, and very likely because a damaged wire in the landing gear was producing sparks, the leaking fuel then caught fire.

The events leading to the ultimate disaster all happened in some three seconds, and must have been very confusing to the crew. The control tower told the Concorde's crew they had flames coming out behind them. Debris and more likely hot gases from the fire caused the performance of the two engines on the left side to fall off, resulting in a yaw to the left. The captain rotated the aircraft early as they deviated to the left of the runway, but no sooner had they lifted off than the fire warning for the No. 2 engine sounded and the flight engineer shut it down.

The No. 1 engine seemed to be recovering and able to help them reach the 220-knot speed to fly at least horizontally with the landing gear down. They tried to raise the landing gear, but were unsuccessful, no doubt due to damage caused by the fire or debris. They attained a height of 200 ft, still with insufficient airspeed. The No. 1 engine began to fail, and with the first officer constantly warning them about the lack of airspeed, the aircraft went slightly nose-up and the left wing dropped down to 115 degrees. The yaw and sideslip meant air was no longer properly entering the good engines on the right-hand side, and they too lost power, though it is possible they were throttled back at the last minute in an attempt to straighten the aircraft's trajectory.

Virtually upside down, the pride of France and Britain crashed on a two-star hotel some 6 kilometers from the end of the runway, and exploded in a fireball. The crash was so violent, with debris scattered widely, that there was no hope of survivors. The death toll was 100 passengers, six cabin attendants, and three aircrew.

Fortunately, the three-storey hotel was almost empty, and, on the ground, 'only' four people were killed and six people injured. (Forty-five Polish tourists staying at the hotel later returned from sightseeing to find a surprising sight.)

## Conclusions

Although it does not say so in so many words, the lengthy BEA report into the crash gives the impression the Air France Concorde team of officials, mechanics, and aircrew were an exclusive lot like those associated with expensive sports cars, and had a somewhat cavalier attitude. With such cars, drivers are liable to take risks when overtaking, in the belief that the tremendous reserve of power will always get them out of difficulties. As already mentioned, the extra distance to New York from Paris meant that Concorde would often be operating just within its safety envelope. To give that 'little bit extra',[4] aircraft would often be loaded with excess fuel on the assumption (or pretext) that taxiing would use it up before takeoff.

Just after the accident, maintenance staff who had replaced part of the thrust reverser mechanism on one of the engines became so distressed at the thought they might have been responsible for the disaster, they had to go to the doctor for medication. One can imagine the anguish they endured until it was discovered that the accident was unconnected with their work, carried out properly. However, the BEA investigators did find other maintenance workers had forgotten a spacer when reassembling the landing gear during earlier servicing.

An article appeared in the British *Observer* newspaper suggesting that omission of the spacer had caused the aircraft to deviate to the left and that the lack of it only made matters worse when the tire failed—causing the aircraft to veer to the left 'like a supermarket trolley with a jammed wheel.' The BEA disputed this, saying the aircraft only started to deviate when the thrust from two engines on the left-hand side fell away.

While saying the lack of the spacer had not played any role in the accident scenario, the BEA were highly displeased with this sign of maintenance failures and lack of written material that procedures had been 'signed off' on completion. They noted that the Air France maintenance people justified working 12-hour shifts by claiming this avoided wasting time briefing others.

The BEA inquiry took extra time because it was run in parallel with, but separately from, the judicial inquiry, which in the end did not come up with anything dramatic. Some of the investigators from England complained it took a long time to see the evidence, and the BEA report has a note saying that this was due to the judicial inquiry.

The French insurers were very pleased to have come to an amicable albeit expensive agreement with the relatives of the German victims, as they wanted to avoid litigation in the US courts. However, the lawyers for the other victims' relatives were not as happy with this quick settlement and asked for extra compensation for their own services.

The direct cause of the accident was running over the titanium strip. There were suggestions that the crew might well have been able to save the aircraft had it not been overloaded with the center of gravity too far aft, and had the flight engineer not shut down the No. 2 engine. However, the intensity of the fire was so great that the left wing and associated control systems would have failed before reaching the nearby Le Bourget Airport. Indeed, there is evidence that failure of the left elevon was what caused the left wing to drop at the end. Aluminum loses much of its strength when heated to a mere 300°C and melts at 600°C, and investigators found molten aluminum under the flight path.

One point that the BEA investigators did make regarding safety in general, was that when something is used so little, improvements do not tend to be made. In particular, this applied to the tires. If there had been hundreds of Concordes in operation, developing much safer tires would surely have been thought worthwhile.

Indeed, when Concorde returned to service:

1. It had new NZG[5] tires developed by Michelin that had new materials making them more resistant to foreign bodies and designed so that only small pieces would fly off if they did happen to fail.

2. In addition, the fuel tanks were lined with Kevlar (used for body armor) impregnated with Viton (an expensive synthetic rubber able to withstand high temperatures). Thus even in the unlikely event of a large piece of rubber flying off the newly developed tires hitting the underside of the wing, the shockwave produced in a virtually full tank would not produce a gaping hole elsewhere.

There had been a close shave, not widely publicized at the time (late 1970s), when the engine on a British Airways Concorde caught fire. The passengers escaped via the emergency slides without too much difficulty except that a passenger wearing shoes with high heels slit the fabric of one of the slides on her way down. A male, and presumably heavier passenger following her, went right through the aperture and found himself with a sore spine on the ground below.

More troubling was the discovery later that the titanium shield above the engine, destined to protect the fuel tanks, had begun to 'bubble' due to the intense heat of the fire. Had more time elapsed even titanium would have failed and there would have been an enormous conflagration. Strangely, there is no mention of this in the individual histories of any of the British Airways aircraft.

The criminal investigation run in parallel with the BEA investigation also concluded that the training of Air France's Concorde aircrew had 'weaknesses'[6] that led amongst other things to the shutdown of an engine before necessary. However, these various failings did not amount to gross negligence or criminal responsibility.

On July 4, 2008, a French judge agreed with a prosecutor's submission that John Taylor (a Continental mechanic who allegedly fitted the non-standard strip), Stanley Ford (a Continental maintenance official), and the airline itself stand trial for involuntarily causing death and injuries.

Also cited for trial were Henri Perrier, 77, the director of the first Concorde program, and Claude Frantzen, 69, a former director of technical services at the DGAC, the French civil aviation authority. They are alleged to have known that the Concorde's wing, which contained fuel tanks, was fragile and vulnerable to damage from the outside.

A spokesperson for Continental, the only accused with real money, stated, 'These indictments are outrageous and completely unjustified,' and said any charges would be defended with vigor.

This court case does not really reflect the overall situation, as the causes of the accident were many and complex.

---

[1] Said to have been 20 million pounds sterling per year—BA and AF did not pay for the aircraft.

[2] The nose usually droops down 5 degrees for takeoff, and 12.5 degrees on landing, so the pilots' view not obscured by the long nose when the aircraft is pointing upwards.

[3] After the accident, the BEA estimated her actual takeoff weight including the 19 extra items of luggage to have been 186,451 kg. This was likely to have been an underestimate, as 20.7 kg was the average for the 103 items on the load sheet, and 84 kg was taken to be the average passenger weight including carry-on luggage. Both averages seem low for this atypical passenger profile.

[4] Thus lessening the danger of having to divert en route and greatly upsetting their most demanding passengers.

[5] NZG stands for Near Zero Growth, meaning they hardly grow at all at very high rotational speeds. Michelin's work was not wasted as their new tires are being considered (along with Bridgestone's) for use with the giant Airbus A380.

[6] *The Independent*, December 15, 2004.

# CHAPTER 8

# PILOT SICK, SUICIDAL, OR INAPPROPRIATE RESPONSE

## BEA TRIDENT CAPTAIN'S HEART ATTACK
## (Staines, London 1972)

### Up-tight Captain—Diffident Rookie First Officer

> Lack of a cockpit voice recording made it impossible to determine who did what in the following incident. As a result, the British Government belatedly faced down opposition from the pilots' union and mandated the installation of cockpit voice recorders (CVRs) in all sizable UK-registered airliners, just as in the United States.
>
> *[British European Airways Flight 548]*

The British European Airways tri-jet Trident had taken off for Brussels from London's Heathrow airport in cloudy and somewhat turbulent weather conditions. Only 114 seconds into its flight, with the aircraft traveling at 162 knots at about 1,500 ft, someone moved the lever controlling the leading edge droops, causing them to retract.

Droops, as their name implies, are like 'upper lips' on the front (leading edges) of the wings that can be made to droop forwards and downwards to change the configuration of the wing and enable the aircraft to fly at low airspeeds. Their function is similar to that of the much better-known 'slats.'

Theoretically, the airspeed would have had to be at least 15–20 knots higher than the 162 knots at which they were flying for the aircraft to be able to fly without the droops deployed. In fact, to allow a safety margin, the pilots would only retract the droops once the airspeed had reached 225 knots, and never when the aircraft was in a turn as it was—an aircraft is more vulnerable in a turn, especially if the turn involves turning away from a strong headwind, as the drop in airspeed can be dramatic.

Every Trident pilot would have had this minimum droop retraction speed drummed into him or her, and could hardly forget it as it was indicated next to the droop lever.

Even so, retracting the droops by mistake need not prove immediately fatal, as even in those days, airliners had good systems to warn pilots of an imminent stall. Sensors on the wings would detect development of abnormal airflow over the leading edge and a stick shaker system would shake the control columns to warn the pilots. According to the flight data recorder (FDR), on that BEA flight the sticker shaker operated less than two seconds after retraction of the droops.

In addition, aircraft such as the Trident, with the engines at the rear and high tails (high horizontal stabilizers) are equipped with a stick pusher system that pushes the nose down in a stall. This is to compensate for the fact that aircraft with engines at the rear and high tails go *nose-up* rather than nose-down in a stall, thus making the stall worse and often irrecoverable if anywhere near the ground.

Apart from in cases of extreme wind shear, an aircraft's airspeed changes progressively, so that in normal circumstances the stick-shaker warning (that the airspeed is falling to such an extent that a stall is imminent) occurs well before the 'last resort' stick-push. However, as this was a 'change of configuration stall' (i.e. not due to a progressive drop in airspeed, but due to a change in shape of the wing), these events took place so quickly that the stick shake warning and stick push must have seemed to have occurred almost simultaneously.

The virtual concurrence of these two events may have confused the pilots, for when the stick push mechanism duly caused the nose to pitch downwards, and so much so, that the aircraft gained almost sufficient speed to recover, *someone* fought against the stick pusher and pulled the nose up. Once again, the stick pusher operated to push the nose down only for *someone* again to use considerable force to resist it, before finally disabling it. As at no point was there an attempt made to increase engine power one must conclude that whoever was at the controls was unaware of the true situation.

With the nose yanked up again without redeployment of the droops and no application of additional power, the Trident did what the stick pusher was trying to prevent—it went into a deep unrecoverable tail-down stall.

Below them, a 13-year-old boy walking with his younger brother along a footpath saw the Trident with its wings level drop out of the cloudy overcast, with the tail weighed down by its three heavy engines striking the ground first and breaking off. The rest of the aircraft then belly flopped onto the field with the sound of crumpling and tearing metal, as the fuselage and wings separated into various pieces. Despite the large amount of fuel carried at takeoff spilling onto the ground, there was no outbreak of fire— no doubt because of the lack of forward speed.

With air traffic controllers not even having noticed the aircraft's disappearance, the boy ran to a house some 400 yards away for help. The occupant rushed to the scene, but her skills as a hospital emergency room nurse were of little avail as only one person showed any sign of life, and that sole survivor later died in hospital, making the total death toll 118. The official report into the crash praised her highly.

There have been survivors in crashes, even with intense fires, where the wreckage must have looked even worse. However, with the wings providing no lift at all and the forward speed dissipated by the drag produced by the nose-up/tail-down attitude, the Trident had belly flopped almost straight down with virtually nothing between the occupants and the ground to cushion the shock. Had the aircraft belly flopped on the nearby trees they might have absorbed enough of the shock to enable some to survive.

With little immediate information about the 'mysterious' cause of the terrible disaster, newspapers resorted to carrying stories about morbidly curious bystanders and gawkers hampering the rescue efforts by blocking the roads. (The official report later denied their presence had affected the death toll.)

The absence of fire facilitated the work of the investigators, and in particular with respect to the post mortems of the crewmembers. They established these key points:

1. **Someone had retracted the droops before the aircraft had reached sufficient airspeed to stay in the air without them and contrary to company regulations when the aircraft was in a banked turn and more vulnerable.**

2. **The built-in stall warnings (stick-shaker) were ignored and the automatic recovery (stick-pusher) resisted several times before being disabled (switched off).**

3. **Inexplicably, at almost every stage of the short flight, prior to and including the fatal retraction of the droops, the airspeed had been lower than it should have been, and this unusually low airspeed had made the retraction of the droops especially lethal.**

4. **The captain, who was handling the aircraft, had had a heart attack, and medical experts concluded from the color of the blood in his heart that he was probably dead even before the aircraft hit the ground.**

The investigators had to resort almost entirely to supposition, as the aircraft did not have a cockpit voice recorder (CVR), even though CVRs had been made mandatory for US-registered airliners much earlier in 1965. [Opposition from the UK pilots' unions had thwarted their introduction in the UK.]

It was impossible to know who did what and why. From terse communications with ATC, it was evident that the captain had been handling the aircraft, but it was not clear who had moved the droop lever.

The initial investigation was followed by a public inquiry with lawyers arguing for days without producing anything of significance that was not apparent from the original investigation. What *were* apparent, as in so many crashes, were the human personality factors that experience has shown increase the likelihood of a disaster.

On the flight deck, there were actually four pilots:

1. **Captain Key, an uptight captain, who supported the company in the ongoing industrial dispute.**

2. **Twenty-two-year-old Second Officer Keighley. He had only very few hours' line experience on the Trident. He was in the first officer's seat next to the captain.**

3. **Twenty-four-year-old Second Officer Ticehurst, who was in the monitoring seat.**

4. **A Captain Collins in the jump seat behind Captain Key. This second captain was deadheading with his own crew to Brussels. Although a freighter captain on another aircraft type he too was qualified to fly Tridents.**

Though technically qualified, Keighley was thought by instructors, both before and after joining the airline, to lack initiative and to be rather diffident. While they thought he would eventually make a good pilot, his relatively young age, unassertive character and inexperience meant he would have trouble coping with a captain known to be uptight and who had shown just before the flight he could get very angry.

Industrial action at the airline meant that some junior pilots had not had the extra training required to permit them to 'legally' occupy the third seat (behind the captain and first officer), which involved monitoring the flying pilot's actions and performing certain technical functions that used to be done by a flight engineer and necessitated the extra paper qualifications. This quirk in the regulations in turn meant that the least qualified pilot was likely to be at the controls next to the captain.

Furthermore, prior to the flight, Captain Key had been involved in a violent argument in the crew room with another pilot about the strike, and Keighley had witnessed the captain's violent outburst of temper. Thus, there would have been good reason for him to be very circumspect in his dealings with him and hesitate to do anything that might provoke him.

In addition, it was said that the considerable air turbulence must have raised Keighley's certainly already high stress level.

The investigators thought the presence of Captain Collins might have distracted the junior pilots. The official report notes that when Captain

Collins was found in the debris he was still holding an air freshener can in his hand. These air fresheners were standard issue for freighter captains, but one wonders what he was doing with it so early in the flight—was Captain Key sweating so profusely that use of the air freshener was deemed necessary? An awful possibility, that no one hitherto has suggested, is that Captain Collins was standing up with his air freshener and this had been a further distraction. He might even have fallen forward when the initial stick push occurred, thus blocking the view of Ticehurst.

In his book *Disaster in the Air*, Jan Bartelski who has worked in senior positions for the International Airline Pilots' Association, says an official accident report should not publicize such details as 'being found dead grasping an air freshener.' However, in the author's opinion, it does seem very relevant, in that many people have said that Captain Collins' body being found without earphones, slumped away from his seat might mean he was trying to get to the droop lever to reset the droops. Would he have done this with the air freshener can in his hand?

Jan Bartelski does postulate very logically that an erroneous airspeed reading on the captain's side might have led him to retract the droops because he thought they were going too fast rather than too slow. This would account for the consistently low airspeeds at the various stages of the short flight, which no one can explain apart from suggesting this resulted from the captain being in pain.

Possible contributory causes of the disaster were said to have been:

1. **The airline's training.**

2. **Reports of 'similar' incidents being overlooked because of bureaucratic muddle, staff absence (holidays), bad luck, and so on.**

The major outstanding questions were:

1. **Why was the aircraft flying more slowly than it should have been at various stages of the climb out?**

2. **Why was the droop lever moved?**

3. **In addition, why, even if the captain was incapacitated, didn't the other two pilots, and especially the monitoring pilot, realize what was happening?**

As already mentioned, the absence of knowledge regarding what the aircrew were saying between themselves demonstrated the need for CVRs. The British Government finally put its foot down and made their installation mandatory despite the opposition from the pilots.

171

# WAS EGYPTAIR FLIGHT 990 SUICIDE?
# (JFK-Outbound 1999)

## Airline Would Not Agree

> Cockpit video recorders would have greatly facilitated numerous investigations, and in particular, the one we describe here where it was thought but not proven to be a case of a pilot committing suicide.
>
> *[EgyptAir Flight 990]*

The EgyptAir 767 crashed in Nantucket shortly after taking off from New York's JFK killing all 217 people onboard. No plausible mechanical-, terrorist-, or weather-related cause was ever found.

Investigators listened to the CVR tape over and over again, and sought the help of Arabic specialists in determining what the words meant. This was not easy as words equivalent to 'God is Great' could be words a person might utter before committing suicide, or words uttered on seeing a crisis developing. US investigators finally decided that First Officer Gamil El Batouty must have crashed the Boeing 767 on purpose, but EgyptAir vociferously opposed that view.

An article on the ABC News website after the EgyptAir crash said:

> *'Although the actions of the Flight 990 copilot may never be clearly understood, the allegations [that the pilot crashed the aircraft on purpose] raise [general] fears about whether pilots may be suffering anything from depression to anxiety, or even a death wish. But are the fears founded? There are, in fact, very few instances in which a pilot or crewmember's deliberate actions are known to have brought down an airplane:*

1. **In 1982, a Japan Airlines DC-8 approaching Tokyo's Haneda Airport plunged into Tokyo Bay. It was determined that the pilot had pushed the nose of the plane down after fighting off the first officer for control. Twenty-four people were killed and 141 injured. The pilot, who survived, was later put into a psychiatric institution.**
   [After this incident, passengers and colleagues would scan the faces of the airline's pilots for any tick suggesting mental problems. This made them self-conscious, and twitchier than usual! (Author)]

2. On Aug. 21, 1994, an Air Morocco jet fell from the sky after its autopilot was disconnected, and 51 people were killed. The cockpit voice recorder suggested that the pilot wanted to commit suicide and deliberately crashed the plane.

3. On Dec. 19, 1997, a SilkAir Boeing 737-300 at cruising altitude went into a steep dive, after its flight data recorder and cockpit voice recorders had been turned off. It crashed in Palenbang, Indonesia, killing 104 people. The pilot had recently been demoted, and was suspected of committing murder/suicide.

4. On Oct. 11, 1999, an Air Botswana pilot recently grounded for medical reasons took off in a company plane and threatened to crash it into company headquarters. He ultimately crashed into two other Air Botswana jets on the ground, destroying all three craft and perishing.

5. The closest such American incident was by an off-duty Federal Express pilot who, while traveling on a FedEx cargo flight on April 7, 1994, attacked the flight crew with a hammer and spear gun in an attempt to take control of the DC-10 and crash it into Federal Express headquarters in Memphis, Tenn. The injured flight crew managed to gain control and safely land the airplane.'

The article went on to say that while airlines carry out tests to determine personality traits, they do not carry out tests to find mental disorders. However, the many pilots from the military would have been subjected to them.

# PILOT SWISHES-OFF AIRBUS TAIL
# (JFK-Outbound 2001)

## Why Him?

> Though wake turbulence was a key factor in this incident, it has been included in this chapter as it was a 'propensity' of the first officer, perhaps accentuated by his training that was most likely the cause.
>
> *[American Airlines Flight 587]*

The 16,000 ft runway at Denver International Airport in Colorado is the longest commercial runway in North America. It owes this distinction to the city literally being a mile high and thus needing an exceptionally long runway to cope with heavily laden aircraft that accelerate less quickly at the lower atmospheric pressures found at high altitudes. The previous record holder, the slightly shorter 14,572 ft (4,441 m) Runway '31L' at New York's JFK Airport probably still holds the record for the best takeoff prospects as it is at sea level as well as being exceptionally long.

A drawback of New York's '31L' is that the city lies straight ahead, albeit in the distance. To avoid areas that are sensitive for noise and other reasons (including terrorist action), aircraft taking off in that north-westerly (310-degree) direction usually have to make a sharp left turn shortly after takeoff, so as to avoid the city and fly mostly over water.

On November 12, 2001, almost two months to the day after 'September 11'—with the images of those two aircraft slamming into the World Trade Center's twin-towers still vivid in people's minds—Japan Airlines Flight JL47 to Tokyo took off from 31L at JFK. It was just after 9 a.m. The shorter parallel runway, 31R, on the other side of the terminal buildings, was being used for incoming aircraft, including the soon expected British Airways supersonic Concorde Flight One from London.

JL47 acknowledged the takeoff clearance from the tower, but waited perhaps 15 seconds longer than usual before beginning its roll. In addition, with the large amount of fuel required for the 13+-hour flight to Tokyo it would have climbed out more slowly than most other 747s just hopping across the 'pond' to Europe. The tower had already warned a police helicopter to exercise caution about wake turbulence from several heavy jet departures over a suburb to the left of the runway extension[1] called Canarsie.

Once well into the air, the Japan Airlines pilots would retract the flaps and commence a high power climb. It is precisely when climbing under high power with a 'clean configuration' (i.e. no flaps or slats sticking out) that a large aircraft such as the 747 produces the most wake turbulence.

This consists of vicious vortices of swirling air produced at the wingtips, where the air squished under the wings meets the lower-pressure relatively fast-moving air above them. These hang behind the aircraft, and, spinning like tops, gradually descend until their energy either dissipates or they are broken up by other turbulence. In fact, turbulent or stormy weather conditions help protect following aircraft from wake turbulence as the turbulence breaks up the spirals. It is in calm conditions that wake turbulence is the most treacherous. That day, aircraft taking off on JFK's 31L were encountering a light headwind of just 9 knots.

The next aircraft in line to take off was American Airlines Flight 587, an Airbus A300 bound for the Dominican Republic with 260 people on board—a flight expected to take some four hours, but which in fact was to last only 104 seconds from lift-off. First Officer Sten Molin was the pilot flying (PF) with Captain Edward States in command. The tower had warned the A300 of the danger of wake turbulence, but this was routine in the circumstances, and was in no way exceptional. In fact, many considered it a phrase used to cover the controllers' backs, with the effect being somewhat like someone crying wolf too often. Nevertheless, Molin was obviously concerned, for he said to the captain:

*You happy with that distance?*

The captain replied:

*Aah, he's... We'll be alright once we get rollin'. He's supposed to be five miles by the time we get airborne. That's the idea.*

First officer:

*So you're happy ... Lights?*

Captain:

*Yeah, lights are on.*

Preparations for takeoff continued.

First officer:

*Takeoff checks complete. I'm on the roll. Thank you, sir.*

The aircraft began its roll, and reached the takeoff decision speed, $V_1$.

Captain:

*$V_1$!*

The aircraft reached rotation speed, $V_R$.

Captain:

$V_R$!

Captain:

> *ROTATE.*

The captain announced they had reached the safe takeoff (climb) speed, $V_2$, and then $V_2$ +10 knots, giving them an extra safety margin.

First officer:

> *Positive rate, gear up, please.*

With the aircraft 500 ft off the ground, the aircraft was banking left as the control tower ordered the crew to turn left and fly the 'bridge climb,' like JL47 ahead of them. However, they had commenced their left turn earlier than JL47, with the result that they were 'cutting the corner' downwind of the Japan Airlines craft rather than following in its precise tracks.

The control tower signed off, telling the A300 to contact New York Departure (Control).

They duly informed Departure they were at 1,300 ft, and climbing to 5,000.

Departure confirmed they had them on their radar, and said:

> *Climb, maintain one three thousand.*

They acknowledged this. The aircraft passed through 1,500 ft at roughly 220 knots, and the bank eased as they completed their turn to the left. The Japan Airlines 747 was 'ahead' of them, but upwind and further out on the curve, and somewhat higher, but not so much higher due its load of fuel.

As Captain States and First Officer Molin passed through 1,769 ft at 239 knots, Departure called, telling them to turn left again.

> *587 heavy, turn left....*

The Cockpit Area Microphone (CAM) picked up a squeak and a rattle.

Captain:

> *Little wake turbulence, huh?*

[Wake turbulence from one of the JAL 747's wingtips.]

First officer:

> *Yeah!*

The aircraft was in a steep, but not excessive bank, as it continued to effect the second left turn as ordered.

Fourteen seconds later and traveling at 238 knots they encountered the wake turbulence from the JAL 747's other wingtip.

In a strained voice, Molin asked for maximum power, and the following exchange took place between the two pilots, with Captain States speaking first:

*You all right?*

*Yeah, I'm fine.*

*Hang on to it. Hang on to it.*

This time the buffeting seemed more serious, and the flight data recorder (FDR) shows First Officer Molin continuously making rapid full-sweep two-and-fro rudder inputs in addition to the aileron inputs that were normal for such a situation.

The cockpit area microphone (CAM) recorded the sound of a snap

CAM:

*[Loud thump]*

CAM:

*[Loud bang]*

Molin:

*[Human grunt?]*

CAM:

*[Roaring noise starts and becomes louder]*

Molin:

*Holy xxxx!*

There followed warning chimes, which were probably first ECAM chimes and then stall warning chimes.

*[Roaring noise decreases and ceases]*

Molin:

*What the hell are we into? ... We're stuck in it.*

[Possibly more chimes lasting some four seconds overall]

Captain:

*'Get out of it! Get out of it!'*

END OF RECORDING

When Captain States was saying, 'Get out of it!,' neither he nor Molin knew the vertical tailfin had broken off some 14 seconds earlier, and was falling into Jamaica Bay below.

The aircraft—minus its vertical stabilizer (tailfin)—continued a little further and crashed onto a narrow band of land separating Jamaica Bay from the Atlantic Ocean, which is part of Queens. None of the 260 people on board the Airbus 300 survived. The death toll on the ground could have been considerable as it was a residential neighborhood, but was limited to five persons as most pieces luckily hit unoccupied property or open spaces.

The big question was why Molin had swished the rudder back and forth in such a manner. Actually, the investigators had some difficulty determining just how extreme Molin's movements had been because of the sampling rate. That is, the frequency with which the FDR measures the angle of the rudder, which was then four seconds, during which time it would have been possible for him to move the rudder back and forth (without it showing up).

Another problem was that the readings, as are many others on FDRs, are filtered to avoid confusing spikes. This averaging would not matter when dealing with a rudder used in virtually one position as would usually be the case, but very confusing when trying to determine the magnitude of the extremes in the present situation.

One major line of inquiry was obviously to find out whether the tailfin had had some inherent weakness, either due to poor design or previous overstressing that had left cracks that had gone undetected. Since it was made of composites rather than the traditional metal, there was much talk that composite tailfins were inherently dangerous, partly because, unlike metal tailfins, cracks are so difficult to detect. Some American Airlines pilots even talked of boycotting the Airbus A300.

In the end, the investigators concluded the accident had not resulted from an inherent weakness but from Molin's aggressive use of the rudder, and in particular his rapidly moving it back and forth.[2]

The next question posed was why Molin had done this. Should the manufacturer have warned that doing so was dangerous? As large sums of money and prestige were at stake, there then ensued a battle between Airbus and American Airlines. Airbus maintained that the airline's training put too much stress on use of the rudder, which the airline denied.

Investigators looked into Molin's personal life so extensively that his father, also a pilot, complained. Inquiries almost got to the point of ascertaining how Molin performed in bed. He was said to be a little immature socially, and his deferential manner in his exchanges with Captain States do hint at this. However, investigators found nothing dramatic.

On the other hand, American Airlines maintained Airbus knew of the dangers, and had done too little to warn pilots.

Airbus maintained that the airline had trained Molin to use the rudder in recovery situations, and being nervous about wake turbulence even before takeoff, he expected it, and over-reacted when it occurred. Following this line of thought, one could say the first encounter keyed him up, so that he was more aggressive the second time.

Some experts said that as he reacted mildly the first time, the turbulence the second time might have been rather different and produced the yawing movement to which he reacted instinctively by using the rudder.

Perverse though it might seem, had First Officer Molin been captain rather than first officer, the subsequent joust with the wake turbulence might have never taken place. When Molin asked the captain just before takeoff whether he was happy with the distance between them and the JAL aircraft ahead, he was evidently thinking it would be better to wait perhaps 30 seconds more. This expression of serious doubt to seniors in the form of a question brings to mind the worst aircraft disaster, at Tenerife, where the flight engineer used the words:

> *Did he not clear the runway then?*

Had Molin been less polite and said forcefully,

> *I think we should wait a moment!*

the captain of flight 587 might have done just that and not tried to justify himself.

Admittedly, the KLM flight engineer at Tenerife would have had to be very assertive to halt that fatal takeoff roll.

Conversely, had Captain States been flying the aircraft, his laid-back attitude would probably have meant he would have let the aircraft have its head, and not have used the rudder so disastrously, if at all. However, his telling Molin,

> *Hang on to it. Hang on to it!*

might have made Molin even more determined to keep the aircraft on a leash, though 'hanging on' was not literally telling him to swish the rudder, but could have been interpreted as that.

With hindsight one can also see that had Flight 587 followed the track of the Japan Airlines 747 more closely instead of cutting the corner as ordered by ATC, they would have missed the turbulence altogether as it would have been blown downwind. In a sense, the required separation was not maintained once the corner was cut. Of course, the 'premature' turn over water would subject built-up areas to less noise.

An article on the website (www.mywiseowl.com) half-seriously says:

> *The primary purpose of Flight Data Recorders (FDRs)*
> *is to reduce the manufacturer's liability by correctly assigning*
> *blame to the failing assemblies or persons, with the famous*
> *secondary purpose being to prevent future accidents.*

Had FDR evidence not been available in this accident, would anyone have thought the first officer would have made those rudder movements?

Thus, the FDR did indeed help save the day for the manufacturer. The airline put considerable pressure on the investigators, making new points until they were told not to make new representations unless based on new *facts*. Whether or not this pressure was a factor in the change made to the order in which the contributory factors were listed, it is notable that Board member Carol J. Carmody, with the concurrence of Board member Richard F. Healing, added a dissenting statement to the report.

While they agreed with the conclusions of the report as regards probable cause, namely the excessive use of the rudder by the first officer, they objected to the fact that the Vice Chairman had changed the order in which the contributory causes were listed from that in the original draft. This gave the impression that more weight should be given to the characteristics of the A300 rudder system[3] than to the nature of the airline's Advanced Aircraft Maneuvering Program (AAMP).[4] They pointed out that Molin had not been known to use the rudder abnormally *before* partaking in the program, and when questioned by a captain about excessive use of the rudder in another incident after partaking in the program, Molin had insisted the AAMP directed him to use the rudder in that manner.

Carmody went on to say:

> *To elevate the characteristics of the A300-600 rudder system in the hierarchy of contributing factors ignores the fact that this system had not been an issue in 16 million hours of testing and operator experience—until the AAMP-trained pilot flew it.*

This puts Molin in a rather different light. Known as a hands-on pilot—some saying his flying was as smooth as silk—maybe his only propensity or quirk was to follow things too much to the letter. In 2012, the NTSB said the A300 should have greater in-built protection against use of the rudder in such an excessive fashion, which suggests that they no longer think another pilot doing likewise is inconceivable.

---

[1] As explained in connection with the collision between an airliner and a Cessna at Milan's Linate Airport, 'runway extension' means the imaginary line that would be drawn if the runway continued.

[2] The NTSB presented a simulated video for the inquiry, showing a side-view of the aircraft and the movements of the controls made by Molin.

[3] Four years earlier, the A300-600 pilot of American Airlines Flight 903 lost control at 16,000 feet on approach to Miami and moved the rudder from side to side to recover, almost tearing off the tail in the process.

Subsequently, an Airbus internal memo noted, 'Rudder movement from left limit to right limit will produce loads on fin/rear fuselage above ultimate design load.' If that memo had been generally circulated, that fact not only might have been incorporated in the AAMP program, but mentioned in the manual.

[4] The AAMP program to enable pilots to right aircraft after upsets included aggressive use of the rudder.

# COLGAN AIR
# (On Approach to Buffalo Niagara International 2009)
## 50% of Flights in US by Regional Carriers

> Readers might well ask why the A330 crash of Air France Flight 447 into the South Atlantic is in the next ('Fly-by-Wire') chapter and the Colgan crash is in this one, when in both cases the inappropriate reaction of the pilot(s) to stall warnings was apparently the cause.
>
> This is simply because the 'Fly-by-Wire' chapter specifically covers aircraft such as the Airbus A330 with sophisticated computer control systems, and until the remarkable recovery of the flight recorders from the depths of the South Atlantic, many assumed these systems were themselves responsible for the disaster.
>
> *[Colgan Air Flight 3407]*

Though not historically a major disaster in terms of the number of lives lost, the Colgan Air Continental Airlines Connecting Flight 3407 crash[1] described here received much attention because fatal air crashes in the US had become rare. Another reason was that it made the American public realize how many flights seemingly flown by the majors (with their flight numbers and even their livery) are actually operated by regional airlines.

Though the Canadian-built Bombardier C4 turboprop airliner[2] used for Flight 3407 had Continental livery (colors), employees of Colgan Air[3] operated and serviced the flight exclusively. Following the accident, legislators passed laws to make purchasers of airline tickets more able to determine on which airline they are actually flying.

Salaries and working conditions at commuter airlines as opposed to the majors are less than generous. The 47-year-old male captain and the 24-year-old female first officer, whose gross salary had been $15,800 during the previous year and was less than that of a bus driver, spent much of the flight discussing the difficulties they had in relation to this. (The cockpit voice recorder or CVR also recorded the captain stating that he earned a gross salary of about $60,000.) The captain resided in Florida and the first officer in Washington State, both on the other side of the country with respect to their New Jersey operating base. Both had at one time considered having proper 'crash pads' at New Jersey but for financial reasons had not done so—there was always the option of resting or sleeping in the crew lounge.

The first officer had come in from Seattle early that morning. She had managed to get a reasonable amount of rest in the crew lounge and on the flight from Seattle. She was suffering from a cold and had stated in an exchange prior to takeoff that had circumstances been different she would have called in sick.
She had said:

> I'm ready to be in the hotel room.

The captain had replied:

> I feel bad for you.

To which she replied:

> This is one of those times that if I felt like this when I was at home there's no way I would have come all the way out here. If I call in sick now I've got to put myself in a hotel until I feel better ... we'll see how... it feels flying. If the pressure's just too much ... I could always call in tomorrow at least I'm in a hotel on the company's buck but we'll see. I'm pretty tough.

The CVR recorded her sniveling and occasionally yawning during the flight. The captain himself suffered from a sleep deficit built up over several days and could be heard yawning on the CVR. The rest that he had had that morning in less than ideal conditions in the crew lounge could hardly have made up for that deficit.

The flight was to be a short 53-minute hop across New York State to Buffalo on the edge of Lake Eerie. Near the border with Canada, Buffalo is the second largest city in New York State, and consequently they were over built-up areas as the aircraft approached the airport.

The CVR recorded the Newark tower controller clearing the airplane for takeoff at about 21:18:23 Eastern Standard Time.

The first officer acknowledged the clearance, and the captain stated:

> All right, cleared for takeoff, it's mine.

The intended cruise altitude for the flight was 16,000 ft mean sea level (msl) and the flight data recorder (FDR) showed that, during the climb to altitude, the propeller de-icing and airframe de-icing equipment were turned on (the pitot static de-icing equipment had been turned on before takeoff) and the autopilot was engaged.

The airplane reached its cruising altitude of 16,000 ft at about 21:34:44. The cruise portion of the flight was routine and uneventful, and the only thing remarkable about it was the rapport between the two pilots, which resulted in them indulging in almost continuous non-essential personal conversation. Although not in conflict with the sterile cockpit rule, which prohibits non-essential conversations within the cockpit during critical phases of flight, as they were above 10,000 ft, it did mean that certain tasks such as checklists were delayed until the very end of the flight when they would be busy.

At about 21:53:40, the first officer briefed the captain on the airspeeds for landing with the flaps at 15° (flaps 15), namely 118 knots as the reference landing speed ($V_{REF}$), and 114 knots as the go-around speed ($V_{GA}$). The captain acknowledged this information.

Determining the so-called reference speed (for landing) is a key aspect of any landing as it is the airspeed needed to ensure a stabilized safe landing. However, the airspeed that the first officer gave was that for normal conditions, not icy conditions under which say an extra 20 knots is added to allow for wings, stabilizers, and control surfaces performing less than optimally.

The flight continued to descend under approach control with the captain confirming in his briefing the airspeed for the 15° flaps landing.

About 22:10:23, the first officer asked whether ice had been accumulating on the windshield, and the captain replied that ice was present on his side of the windshield and asked whether ice was present on her windshield side. The first officer responded, '*Lots of ice.*' The captain then stated, '*That's the most I've seen—most ice I've seen on the leading edges in a long time. In a while anyway I should say.*' About 10 seconds later, the captain and the first officer began a conversation that was unrelated to their flying duties.

At about 22:12:18, the approach controller cleared the flight crew to descend and maintain 2,300 feet, and the first officer acknowledged the clearance. Afterward, the captain and the first officer performed flight-related duties but also continued the conversation that was unrelated to their flying duties. About 22:12:44, the approach controller cleared the flight crew to turn left onto a heading of 330°. At about 22:13:25 and 22:13:36, the captain called for the descent and approach checklists, respectively, which the first officer performed. About 22:14:09, the approach controller cleared the flight crew to turn left onto a heading of 310°.

The altitude hold mode became active as the aircraft was approaching the preselected altitude of 2,300 feet, which was reached about 22:14:30 with the airspeed about 180 knots at the time.

The captain began to slow the aircraft less than three miles from the outer marker to establish the appropriate airspeed before landing. According to FDR data, the engine power levers were reduced to about 42° (flight idle was 35°) at about 22:16:00, and both engines' torque values were at minimum thrust at about 22:16:02. The approach controller then handed them over to the BUF ATC tower controller. The first officer's acknowledgement of this instruction was the last communication between the flight crew and ATC.

When the first officer at about 22:16:21 told the captain that the gear was down the airspeed was roughly 145 knots. The reduced airspeed meant the autopilot had to apply additional pitch trim in the aircraft-nose-up direction to maintain the 2,300-ft altitude. An 'ice detected' message appeared on the engine display in the cockpit. About the same time, the captain called for the flaps to be set to 15° and for the before landing checklist. The airspeed was then about 135 knots.

At 22:16:27.4, the CVR recorded a sound similar to the stick shaker. (The stick shaker warns a pilot of an impending wing aerodynamic stall through vibrations on the control column, providing tactile and aural cues.) The CVR also recorded a sound similar to the autopilot disconnect horn, which repeated until the end of the recording.

When the autopilot disengaged, the airspeed had dropped to 131 knots. FDR data showed that 0.4 seconds later the control columns moved aft and that the engine power levers were advanced to about 70° (the rating detent was 80°) 1 second later. The CVR then recorded a sound similar to increased engine power, and FDR data showed that the engine power had increased to about 75% torque.

The stall warning (stick shaker) activates 7 knots or so before an actual stall. However, as the 'reference speed' switch on the 'icing panel' had been turned to 'Increase,' the stick shaker would activate at about 20 knots higher than it otherwise would have done. In addition, the airspeed indicator would have shown the low speed red markings coming up on the band. Surprisingly, in view of all the talk about icing, the pilots had not even considered increasing their reference landing speed.

The captain had not called out 'stall' when the stick shaker activated, nor had the first officer called out 'positive rate' when the aircraft climbed in response to the captain (presumably) pulling back on his control column. While the increase in power (not to the maximum) could not immediately influence the airspeed, putting the aircraft into a climb certainly did, and it declined rapidly.

After pitching up, the aircraft rolled to the left, reaching a roll angle of 45° left wing down; and then rolled to the right. As it rolled to the right through wings level, the stick pusher[4] activated at about 22:16:34, at which point flaps 0 was selected.

At about 22:16:37, the first officer told the captain that she had put the flaps up, even though she had not been ordered to do so, and in so doing had made recovery from the stall even more difficult as the aircraft would have to fly even faster in a no flaps configuration.

FDR data confirmed that the flaps had begun to retract by 22:16:38; at that time, the aircraft's airspeed was about 100 knots. FDR data also showed that the roll angle reached 105° right wing down before the aircraft began to roll back to the left and the stick pusher activated a second time (about 22:16:40). At the time, the aircraft's pitch angle was -1°.

At about 22:16:42, the CVR recorded the captain making a grunting sound. The roll angle had reached about 35° left wing down before the aircraft began to roll again to the right. Afterward, the first officer asked whether she should put the landing gear up, and the captain stated '*gear up*' and an expletive. It was too late. The aircraft pitched about 25° nose down, with a roll angle of 100° right wing down, respectively, with the aircraft entering a steep descent. The stick pusher activated a third time (about 22:16:50), and two seconds later the FDR data showed that the flaps had retracted fully. About the same time, the CVR recorded the captain stating, '*We're down*,' and the sound of a thump.

The aircraft had come down on a single-family home and a post-crash fire ensued. The death toll was 50: 1 person killed in the house, and all 49 occupants of the aircraft. The fire, partly augmented by escaping gas from a gas main to the house, destroyed much of the aircraft, making recovery of the bodies and evidence very difficult. However, finding the extremities such as the nose, wingtips and tail showed the aircraft had not broken up prior to hitting the ground. Investigators quickly recovered the FDR and the CVR, and found them to be in good condition.

## Probable Cause

The NTSB ultimately determined that the probable cause was:

1. **The captain's inappropriate response to the activation of the stick shaker, which led to an aerodynamic stall from which the airplane did not recover.**

Contributing to the accident was:

1. **The flight crew's failure to monitor airspeed in relation to the rising of the low speed cue.**

2. **The flight crew's failure to adhere to sterile cockpit procedures.**

3. **The captain's failure to effectively manage the flight.**

4. **Colgan Air's inadequate procedures for airspeed selection and management during approaches in icing conditions.**

There were differing opinions at the NTSB as to how much fatigue was a factor, with some believing it should have been included in the contributing causes. After publication of the official report, a lawyer for families suing over the crash said that newly released emails showed Colgan Air doubted the captain's ability to fly the plane six months before it crashed. These emails were not made available to the NTSB in the course of their enquiry. Colgan Air had admitted that they might well not have employed the captain had they been aware of all the checks that he had failed before they engaged him.

The NTSB recommended that there should be a limit to the number of failed checks a pilot was allowed before his or her dismissal. However, the FAA considered this to be too arbitrary and impractical. Yet, there have been a number of cases, including a recent Nigerian one, where pilots responsible for crashes have been found to have a checkered history as regards check rides, and with hindsight should perhaps have been let go. Instead of being fired, such pilots are generally sent for remedial training, but one wonders whether any amount of remedial training can make up for a lack of innate aptitude or ability to analyze while under stress. At one time, many commercial pilots in the US came from the military where the weak ones were quickly weeded out.

Ironically, it was the extra 'safety feature,' namely the special switch for increasing the reference speed setting for icy conditions that caused the stick shaker to operate and the captain to react perhaps in panic, which bears out the contention of Charles Perrow that the safety systems can cause accidents.

The first officer, who was considered to be above average for her level of experience, did not help matters by raising the flaps. Her failure to note the rising low-speed cue with its red markings on the band of the airspeed indicator was attributed to the fact that she was preoccupied with other tasks.

Gossiping had delayed tasks such as checklists. Then the lowering of the flaps and undercarriage would have diverted her attention from the altimeter to the central console. Of course, the captain should have been monitoring the airspeed himself and picked up on the rise of the red low speed cue. Could his alleged tendency to rely more than usual on the autopilot to do the flying have got him out of the habit of monitoring airspeed? His failure to call out 'stall' possibly led to the first officer to react incorrectly by raising the flaps (to which the captain did not object). To what extent her bad cold and fatigue impaired her monitoring and decision-making is difficult to determine.

---

[1] The previous disaster had similarly involved a commuter airline, the Comair Flight 191 crash in August 2006, where the aircraft with 50 people aboard had taken off on the wrong (much too short) runway. Only the first officer survived, having suffered terrible injuries.

[2] Designed to carry 74 passengers and 4 crewmembers (2 pilots, 2 cabin crew).

[3] Colgan Air was a regional carrier that flew routes under contract for US Airways, United, and Continental. Pinnacle Airlines Corp, the parent company of Pinnacle Airlines and Colgan Air, filed for bankruptcy protection on April 1, 2012. Pinnacle said it would rework contracts with Delta and end flying for United and US Airways. The company also said it wanted to cut its labor and operating costs.

[4] As a last resort, it pushes the nose down so the aircraft can gain speed. It can be countered and overridden by the pilot.

# CHAPTER 9
# 'FLY-BY-WIRE'

## NEW A320 CRASHES AT AIR SHOW
## (Habsheim 1988)
### Did the Computer Crash The Aircraft?

> The crash of a brand-new Airbus 320 at a tiny air show seemed a
> bad portent for what was to be one of the most successful aircraft
> and led to years of argument. Was the pilot responsible? On the
> other hand, was it the computer?
>
> *[Air France Sightseeing/Air Show Demonstration flight]*

Air France had planned a sightseeing charter flight with what they hoped
would be yet another impressive air show demonstration of their new
extra-sophisticated A320 Airbus. This time the A320 was to be shown off at
Habsheim, a tiny airfield situated close to the border with Germany and
Switzerland. On its way from Paris, the A320 would stop off at nearby Bâle-
Mulhouse Airport. There sightseers would board with the prospect of being
taken to see France's highest mountain, Mont Blanc, 25 minutes' flight time
to the south, after the demonstration at the air show.

Provided the pilot did not sink below the minimum permitted height of
100 ft (30 m) given in his instructions and his track kept to that of the
3,300-ft (1,000-m) paved runway with an obstacle-free (i.e. no trees)
overrun space extending some 650 ft (200 m) beyond the end, the site was
reasonably acceptable.

However, unbeknown to the Airbus pilots, the show's organizers had
placed the spectators facing a grass landing strip (destined for ultra-light
aircraft and gliders) set at a 40-degree angle to the paved runway. Besides
being only 2,500 ft (765 m) in length, this grass landing strip ended a mere
200 ft (60 m) from the edge of a dense forest of young oak and birch trees,
with many reaching to a height of 40 ft (12 m)!

Some say that a quick glance from above and afar might well have given
the impression the closely packed trees represented a different color field
or mere bushes. However, it would seem quite probable that the pilots—
with no time to assess the situation—presumed the spectators would be

located along a landing strip suitable for flying demonstrations with no immediate obstacles.

Air France management had officially approved the application from the organizers of the air show, but final arrangements were hurried and seem somewhat haphazard. The company only gave the file with the details of the operation to the pilots just before they left Paris, with no verbal briefing about conditions. The map of the airfield did not have a key to the symbols used, which might have been obvious had it not been a black-and-white photocopy of a colored map. However, Air France had previously done flyovers at Habsheim air shows, and it may have seemed a routine affair.

Since the two pilots chosen for the jaunt, Captain Michel Asseline (44) and copilot Captain Pierre Mazières (45) were both management captains rather than line captains—always a dangerous proposition—Air France staff perhaps too easily assumed they would be able to responsibly assess the situation for themselves and be able to perform the task without much oversight. However, neither of them were test pilots, nor pilots with any experience of giving demonstrations at air shows.

As head of Air France's A320 training division and as one of the people responsible for liaising with the manufacturer over the technical aspects of the introduction of the A320 into Air France's fleet, Asseline had experience of executing the dramatic maneuver he was planning. He told his doubting first officer he had done it 20 times. While true, this would certainly have been over airfields with plenty of space and in an A320 probably carrying much less weight in terms of fuel and passengers, if any.

Their instructions were to pick up the sightseers at Bâle-Mulhouse airport and, in the mere *five minutes* it would take them to fly from there to Habsheim, to lose height and speed, lower the flaps and landing gear, before performing a low-level pass at 100 ft (30 m) followed by that dramatic climb out to impress the spectators. Asseline intended to make this maneuver even more impressive by using the ability of the computer to fly closer to the stall limit than a human could normally manage.

He would reduce the airspeed to just above the minimum needed to maintain horizontal flight, and let the computer do the rest—namely raise the nose very high to keep the aircraft flying parallel to the ground. Of course, to do this he would have to disengage the Alpha floor safety mode designed to rescue the aircraft from dangerously high angle of attack situations (such as might develop in wind shear and the operation in question). The Alpha floor safety mode would otherwise apply full takeoff/go-around power via the auto-throttle and spoil the party.

Though the computer could be relied on to not let aircraft stall at the minimum airspeed, it would be a risky procedure if there were any obstacles in the aircraft's path as it would be difficult to climb away at that minimal airspeed, and especially so if the engines were still idling and would therefore take time to spool up.

It is a tenet of both airlines and the military that pilots making a landing (which this maneuver resembled) conduct a *stabilized* approach. Stabilized means the aircraft should have steadied and be properly lined up, and, as far as possible, be at the right speed well before the runway. Hurried last minute, possibly ill-judged, maneuvers are to be avoided.

The short distance between Bâle-Mulhouse (where they were to pick up the passengers) and Habsheim would give the pilots scant time to descend and stabilize in the best of circumstances. In addition, their unfamiliarity with the area would mean they would be looking for landmarks.

With the sightseers picked up at Bâle-Mulhouse Airport on board, and Asseline announcing, '*I am going to demonstrate the progress made by*[1] *French aviation,*' the jaunt was taking on the trappings of a trip to the circus—which is in fact what it turned out to be. A circus act shown on TV worldwide. The subsequent inquiry suggested the presence of the sightseers had created a 'holiday' feeling in Captain Asseline.

The A320 turned towards Habsheim with maximum bank and climbed to the 1,000 ft altitude authorized by the Bâle-Mulhouse Airport control tower. Still at almost 1,000 ft, they lined up with Habsheim with only two minutes to go.

As he dropped to 100 ft (30 m), and simultaneously tried to reduce speed, Asseline suddenly realized that the spectators were placed to view performances along the axis of that grass landing strip set at a 40-degree angle to that of the paved runway, and some distance away.

Just when he should have been stabilizing the aircraft at 100 ft, he had to adjust his course, and as aircraft tend to lose some lift when banking, the A320 came in losing further height. Adding to its vulnerability was the fact that the engines were throttled back to idle so Asseline could get the airspeed down to that 'minimum flyable airspeed' in time for the computer to 'show off' by pushing the nose up at the sharpest possible angle without stalling.

The aircraft did just as it was expected to do, ending up with its nose pointing upwards at a maximum of 15 degrees, and with its trajectory virtually horizontal over the grass landing strip, which would have been fine except that the pilots had started the maneuver too low. The dangling main wheels were just 30 ft (10 m), instead of 100 ft (30 m), above the grass strip. Some have suggested that having the nose so high up and the tail so low made the pilots feel they were higher than they were. The small scale of the airfield might also have deceived a captain used to runways four times as long and control towers three times as high. Others contest this.

Moments earlier, Mazières had warned Asseline about electricity pylons carrying power lines some three kilometers ahead and the captain told him not to worry as he had seen them. What neither of them had realized was that the dark green patch just before the pylons was a forest with trees so densely packed together that they did not stand out when viewed from above from a distance. As mentioned, some were *40 ft (13 m) high*.

With the trees dead ahead and as high if not higher than they were (in the nose-up cockpit), Mazières was the first to see the danger.

He shouted '*Go-around!*' and they applied maximum power, hoping to climb away.

However, the aircraft was performing at the limit of its flight envelope and having had to lose height with the engines throttled back, it had no immediately available reserves of energy, either in terms of (1) momentum (airspeed) or (2) engine thrust.

### 1. Momentum (airspeed)

If an aircraft is flying well above its stalling speed and flying normally, simply pulling back on the controls will make it rise almost immediately. However, here the computer had been 'told' to fly at a speed so close to stalling speed that it would have to put the nose up in the air just to stay level. Even were the computers to allow the pilots to push the nose up further which is doubtful, the aircraft would have doubtless stalled. In addition, that nose-up attitude would already have been producing considerable drag and preventing it from gaining forward airspeed.

### 2. Engine thrust

With nothing available in terms of airspeed, the only hope was to power up the engines. However, unlike the engines in a car with an internal combustion engine, jet engines do not give instant power, and this is particularly true when idling, as indeed these were.

This meant the engines would take six if not eight seconds just to spool up, and *begin* accelerating the aircraft, which was probably slowing even more due to the attempt to climb over the trees.

Videos show the preening Air France A320 approaching and passing in front of the camera. Then, just above the ground, it continues, preening even more to try to maintain its height. Heading straight for the trees, the bird must surely be going to heave itself up, but its resources seem to fail it. As if making a perfect landing, the A320's rear underside brushes the trees, with it still seeming possible it might lift off. It then sinks into the foliage like a drowning swimmer engulfed by the waves. A few moments later a dense cloud of smoke billows up from a point slightly further on.

The two airfield fire appliances and an ambulance with a doctor attending the show, rushed to the scene. Appliances from local fire departments tried to join them, but the larger vehicles were unable to get through the closely spaced trees.

Amazingly, 133 of the 136 people on board managed to escape before fire consumed the entire aircraft except for the tail and part of a wing. The passengers owed their relative 'good fortune' to their lack of hand luggage (a point to remember!) and the fact that many were young physically able, first-time flyers, who had noted the location of the exits during the pre-flight briefing. Unfortunately, this meant some would not know how to release their seat belt buckle (another point to remember as they differ from those in cars).

The three that perished were a handicapped boy, a young girl who had been unable to undo her seat belt perhaps because she had not been able to do it immediately and people behind had pushed her forward trapping her against the belt, and a courageous woman who came back to help her. A female flight attendant helping people exit from the front apparently went back into the cabin to check there was no one left. Not being able to see because of the smoke, she called out and got no reply—perhaps the three were already unconscious due to smoke inhalation.

Thirty-four passengers required hospital treatment for burns and injuries. In addition to suffering from shock and smoke inhalation, the two pilots were briefly hospitalized for minor injuries to the head and collarbones.

TV news bulletins around the world replayed and replayed the dramatic footage of the crash—much to the chagrin of the aircraft's manufacturer (Airbus Industries) and Air France who had only taken delivery of the aircraft some three days earlier. The media and particularly competitors made much ado about the crash of this innovative aircraft representing the new so-called 'fly-by-wire' technology, which, thanks to computers, was supposed to enable aircraft to fly more safely. Some people, particularly in America, mocked Airbus, saying it seemed their computer had been making a perfect landing—on the trees.

With this very public loss of their 'new generation' aircraft, the manufacturer and Air France went into a panic. Many prospective orders were at stake. The reputation of Airbus Industries (a consortium of France, Germany, Britain, Spain and West German companies) was at stake. For the French, it was considered, no doubt justifiably, an Affair of State, as it threatened their budding aircraft industry at a delicate moment. Many jobs, not to mention prestige, depended on it.

### The aftermath

For a crash where 'only' 3 people died and 'merely' 34 were injured enough to require some degree of hospitalization, a surprising amount of controversy and bitterness ensued for more than a decade. The fact that investigators recovered the black boxes intact, the fact that they had the benefit of the pilots being able to explain their actions, and the fact that there were several video recordings of the event (some audio) did not hasten a resolution. Nobody trusted anybody.

Court cases continued, on and off, for some ten years. The various parties—Captain Asseline, the survivors and the injured, Air France, Airbus Industries and even the French Government—fought legal battles and exchanged insults over it.

An exasperated Air France official was reported as saying, with more than a grain of truth,[2] something like:

*There would have been less trouble had the people died.*

There were accusations that officials had tampered with the 'black boxes.' Air France sidelined as 'unfit for duty' a pilot who came out in support of Captain Asseline. The man in question thereafter remained an implacable foe of the airline and the aviation authorities. He has had no end of trouble ever since on account of his comments and the critical books he wrote—even accusing a Cabinet Minister of being involved in the alleged tampering of the digital flight data recorder (DFDR) and cockpit voice recorder (CVR) tapes. Reduced almost to the state of a beggar, he pursued the fight on the Internet to keep life and soul together.

As is the case in so many dramatic events—even President Kennedy's assassination—securing the 'crime scene' and evidence is not usually uppermost in people's minds at the time. In the rush to analyze the CVR and DFDR tapes, those involved were casual in their handling of those valuable items of evidence. Then, when a judge later ordered their surrender to him, they were not immediately available—leading to increased suspicion that the authorities had been in the process of doctoring them.

Captain Asseline first maintained that the accident had occurred because the engines failed to spool up. Then on seeing video showing how low he was, he suggested the barometric altimeter might have been giving the wrong reading because of a bug in the software. He also said he pulled the throttles back for a moment when the engines did not respond, as from his experience, he knew that was the way to 'reset' the system.

The subsequent inquiry laid the blame for the disaster largely on Captain Asseline, but also criticized Air France for their casual approach to the whole operation. His pilot's license was revoked, and Air France dismissed him while retaining the services of Mazières. Asseline then wrote a book called: *Le Pilote–Est-il coupable?* (The Pilot—Is he the guilty one?).

## An Affair of State

It was an *Affair of State*, whatever way one looked at it. A number of people maintaining there was a cover up admit that if there were one, the government officials involved did so not for personal gain but with the best of motives.

Regardless of whether any credence can be given to the conspiracy theorists, Asseline's envisaged maneuver, which Mazières questioned at the time, was a reckless act over a tiny airfield.

Furthermore, Asseline was literally playing to the gallery—even making an additional announcement in perfect German for those of his sightseeing passengers unable to understand French. His statement that *'he was going to demonstrate the evolution of French aviation'* was almost the language of a stunt or test pilot not an airline pilot. However, stunt and test pilots risking their lives are careful individuals who study venues very carefully beforehand. In addition, at Bâle-Mulhouse Airport he had been taking part in a press conference rather than concentrating on the operation on hand.

Having made showing off so important, one can understand how difficult it would have been for him to perform his stunt away from the spectators.

Admittedly, Air Frances's idea of combining sightseeing and an air show demonstration was not a good one and could have contributed to his buoyant mood.

Apart from the rashness of undertaking such a maneuver at an unfamiliar site with an almost full load of passengers, another fault would seem to be that Asseline took the Air France regulations regarding the 100 ft fly-past height in a landing configuration (i.e. landing gear and flaps lowered) too literally.

The 100 ft minimum height was surely set for large flat open areas such as major airfields or airports. In a confined area such as Habsheim airfield, the height of nearby obstacles such as the trees and the electricity pylons in the distance obviously should have been taken into account.

Asseline probably would have missed the trees had he aimed to fly at that 100 ft + 35 ft to allow for obstacles in the general area. This would no doubt have been so, regardless of whether as he later claimed, his altimeter had misled him, his engines had not spooled up *quite* as fast[3] as claimed by the investigators, and the aircraft did not lift when it should have done.

In any case, as it was not a large airfield he should have maintained a greater safety margin and have been prepared for, say a bird strike affecting an engine, in such a confined space.

Some people find his fight over the years to prove he was right—harming Airbus and Air France in the process—difficult to comprehend. However, as any 'good driver' involved in even a minor road accident knows, one tends to replay and replay events, finding things in one's favor. This must be especially true when the individual has so much at stake.

While Air France management surely had much to answer for, the captaincy of a ship or aircraft is associated with the concept of 'command responsibility.' That is to say, the captain should exercise good judgmentand make appropriate decisions regardless of the pressures to which he or she may be subject, and regardless of the poor decisions made by others. In that sense, Asseline's flamboyant Master-of-Ceremonies approach seemed inappropriate. The title of Asseline's book asking whether the pilot is guilty seems to go against this command responsibility principle.

As for Air France management, one can surely say that Asseline would never have been placed in the situation he was had things been properly planned and better executed.

The present author remembers how in the early 1960s, a young Frenchman told him he was going to be a pilot with Air France. The conversation went on as follows with the author speaking first:

*That must be difficult! Why are you so certain?*

*J'ai du piston!*[4] *(I know the right people)*

Pilots are required to have high minimum standards, so probably there was not much to worry about, and the young man in question did look as if he would make an excellent pilot. However, selection of people on the management side may not have been so rigorous. If true, Air France would not have been the only 'piston' airline flying jets. While Air France has perhaps raised its game since then, those other airlines may not have done so.

Once again, although one can fault Captain Asseline, it was an accident where many factors came into play.

---

[1] He used the French word '*continuité*' (continuity), which is difficult to translate. 'Progress made by' seems closest.

[2] Proved right in the case of the Concorde crash where everyone died and claims were settled easily.

[3] The manufacturer of the engines subsequently improved their reaction time.

[4] *Piston(fr.)* is a familiar word in French meaning to know someone who can give you an (unfair) advantage in obtaining a post or similar.

# INDIAN AIRLINES AIRBUS A320
# (Bangalore 1990)
### Another A320 Crash

> The A320's engine manufacturer subsequently improved reaction time, and the aircraft operated for a time without further crashes.
>
> However, just as Airbus seemed to be leaving the bad publicity of the Habsheim crash behind it, there was another Airbus A320 crash.
>
> *[Indian Airlines Flight 605]*

The Indian Airlines[1] A320 Airbus had taken off from Bombay (Mumbai) with 146 people on board, including two captains in the cockpit. Both captains were experienced, but had comparatively few flying hours on the A320, which with its sophisticated computer systems differed considerably from the aircraft they had previously flown, notably turboprops and 737s.

On the final part of the flight into Bangalore in Southern India, the route-checking captain in the right-hand seat was the pilot flying (PF). This was a strange state of affairs as the check captain had only flown about 68 hours in the A320 and was not certified by Airbus Industries to be a check captain on the A320. Furthermore, the Indian civil aviation authorities had instructed the airline that the captain in question be *positively monitored* with regard to matters such as the sophisticated Flight Management Guidance System (FMGS) on the A320. Not only that, the people instructing him on the A320 had observed 'numerous small errors and omissions ...' regarding the use of the FMGS and operation of the power controls.

At one point, the captain undergoing the check asked whether the check captain flying the aircraft realized they were in the OIDM Mode and suggested they switch to the Heading Vertical Speed Mode. The suggestion was apparently ignored.

Making its final approach to Bangalore with its landing gear already lowered the A320 was descending, but as it descended, it started sinking rapidly and was soon below the intended glide path—with its speed less than it should have been for an approach. Although it was obvious they were not going to make the runway, the pilots took no action, despite two sink rate warnings and four altitude alerts.

Only when they were at 140 ft, still sinking rapidly, and with the computer pushing the nose up to a high angle of attack to compensate for the minimal airspeed, did the pilot non-flying (NF) shout, '*Hey, we're going down!*' and push the throttle levers for a TOGA (takeoff-go-around). In fact, the Alpha floor safety mode (disabled at the Habsheim air show) ensured the computer was already spooling up the engines.

Even with the engines speeding up faster than certified—and perhaps faster due to improvements made in the light of the Habsheim disaster—the high sink rate combined with excessively low airspeed meant saving the situation would prove impossible in the 100 or so feet available.

With the nose pointing upwards—but less than it would have been had the computer not prevented the aircraft from going into a stall when the pilots pulled their sidesticks back fully—the aircraft came down hard on a golf course over half a kilometer from the runway. After bouncing and forcing its way through some small trees, it skidded over a green. Slowing more, but not enough to prevent the embankment around the course shearing off the engines, the aircraft finally ended its headlong charge just before the airport's perimeter wall and caught fire.

Despite the proximity of the airport, the fire service took more than 20 minutes to reach the scene. This was due to the locking of a gate for security reasons, a bad airport road, and lack of a radio link with the control tower.

By the time the fire services arrived, there was nothing they could do except help those who had already escaped. At Habsheim, almost everyone on board escaped even though the A320 had caught fire immediately. This was largely due to them being able to save themselves thanks to the soft 'landing.' At Bangalore, 54 people out of 146 survived. Many were seriously injured. Both pilots perished.

The inquiry found that, contrary to instructions in the operating manual, the aircraft had been descending in *Open/Idle Descent Mode (OIDM Mode)* with too low an airspeed for an approach. It should have been the *Heading/Vertical Speed Mode* coupled with the Flight Director System to keep the aircraft pointing in the desired direction and most importantly control the rate of descent, not letting dangerously high rates of descent develop.

Thus, once again, it seemed an A320 had crashed because a senior pilot had not used the sophisticated systems wisely and appropriately. Some say, the aircraft was too sophisticated for Indian Airlines at the time.

Some of the information in this section is from Macarthur Job's *Air Disaster* (Vol. 3) and it is perhaps worth mentioning that Job says:

> *Both crewmembers instinctively pulled their sidesticks to full nose-up elevator, a control input which in any other aircraft, would have resulted in a catastrophic stall.*

> *But the computerized flight control system limited the nose-up attitude to the maximum permissible angle of attack.*

On the other hand, as the Indian aircraft was almost on the ground and sinking fast, a much higher angle of attack leading to a stall might have given a little extra lift and forward deceleration, thus making the aircraft come down less hard and with less forward momentum. It would have been like the 'flare' pilots perform on landing, but an excessive one with the tail striking first. Without more information, it is not possible to say whether this speculation is valid. It just goes to show how difficult it is to program the computer for every eventuality, especially when an unexpected situation develops due to human error or exceptional circumstances (see Bilbao).

## Bilbao

An incident on February 7, 2001 at Bilbao in Spain in which no one was killed, but was serious enough for the aircraft to be written off, was principally caused by wind shear, the airport not being equipped with wind shear detection equipment and the failure of the air traffic controllers to warn the pilots of the conditions. However, it is interesting in that it prompted Airbus to remove a 'safety feature' and go back to an earlier version of their software. The safety feature had been brought in because it was believed it would be advisable to incorporate a feature that would keep the nose down in the event of the angle of attack (alpha) increasing too rapidly—ironically as might happen in the case of wind shear.

In the Bilbao incident, this feature hindered a recovery, in that the pilots were unable to break the extremely high sinking rate (1,200 fpm) by pushing nose up to make the aircraft flare sharply just above the runway. The nose wheel collapsed and the aircraft skidded 3,280 feet (about 1000m) down the runway before coming to a halt.

## Recriminations

After the crash, the Indian Government claimed Airbus was 'undermining' the reputation of the Indian Airlines pilots, and said the check captain was an excellent pilot (even though not certified by Airbus to be a check captain).

A French newspaper 'countered' by claiming that C. A. Fernandez, the pilot being checked out, had performed badly in stress situations, had been referred for extended basic training in India and had not been certified as passing. As mentioned, the check captain actually flying the aircraft had been found wanting by Indian government officials during tests.

Despite this early scare and spat, which led to the temporary grounding of the airline's A320s, the company has since purchased or leased many A320s.

---

[1] Indian Airlines was mainly a domestic airline, but has recently merged with the also state-owned Air India.

# QF72, INFLIGHT UPSET OF QANTAS A330 (Off N. Australia 2008)

## Unbuckled Passengers Hit Ceiling Panels

> The following incident is of particular interest because it highlights the problems *possibly* caused by a failure of the Air Data Inertial Reference Unit (ADIRU), which is a key component of *fly-by-wire* aircraft.
>
> Lawyers representing relatives of victims of the Air France A330 crash (see next narrative) are attempting to draw parallels with this incident. However, in that case problems with the pitot probes seem to have been a factor, not mentioned at all in this case.
>
> *[Qantas Flight 72]*

As in the case of the Qantas Bangkok overrun, the Australian Air Transport Safety Bureau (ATSB) has produced very comprehensive reports, namely a fact-giving interim report and a final report. As the nub of the reports is technical, namely the performance of the Air Data Inertial Reference Unit (ADIRU) and the way the computers were programmed rather than human actions, it is really for techies wanting to know how fly-by-wire aircraft work or those who think it might have some relevance to the Air France A330 crash described next.

### In the Passenger Cabins

The Qantas Airbus A330, with 303 passengers, 9 cabin crew and 3 flight crew on board, had taken off from Singapore for Perth on October 7, 2008 at 09:32 local time. It was a regular scheduled flight with flight number QF72.

Having completed almost two thirds of their journey and with the aircraft cruising at 37,000 ft, the passengers were relaxing after their meal, with some on their feet to visit the toilet, when the aircraft suddenly pitched slightly downwards before pitching nose-down even more. After leveling out and climbing to regain height, the same thing happened again, except that the upset was less violent.

The first upset was particularly brutal; passengers were thrown about, with one woman hitting the fascia above her so hard that it left a dent, before falling back with a bleeding head wound. Most of the injured were those who had left their seat belts unbuckled. A few whose seat belts were loosely attached (and often near the limit of their extension) claimed they became unclasped as they were thrown upwards—it seems the clasp got snagged under the arm rest. Those standing were injured, as were the two in the toilet—one seriously, the other less so.

Altogether, one member of the cabin crew and 11 passengers suffered serious injuries. Eight members of the cabin crew and 95 passengers received minor injuries, leaving 200 persons[1] (3 crew and 197 passengers) relatively unscathed, though the roller coaster experience must have been quite traumatic.

## On the Flight Deck

At 12:40:28, and a couple of minutes before the first upset, the autopilot disconnected. There followed a series of warnings that this or that system had failed.

At 12:42:27, and with the pilots having had to take control while still trying to evaluate the confusing situation, the nose of the aircraft pitched downwards without any such input command from the pilots. The maximum pitch-down angle was about 8.4° with the aircraft dropping 650 ft. The crew brought the aircraft back to its cruising height of 37,000 ft, all the time trying to deal with the cascade of failure messages. At 12:45:08, the aircraft made an uncommanded pitch down again. However, this second time, the pitch-down angle only attained about 3.5°, with the drop in height less too, at just 400 ft.

The aircrew made a 'Pan ... Pan ... Pan...'[2] call and diverted to Learmonth, a back-up Australian Air Force base also used by civilian aircraft. When informed by the cabin crew of the gravity of some of the injuries, the pilots made a Mayday call.

Because they were unable to enter a GPS approach into the flight management computer, they made a straight-in visual approach from about 15 nm, acquiring the precision approach path indicator (PAPI) at about 10 nm. They touched down safely at Learmonth at 13:50, with the passengers somewhat apprehensive due to the time taken making orbits before landing.

## The Investigation

Though much information about what happened was available from the pilots, from the digital flight data recorder (DFDR), from the Cockpit Voice Recorder (CVR), from the quick access data recorder (QAR), from the onboard fault monitoring systems and from data stored in the various units, it is proving difficult to determine every detail of what happened and why.

Adding to the problem is that it was not quite possible to say why the No. 1 ADIRU seemed to have malfunctioned in the way it did, with the investigations even looking at possible extraneous causes such as special military radio transmissions. Another aspect was that how the computers react to the (possibly false data) they receive from a failed ADIRU depends on how Airbus programmed them.

To see the great lengths to which the investigators have already gone and to learn much about the A330 fly-by-wire control systems, the author suggests the reader download the actual preliminary report, which as mentioned is more for the technically minded. As it gives the facts and details of the work done without conclusions, one cannot sum it up, and to do so would risk distortion.

## Other Incidents

Virtually any device can fail, and this is why essential ones such as ADIRUs are in triplicate, so that the computers can identify the faulty one as the odd one out. The report said the manufacturer in question stated the mean time between failures (MTBF) for the ADIRU model used on the aircraft in question was about 17,500 flight hours. According to the author, that would put the chance of two failing together at a very low figure. Even if they did, that should not affect the flight controls as they did, and Airbus has apparently stated they know of no such case where the ailerons have been affected—though it seems this aspect was a matter of programming and a rare data input combination.

The ATSB investigated an in-flight upset occurrence related to an ADIRU failure on a Boeing 777-200 aircraft, which occurred on August 1, 2005, 240 km north-west of Perth. The ADIRU on that aircraft was made by a different manufacturer and of a different type to that on QF72. Further details of that investigation can be found on the ATSB website.

The ATSB investigated other incidents where the ADIRUs had problems on Airbus A330s, with one occurring geographically rather near, and the other somewhat less near the location where this upset happened, leading to speculation that there might be some factor such as electromagnetic waves at play. However, this is thought to be most unlikely.

The ATSB's final report, dated December 19, 2011, attributed the incident to the combination of a design limitation in the flight control primary computer (FCPC) software of the Airbus A330/A340, and a failure mode affecting one of the aircraft's three ADIRUs. This meant that, in a very rare and specific situation, multiple spikes in angle of attack (AOA) data from one of the ADIRUs occurring more than 1.2 seconds apart (i.e. longer than the system would retain historic data on the assumption a spike was abnormal) could result in the FCPC commanding the aircraft to pitch down.

---

[1] As these were the officially reported figures, they may not give the full picture.

[2] Used instead of the well-known Mayday call to signify difficulties rather than a full emergency. The Swissair flight that caught fire after leaving New York used it, as they had not realized the gravity of the fire.

# AF447, A SEMINAL ACCIDENT
# (S. Atlantic 2009)
### The 'Startle Effect'

> Though it can be of scant consolation to the relatives and friends of those who lost their lives, the catastrophic drop of Air France Flight AF447 into the South Atlantic may have made flying safer, just as the series of crashes of the world's first jetliner, the de Havilland Comet, described in the next chapter, did in their day.
>
> The Comet crashes alerted manufacturers to the danger of cyclical stress concentrating at particular points of the fuselage. The AF447 Airbus A330 crash has now alerted airlines and their pilots to the danger of startled pilots being at a loss, and worst still, doing the wrong thing, on suddenly finding they must fly the aircraft manually when blissfully cruising at high altitude under autopilot.
>
> In the AF447 case, the pilots did not understand what was happening. The captain had gone for his rest ostensibly leaving the less experienced of the two copilots in charge.
>
> *[Air France Flight 447]*

At around 10:30 p.m. local time on August 31, 2009, Air France Flight 447 took off from Rio de Janeiro at almost its maximum takeoff weight. On board the twin-engine Airbus A330 were 216 passengers, and 12 crewmembers. The aircrew consisted of the captain and two first officers. The extra pilot was to allow them to take turns in having a rest over the long flight to Paris lasting some 11 hours.

The captain, 58-year-old Marc Dubois, had approximately 11,000 flight hours, of which 1,700 had been on the Airbus A330. The first officers were 37-year-old David Robert, with 6,500 hours, and 32-year-old Pierre-Cédric Bonin, with 2,900 hours.

Two and a half hours after liftoff, the A330 made its final radio exchange with Brazilian air traffic control (ATC) before reaching airspace over the Atlantic not covered by their radar. Later it would link up with Senegalese ATC in Africa on the other side of the South Atlantic.

The gap in radar coverage and the fact that they had not filed a definitive flight plan with the Senegalese meant that there was some confusion when to everyone's surprise the aircraft failed to appear on the radars on the other side of the ocean, with the various FIR (Flight Information Region) controllers questioning each other as to its whereabouts.

When it became clear none of them had been able to contact the aircraft, fears grew that some mishap had befallen it. Air France knew more than it was letting on, having received, independently of the pilots, automated maintenance messages beamed via satellite indicating abnormalities, including airspeed discrepancies and abnormal cabin pressure change.

The arrivals boards at Paris' Charles de Gaulle Airport had switched to indicating a delay, but with the 'delay' becoming interminable, it was obvious that something was seriously wrong. Air France had to admit the aircraft was lost. However, apart from those maintenance messages beamed via satellite there was no clue as to what had happened to it. It was a mystery, and there were many theories as to what might have happened, with many pointing out that it was flying in 'coffin corner'—that is at great height in very thin air where the safety margin between flying too fast and too slow is small.

A few days later, the Brazilians began recovering small amounts of wreckage, including the vertical stabilizer (tailfin), from the ocean surface. They also retrieved some 50 bodies, including that of the captain. A French submarine and vessels trawling with sideways-scanning detectors began searching for the locating signal of the digital flight data recorders (DFDR) and cockpit voice recorders (CVR). The localizers transmit for a month. It was claimed this search was unsuccessful because the water was almost 4 kilometers (2.5 miles) deep and the ocean floor very uneven in places.

Without the recorders, the accident might never be properly explained. However, the limited amount of wreckage and particularly the bodies recovered were sufficient to confirm the disaster had not been caused by an on board bomb.

This was the first disaster where automated messages sent via satellite for maintenance purposes looked as though they would be the main clue as to what actually happened. This led to proposals that aircraft flying in isolated places over oceans where recorders might never be recovered should transmit the extra data for air accident investigations purposes in addition to that required for maintenance.

Two major and other searches were undertaken without success, and after almost two years and much wild speculation as to the cause of the accident, it seemed there would be no definitive answers regarding what actually happened. Then to everyone's surprise a final effort to find the wreckage and recorders proved successful. The fact that it was found on a relatively flat part of the ocean bottom not far from the aircraft's last known position raised some questions regarding the failure to find it right at the beginning. The recorders revealed what had happened, but not for sure, why.

Before continuing, we should explain some key technical and other terms found in the BEA material and our narrative.

**Alternate Law** simply refers to the flying mode where the computers controlling (flying) the aircraft, having determined that the data (such as airspeed) they are receiving must be unreliable, switch to a 'simplified' operating law where many of the protections, such as preventing the pilot stalling the aircraft, or doing something that could otherwise endanger the aircraft, are suspended.

At the same time, autopilot and auto thrust are disengaged and control is passed to the pilots, who without warning—hence the so-called 'startle effect'—are confronted with the task of flying the aircraft with no computer to hold their hand when their minds up until then have been preoccupied by other matters. If very high up, in thin air where they have had little or no practice, this would be particularly difficult in the best of circumstances.

**Pitch is** the geometric attitude relative to the earth's surface of the aircraft in the longitudinal plane. (Degree of bank is the attitude in the lateral plane.)

The **Angle of Attack,** called $\alpha$ by Airbus, is the angle of the airflow striking the wing. If the aircraft is cruising normally at an appropriate speed, it is often not so very different from the pitch. However, if the aircraft is sinking, say in a stall where the wings are not providing enough lift to keep it up, the pitch can say be 5 degrees and the angle of attack perhaps 40 degrees. Like a high-speed elevator (lift), the aircraft can be dropping precipitously without those inside feeling it. Up until now, modern transport aircraft have not been equipped with an instrument showing the pilots the angle of attack.

The **Flight Director (FD)** is a sophisticated system that takes much of the hassle out of today's piloting. The pilots tell it what they want to do, say at what heights they want to fly at various stages of the flight and the waypoints they want to pass over and so on.

The FD on the one hand tells the autopilot what is wanted and on the other hand superimposes a crossbar on the attitude indicator to tell the pilots the pitch, bank, and so on required should they be flying manually. Ideally, pilots should switch it off in the case of 'unreliable airspeed data' to prevent them following it out of habit, as it cannot give them correct guidance without such data.

The **Electronic Centralized Aircraft Monitoring (ECAM)** device is a screen detailing problems, faults, and advising. Problem is that it can show too many items in a crisis. Showed irrelevant maximum speed permitted when aircraft was stalling due to going too slowly.

## Timeline [in Hours, Minutes, and Seconds] based on Cockpit Voice Recorder and Digital Data Recorder

*Negative time in square brackets is the time remaining before the moment [00:00:00] the autopilot disengages and the PF (pilot flying) takes over the controls. Positive times are the elapsed time from then. These times, rounded to the nearest second, give the reader a better idea of the timeline than the UTC times used in the official report.*

*Readers should bear in mind that what follows is only a highly selective extract from the cockpit voice recording and data recorder to enable them to situate events relatively in time. This partial rendering should not be used for detailed analysis of the pilots' actions as, even during the latter part, many possibly significant remarks are omitted to save space.*

*The BEA documentation simply refers to the first officers as the PF (pilot flying) and PNF (pilot not flying), or sometimes as the pilot in the right seat or the pilot in the left seat or captain's seat. This is confusing, especially when the roles switch. To make the accounts easier to follow, we hereafter refer to them as the senior FO and the junior FO, where 'senior' and 'junior' merely signify their relative ages and flying experience. The junior FO, who was for the most part the PF, was in the right-hand[1] seat.*

**[-02:00:51] (i.e. 2 hrs 51 sec before autopilot disconnection)**
**Beginning of the CVR recording**

Captain Marc Dubois and the junior first officer, Pierre-Cédric Bonin, were alone on the flight deck. Senior First Officer David Robert was resting in the rest station. Most of what is on the early part of the CVR is routine and has been omitted.

**[-01:11:58]**
**Captain suggests junior FO gets some rest**

> *Try maybe to sleep twenty minutes when he (the senior FO) comes back or before if you want.*

> *Ok that's kind, for the moment I don't feel like it but if I do feel like it, I will.*

> *It'll be a lot for you.*

The captain was justifiably concerned about the junior FO getting some rest, but it seems odd to the author that the senior FO is allotted proper rest time in the rest station and not the junior FO. Of course, neither FO was particularly sleepy at that time early in the flight. The captain would have the best time for a proper rest.

When the captain said 'it'll be a lot for you,' he would have been thinking of the total flight time of some 11 hours, not to mention the time on duty before takeoff. He suggests the junior FO doze off in his seat, either while the y are together or later when the senior FO returns.

**[-00:18:07]**
**Captain comments on weather conditions ahead**

> *It's going to be turbulent (bumpy) when I go for my rest*

**[-00:14:08]**
**Captain notes it is time to wake up the senior FO**

> *Well, right, we just have to wake him up that's all eh*

**[-00:13:59]**
**Sound of high/low cabin chime [-00:13:55]**
**+ Noise like a knock on the partition of the rest station**

**[-00:13:49]**
**Captain asks junior FO about who is landing the aircraft**

> *Err, who's doing the landing, is it you? Well right, he's going to take my place.*

The junior FO does not reply.

**[-00:13:45]**
**Captain confirms FO is a PL + change in background noise**

> *You're a PL (licensed), aren't you?*

**[-00:13:44]**
**Junior FO replies in affirmative**

> *Yeah.*

It was quite logical for the junior FO to land the aircraft on their return to Paris as the senior FO had performed the landing on the way out to maintain his currency (minimum number of landings required keep his license valid).

**[-00:11:36 to -00:11:34]**
**Private conversation**

> *...   ...*

The BEA has deleted this exchange, considering it to be of a private nature. However, with it being so close to the handover it might have thrown useful light on the relationship between the captain and the junior FO.

**[-00:11:06]**
**Captain makes colloquial remark indicating his stint is over + sound of chair adjustment**

> *That's it.*

**[-00:10:39]**
**Noise of cockpit door opening**

**[-00:10:33]**
**Captain addresses senior FO**

> *OK?*

**[-00:10:29]**
**Junior FO addresses senior FO**

*Did you sleep?*

**[-00:10:27]**
**Senior FO replies**

*So-so.*

**[-00:10:21]**
**Captain addresses senior FO**

*You didn't sleep, then.*

**[-00:10:18]**
**Junior FO addresses captain**

*He, he said so-so... so-so.*

**[-0:09:57]**
**In a very colloquial manner, captain announces he is going for his rest**

*Well, I'm out of here (approximate translation—French very colloquial, like 'I'm off.')*

**[-00:09:46]**
**Senior FO replies to junior FO's comment, 'He, said so-so ... so-so.'**

*I... I was dozing in fact.*

Senior FO asks junior FO whether he is OK.

**[-0:09:29]**
**Junior FO replies**

*OK.*

**[-0:09:32]**
**Junior FO briefs senior FO on situation in presence of captain**

*Well the little bit of turbulence that you just saw we should find the same ahead we're in the cloud layer unfortunately we can't climb much for the moment because the temperature is falling more slowly than forecast. So, what we have is some REC MAX a little too low to get to three seven.*

**[-0:08:34]**
**Captain informs junior FO of the frequencies to use**

*Err, sixty six forty nine fifty five sixty five and after it's sixty five thirty five.*

**[-00:08:19]**
**Noises in cockpit**

**[-01:08:05 to -00:06:28]**
**The FOs discuss diversion airports available**

**[-0:06:21]**
**Junior FO**

> *The inter-tropical convergence there, well we're in it between SALPU and TASIL*

**[-0:04:10]**
**Junior FO**

> *We'll call them in the back to tell them anyway because ...*

**[-0:04:00]**
**Junior FO talks to cabin crew**

> *yes (...) it's (...) in front tell me in two minutes. There we ought to be in an area where it will start moving about a bit more than now, you'll have to watch out there .*

**[-00:03:52 to 00:03:46]**
**Dialog between cabin crew and junior FO**
**Cabin crew (first to speak)**

> *All right, are we to sit down?*

> *Well I think that it might be a good idea to tell your ... ?*

> *Yeah, okay. I'll call the back, thanks a lot.*

> *Thanks, I'll call you when we're out of it.*

**[-00:03:04]**
**Junior FO**

> *See, we're really on the edge of the layer (and under the squall).*

**[-00:02:02]**
**Senior FO**

> *Don't you maybe want to go to the left a bit?*

**[-00:01:58]**
**Senior FO**

> *You can possibly go a bit to the left. I agree that we're not in manual eh?*

The senior FO suggested changing course a little to the left to avoid turbulence they could see on their weather radar and they altered the heading to a setting minus 12° off their preset route.

**[-00:01:24]**
**Junior FO**

*What's that smell now?*

**[-00:01:22]**
**Senior FO**

*It's ... It's ozone.*

**[-00:01:21]**
**Junior FO**

*It's ozone that's it, we're all right.*

**[-00:00:19]**
**Background noise increases (typical noise of impact of ice crystals, identified by A330-340 pilots)**

Neither pilot alluded to it. The BEA noted that at the time pilots had little knowledge regarding the phenomenon. Nevertheless, the senior FO (PNF) took it upon himself to reduce the airspeed down towards Mach 0.8 and switched on the engine anti-icing—no doubt in response to the indication of ice shown by the instruments.

------------------------------------------------

**[00:00:00]**
**AUTOPILOT DISCONNECTS DUE TO ICING UP OF PITOT PROBES**

------------------------------------------------

**[-0:00:02 to 00:00 (2 h10 min 05 UTC]**
**Sound of cavalry charge warns that autopilot is disconnecting**

**[00:00:01]**
**Junior FO (pilot flying (PF))**

*I have the controls.*

**[00:00:03]**
**Senior FO (pilot not flying (PNF))**

*All right.*

Unlike Boeing aircraft, which have 'traditional' control columns that move in unison on both sides of the cockpit, Airbuses have sidesticks with no mechanical or simulated interconnection. In addition, as these are located on the far side of the pilots, it is very difficult for the other pilot to see what his colleague is doing, and particularly so in relative darkness.

Thus, the senior FO did not see that the PF had pulled back his stick and put the aircraft into a climb taking it from 35,000 ft to ultimately its maximum operating height of 37,500 ft. Without application of additional power, the aircraft could only achieve this climb by using up kinetic energy in the form of airspeed, and on reaching its maximum height it had lost so much that it stalled. Even so, the junior FO was still for some reason keeping the nose up, thus preventing it from diving and regaining essential. It began sinking faster and faster. When the junior FO had taken over the aircraft had been flying all right and would have continued to do so with minimum input. Unfortunately, his excessive inputs had created a crisis.

**[00:00:05]**
**Two SV (synthetic voice) stall warnings (BEA calls it STALL 1 warning)**

*Stall.*

*Stall.*

**[00:00:06]**
**Senior FO**

*What is that?*

**[00:00:08]**
**Two SV stall warnings, last one truncated**

*Stall, S ...*

**[00:00:09]**
**Junior FO**

*We haven't got a good display...*

**[00:00:10]**
**Junior FO**

*We haven't got a good display...*

*... of speed.*

**[00:00:11]**
**Senior FO**

*We've lost the speeds ...*

**[00:00:17]**
**Senior FO**

*Alternate law protections- (law/low/lo).*

**[00:00:19 to 00:00:23]**
**Senior FO**

*Wait we're losing ...*
*Wing anti-ice.*
*Watch your speed.*
*Watch your speed.*

**[00:00:23]**
**Junior FO**

*OK, OK, OK, I'm going back down.*

**[00:00:26]**
**Senior FO**

*Go back down.*

**[00:00:27]**
**Senior FO**

*According to that, we're going up.*
*According to all three, you're going up,*
*so go back down.*

**[00:00:30]**
**Junior FO**

*OK.*

**[00:00:31]**
**Senior FO**

*You're at ... Go back down.*

**[00:00:37]**
**Junior FO**

*We're in a ... We're in a climb.*

**[00:00:45]**
**Senior FO**

*(Expletive) Where is he?*

Seems senior FO had already called the captain. Anyway, from this time onwards, he tried several times to call him back and maybe this drew his attention from what the junior FO was doing.

**[00:00:46]**
**Start of almost continuous stall warnings (BEA calls it STALL 2 warning)**

**00:01:01]**
**Senior FO**

*(Expletive) Where is he?*

**[00:01:05]**
**AIRCRAFT REACHES MAXIMUM HEIGHT OF 37,924 FT**

The PF made nose-down inputs alternately to the right and to the left. The climb speed, which had reached 7,000 ft/min, dropped to 700 ft/min and the roll varied between 12 degrees to the right and 10 degrees to the left. The speed indicated on the left side increased suddenly to 215 kt (Mach

0.68), while the speed displayed on the left primary flight display (PFD) remained invalid for 29 seconds. The aircraft was by then at an altitude of about 37,500 ft and the recorded angle of attack around 4 degrees. Stall 2 warnings continued.

**[00:01:20]**
**Senior FO**

> *Do you understand what's happening, or not?*

**[00:01:28]**
**Junior FO**

> *(...) I don't have control of the airplane any more now.*

**[00:01:30]**
**Junior FO**

> *I don't have control of the airplane at all.*

Stall 2 warnings still continuing.

**[00:01:37] RETURN OF THE CAPTAIN**
**Noise of cockpit door opening**

The captain's return to the cockpit coincided with the aircraft falling through 35,000 ft, the altitude it had been when he had departed a little earlier. Apart from the alarms and the senior FO's expression of concern, a quick glance at the altimeter might have led him to believe that not much had changed. He was not to know that it had climbed to 37,924 ft without additional power being applied and that the stall warnings were therefore believable.

   The action required was to throttle back the engines to stop them pushing the nose up, push the sidestick forward to try to push the nose down and the aircraft into a dive. Then once it had gained enough airspeed for the control surfaces to stop the engines from pushing the nose up, gradually applying engine power until the aircraft came out of the stall and could be piloted to break[2] the rapid rate of descent, hopefully before hitting the sea. As it was, the junior FO was, unknown to the others, more or less continually pulling back on his side stick. Doing the opposite of what was required.

**Captain**

> *Er, what are you (doing)?*

**[00:01:39]**
**Senior FO**

> *What's happening? I don't know I don't know what's happening.*

**[00:01:42]**
**Junior FO**

*We're losing control of the aircraft there.*

**[00:01:39]**
**Senior FO**

*We lost all control of the aircraft. We don't understand anything. We've tried everything.*

**[00:01:48]**
**Captain**

*So take that.*

**[00:01:50]**
**Senior FO**

*Take that, take that.*

**[00:01:53]**
**Junior FO**

*I have a problem; it's that I don't have vertical speed indication.*

**[00:01:59]**
**Junior FO**

*I have the impression that we have some crazy speed, no, what do you think?*

He possibly had the impression of a crazy speed due to the tremendous noise generated by the aircraft belly flopping downwards through the air with the air 'whistling' as it splayed off the wings.

**[00:01:42]**
**Senior FO**

*No, above all don't extend (the air brakes).*

**[00:02:09]**
**Senior FO**

*What do you think about it, what do you think, what do we need to do?*

**[00:02:10]**
**Captain**

*There I don't know, there it's going down.*

**[00:02:22]**
**Senior FO (stall alarm still sounding)**

*You're climbing.*

**[00:02:23]**
**Senior FO (stall alarm still sounding)**

*You're going down, down, down.*

**Captain**

*(Expletive) (Going down)*

[00:02:25]
**Junior FO**

*Am I going down now?*

[00:02:27]
**Senior FO**

*Go down.*

**Captain**

*No, you climb there.*

[00:02:34]
**Junior FO**

*OK, we're in TOGA.*

TOGA (Takeoff Go Around) is a button that sets the engines to high power as well as the control surface configuration so that the aircraft can suddenly climb out and away should they for instance have to abort a landing because another aircraft is on the runway. Not quite what required here where first requirement would be to get the nose down and the aircraft into a dive.

[00:02:37]
**Junior FO**

*On alti what do we have here?*

[00:02:39] **stall warnings ongoing.**
**Captain**

*( ...) It's impossible.*

The junior FO again asked about altitude, without getting a reply, and in the following 20 seconds the captain's main concern was to tell him to get the wings horizontal as the SV stall warnings continued.

[00:03:13]
**Junior FO**

*We're there, we're there, we're passing level one hundred (10,000 ft).*

[00:03:20]
**Junior FO**

*What is ... how come we're continuing to go right down now?*

The stall warnings ceased, because to avoid them giving spurious warnings when landing and taking off, the software is programmed to switch them off when the airspeed is below 60 knots. The odd result in this context was that when the pilots did something appropriate, such as raising the airspeed above 60 knots, the warnings would restart, making them think their action might be wrong.

**[00:03:35]**
**Junior FO**

*But, I've been in maxi nose-up for a while.*

This remark, for the first time, makes the captain realize what the junior FO has been doing (wrong) all along. However, it is really too late.

**[00:03:38]**
**Captain**

*No, no, no, don't climb.*

**[00:03:40]**
**Senior FO**

*So give me the controls; the controls to me; the controls to me.*

**[00:03:41]**
**Junior FO**

*Go ahead, you have the controls, we are still in TOGA, eh.*

**[00:03:50]**
With the senior FO taking control, the stall warnings recommenced even though the situation was improving as explained above. However, the high rate of descent and the little height remaining meant it was too late anyway.

**[00:04:00]**
**Captain**

*Watch out, you're pitching up there.*

**[00:04:02]**
**Junior FO**

*Well we need to; we are at four thousand feet.*

**[00:04:11]**
**SV (synthetic voice) sink rate warning**

[The 'PULL UP!' warning continues until the aircraft hits the sea.]

**[00:04:21]**
**IMPACT WITH THE SEA**

The recordings stopped at 2 h 14 min 28 UTC, that is four minutes and twenty-one seconds after the autopilot disconnect. The last recorded values were a vertical speed of -10,912 ft/min, a ground speed of 107 kt, pitch attitude of 16.2 degrees nose-up, roll angle of 5.3 degrees left, and a magnetic heading of 270 degrees.

Though some of the passengers, not forgetting the cabin crew, would have been aware something was wrong, the fact that the nose was pointing upwards may have reassured them. The deceleration on hitting the sea with the aircraft dropping at 10,912 ft/min would have been so great that they would have lost consciousness instantaneously.

## A SEMINAL ACCIDENT WITH MANY FACETS

In his first appearance on CBS News as their new aviation and safety expert, 'Sully' Sullenberger[3] called this disaster a seminal accident that would be studied for years. He said one needs to look at it from a systems approach, a human/technology system that has to work together. This involves aircraft design and certification, training and human factors. He claimed that if you look at the human factors alone, then you are missing half or two-thirds of the total system failure.

To make the factors and their interplay easier to grasp, we have divided our analysis into facets, making many of the points that the BEA make and those that Sully make without citing him.

### Facet 1 Junior FO's actions

Almost immediately after disengagement of the autopilot and auto throttle, the PF (junior FO) took the controls and pulled back on his sidestick more than was warranted in the thin air at that great height where one needs to go easy on the controls. The BEA attributed the abruptness of his input to the startle effect of suddenly having to take over and lack of experience/training for manual flying at that height.

The BEA conjecture that he might have put the aircraft into a climb as the aircraft had apparently (but perhaps not in reality) sunk a few hundred feet below its 35,000 ft cruising height, the clear sky could be viewed above, and previously they had wanted to climb but had ruled out doing so due to the low temperature

In that rapid and unnecessary climb to almost 38,000 ft, the aircraft slowed and stalled, but the junior FO continued to pull back on his sidestick for most of the time thereafter, thereby making recovery impossible. It is likely that for much of the time the junior FO followed the crossbars of the flight director (FD) when they reappeared. With the computers not receiving the proper data, the FD could not be a viable guide and should have been disabled.

The BEA even checked the junior FO's salvaged seat to see whether it might have been badly adjusted and made him pull back on his sidestick, and found that not to be the case.

### Facet 2 Senior FO's actions

The PNF (senior FO) could see the PF was initially climbing on taking over and told him unsuccessfully several times to go down, but then did not pursue the matter, perhaps because he was distracted by calling back the captain and trying to find out the root of the problem with the instruments. Furthermore, the senior FO could not see what the PF was doing with his sidestick as they are not linked (Facet 6). However, almost right at the end, he did tell the junior FO to go down.

## Facet 3 Captain's handover to the two FOs—CRM

Before going for his rest, the captain handed over authority in a most perfunctory manner and not even in the presence of the senior FO, even having to confirm as an afterthought whether the junior FO was qualified (to make the landing in Paris or take command?).

Shortly before the publication of the June 5, 2012 BEA report, someone revealed the captain's female companion had been on the aircraft. The BEA retorted this was not relevant to the accident, and there seemed to be a consensus that even suggesting such a thing might have been a factor was disgraceful. Nevertheless, the fact that both the captain and the junior first officer had their female companions on board raises a statistical flag—in the junior FO's case it was his wife. Had the captain and junior FO arranged it thus, and even without that being so, had they relaxed as a foursome with the result that the captain was particularly well disposed towards the latter to the extent that this cozy relationship undermined the senior FO? Certainly, the relationship between the captain and the junior FO while the senior FO was resting seemed very close.

Surprisingly, in checking whether the crew had had adequate rest beforehand, the BEA maintains it was impossible to establish how any of the pilots had spent their free time before the flight. All the BEA could say was that the CVR showed no sign of them being excessively tired. In that connection, it has been said that Air France pilots regarded the long flight back to France as a good chance to have a good rest and recuperate after having fun in Rio de Janeiro.

The senior FO had more experience and was considered to be something of an expert at Air France. Indeed the junior FO seemed to defer to his judgment even though he did not always follow his advice in practice. The BEA said this resulted in the perverse situation where the PF deferred to the PNF without the latter having executive authority. Had the senior FO had such authority, *might* he have taken over the controls himself (as a captain would usually do in an emergency) when the stall warning and other alarms sounded, with the result that the nose would not have been kept pointing upwards with disastrous results.

## Facet 4 The actions of the captain

The BEA was not happy with the manner of the handover when the captain departed, in that it was too vague, though at the time the airline did not have a protocol for it.

As mentioned, the captain's return coincided with the aircraft falling through the altitude it had been when he departed, so for a moment he might have thought nothing much had really happened. Had he returned some thirty seconds earlier, the aircraft would have been at its apogee, making him realize what the PF had done, and understand why the stall warning was continuously sounding. Even 15 seconds earlier would have made a great difference.

As it was, his input was limited, and it was only at the end when the junior FO told him he had been in 'maxi nose-up for a while,' that the captain realized what had been happening, and told him not to climb.

### Facet 5 Neither of the FOs, nor the captain reacted to SV stall warnings

The crash occurred because the aircraft stalled, but at no point did any of the pilots mention the word 'stall'. These stall warnings went on for a very long time, and the captain must have heard them even though they stopped when the airspeed fell below 60 knots as explained.

One possible reason suggested by the BEA and others is that when a stall warning sounds in normal flying conditions it is usually of little concern to the pilots as the computer—under normal law—is there to protect them.

On the other hand, if the pilots thought the instruments were incorrect, maybe they just did not believe the stall warnings.

### Facet 6 Pilot/machine interface—euphemistically called 'ergonomics' in BEA's conclusions and recommendations

A few days after the publication of the 2011 interim report, Air France, and its pilots' union, accused the BEA of removing at the last minute a recommendation that the stall warning system be improved, and notably that it should not switch off as it did when airspeed values fall below 60 knots. They claimed excision of the recommendation was to bolster the position of Airbus and lay all blame on the pilots. The union went as far as to say the BEA could not be trusted and they would no longer cooperate with the inquiry. The BEA responded, saying they were leaving out that recommendation until the final report made after further study.

Airbus, thinking of possible litigation, would argue that one could not expect them to program for situations where pilots do something totally out of the norm. In this respect, there is some parallel with the crash of an A300 flight outbound from New York's JFK in 2001 (see page 174) in which the PF reacted to wake turbulence generated by a preceding Boeing 747 by swishing the rudder back and forth from extremity to extremity with the result that it was torn off. Investigators thought one reason why he did so was that he had attended a course run by the airline on how to recover from upsets using the rudder aggressively (but not swishing it from stop to stop). The airline argued that there was too little feedback in the controls to indicate the stresses imposed, that it was too easy to do so, and that Airbus should have made doing such a thing impossible. Though there was never any agreement on who was right, the NTSB quite recently insisted Airbus incorporate such protections on the A300.

Sullenberger and others, and even the BEA, have mentioned possible improvements, not all really coming under ergonomics.

Firstly, there should be a clear indication of the reason when the autopilot disengages of its own accord. This would have meant the pilots would not only have faced less uncertainty, but perhaps more importantly would have meant the PNF could have concentrated on what the aircraft was doing rather than wasting his time trying to fathom what was happening and reading out irrelevant messages appearing on the ECAM.

Secondly, it seems that in a crisis, people pay more attention to visual cues, and therefore stall warnings should be portrayed visually as well. Thirdly, and this follows on from the previous point, airliners should be equipped with an instrument showing the angle of attack that would confirm the stall and give pilots a better indication of what is happening. Its installation on certain military aircraft apparently significantly reduced accidents.

Fourthly, in a crisis humans pay more attention to visual cues than to aural cues often lost amongst a cacophony of other aural warnings, and that there should be a visual cue in addition to the one on the airspeed indicator tape which was not valid anyway.

Fifthly, this visual warning of the stall could be on the ECAM as well as the reason for the autopilot disengagement. As it was, the ECAM was giving warnings about the maximum speed, which was irrelevant in the circumstances, and worse still contributing to the idea of overspeed. In general, the system tends to inundate the pilots with aural and visual warnings so they cannot determine what is important. Interestingly, when the Roll-Royce engine on a Qantas A380 out of Singapore exploded damaging a number of important lines and parts, there were over a hundred such warnings, and the very able flight crew turned many of them off and concentrated on the important ones. Of course, they had plenty of time, unlike the pilots of AF447.

Fifthly, as already mentioned on page 208 ('Unlike Boeing ... '), the sidesticks do not move in unison, making it difficult if not impossible for the PNF to see what the PF is doing. Some means of indicating this should not be difficult. Likewise, the throttles do not move to remind pilots of what the engines have been told to do. Eliminating such features has some pluses, but the case needs to be argued.

## Facet 7 Training

The BEA very much exculpates the pilots because Air France had not trained them to cope with such a situation. That said, Sullenberger pointed out that up until this accident hardly any airline fully trained their pilots to handle high-altitude stalls.

Anyway, in the year or so prior to the disaster we are discussing, Air France had nine instances of problems with the A330/A340 pitot probes, but took no apparent action, and presumably because the pilots had been able to resolve the situation as perhaps these should have.

Post disaster, Air France, not to mention many other airlines have been training their pilots to handle such situations and high-altitude stalls.

## Facet 8 Pitot probes & choice thereof

Based on the 300-year-old idea of French Professor Henri Pitot, the pitot tube is basically a forward-facing protruding tube (probe) with a hole at the front into which the oncoming air (referred to as *ram air*) rushes and a sideways-facing hole measuring the static air pressure independently of the speed of the aircraft. The full name for these is *pitot static tubes*. The sideways-facing *static* ports need not be on the tube itself, there being other ones anyway for measuring air pressure as an indication of height, air temperature and even for determining whether the aircraft is about to stall.

The pitot tubes are like eyes telling the aircraft how fast it is going by comparing the two pressures. Flying with blocked pitot tubes is like walking unsteadily, or worse, with one's eyes shut. There are normally three, so that the onboard systems can detect failure by noting the odd man out.

Two examples of what can happen when the pitot tubes fail to provide the correct data to the pilots and computerized systems are:

1. **The crash into the sea of the Peruvian airliner described on page 268.**

2. **The crash of a US Air Force B2 stealth bomber on taking off from Guam on February 23, 2008.**

In the case of the *B2 bomber*, the humid climate at Guam resulted in the presence of moisture in the sensors (performing the pitot tube function[4]), which made the maintenance staff calibrate them wrongly. They could have removed the moisture by turning on the pitot heaters but did not do so due to poor communications between staff.

As a result, the bomber rotated early on takeoff, which in itself would not necessarily have been fatal except that further erroneous data made the flight control system believe there was a negative angle of attack and tilt the nose up 30°. Unable to fly the machine at that angle and speed the two pilots ejected whilst still just above the ground, and survived with limited injuries. The aircraft crashed at the side of the runway and exploded at a cost of US$1.4 billion. The B2 bomber case demonstrates how important it is that the pitot tubes and units for sensing the angle of attack provide true and accurate data when *interfacing with computerized control systems.*[5]

Following this loss of the Air France A330 fitted with Thales pitot tubes, Airbus in July of that year urged airlines to switch to Goodrich pitot tubes for at least two of the three pitot tubes on the A330/A340 series of aircraft, pointing out that Goodrich already supplied the pitot tubes for 80% of the A330/A340 aircraft. With 1,000 aircraft in operation, the 20% remaining represented some 200 aircraft with sensors supplied by Thales.

The European Air Safety Agency (EASA) found that *'although this (Thales AB probe) has shown an improvement over the previous P/N C16195AA standard, it has not yet demonstrated the same level of robustness to withstand high-altitude ice crystals as the Goodrich P/N 0851HL probe.'*

In consequence, as a precautionary measure EASA issued an Air Worthiness Directive on August 31, 2009, which in essence said that:

> *... at least two out of the three pitot tubes should be the ones supplied by Goodrich and that they should be installed in positions 1 (captain) and 3 (spare) with the Thales one (should that option be taken) in position 2 (first officer). The Thales probe should be the AB and not the AA.*

To really understand the background factors affecting the choice of pitot tubes on Air France A330/A340 aircraft, mention should perhaps be made of a project called ADELINE (**A**dvanced air-**D**ata **E**quipment for air**line**rs) initiated in 2005 regarding the development of pitot tubes and the aspiration to wrest leadership in that field from the Americans.

The Executive Publishable Summary (Draft) says:

> *The objective of ADELINE is to develop new architectures and technologies of air data systems for implementation in new aircraft on the horizon of 2010.*

> *Actual air data equipment is composed of a large number of individual probes and pressure sensors. This equipment delivers vital parameters for the safety of the aircraft's flight such as airspeed, angle of attack, and altitude. The loss of these data can cause aircraft crashes especially in case of probe icing.*

> *The main project targets are: to reduce present equipment costs by 50% including purchasing and exploitation costs, to increase aircraft's [sic] safety by drastically reducing air data system failure.*

> *These targets will be achieved by developing simpler, more reliable, and safer equipment than the American systems that dominate the market.*

One cannot blame Thales for promoting their pitot probes commercially but one can ask why Air France chose them, not forgetting Airbus was associated with Thales in their development. Was it patriotism, or something else?

## Facet 9 Investigative and supervisory bodies, BEA, DGAC, and EASA

When the BEA announced that while the pitot tubes may well have been a factor in the crash, but were surely not the only factor, the Air France pilots' union said they were only trying to cover up their own failures and those of the DGAC (French Directorate General of Civil Aviation). The argument was that they had failed to pick up on problems with the Thales pitot tubes and the European Air Safety Agency had not been diligent in applying the latest lessons in certifying them.

According to the BEA report, the A330s had originally been fitted with Goodrich probes, but the DGAC on finding some problems ordered that they be fitted with a more advanced Goodrich probe or with the Thales probe that iced up on AF447. Thus, the French DGAC opened the door for the Thales probe, but Air France was still responsible for going through it.

## Facet 10 Culture of the airline

See page 68 for the points made by the freelance French aviation writer François Hénin regarding laxness (easy-going attitude) at the airline in connection with the Air France overrun at Toronto. Hénin says Air France was making serious efforts to rectify this, which cannot be easy in the face of the entrenched incumbents, labor laws, union power, not to mention the French way of doing things. The same would be true to some extent for any Western legacy airline. Lest readers get these remarks out of proportion, one should remember that, unlike Qantas, the very nature of many of Air France's long-haul routes means exposure to more difficult flying conditions and the likelihood of more, if not so many, incidents.

## Judicial Inquiry

In an interview with the author, Healy-Pratt, a London-based aviation lawyer representing many of the families, said that all air accident investigations are to some extent political. He has suggested the judicial inquiry might prove quite enlightening. Others have already dismissed the judicial inquiry out of hand, saying *all* the delegated experts are establishment figures linked in some way to the parties involved.

## Conclusion

In the Acknowledgements (page xii), we said we wasted much time on cases where officials and the like have been accused of hiding if not falsifying facts, but that in the end even that often did not matter because those responsible, such as the manufacturer, would surreptitiously or otherwise ultimately take remedial measures. We are not saying that is the case here. Indeed, the BEA took great care to avoid such accusations by having witnesses present at key moments and video recordings registering the handling of the recorders.

With litigation pending, it is understandable that Airbus is fighting its corner, and Airbus ironically may be right in that some of the 'ergonomic improvements' proposed, although generally desirable, may not be required to prevent a repeat, as airlines, manufacturers, and pilots will have learnt from this disaster and pilots will be trained to never do the same again.

One final point on which this book and the US's NTSB keeps harping is having video camera(s) on the flight deck. One advantage is that they would be able to show in real time what the instruments are telling the pilots. The BEA interim report in 2011 said that a cockpit video recorder would have greatly facilitated their enquiries. Perhaps out of consideration of the French pilots' union, the latest report published on July 5, 2012 has watered down these comments, the only suggestion being that a video should be taken of instruments with the strictest possible measures taken to ensure that its use is not abused (i.e. show the pilots). Recently, a captain told the author he would have no objections to being videoed as 'We are already monitored in almost everything we do.'

As Charles Sullenberger said, it was a seminal accident with lessons for years to come, especially as regards the association between humans and ever more perfectionist computers. The danger being that perfection the pilots are losing their ability to fly manually when overwhelmed in a crisis. In cases where the pitots are not working such as in the case of the Aeroperú flight described on page 268 that flew into the ocean with the pilots thinking it was at 9,700 ft, it is easy with hindsight and time to see what needed to be done. However, it is not so easy when in the cockpit with all sorts of alarms going off and unbelievable instrument readings.

Nevertheless, in the AF447 case, had any of the above ten facets materially differed, the accident probably would not have happened. Therefore, as the BEA maintains, it would be wrong to attribute it to one in particular.

---

[1] The captain's seat is always on the left because holding patterns and approaches to airports traditionally involved left-hand turns and looking out of his or her side window the captain can see where they are going.

[2] Even though the pilots may regain control before hitting the sea or ground, they still need sufficient height to break the rapid rate of descent—10,000 ft per minute in this case—in time. See 'So near Salvation' on page 285.

[3] Made famous by his successful ditching of his Airbus A320 on New York's Hudson River described in the first chapter of this book,

[4] Stealth bombers do not have protruding pitot tubes (probes) as such, since they could be visible to the enemy radar but their inset sensors act in a similar fashion.

[5] Stealth aircraft have unconventional shapes to make them invisible to enemy radar, which in turn make them inherently unstable and dependent on computers for stability control.

# CHAPTER 10

# METAL FATIGUE
# & STRUCTURAL FAILURE

## THE FIRST JETLINER, THE COMET
## (Comets 1954)

### Front Runner Falls—Others Learn

> It does not always pay to be first with a radically new aircraft concept, and the example of Britain's brief stand on the pedestal with the world's first jetliner rather proves that.
>
> *[BOAC Comet 1 G-ALYZ]*
> *[Canadian Pacific Airways delivery flight]*
> *[BOAC Comet 1 G-ALYV]*
> *[BOAC Flight 781]*
> *[South African Airways Flight 201]*

At the end of the Second World War, and before sky-high taxes made it better to be an accountant rather than an engineer, the British still expected to be in the forefront of aviation technology and aircraft production. The problem was that while the British had excelled in producing fighters such as the Spitfire and the Hurricane, the Americans had built up an invincible lead in bombers and heavy transport aircraft that they could switch to work as civilian aircraft at little cost.

With no hope of challenging on that front, the British set about designing an airliner that would exploit a domain where Britain had some sort of lead—jet engines. This would enable them to leapfrog the Americans with an airliner able to fly almost twice as fast. This project, envisioned by a government committee even before the war ended, had strong governmental support.

As the key feature was to be the use of a jet engine, the government perhaps unfortunately placed its support behind a distinguished aircraft company that produced its own engines—the de Havilland company, maker of the famous all-wood Mosquito, as well as the later Vampire jet fighter.

The major concern from the design point of view was conceiving an airliner that would handle well on takeoff and landing, as well as at the much higher cruising speeds contemplated. Not enough thought was given to the fact that flying an airliner at 35,000 ft or more put it in a completely different category as regards pressurization and the effects thereof, and notably metal fatigue.

Passengers do not require cabin pressure to be the same as that on the ground, but for them to be comfortable it should not be lower than that at about 7,000 ft, a height at which even people with asthma are comfortable.

For post Second World War piston-engine airliners, such as the very successful and beautiful Lockheed Constellation, cruising at 21,000 ft, having the cabin pressure equivalent to that at 7,000 ft meant the pressure difference between the inside and outside corresponded to *14,000 ft* (21,000 – 7,000). The difference for a jet such as the Comet cruising at 35,000 ft would be double that (35,000 – 7,000 = 28,000 ft).

In addition, there is a world of difference between a fighter with no passenger cabin and an airliner destined to carry (then) dozens of passengers. Indeed, it took de Havilland four years to get a prototype into the air and two and a half years more to have a certified aircraft. A limited scheduled service between London and South Africa finally began on May 2, 1952.

With airlines worldwide showing keen interest, de Havilland soon realized their jetliner should have been larger, and proposed a Comet 2, followed by an even larger Comet 3 for what should have been highly profitable transatlantic services. Affluent passengers were boasting about their flights, not only stressing their speed, but also their comfort and smoothness. *'One could stand a pencil on end without it falling over!'* they boasted.

### The First Accident (No Fatalities)

On October 26, 1952, less than six months after the start of commercial flights, the first mishap occurred. A Comet taking off in rain at night from Rome's international airport with a full complement of passengers started juddering and buffeting just as it was reaching the rotation speed ($V_R$) of around 112 knots. Sensing the aircraft was stalling and would not gain enough speed, the captain pushed the control column forward, but finding that did not solve the problem, cut the engines and applied maximum braking.

The aircraft exited the end of the runway at high speed, and ended up some distance away with the landing gear ripped off and fuel leaking onto the ground from a ruptured fuel tank. Fortunately, there was no fire and all the occupants survived—very shocked, but unscathed. The aircraft was a write-off.

Somewhat like the Qantas overrun at Bangkok, the absence of fatalities or even injuries meant the incident received little publicity. The Italian investigators did not even publish their report. Having found marks on the runway showing the tail had struck it a number of times even before reaching the point where the aircraft would normally rotate for takeoff, the investigators concluded it was not the aircraft's fault but the pilots' for prematurely raising the nose on the takeoff run.

Group Captain John Cunningham, de Havilland's highly publicized chief test pilot, carried out tests that showed raising the nose too early increased drag so much that the aircraft could never reach takeoff speed. One wonders whether this shortcoming was not in part due to de Havilland previously working mainly in designing fighters with surplus power where a tiresome quirk like that would not matter.

Early jet engines did not have the abundant power they have today enabling them to soar into the sky at a considerable angle. They were not much different from piston-engine aircraft such as the Lockheed Constellation that seemed to take off like swans with their 'flippers flicking over the water's surface.' Manufacturers had not yet fully considered exploiting leading edge devices able to give extra lift without excessive drag at low speeds. Even the early Boeing 707-100s that stepped into the Comet's shoes only had partial slats inboard of the outboard engine pylon. Full-wing slats only came in later versions of the 707.

All Comet pilots were told to keep the nose down until reaching takeoff speed, but with no dedicated attitude indicator showing the attitude in degrees, any abnormal nose-up attitude proved difficult to detect when concentrating on the runway ahead and occasionally glancing at an artificial horizon that would only give a rough indication. In addition, the hydraulic controls of the day did not simulate a 'feel' and the pilots could be pushing the tail down with the elevators without realizing it.

## The Second Accident

When the first of three Comets ordered by Canadian Pacific Airlines was ready for delivery early in 1953, de Havilland persuaded the Canadians to have it delivered via Australia. This would provide a chance to demonstrate it 'down under' and produce worldwide publicity if they could break the record for the time taken to fly from England to Australia in the process.

The aircraft took off from England on March 2, with a five-man flight crew headed by Canadian Pacific's overseas operations manager, Captain Pentland, who, as a busy manager, had little experience of flying the Comet and had never taken off at night at its controls.

Early the next morning, and while still dark, the Comet was taking off from Karachi at its maximum permissible takeoff weight only to find the Rome scenario repeated but with a less favorable outcome. After failing to lift off either on the runway or on the 180-meter overrun, the Comet exploded on encountering a number of obstacles situated beyond. The five-man crew and six de Havilland technicians, who were traveling as passengers and were due to assist Canadian Pacific with the aircraft, were killed.

Again, witnesses noted the unusually high nose-up attitude maintained for most of the takeoff run. Just as at Rome, the runway marks showed the tailskid had scraped the runway at several points. It seemed the pilots corrected the nose-up attitude at the last moment and almost succeeded in lifting off.

Investigators concluded that fatigue and pressure to beat the record had been contributing factors to what they classed as 'pilot error.'

Canadian Pacific immediately canceled their order for the two aircraft de Havilland was prepping for delivery. The accident was bad publicity for de Havilland, but they could still attribute it to pilot error and argue that with some modifications and better training there should be no more such silly accidents. It was fortunate that up to then the number of fatalities had been mercifully small.

However, this would not prove true for the next accident to a Comet that was to occur only two months later, and attributed to the 'exceptional circumstances,' namely the weather.

**The Third Accident**

The Comet bound for Delhi had taken off from Calcutta in mid-afternoon on May 2, 1953. There had been no problem lifting off as the aircraft was quite light, with a crew of 6 and 37 passengers, and only the fuel required for the two and a half hour leg to Delhi.

Twelve minutes after takeoff, the crew duly reported to Calcutta that they were climbing to 32,000 ft, before calling the controller at Delhi, who replied, without getting a response.

Repeated efforts failed to get any response, and nothing more was heard radio-wise from the aircraft.

Witnesses later reported hearing a bang in the sky during an exceptionally severe thunderstorm, and seeing a 'blaze in the sky' around that time and at the location of the aircraft.

The aircraft had, in fact, disintegrated in the sky. Based on evidence that the tailplane had failed due to an exceptional downwards force, an Indian High Court judge concluded the accident was due to the storm, and that any aircraft would have broken up in the same circumstances.

Experts re-examining the debris in England drew the same conclusion. They thought it possible the 'lack of feel' in the controls had led the pilots to over-control; especially as the captain had for much of his career flown flying boats, where heavy control inputs were the norm. It was thought the explosive decompression (presumed to have followed separation of the tailfin) occurred as the aircraft was climbing through 27,000 ft.

People were getting apprehensive, but there was no *proof* that there was anything inherently wrong with the aircraft itself. The eight accident-free months that followed seemed to confirm this.

## The Fourth Accident

Then, south of the island of Elba on January 10, 1954, a Comet 'inexplicably' disintegrated in mid-air.

The aircraft with six crew—in those days the pilot and first officer were complemented by an engineer and a radio officer—and 29 passengers had taken off from Rome for London on the last leg of the run from Singapore. The fact that the aircraft had disintegrated in mid-air probably while climbing through 27,000 ft, just as in the Indian case, was thought to be a mere coincidence.

De Havilland had tested the Comet's cabin under high air pressures and severe conditions prior to production and concluded that it should have been able to withstand 15 times more flights than the 1,200 that the aircraft had done. Nevertheless, to rule out that possibility, officialdom decided that one of the older models should be tested to destruction in a water tank— the advantage of using water instead of air would be that when the cabin ultimately failed, metal at the point of failure would stay more or less in place.

The Comets were withdrawn from service for modifications made on the basis that the cause was most likely an in-flight fire or engine fan blade separation.

## The Fifth Accident

Eleven weeks after the Elba accident, the Comets were put back into service, only for yet another 'inexplicable' accident to occur two weeks later.

Again, the aircraft happened to have taken off from Rome. It was the evening of April 8, 1954. The Comet in question was one leased to South African Airways and crewed by staff from that company. With only 14 passengers, the flight can hardly have been a profitable one—memories of the Elba accident had no doubt dampened people's enthusiasm.

After reporting that it was climbing to its cruising height of 35,000 ft and seven minutes later calling Cairo to report its ETA, nothing more was heard of it. It had disintegrated 20 nm off the Italian coast southeast of Naples. The disintegration had occurred at roughly the same time after departure and at a similar height to the previous one off Elba.

## The Cause and Aftermath

With Britain's dream shattered, the aircraft's Certificate of Airworthiness was withdrawn. Until the exact cause of the disasters could be definitively determined and adequate steps taken to prevent any chance of a reoccurrence, the Comet bandwagon was halted in its tracks. Meanwhile, other countries, and especially the US, were catching up.

The wreckage of the last disaster had fallen in such deep water that, with the technology of the time, little could be done to recover it. However, the Elba wreckage was more accessible, and a crucial piece of evidence was found. This was the tail with paint marks on it indicating it had been hit by a passenger seat ejected from the cabin, which could well have happened due to a pressurization failure of the cabin.

In late June, the fuselage that was being tested to destruction in the water tank finally failed. The failure had occurred at a rivet hole adjoining one of the square escape hatches. More detailed inspection revealed fatigue cracks that could have been the failure point in rivet holes in the vicinity of the cutout for the ADF antenna in the roof of the cabin.

If the failure had not occurred at the escape hatch, which they had recovered intact, it in all likelihood occurred in the vicinity of the ADF cutout. Assuming that the failure had occurred there, they tried to work out where the part in question would have fallen, and finally recovered it. The telltale fatigue cracks were duly found and they had the definitive answer they wanted.

The five remaining Comet 1s had become junk. A number of Comet 2s in the course of production were modified and bought by Britain's Royal Air Force. They had the safer round smaller windows. With the RAF operating them at a slightly reduced cabin pressure as a precaution, these aircraft performed without any serious problems over a number of years. Indeed, the RAF has modified several Comets to serve as AWACS[1] and ELINT[2] aircraft under the NIMROD designation.

In October 1958, BOAC launched a transatlantic service with the larger radically redesigned and strengthened Comet 3s. What was to be the Comet's second honeymoon was cut short three weeks later by the arrival of Boeing's much larger 707 with its longer range, greater speed and greater economy—developed in tandem with the KC-135 air refueling tanker funded by the US Air Force Strategic Command.

Not only was the 707 as everyone knows an outstanding success, so was the KC-135 with perhaps as many as 900 being produced in various versions over the years. Boeing and other US makers such as Douglas had learnt much from the Comet disasters with the help of the British who made information freely available.

De Havilland's last stab at the big time was with the rear-engine Trident tri-jet. However, there again Boeing spoilt the party with its similar 727 tri-jet, not because the Trident had serious technical faults but because it had been designed solely with the needs of British European Airways, or rather its chairperson, in mind.

Only 117 Tridents were made, with some ending up in China where they served creditably. The 727 remained in continuous production for 22 years, with the last one, the 1,831st, coming off the line in August 1984.

## Final Comments

With the aircraft being small and increasingly shunned by passengers, the total number of fatalities was mercifully low. From that time on, engineers and metallurgists in fields where failure could have disastrous consequences such as aviation and not least nuclear power, became obsessed with the dangers of metal fatigue and corrosion-assisted fatigue.

## Epilog—Nimrod

While the lessons learnt from the Comet disasters no doubt saved many lives in the early years of the jetliner age, it may come as something of a surprise that a Comet variant, the above-mentioned Nimrod, not only crashed as recently as September 2, 2006 but that the incident led to an inquiry providing many useful lessons regarding safety. However, this time the lessons are organizational rather than technical.

How could an aircraft of such a vintage still be in service 50 years or more after its conception? The reason is that in a project that has cost—the author would say wasted—billions of pounds, the Comet airframe was used as the basis for a maritime patrol aircraft, principally to look for submarines, though the various variants had many military and even civil roles.

What is more, the Conservative Government of the day gave Nimrod a new lease of life in the 1990s by ordering the Nimrod MRA4 based loosely on the old airframes. However, with cost and time overruns and only one out of the four aircraft ready to fly when the project was cancelled in late 2009 by a subsequent Conservative government (with the Liberals as very junior partners), the Nimrod MRA4 could be said to be the most expensive aircraft ever—£4.1 bn. Even dividing that sum by the four on order almost puts them on a par with the B-2 Stealth Bomber. Part of the reason for the cancellation was that the use of such an old airframe meant spare parts would have to be specially made and maintaining it in service would be extremely expensive. Besides, much of its equipment was out of date.

In fact, the airframes were of an earlier era, having been coach-built with the plans only used as a guide so that they all differed dimensionally, which made fitting additional sections and equipment to them so time-consuming and expensive.

When Nimrod XV230, the first Nimrod to enter service with the Royal Air Force on October 2, 1969, exploded during midair refueling over Afghanistan in 2006 killing 12 airmen, one marine and one soldier the immediate cause—the leaking of fuel—was pretty evident. The indirect cause, namely why safety had not been given due weight, became a scandal.

The Oxfordshire coroner, Andrew Walker, handed down a narrative ruling that the aircraft had 'never been airworthy from the first time it was released to the service nearly 40 years ago.'

On December 13, 2007, Mr. Haddon-Cave QC was appointed by the then Secretary of Defense to conduct a review into the wider issues surrounding the loss of Nimrod XV230 in Afghanistan. While this book has looked at incidents very much in terms of what happened at the coalface, Haddon-Cave, who had distinguished himself as a top lawyer handling aviation and commercial litigation, was able to look at the organizational aspects of safety taking the broader view.

His final report[3] into the disaster was highly critical of the British Royal Air Force and of certain senior officers, with some saying it could even have gone higher up. In essence, the disaster should never have happened and an earlier safety review prior to the disaster had been a farce.

With almost two years and a broad mandate, Haddon-Cave was able to render a remarkably perceptive analysis of the lessons to be learnt from not only the Nimrod disaster, but also from other notable complex organizational disasters, such as the Challenger Shuttle disaster.

He made too many points to cite them all in this book, but some are listed in Chapter 16 under the heading 'A Just Culture.'

---

[1] Airborne early warning and control (AWACS). Special aircraft equipped with sophisticated radar, electronic surveillance and communications equipment that hover over an area or aircraft carrier to detect attacks or to control and guide attacks.

[2] Electronic Intelligence (ELINT).

[3] *The Nimrod Review: An independent review into the broader issues surrounding the loss of the RAF Nimrod MR2 XV230 in Afghanistan in 2006*, 587 pages.

# SECTION OF ROOF BLOWN OFF ALOHA 737 (Hawaii 1988)

## Flight Attendant Sucked Up into Venting Flap

> Learning from the Comet disasters, aircraft designers made windows smaller and rounded, and avoided having points where stress would concentrate. They also used cross-plinths to prevent any fuselage failure from spreading like a failed zip fastener.
>
> In the 737, Boeing designed the fuselage so that in the event of a failure, a 'structural flap' would open to release the cabin air without destroying the entire structure. This failed to serve its purpose in this case because the updraft sucked a female flight attendant standing below up into the aperture. As the opening blocked by the hapless flight attendant could no longer serve its purpose, the whole of the passenger cabin roof was blown off in the vicinity.
>
> Pictures of the Aloha jet with passengers sitting in the open as if on an open-top sightseeing bus received worldwide publicity.
>
> *[Aloha Airlines Flight 243]*

Used for inter-island hops, the 18-year old Boeing 737 had 89,680 cycles to its credit, or rather debit. Dividing the number of hours it had been airborne by that number, the average flight time worked out as 25 minutes. Only one other 737 in the world had as many cycles.

Admittedly, the impact of these cycles on the structure was theoretically less than usual in that the short distances meant the maximum height reached was less than it would normally be. However, this 'plus' was negated by the fact that the aircraft was operating in, and parked in, the warm, salty and humid environment associated with the Hawaiian Islands.

Furthermore, the airline operated within tight financial margins, and extracted the most from its geriatric fleet by doing important fuselage checks piecemeal overnight, it being imperative to have the aircraft back in the sky early the next day.

Some operations such as checking rivets and the bonds holding the fuselage together require not only very diligent and tedious work, but also setting up gantries and safety harnesses if upper parts of the fuselage are to be checked safely, all limiting the effective inspection time. Perhaps worst of all, workers suffering from upset sleep rhythms can very easily miss defective areas.

On boarding in the good light of the early afternoon, one of the passengers had noticed a small horizontal crack along a line of rivets to the right of the forward left-hand door and had even thought of reporting it to the crew, but did not do so for fear of being thought foolish.

The aircraft was already making its ninth flight of the day, this time the 35-minute leg from Hawaii's Big Island (Ito) to Honolulu on Oahu Island. Their route would take them close to several other islands in the Hawaiian chain, including Maui.

Twenty minutes after takeoff, they had leveled out at their cruising height of 24,000 ft with 37-year old First Officer Madeline (Mimi) Tompkins, at the controls. She had 8,000 hours' flight experience and hoped soon to be promoted to the rank of captain, like Captain Schornsteimer sitting next to her, also with a similar amount of flying experience.

A loud bang behind the pilots signaled the beginning of an explosive decompression. Madeline Tompkins later said the decompression was so rapid that the displacement of the small amount of air in front of her was enough to throw her head back. Donning their oxygen masks according to regulations, and the captain taking over control as is usual in an emergency, the two pilots tried to assess the situation.

Glancing behind him, Schornsteimer had been shocked to see some blue sky through the doorway where the blown-off flight deck door had once been. Had he been able to see the full extent of the damage, he might not have made such a rapid emergency descent with the airspeed attaining 280 to 290 knots even with deployment of the air brakes. This is standard practice in the case of a decompression so the passengers can breathe more easily, but is contra-indicated when doing so might lead to the structural breakup of the aircraft.

Having seen the sky through the cockpit doorway, the captain would have realized some passengers would not have oxygen masks, and felt a rapid descent was necessary for their benefit. He could not see enough to realize that with so much of the upper fuselage missing, he was exposing them to a vicious slipstream and, worse, going so fast could bring about the breakup of the structurally impaired aircraft. Schornsteimer later received many plaudits for his airmanship, but was criticized by the investigators on this point.

As the aircraft slowed at a height where breathing was easier for all, the plight of the 89 terrified passengers and the remaining (two) female cabin attendants became more bearable. Some had seen the shocking sight of Flight Attendant Clarabelle Lansing, who had been working at the airline for 37 years, sucked upwards into a hole (the famous 'safety flap') that opened up in the left of the roof near row 5, before the whole section around it came away.

Another flight attendant, Jane Sato-Tomita, who had been standing three rows further forward not far from the flight deck door had been severely injured by flying debris and notably that missing door. The other flight attendant, Michelle Honda, had been thrown about and had suffered bruising, but being much further back in the part of the cabin that still had a roof, was relatively unscathed. Dragging herself on her hands and knees up the aisle against the slipstream, she had to shout in passengers' ears to communicate. Unable to contact the flight crew over the intercom, she at one moment thought the pilots might be incapacitated and asked likely prospects whether any of them could fly a plane!

Unlike the flight attendants standing in the forward part of the aircraft briskly serving drinks in the little time available before their expected arrival at Honolulu, the seated passengers there had seat belts to save them from serious injury or even death.

The pilots, who were very much alive and the least subject to the elements, found the aircraft was controllable, albeit somewhat abnormally. Apart from the distortion of the airflow over the fuselage caused by the 'gap,' the nose was, in fact, drooping down about a meter below where it should have been and springing up and down. Some maintained only the seat-fixation rails running longitudinally along the cabin floor were holding the aircraft together—hence the springiness.

The pilots decided to divert to Maui Island's Kahului Airport by then only some 20 nm away. This was on the opposite side of the island and involved an approach between two high mountains, which, though not inherently difficult, could have been fraught with danger for an aircraft in their condition, as the violent wind and turbulence could easily break the fuselage apart. Luckily, the wind was much weaker than usual.

Their immediate problem was radio communication, largely due to the wind noise, which made it virtually impossible to hear or be heard. It took some time even for the Maui controller to get their flight number right and then to grasp the seriousness of their predicament, of which even the first officer handling the radio was unaware as she had no intercom contact with the passenger cabin and had to assist the captain. Maui ATC asked them to switch frequencies as if they were a normal flight.

The investigators criticized this obligation to change radio frequency on the grounds that aircrew dealing with an emergency should not be distracted by this task, which had the added risk that contact with the aircraft might be lost altogether. This reminds one of the criticisms leveled at ATC in connection with the famous crash of a 737 at Kegworth in the UK the following year, where the pilots shut down the good engine instead of the bad one and incidentally had to hop from frequency to frequency.

On lowering the landing gear, they found there was no green light to confirm the front nose wheel was down and locked. Fearful that the aircraft would break up if they delayed, they decided to forgo the usual procedure of overflying the airport for the tower to make a visual check, which would entail a circuit to bring them back to the touchdown approach. The captain decided to come in anyway.

As they came in, the control tower was able to confirm the front wheel was down, but obviously could not be sure it was locked. As the amount of flap was increased to 15 degrees for the landing, the aircraft began to misbehave, and the setting was quickly reset for 5 degrees with the first officer having to consult her manual and make quick calculations to work out the $V_{REF}$ (landing airspeed) for that configuration, which was 152 knots. However, finding the aircraft unstable at that speed, the captain opted for 170 knots, but as he moved the throttles, the port engine failed and would not relight.

With the other engine, he was still able to bring the aircraft in at the higher speed, telling the first officer, who suggested increasing the flaps to 40 degrees detent at the last moment, to wait until they were on the ground before doing so. Despite, or thanks to the higher than usual speed, the aircraft touched down smoothly with the nose wheel holding. Observers saw the fuselage flexing as if it might snap at any moment. Using the brakes and reverse thrust on the operable starboard engine, the captain successfully brought the aircraft to a halt on the 6995-ft (2,133-m) main runway.

It was only after shutting everything down and moving back to assist with the evacuation that the pilots realized how close they had been to the aircraft snapping in half at any time or tearing itself apart during their rapid descent to a level where passengers could breathe without masks. With no upper fuselage to take the compressive forces, the fuselage could have snapped upwards at the last moment had they come down too hard on the nose-wheel. It is not clear whether anyone has mentioned that the 'lack of a green' to confirm the nose-wheel was locked might have made the captain more careful than he would have been to bring the nose down gently and may have been a blessing in disguise.

The only passengers unscathed, apart from eardrum problems, were those sitting right at the rear of the passenger cabin, which had retained its roof. Those immediately behind the break had been hit by debris and were suffering from lacerations, often to the face. Worst affected were those sitting in the area exposed to the elements, some of whom were trapped in their seats in places where the floor had buckled upwards beneath them due to the air pressure in the hold below.

Those able to vacate their seats and walk, either evacuated via the stairs at the rear or the emergency slide at the main door at the front, with at least one dithering passenger having to be pushed onto the slide by the first officer. The fire crew was able to extract and evacuate the others in less than half an hour, and dispatch them to hospital by ambulance

There was a whole range of major and minor injuries, including lacerations from flailing wires and even electrical burns occasioned by contact with them. It took time and therapy, for once justified, for some to recover psychologically.

Search of the ocean where the explosive decompression had occurred failed to produce either the body of the ejected flight attendant or any useful material evidence. With key evidence missing, investigators had to work out what had happened from cracks and disbonding on the periphery of the hole.

To understand the conclusions of the investigators one needs to know how the fuselage of those early 737s was assembled or rather riveted and glued together.

To save weight, the skin of an airliner is often only the thickness of a credit card. Even the thickness of the paint or lack thereof, can make quite a difference to the overall weight of the aircraft.

The fuselage consists of overlapping panels mounted on a frame and riveted together. However, unlike a ship's hull where the rivets can hold the thick plates together with tremendous force, rivets holding the outer skin of an airliner can only get a limited purchase, as they have to be countersunk to ensure a clean airflow over them. If subjected to repeated stresses, cracks develop in the skin around them.

Therefore, Boeing and other manufacturers decided to bond the overlaps with epoxy resin—in principle using the rivets solely to hold the surfaces together while the resin cured (set) and bonded the joint. Of course, the rivets would provide residual strength to the joint in the event of failure of the bond, and allow time to discover the problem during maintenance.

As many who have used epoxy glues know, mixing the two resins together in the right quantities with adequate mixing every time is no easy task. Boeing thought it had solved the problem by putting the mix on a scrim tape. Kept in a refrigerator to prevent curing, the tape would be used as needed and sandwiched between the overlaps before riveting. In theory, it should have produced a perfect bond, but in practice, this was not always true for a number of reasons, including dirt and humidity.

If an aircraft is being operated in a hot, salty and damp environment, corrosion in the poorly bonded areas can push the bonded parts apart so that they in turn disbond until only the rivets are holding the assemblies together. Then, with all the stress and weakness concentrated along that line, a long crack can result.

Boeing was well aware of the problems associated with the bonding in the earlier models of the 737, but largely dismissed the possibility of a failure leading to a catastrophe as it had devised a 'safety flap' system. This consisted of having the skin crisscrossed by 'tear straps' that would arrest and divert any crack that was actually opening up (called the 'lead crack') at right angles, thus creating a triangular flap that would blow out and relieve the pressure before further damage was done. These tear straps created 10-

inch squares, big enough to relieve the pressure but not so big as to significantly weaken the structure in the process.

Not everyone agreed this would work, thinking it might not save the situation in the event of a crack along a line of rivets extending over several potential 'flaps.'

From evidence from the passenger mentioned above and signs of a crack on the same horizontal line of rivets on either side of the gap the NTSB investigators concluded that this was what had indeed happened. They later accepted as theoretically possible but unlikely, a scenario put forward by Matt Austin, a non-aeronautical engineer specializing in pressure vessel explosions, which suggested that the safety flap mechanism did initially work as intended but subsequently failed because the lost flight attendant, Clarabelle Lansing, was sucked into it in the process.

Austin was basing this on his experience of pressure vessels, where an initial rupture can be forced wide apart by a 'fluid hammer' effect when debris, for example, blocks the orifice, the powerful hammer effect around the hole being similar to that produced when one replaces the plug in one's bath while water is still flowing out. According to Austin, Clarabelle Lansing was the 'plug.' There is certainly some evidence that that was what happened as some passengers saw her being sucked leftwards and up into an 'opening.' Signs of blood spatter found (possibly seen in photos) on the remaining part of the fuselage aft of that point seem to be a good indication that she was caught there for a moment. If she had gone straight out as the roof opened up there would not have been any blood.

However, the NTSB's investigators stood by their initial findings as to the initial cause of the failure and their recommendations remain valid. Adding such grisly details would not change much. Should they have recommended that such safety flaps be considerably larger than just 10 inches square? Tests might show that the individual would have to be standing up and wearing a skirt to be sucked sideways and up into the venting flap.

The Aloha incident had a galvanizing effect in aviation circles with the realization that many had been complacent regarding aging aircraft. Outside those circles, the pictures of the roof of an airliner blowing away as if it were a tent in the wind produced tremendous pressure from both the public and the media on the US Congress, which in turn pressured the FAA, with the threat that if nothing were done, aircraft over a certain age would be banned outright.

The Aloha incident and subsequent accidents had the beneficial effect of getting Congress to fund the employment of additional FAA field inspectors, their number having dwindled from 1,672 to a low of 1,331 in 1984, despite the need for more stringent checks to prevent airlines cutting corners to maintain profitability in the face of deregulation.

One problem was that the airlines were not following the directives and advice provided by the manufacturers and the FAA. In their defense, one should point out that the FAA had drafted its directives in something resembling legalese and that a small airline, like Aloha, would have needed someone to translate these into a form the mechanics could grasp.

As regards the Aloha incident, many said some other airlines were as bad, and that Aloha was merely the first to have a failure because their old high-cycle aircraft were operating in the particularly hot, salty and humid environment in the Hawaiian Islands.

The incident and the strained relations with John Maple, the Principle Maintenance Inspector, assigned by the FAA to Aloha, made Boeing rethink its confidentiality policy. Boeing, thinking like medical doctors, felt that 'patients' might hesitate to come to them with problems if they thought they would be reported to the regulators.

FAA inspector Maple, who said he had prompted Aloha to get Boeing to review its maintenance procedures, was furious to find himself excluded from the meeting at which Boeing reported the results. Since then Boeing has told airlines to report problems themselves as it will do so anyway within 24 hours.

Boeing might have been justified in its thinking about confidentiality, but now with lawyers avid to find any cover-up and sue, the downside risk of that informal approach is now probably too great anyway.

Although not in any of the official reports, it is alleged Boeing staff traveling as passengers on the aircraft in question felt it was in a pretty bad way due to the rattles, as did another frequent traveler who said it felt like an 'old car.'

The excellent article by Martin Aubury in the BASI journal from which some of the information here is drawn finishes by saying the teams setting out to investigate the problems with aging aircraft concluded that checking the obvious was not enough, and that:

1. If signs of corrosion are found, it must be assumed the state of the whole aircraft is questionable.

2. If a problem is found, a proper fix is essential. They point out that repairs are sometimes badly done with questionable techniques. These probably seem strong at the beginning but may fail later, as happened in the case of the repairs to the aft pressure bulkhead in the JAL 747, which resulted in the worst single-aircraft disaster ever.

3. A repair making one part too strong may produce stress elsewhere. In addition, repairs may hide other defects or make them difficult to see. They therefore need especially careful and thorough checking.

# CARGO HOLD DOOR FAILS ON 747
# (Honolulu 1989)

### Business Passengers Blown Out

> The problem of aging structures highlighted by the Aloha incident may have diverted attention from another aging problem—aging wiring. Sometimes hasty repairs to those worrisome fuselage structures have led to metal shavings falling into wire bundles.
>
> The incident described below, involving the 89th production line Boeing 747 manufactured in late 1970, shows that short-circuits not only present a fire risk, but also the risk of triggering something more unexpected—in this case the unlocking of a cargo door prior to takeoff.
>
> *[United Airlines Flight 811]*

The aircraft used for United Airlines Flight UA811 from Honolulu to Auckland, New Zealand, on February 24, 1989, with 337 passengers on board, was an old Boeing 747 that had seen considerable service. Honolulu was essentially a refueling stop—the airline also had a non-stop Los Angeles to Auckland flight for which they used a newer long-range 747.

The aircraft received clearance to take off at 1:52 a.m. local time, and climbed out as usual except for deviating somewhat from the normal course to avoid some thunderstorm cells—their presence ultimately proving fortunate as they made the captain keep the 'attach seat belt!' signs switched on.

Sixteen minutes into the flight, with the aircraft having passed 22,000 ft on its climb to its 30,000+ cruising height for the long trans-Pacific leg to Auckland, the aircraft juddered, and the aircrew heard a thud that appeared to have come from behind and below them. There followed a tremendous explosion, which for a moment tilted the aircraft leftwards.

The roar of the wind became unbelievably loud, and the misting of the air confirmed that the aircraft had suffered a rapid decompression. Failure of the lights added to the fears of many that this was to be another Lockerbie.

However, the emergency lighting soon kicked in and people began to realize the aircraft was not (at least for the time being) in the process of breaking up. The cabin pressure warning horn prompted the crew to put on their oxygen masks, but to their consternation, they found there appeared to be no oxygen.

In putting the aircraft into an emergency dive to get to a level where they could breathe more easily, the captain might, as in the Aloha case, have been putting the integrity of the aircraft at risk. At the time, there was no way he could have known the extent of the damage. In fact, even without an emergency dive, the flight crew should have been able to stay operational until reaching a reasonably comfortable height.

The first officer entered 7700 (the emergency code) into the transponder, and called Honolulu Approach Control to formalize the emergency. While able to communicate with far-off ATC, the pilots could not communicate with the cabin crew just behind them. Meanwhile, the instruments were showing the No. 3 engine was failing and would have to be shut down. After that was completed, the flight engineer went back to inspect the damage.

In the early 747s, the upper cabin behind the flight deck was quite small. The engineer was astounded to see a 3-m wide section of the skin below the windows had separated from the stringers and formers on the right-hand side, and the open sky visible between the gaps. This accounted for the noise of the wind in the cockpit. Worse was to come.

On descending to the larger lower deck Business Class cabin below, the flight engineer saw that, there, the stringers and formers had disappeared as well, leaving a 3-m wide gaping hole extending from floor-level to the ceiling. What is more, the floor had failed just above the cargo hold door below, and the five rows of twin seats that had been attached to it there had disappeared—presumably together with a number of passengers as the aircraft had been quite full.

The remaining Business Class passengers had tried to move back to the main cabin where the scene was almost unimaginable. People were screaming; some were hysterical; and others were already in the brace position waiting for the aircraft to crash. Because the volume of air in the main passenger cabins had been so much greater, the effect of the mass of air rushing forwards when the sudden decompression occurred had been even greater too. The escaping air had hurled meal trays and glasses with such force that some were even embedded in the bulkheads. It had also dislodged wall and ceiling panels and there was dust and debris everywhere. The projectiles had injured a number of passengers, and even those that were unscathed seemed distressed because of the wind and the stress.

The cabin crew valiantly tried to get the situation in hand but the noise of the wind made communication with the passengers virtually impossible. One positive was that having descended to a lower altitude, the passengers, whose oxygen masks were not working, were coping.

In assessing the damage, the flight engineer was particularly concerned to see long streaks of flame emanating sporadically from the No. 4 engine (the one on the extreme right). The violence of the decompression had ejected debris, or possibly a passenger, not only into the No. 3 engine that had been shut down, but even as far as the outboard engine. Hurrying back to the flight deck, the flight engineer found his colleagues waiting for him to assist with the shutdown of that engine shutdown, which they duly carried out.

With engine power on only one side, the 747 limped back towards Honolulu, with the reduced speed having somewhat lessened the disturbing noise of the wind. Twenty minutes later the distraught and terrified passengers had their spirits raised by the sight of Honolulu that they had left shortly before.

As they lowered the flaps to land, a flap asymmetry appeared, and the captain had to limit the amount of flap to 10 degrees. He decided to come in at 190 to 200 knots not only because of the limited amount of flap, but also because the aircraft might be difficult to control at the normal lower speed due to damage to some control surfaces, having both engines on one side shut down, and the gaping hole. He made a perfect landing and managed to bring the aircraft safely to a halt using the wheel brakes and idle-reverse thrust on the two 'good' engines.

The captain ordered an emergency evacuation in the course of which some passengers, and surprisingly it is said all the cabin crew, sustained some form of injury. A number of the passengers had been injured when the decompression occurred.

Nine Business Class passengers had been ejected altogether—eight in the seats they were sitting in and the ninth, who had been sitting just across the aisle from that block of seats, without his seat, making one wonder whether he was properly strapped in.

Things could have been much worse and the fact that the aircraft remained intact is perhaps a credit to Boeing, especially as it was an early model 747. Both the flight crew and the cabin crew performed well in very difficult circumstances. Valuable lessons were learnt, such as ensuring the pilots and cabin crew are guaranteed to have oxygen available—oxygen requirement is much greater for someone engaged in physical activity and needing to be able to think clearly.

It was immediately obvious that the untoward opening of the cargo hold door on the front right-hand side had been responsible for the explosive decompression and associated structural damage.

Cargo hold doors are by their very nature a potentially vulnerable part on an aircraft. To save room, they generally open outwards and have to be wide enough to allow pallets and containers to pass through. In addition, they are the doors most frequently opened and shut on an aircraft.

An extremely complicated mechanism consisting of pushrods, cranks, cams, and latches, to mention only a few of the items, is required to cope with the width. In addition, on large aircraft, an electric motor is usually incorporated to do the basic locking and unlocking, with manual locks completing the process. There should be no danger of the unlocking function operating in flight as the motor uses electrical power only available on the ground either from the APU (Auxiliary Power Unit) at the rear of the aircraft, or from the airport electricity supply.

The incident occurred in February 1989, and it was not until September the following year that by an incredible feat of technology the US Navy recovered the cargo door (in two pieces) from a depth of 14,200 ft. The recovered door showed it had been unlocked electrically and the manual locking pins had insufficient strength to prevent the door opening. This contradicted the NTSB 'Final Report' saying the electrical unlocking of the door prior to takeoff could only be considered a remote possibility.

This shows the danger, in the absence of definitive evidence, of assuming that 'what was the most probable cause by far' was actually the cause. The NTSB published a correction.

Meanwhile, the inquiry had made the following points:

**1. Questions concerning the door's design and approval by the FAA.**

**2. Doubts concerning maintenance by the airline and their failure to detect trends.**

**3. The airline's failure to realize that the FAA directive concerning the doors was safety related and that its execution should not have been postponed, even though the airline was not exceeding the proscribed time limit.**

**4. Contributing to the accident was a lack of timely corrective actions by Boeing and the FAA following a 1987 cargo-door-opening incident on a Pan Am B-747.**

Thinking of how there had been a previous alert makes one think of the DC-10 cargo door incidents in 1972 and 1974 where a known cargo door problem was left unresolved. Following the DC-10 disaster outside Paris, airliners, including the Japan Airlines Boeing 747 featured in the chapter on uncontrollability, were fitted with vents in the floor to release pressure differentials.

The 747 in question had been manufactured earlier in 1970, and the situation regarding floor vents then was uncertain. However, the floor did buckle near the failed cargo door—damaging the pipes feeding oxygen to the pilots and passengers, as well as the intercom system, but not affecting vital controls. The fact that a 'flap' opened in the side of the Business Class cabin and let much of the air out helped prevent the more extensive damage that might have led to the loss of the aircraft.

Improvements, too late for those nine Business Class passengers, were subsequently made, and there has not been an accident since due to the opening of a Boeing 747 cargo door.

# CHINA AIRLINES/EL AL 747F ENGINE MOUNTS (1991/1992)

## Boeing Redesigns Engine Mounts at Great Expense

> It is not so widely known that Boeing spent a considerable amount of money redesigning the engine-supporting pylons on its early 747s and refitting many aircraft following two crashes of the cargo versions.
>
> In both crashes, an engine separated taking the neighboring one with it. This crash of an El Al 747 into a block of high-rise apartments in an Amsterdam suburb received much publicity because of the mysterious nature of its cargo.
>
> *[China Airlines 747 Freighter]*
> *[El Al 747 Freighter]*

The supporting pylons for engines mounted under the wings of airliners are usually designed to allow the engine to possibly fall off in certain circumstances, such as:

**1. When exceptional torque is produced by an engine seizing up.**

**2. When an engine is seriously on fire.**

**3. When ditching in water, so the wing is not torn off, or so the aircraft does not spin round disastrously and cartwheel.**

On December 29, 1991, the in-board No. 3 engine came off an 11-year old China Airlines Boeing 747-2R7F (Freighter) as it was climbing out under high power from Taiwan's Chiang Kai-Shek International Airport. It glanced off the outboard No. 4 engine (set further back), which in turn also fell off. The aircraft subsequently crashed, killing all five occupants.

Though the No. 3 engine was retrieved from the sea some distance from the main debris, the pylon was only discovered seven months later.

Nine months after that disaster, an El Al Cargo 747 suffered a similar separation of engines 3 and 4 when climbing out of Amsterdam's Schiphol Airport. Vital control parts were affected and the aircraft became uncontrollable with the pilots trying to solve the problem by raising all the flaps. After seeking to return to the airport to make an emergency landing, the aircraft ploughed into an 11-storey apartment complex in Amsterdam's down-market district of Bijlmer.

The last words from the crew were disturbingly matter-of-fact:

*Going down...eh...1862, going down, going down, copied going down?*

In addition to the four occupants of the aircraft, 47 people were killed on the ground, with the total perhaps more as the building housed a number of unregistered illegal immigrants. The disaster immediately received considerable publicity because the dramatic pictures probably made people consider just how much damage an aircraft plunging into a building can cause.

However, the mystery surrounding the nature of the aircraft's cargo was to give the story legs.

Amsterdam's Schiphol Airport was one of several European airports allowing El Al to transship cargo unsupervised, and as a result, the details of the manifest were not public knowledge. After saying the freighter had been carrying innocuous flowers and perfume, the Israeli Government eventually admitted that a precursor for making nerve gas (sarin) had been onboard, but claimed it was for testing filters and the amount was small. It was a very sensitive matter, especially as the aircraft had come from the USA and it would look bad if the Americans were seen to be providing Israel with materials for chemical warfare. Depleted uranium was also present.

Residents reported seeing men in white suits sifting through the wreckage. The flight data recorder (FDR) was never recovered, leading to suspicions that it had been spirited away by Mossad (the Israeli secret service), though why they should do so is not easy to comprehend, unless they feared the accident was due to the cargo.

People and notably rescuers in the area of the crash—where the debris burnt for an hour and smoldered for several more—reported all sorts of ailments and depression, and there were accusations of a cover-up. As in the case of 9/11, people would anyway have been affected by the untold number of constituents in the cloud of smoke and dust when an aircraft, laden with fuel just after takeoff, hits a building. The nature of the cargo is not very relevant here, except to remark that some very nasty things probably pass over our heads from time to time, in aircraft cargo holds and diplomatic bags.

A 14-inch crack was found in one of the 'fuse pins' used for attaching the engines on the El Al freighter, and designed to shear as a safety measure under the special circumstances mentioned above, but not in normal service. Such cracks can develop when metal is under repetitive flexing conditions, especially if there is an initial pit on the surface due to corrosion, in a phenomenon called stress-assisted corrosion where the stress facilitates the penetration of the corrosion. The initial pit would probably have been due to the surface being left vulnerable to corrosion (passive) due to lack of primer or faulty coating during manufacture. Incidentally, shortly before, Boeing had issued warnings concerning the pins used for attaching the Pratt & Whitney engines in question.

Following these two incidents, Boeing notified users about the necessary checks and then redesigned the entire mounting system.

Modifying existing aircraft cost the company a considerable amount of money, as it involved a lengthy task—said by one commentator to be 40 days. In addition, a considerable number of susceptible 747s had been delivered.

On the basis that the El Al pilot initially talked about an engine being on fire, it has been suggested that the two accidents just described were caused by a door breaking off and entering the No. 3 engine. If true, would Boeing have gone to such great expense to redesign the attachment?

One final point worth making is how a mistake, oversight, or carelessness in a manufacturing process can have disastrous results years later, of which there are number of examples in this book. Of course, better design and checks should have prevented one failure leading to a disaster.

# CHAPTER 11
# INVISIBLE DANGERS—TURBULENCE

## SIGHTSEEING BOAC 707 BREAKS UP
## (Mt Fuji, Japan 1966)

### Voyeurs Caught up in Beauty's Swirling Skirts

> In the 1970s, when air travel was relatively novel, at least to non-Americans, British airline pilots would regale their passengers with details such as the 'incredible' quantity of fuel on board, and expect them to be in awe. Soon they were to find the extortionate price of their ticket set by the officially endorsed IATA[1] cartel even more awesome!
>
> As compensation for this, or because flying still had something of the frontier spirit about it, a BOAC captain might sometimes offer his passengers a treat. What better treat could there be than giving them a close-up view of Japan's renowned Mount Fuji?
>
> *[BOAC Flight 911]*
> *[Canadian Pacific Airlines Flight 402]*

Weather conditions that day were so good that from Tokyo, one could clearly see the ice-capped cone of 12,390 ft Mount Fuji some 80 km or more away. This prompted the captain of the British Overseas Airways Corporation (BOAC) flight to Hong Kong to change his flight plan at the last minute.

Instead of the usual 'Jet Green 6' airway from Tokyo's Haneda Airport, out over the sea to Oshima Island and on to Kagoshima in the south, he would take the scenic overland 'Red 23' airway skirting Mount Fuji and onwards to the industrial city of Nagoya. The 75-strong American tour group he had onboard would surely be highly appreciative.

Despite the bright sky overhead, the atmosphere at Haneda Airport was more than somber. Only a month earlier, an All Nippon Airways Boeing 727 had crashed 15 km away from the airport.[2] As if that had not been enough, the previous night, with many aircraft diverting due to visibility just below the 1.0 km minimum, a Canadian Pacific DC-8 whose captain was determined to land there had circled for 45 minutes until visibility improved just enough for him to be allowed to make an attempt.

In their haste to seize the opportunity before the weather closed in again, the pilots of the DC-8 had descended too steeply. The tower told them they were too low for the distance they were from the runway and instructed them to abort the landing. Disregarding this, the pilot continued, his aircraft first snapping off a number of the frail posts set in the sea to support the approach lights before smashing into the unforgiving concrete of the airport perimeter sea wall, somewhat higher than the runway to keep the sea out. Only eight of the 72 occupants survived the ensuing blaze.

The next day, the pilots and passengers of the BOAC Hong Kong flight could hardly have failed to gaze at the charred debris of that DC-8 as they turned onto the runway to line up for their takeoff for Hong Kong. According to some imaginative Japanese newspapers, this horrific sight might have contributed in some way to the deadly accident that was to befall the BOAC flight, in that it must have unnerved the pilots.

Leaving the charred debris behind, the BOAC 707 lifted off and made a wide turn to join Airway Red 23. Instead of continuing his climb to cruising height, the captain initiated a gradual descent on reaching almost 17,000 ft. Then in what must surely have been an intended deviation from the airway that for safety reasons skirted Mount Fuji, the aircraft apparently then veered from a heading of 246 degrees to a heading of 298 degrees magnetic, taking it towards the conical peak of the mountain, then only some 10 miles distant. Possibly, the captain intended to 'snake' so passengers on both sides would get a view, without rushing to one side and possibly risking upsetting the aircraft.

Just as the passengers were about to get the wonderful close-up view of the mountain, a violent force of air pushed the vertical tailfin (vertical stabilizer) so sharply to the left that it broke off, taking the horizontal stabilizer on the left-hand side with it.

This—possibly with the help of the violent air turbulence—destabilized the aircraft so that it immediately began to break up. People below could see it falling from the sky trailing vaporized fuel, which many thought to be smoke. Some even took photographs. No Mayday call or any other radio transmission was made.

Authorities diverted a US Navy A-4 fighter from the nearby Atsugi air base to look for signs of wreckage. It encountered such violent turbulence in the area that the pilot almost lost his own craft.

According to Macarthur Job (*Air Disaster* Vol. 1), the Navy pilot said afterwards:

> *I flew into the same turbulence, and truly thought the airplane was going to come unglued ...*

> *My oxygen mask was pulled loose, my head was banging on both*

*sides of the cockpit canopy, the instruments were unreadable, and the controls about useless.*

*Somehow, I managed to get the nose pointing up more times than down, and eventually climbed out of the turbulence. When I got back to Atsugi, the A-4's g meter had registered +9g and -4g, and the fighter was grounded for inspection.*

Other aircraft flying nearby, but not quite so close to the mountain, also reported severe turbulence.

Ultimately, searchers found the wreckage of the BOAC 707 scattered in a wide path some 16 km long. As the aircraft had broken up at a considerable height, there was no possibility of survivors despite much of the fuselage hitting the ground in one piece. For the investigators, finding out precisely what had happened was difficult because searing heat from burning fuel had seriously damaged the flight data recorder (FDR) located, in those days, in the nose.

The aircraft did not have a cockpit voice recorder (CVR), despite their installation being made mandatory in the United States the year before (1965). In the United Kingdom, the pilots' union, like that of their North American counterparts, had long opposed the introduction of a 'spy in the cockpit,' and their installation only became mandatory for UK-registered airliners eight years later following the crash of the Trident airliner where the captain had had a heart attack (see page 167). Without a CVR to help them, investigators were unable to determine what transpired in the cockpit.

Thus with no FDR or CVR, air accident investigators had to try to work out what had happened to the 707 through careful examination of the wreckage and analysis of reports from 'amateur' eyewitnesses, who from the ground could hardly make accurate estimates of the initial height and course of the aircraft. Luckily, the film recovered from a passenger's 8-mm movie camera seemed to answer that question, and is indeed the basis for the aircraft headings just cited.

As mentioned, it was ascertained that the vertical stabilizer (vertical tailfin) had snapped off in a leftwards direction, and had struck the left horizontal stabilizer causing that to break off too. The ventral stabilizer (an inverted 'shark's fin' under the belly beneath the tail) also broke off in a leftwards direction, suggesting a powerful leftwards gust was responsible rather than over-aggressive use of the rudder as in the case of the Airbus 300 taking off from JFK in 2001.

The passenger's 8-mm movie camera had been filming out of the window when it received a shock sharp enough to skip two frames. Still working, it fell to the floor and showed seats and carpet before stopping.

From the footage, investigators estimated that the aircraft had been traveling at a speed of 320–370 knots.

They found some pre-existing cracks in the tail area, but tests showed these did not significantly weaken the tail and that some exceptional force must have been at work. [Nevertheless, inspections revealed similar cracks in other 707s, and in consequence design changes were made and more frequent inspections were ordered.]

The loss of two Japan Air Self Defense Force fighters due to severe turbulence near Mount Fuji in February 1962 should have been lesson enough, but it was only after this tragic and unnecessary sightseeing accident that the 'Scenic Airway' option was withdrawn.

Before the year was out, yet another major air disaster occurred in Japan. That November, a small domestically built All Nippon Airways YS-11 overshot the runway at Matsuyama causing 50 fatalities. Now, years sometimes go by without a single significant disaster in Japan, proving that flying there is much safer.

---

[1]IATA, the International Air Transport Association representing the world's airlines, regulated tickets prices. It acted very much as a cartel, keeping ticket prices artificially high. Having largely lost the battle with deregulation in the US, Europe, and elsewhere, it is shifting its focus to other aspects of commercial aviation such as safety.

Both IATA and the UN's ICAO, International Civil Aviation Organization have their headquarters in Montreal, Canada.

[2] Investigators later concluded a spoiler *might* have deployed and caused the aircraft to stall.

# WIND SHEAR & MICROBURSTS (1982/1985)

## Dangers of Wind shear

> The 'hidden danger in the sky' of most frequent concern to pilots is wind shear as it may well affect them when they are taking off and landing, and consequently flying slowly and near the ground with little height for recovery.
>
> After a series of wind shear disasters in the United States, airports most prone to wind shear have been belatedly equipped with extremely expensive devices to detect the phenomenon. They have proved highly effective.
>
> *[Pan American World Airways Flight 759]*
> *[Delta Flight 191]*

Wind shear occurs where two bodies of air moving in different directions come together. This can result in a dramatic drop in airspeed.

Not only can an aircraft find itself going too slowly and stalling, the air in the second body may be going downwards as well, thus tending to slam the already vulnerable aircraft into the ground.

One particularly nasty form of wind shear is the 'microburst.' It has a life span of about 5 to 10 minutes and affects an area normally no more than 2.5 miles (4 km) across. It consists of a small, very intense downdraft that descends to the ground and spreads out in all directions from the point of impact rather like water from a faucet (tap) falling on a flat surface.

Thus a pilot might take off at the 'correct' airspeed into say a 20-knot headwind, with it also pushing him upwards, and having gained a modicum of height, suddenly find himself in a 30-knot tailwind that is also pushing him down faster than the wind that pushed him upwards.

The 50-knot drop in airspeed could result in at worst a stall, and at least a high sink rate compounded by the effect of the downwards draught, giving the pilot little time to recover, especially if obstacles such as trees or perimeter fences lie in his path.

Two incidents occurring in a three-year period made the American traveling public very aware of wind shear and somewhat nervous of flying. Many phoned their Member of Congress insisting that they do something so that pilots could be forewarned.

## Boeing 727 (New Orleans International Airport 1982)

ATC had warned of wind shear in 'all quadrants' as the Pan American World Airways Flight 759 prepared for takeoff. The captain told the first officer to let the speed build up on takeoff and said they would switch off the air-conditioning so the forward engines would be able to provide more power.

These precautions were to no avail, for after takeoff the aircraft rose to roughly 100 ft (60 m) and then began to sink. It seemed it might manage to stay in the air especially as the ground effect would come into play, but at an altitude of some 50 ft (15 m) it struck some trees 2,376 ft (724 m) from the end of the runway. Losing further height, it continued, clipping trees and houses, before crashing in a residential area 2,234 ft (681 m) further on—destroying six houses and substantially damaging five more.

The impact, explosion and fire that followed resulted in the deaths of all 145 on board and 8 people on the ground, making a final death toll of 153.

The inquiry concluded that the accident was due to microburst-induced wind shear and that part of the problem would have been the pilot being unaware of what was happening, notably the reversal of wind direction and downwards push associated with the microburst phenomenon.

The fact that the total distance from the end of the runway to the crash site was about 4,610 ft (1,405 m) shows how they might very easily have been able to recover. No doubt the initial strike with the trees, and further clipping of trees and houses impaired the performance of the aircraft.

This was an example of what can happen when taking off. In an incident three years later, the aircraft was attempting to land.

### TriStar (Dallas Ft Worth 1985)

Thunderstorms were in the area of the Texas airport as Delta Flight 191, an L1011 jumbo jet with 163 passengers and crew on board, approached Runway 17L (i.e. the left of two or even three parallel runways in 170-degree direction) for landing. There was a rain shaft and scattered lightning coming from a thunderstorm cell in the airliner's final approach path, but the pilots decided the weather was passable and continued the approach.

Some 15 to 30 seconds after the L1011 entered the weather, however, the rain and lightning intensified, and the airplane was buffeted by a violent series of up and down drafts. The headwind increased rapidly to 26 knots, and then, just as suddenly, switched to a 46-knot tailwind, resulting in an abrupt loss of 72 knots of airspeed. The jet was only 800 ft above the ground when this happened, leaving the pilots little room to maneuver when the airplane began to lose airspeed and altitude at the same time. Thirty-eight seconds later, Delta Flight 191 crashed into the terrain short of the runway, killing all but 26 of those onboard.

### Wake Turbulence

One phenomenon, wake turbulence—that is mini-tornadoes coming off the wingtips of large aircraft—can prove troublesome, and sometimes fatal, for following aircraft. Surprisingly, the calmer the weather conditions, the more dangerous these are likely to be, as without turbulence to break them up, they can float for miles.

The worst scenario is generally when a large aircraft heavily laden with fuel and passengers is climbing out after takeoff under high power in clean configuration (i.e. with flaps and undercarriage retracted—nothing sticking out). Large jets use the word *heavy* in their call signs as an extra warning to air traffic controllers.

The amount of turbulence generated does not depend purely on size, with the Boeing 767 being well known for nasty turbulence. Airbus is trying to demonstrate that the wake turbulence generated by its superjumbo A380 is not commensurate with its size and that it should not be penalized by being designated as requiring extra separation from following aircraft.

## UA 747-100 FLIGHT 826 DROPS 1,000 FT (Off Japan 1997)

### Why Passengers Should Keep Seat Belts Attached

> Passengers scoffing at their captain's suggestion that they keep their seat belts attached 'just in case,' do not realize that a smash against the ceiling panels or other solid object could quickly wipe that know-all look from their faces.
>
> Though pilots try to avoid clear air turbulence, it can occur unexpectedly.
>
> *[United Airlines Flight 826]*

Most of the passengers on the United Air Lines 747-100 that had taken off from Tokyo's Narita Airport for Honolulu at 9.05 p.m. local time were Japanese holidaymakers planning to spend the extended New Year holiday period in the warm climes of Hawaii rather than in wintry Japan. Two hours out of Narita, they were flying above the Pacific at the economical cruising height of 33,000 ft. Some people were moving about the cabin even though the 'Fasten Seat Belts!' signs were on. These included cabin crew with their trolleys as the passengers had just finished dinner.

Without warning, the aircraft suddenly dropped and dropped and dropped. So abrupt was the descent that heavy food trolleys hit the ceiling with a crash, making an indentation before crashing back on some passengers. One Japanese woman hit the ceiling and fell back in such a contorted way that she subsequently died from the injuries sustained. Japanese TV later broadcast a video taken by a passenger showing screaming passengers being thrown about the cabin.

A pilot reassured the frightened passengers over the PA, saying:

*We have just hit air turbulence and the aircraft descended 300 meters (almost a thousand feet). There is no danger of a crash.*

The aircraft then turned back to Tokyo so the injured could receive medical attention. Though 110 out of the 374 passengers were said to have been injured, only 10 were kept in hospital. Nine of the 19 crewmembers were said to have been injured, with three of them in a serious condition.

New technology based on lasers should soon make it possible to detect clear air turbulence, which very occasionally can be more than unpleasant as the above case so well proves. It is difficult to detect because, unlike storms, it does not contain the raindrops that can be seen on the aircraft's weather radar. Reports from aircraft ahead are helpful, at least in so much as giving pilots a chance to warn passengers to fasten their seat belts.

252

# CHAPTER 12

# CONTROLLED FLIGHT

# INTO TERRAIN (CFIT)

## FAILED INDICATOR BULB
## (Everglades (Florida) 1972)

**No One Flying Aircraft**

> The 1972 crash of an Eastern Airlines TriStar into Florida's Everglades is often cited as the classic disaster where an aircraft under control hits the ground.
>
> On coming in to land, the lamp confirming the nose wheel was 'down and locked' failed to show. As the flight crew flew around trying to work out why, the autopilot set to keep them at a constant height partially disengaged. Only when it was too late did they notice they had been losing height at a dangerous rate.
>
> *[Eastern Air Lines Flight 401]*

As the Eastern Airlines Lockheed TriStar with 176 people aboard, and with the captain, first officer, flight engineer and a company technician on the flight deck, came in to land at Miami, everything was normal except that the lamp confirming the nose wheel was 'down and locked' had failed to light up. The crew consequently informed ATC they wanted to abort the landing and investigate the nature of the problem. ATC told them to turn off and proceed northbound at 2,000 ft.

With the autopilot set to maintain that height, the two pilots fiddled with the bulb, ultimately trying to remove it from its socket to see whether it had blown. Meanwhile, the captain had told the flight engineer to go down to the avionics bay below to look at the wheel via the observation port. He came back saying he could not be sure, and went back to look again accompanied by the company technician.

While the flight engineer was away in the avionics bay, the chime indicating a deviation of more than 250 ft from the set height sounded just near the seat he had vacated, which he would have heard had he been there. The two pilots wearing headsets evidently did not.

ATC was also getting worried about their height, which was down to 900 ft, but instead of warning them, he politely asked them:

*How are things coming along out there?*

The Eastern Airlines TriStar captain's reply that they were returning to land suggested they were in control of the situation. The aircraft continued in the darkness over the Everglades swamp, with nothing on the ground to indicate how near it was—rather like the Peruvian aircraft over the sea.

Turning the aircraft southwards, the first officer noticed the lack of height despite the fact that the autopilot light was on.

First officer:

*We did something to the altitude!*

Captain:

*What? ... We're still at 2,000...right?*

The captain, evidently looking at his instruments, exclaimed:

*Hey...what's happening here?*

It was too late to save the situation. There was a bleep from the radio altimeters indicating the proximity of the ground, followed by the sound of the left wing hitting the ground as they had been in a left bank turn. The left landing gear struck next, and then the aircraft began to break up with wreckage spread over a swathe of flat marshland 1,500 ft long.

It took rescuers 30 minutes to reach the scene in helicopters and airboats.[1] Only two sections of the aircraft were intact—the tail and a section of the cabin. The rest was in pieces.

It is remarkable that 77 out of the 176 persons on board survived. The death toll was 99. The two pilots and the flight engineer were among the fatalities, though the company technician in the jump seat who had absented himself from the flightdeck and was in the avionics bay to try to check visually from there whether the wheel was down did survive. The press noted that this was an accident involving the new breed of wide-body airliners and wondered whether it heralded deadlier accidents in terms of the number of lives lost at one time.

The investigators attributed the disaster to 'pilot error.'

They said:

> *It seems that in turning around to tell the flight engineer to go down to the avionics bay, the captain must have exerted a strong force on the control column (equivalent to 15 lb) thus disengaging the autopilot on his side.*

[To enable pilots to react instantly to an emergency, autopilots automatically disengage if a strong force is applied to the control column or sidestick. Unfortunately, the autopilot on the first officer's side was mistakenly set to only disengage if the applied force exceeded some 20 lb, compared with rather less on the captain's side. As a result, the light on the first officer's side would have stayed on, giving him the impression that the autopilot was maintaining them at 2,000 ft.]

Contributing factors could have been:

1. **The captain with over 30,000 hours' flight experience was in a sense being extra careful.**

2. **The fact that the indicator lamp was on the first officer's side meant that he had to fiddle with it and was thereby taken away from flying the aircraft.**

3. **The flight engineer might have been afraid to confirm the front wheel was down properly.**

4. **With hindsight, the air traffic controller should have expressed his concern about their excessively low altitude rather than just politely asking, 'How are things coming along out there?'**

5. **The last point about the danger of expressing concern obliquely and politely has been borne out in a number of tragedies in this book, including the worst ever multi-aircraft crash when two Boeing 747s collided on the runway at Tenerife.**

---

[1] Airboats are shallow draft flat-bottom boats with a fan at the back that can skim over the swamp.

# PRE-PROGRAMMED TO HIT MT EREBUS
# (Antarctica 1979)

## A Question of 'Command Responsibility'

> The accident at the South Pole in which a DC-10 full of sightseers flew into a mountain took place at a time when the advantage of using computers to manage the flight was being exploited, but well before development of the enhanced ground proximity warning systems just mentioned.
>
> Apart from the technical aspects, there is some similarity with the case already described where the A320 Airbus crashed at the air show with sightseeing passengers on board, in that the pilots got carried away by the joviality of the jaunt.
>
> *[Air New Zealand Flight 901]*

Staff at Air New Zealand's Flight Operations Division had a sinking feeling of culpability in their stomachs on learning their sightseeing DC-10 had flown straight into a mountain at the South Pole, for that was precisely what they had programmed it to do.

Without informing the pilots, they had made a 'correction' to the final waypoint the night before, moving it from the end of McMurdo Sound, where the track to it passed over water, to a point behind Mount Erebus where the track would pass right over the 12,450-ft high mountain.

The airline's Chief Executive then compounded the scandal by appropriating and shredding documents to try to cover up the mistake.

The scandalous aspect that made the affair a cause célèbre in normally uneventful New Zealand is not why this disaster is of particular interest here. Rather, it is because it highlights three common elements essential for preventing air accidents:

1. **Command responsibility**

2. **Cockpit Resource Management (CRM)**

3. **Consideration of all possibilities when something odd happens and taking conservative action if any doubt remains**

*Command responsibility* is the tenet that the captain of a ship or aircraft has the ultimate responsibility for ensuring his passengers' and vessel's safety, whatever the pressures put on him by management or circumstances. There are no excuses. It is responsibility to a higher God—

'professionalism' in the best sense of the word. Something the captain of the *Titanic* apparently did not demonstrate.

CRM is the concept that the crew works as a team with even the 'lesser players' able to contribute. In this case, that person's contribution came 26 seconds before the impact, with a flight engineer registering his increasing disquiet by saying:

*I don't like this!*

In fact, both flight engineers had been getting increasingly concerned.

*Consideration of all possibilities* relates to the fact that the crew assumed they could not receive the VHF radio transmissions from the US base for some technical reason without thinking that their inability to receive them—they only work in 'line-of-sight' situations (unless the parties are very close)—might be because high land, possibly a mountain, was blocking their path.

### The Disaster

As in the case of the BOAC 'sightseeing' disaster near Japan's Mt Fuji and the Airbus crash at the Habsheim Air Show, 'jaunts' with sightseeing passengers on board are inherently more dangerous than serious commercial flights as they tend to generate an easy-going attitude and involve unfamiliar routes and circumstances.

Air New Zealand's sightseeing trips to the South Pole were no exception. However, involving a 6,000-nautical mile flight lasting up to 12 hours, they represented a major operation.

Weather conditions permitting, the aircraft would descend to 2,000 ft near the Pole for a better view. This low-level flying would consume fuel at a high rate, and even with a virtually full load of fuel at takeoff, the DC-10 would be operating without much margin for playing around before the long return leg home.

Before the introduction of GPS, navigation on long routes over water with no radio beacons depended upon Inertial Navigation Systems (INS), which were (and are) also used for guiding intercontinental ballistic missiles (ICBMs).

The idea behind INS is quite simple.

1. **A combination of gyroscopes measures changes of direction.**

2. **Sensors attached to inertial weights detect acceleration and deceleration.**

3. **A computer integrates the two to calculate the position.**

The system is in triplicate, allowing the computer to ascertain if one has failed, as it will be the 'odd man out.'

As with ballistic missiles, users can program the desired route into the system so the aircraft flies to the destination automatically.

In airline use, the system works very well *provided* the pilots put in the correct coordinates. This has perhaps not always been the case (see Korean Airlines 747 shot down over Russia).

The INS system is a form of dead reckoning, so, unlike the GPS system based on satellites, accuracy decreases with time and distance. Some versions are referred to as AINS (Area INS), in that they are considered accurate over a specific area.

These Air New Zealand trips to Antarctica were popular with airline staff and in consequence rather than choosing pilots with experience of polar flying, the treat was ill advisedly shared out as a perk. The captain chosen that time was 45-year-old Captain Collins. He had 11,000 hours' flying experience, 3,000 of them on the DC-10. A qualified navigator, he was regarded as a very capable pilot exercising good judgment, but lacked experience of flying in Arctic conditions.

The rest of the flight crew consisted of two first officers, Cassin and Lucas, and two flight engineers, Brooks (44) and Moloney (49). Brooks had been on one previous flight to the Antarctic, while Maloney had the most airline experience.

As usual on these trips, a celebrity was included, his role being to give a commentary to the passengers on approaching the South Pole. This time it was Peter Mulgrew, a well-known New Zealand adventurer, who had walked from McMurdo (the DC-10's first objective) to the South Pole on an expedition led by Sir Edmund Hillary, famed for climbing Mt Everest.

On board the DC-10 were 237 passengers. Though most were New Zealanders, other nationalities, including 24 Japanese and 23 Americans, were present. There was also a sizable cabin crew to indulge them. In all, 257 excited souls were departing from Auckland that November 28, 1979 morning, never to return.

McMurdo is a US exploration base 2,384 miles from Auckland. With 1,000 visitors in summer and 200 or so 'residents' in winter, it had long been the main point of entry for those venturing into Antarctica. Late November would be summer with daylight lasting 24 hours a day. Nearby is the much smaller New Zealand Scott base.

McMurdo has an ice runway able to take certain types of aircraft—weather conditions permitting. There was no question of the DC-10 touching down there—they only wanted to avail themselves of the base's radar facilities, so they could be (safely) talked-down to get a better view.

Next to McMurdo was Ross Island with various peaks, the highest being Mt Erebus (12,450 ft) and Mt Terror (10,700 ft), named after the two ships under the command of Englishman Captain Ross who came to the area in 1841, and, fearful of being iced-in, did not attempt to make land.

Mt Erebus is actually an active volcano. In satellite photos, the red-hot magma at the peak looks scary against the snowy whiteness of the surrounding slopes. Despite appearances, Ross Island is a true island, being joined to mainland Antarctica only by a vast ice shelf.

The planned outward route from Auckland would take the DC-10 out over the sea, over New Zealand's south island and on to the Antarctic. They would pass over a number of waypoints, including a couple of tiny islands that would enable them to confirm their position and hence the accuracy of their INS navigation system. Interestingly, the nearer they got to the South Pole the greater the discrepancy between their true heading and magnetic heading would become, attaining as much as 160 degrees at McMurdo. Indeed, at McMurdo anyone on the ground would find the compass needle pointing downwards!

The last waypoint before McMurdo was Cape Hallet. According to the (unrevised) map the pilots had worked on prior to the trip, the McMurdo waypoint was on low-lying ground, with just sea in between the two waypoints. The nearest they would come to Mt Erebus should have been 20 to 25 nautical miles, and with relatively little distance covered after passing over Cape Hallet, there could hardly be an INS error of that magnitude.

In fact, it was a pity the INS was performing so well. With the McMurdo waypoint reprogrammed to be 2 degrees 10 seconds of longitude further east. The direct track to it from Cape Hallet passed, not over the sea, but right over the mountain!

While still some way off McMurdo, the DC-10 was able to contact the base on VHF, but as the base replied on HF, both parties opted for HF, as that is less affected by distance and obstacles. In addition, being so far from anywhere, there would not be the usual interference from other transmissions.

McMurdo informed them that there was still low overcast at 2,000 ft with some snow, but that visibility remained about 40 miles. The DC-10 asked permission to descend to Flight Level 160 (16,000 ft), but was only authorized to descend to Flight Level 180.

McMurdo then said:

> Within range of 40 miles of McMurdo we have radar that will, if you desire, let you down to 1,500 ft on radar vectors. Over.

This pleased the DC-10 captain and first officer who were getting worried their trip would be a washout.

Thinking that the visibility was good enough for them to make a descent, perhaps performing an orbit (circle) to keep out of the cloud ahead, the captain said:

> Well actually it's clear out here if we get down.

To which the flight engineer commented:

> *It's not clear on the right-hand side here.*

The first officer said:

> *No.*

Despite the comment by the flight engineer, the first officer called McMurdo at the captain's request, saying:

> *We'd like further descent and we could orbit in our present position which is approximately 43 miles north, descending in VMC [Visual Meteorological Conditions].*

McMurdo gave permission and asked to be kept informed of their height, and the DC-10 acknowledged and confirmed they were vacating Flight Level 180.

With only three miles to go before they should be on the McMurdo radar, it is surprising that the captain should opt to go to the trouble of circling to descend in a clear part of sky where visibility on the right was not so clear. Was he trying to give his passengers a better view?

For a brief moment, the VHF radio seemed to be working. They then reverted to HF without considering that the inability to communicate by line of sight VHF could be because they were in the wrong location.

They then called McMurdo on HF:

> *901... still negative contact on VHF. We are VMC and we'd like to let down on a grid of one eight zero and proceed visually to McMurdo.*

McMurdo replied:

> *New Zealand 901, maintain VMC. Keep us advised of your altitude as you approach McMurdo ...*

Conversing in the cockpit, the captain said he had VMC 'THIS WAY,' and that he was 'GO(ing?).'

At the same moment, Mulgrew (the guide), frustrated at not being able to earn his keep, was saying to the others in the cockpit:

> *Ah well, you can't talk if you can't see anything.*

Adding:

> *Here you go. There's some land ahead.'*

The first officer informed McMurdo that they were descending from 6,000 ft to 2,000 ft, and that they were VMC.

The captain said he had heard there was clear weather at a place called Wright Valley and seemed to be asking Mulgrew whether he could get them there. He thought he could.

Perhaps getting worried, the flight engineer said:

*Where's Erebus in relation to us at the moment?*

After saying, *'Left, about 20 or 25 miles,'* and some discussion, Mulgrew admitted he did not really know. They then finally all agreed that conditions did not look good.

The flight engineer, expressing his concern more strongly, said:

*I don't like this.*

The captain (presumably relying on the INS) said they were 29 nautical miles north and that they would have to climb out of it.

First officer:

*You're clear to turn right. There's no high ground if you do a one eighty.*

Thereupon the GPWS (Ground Proximity Warning System) operating with a six-second delay to prevent spurious warnings went:

*Whoop, whoop. Pull up. Whoop whoop.*

The first officer announced they were at 'Five hundred feet.'

GPWS:

*Pull up!*

The first officer declared:

*Four hundred feet.*

GPWS:

*Whoop, whoop. Pull up. Whoop, whoop. Pull up.*

*Politely*, the captain asked for go-around power—he did not push the throttles 'through the gates' (to get maximum power at the sacrifice of engine life), so he could not have seen anything to indicate a mountain was ahead.

The last words on the CVR tape were from the GPWS:

*Whoop, whoop. Pull—.*

Five minutes later, the McMurdo controller, wanting to find out why they were taking so long to confirm their descent to 2,000 ft, called them both on VHF and HF, and repeatedly thereafter to no avail.

The DFDR showed the aircraft had made two descending orbits either side of its track as it descended and leveled out at 1,500 ft.

Continuing on at that height it had impacted the 13° upwards slope of Mt Erebus at 240 knots, with a nose-up angle of 10° as the pilots attempted their last minute go-around.

It was not until the next day and 11 hours later that a USN Hercules searching the northern part of Ross Island reported the finding of the wreckage and the absence of survivors.

With the landing gear up, and only a thin layer of powdery snow covering the hard layer of ice coating the slope, there was nothing to cushion the shock and the aircraft skidded up the slope for a distance of some 550 meters, breaking up as it went. Traces of fire showed on the ice.

Unlike crashes where there is some warning of impending disaster, passengers in CFIT disasters are not usually wearing seat belts, and certainly not in the brace position. In this case, many were thrown clear as the aircraft broke up. A large number of the bodies were surprisingly intact, but post mortems maintained they died from the initial impact.

Had the pilots seen the slope ahead, raised the nose earlier and more sharply, the aircraft might have been climbing and losing speed, making the shock of the impact with the incline much less severe, and raising the possibility that there might have been survivors. However, one wonders, as with the JAL crash, how many traumatized survivors could last a whole night in the cold.

So great was the shock to that small nation, and so great was the scandal, that two inquiries were launched:

1. **The usual New Zealand Office of Air Accidents inquiry, led by Chief Inspector Chippendale.**

2. **A Royal Commission of Inquiry, under the Royal Commissioner, Mr Justice P.T. Mahon, who overturned the findings of the aviation experts of the Office of Air Accidents.**

The former attributed the accident to:

The decision of the captain to continue the flight at low level towards an area of poor surface and horizon definition when the crew were not certain of their position, and their subsequent inability to detect the rising terrain which intercepted the aircraft's flight path.

The Royal Commissioner summed up his findings as follows:

In my opinion: ... the single dominant and effective cause of the disaster was the mistake made by those airline officials who programmed the aircraft to fly directly at Mt Erebus and omitted to tell the aircrew. That mistake is directly attributable, not so much to the persons who made it, but to the incompetent administrative airline procedures, which made the mistake possible.

*In my opinion, neither Captain Collins nor the flight engineers made any error which contributed to the disaster, and were not responsible for its occurrence.*

The fact that aviation experts and legal experts could come to such different conclusions is interesting. In the author's opinion, the truth lies somewhere between these two extremes, and is tipped against the pilots.

The airline's mistake in not informing the pilots of the 'revision' they had made is blatant, and it is understandable that the Royal Commission was revolted at the way the Chief Executive had attempted to cover it up. They were also dismayed that the flag carrier, albeit of a tiny country, was run close to the CEO's chest like a private fiefdom. These sentiments rather than technical matters were bound to influence 'professionals used to working in the judicial domain.'

The actual key to the accident was a phenomenon called 'whiteout,' well known to pilots operating in areas with snow and mountains, whereby the snowy slopes merge with the clouds giving the impression there is just thin cloud in the distance. The horizon disappears. A pilot without experience of the phenomenon or proper training in Arctic flying would be left with the impression it is safe to fly visually (VMC) as he *believes* he can see in the immediate vicinity. Under visual flight rules this gave the pilots the regulatory justification for descending, as Captain Gordon Vette,[1] author of *Impact Erebus*, pointed out at the Tribunal.

If the key to the disaster was whiteout, then the airline should be faulted for treating the Antarctic flights as 'perks' to be shared around and not choosing pilots with Antarctic experience. Failing that, briefing on whiteout and Arctic flying should have been better.

On the other hand, it is difficult to understand why the pilots did not become concerned not only at their inability to communicate with McMurdo by VHF but also at their failure to lock on to either of the (VHF) radio beacons there.

The two flight engineers were getting increasingly worried, and finally the captain agreed they should go around. However, this decision came too late.

The captain was known to be methodical and to show good judgment. One can only conclude that the wish to please the passengers got the better of his judgment, with the lack of knowledge of how deceptive a whiteout can be as a mitigating factor.

He evidently thought he had adequate visibility (VMC), and the fact that he performed two orbits to remain under VMC proves he wanted to stick to regulations and not fly blindly into cloud. As he was just three miles from the '40 miles out' from where the base radar would have been able to talk him down, he must have been pretty sure of the weather conditions.

When they realized they could not see where they were, they should have acted immediately. Possibly, the presence of the tour guide in the cockpit, and his interceding to give his opinion as to where they might be slowed decision-making. In normal flying, pilots wisely try to avoid being disturbed at critical moments by anyone. In fact, it is a legal obligation under 'sterile cockpit' rules.

The airline's monumental blunder was just one factor in an accident that would not have happened had due weight been given to command responsibility, cockpit resource management (CRM), and the need to explore all possibilities when something (in this case the VHF radio and radio beacons) is not working—a dramatic and sorry lesson for everyone.

---

[1] New Zealand Airline's Captain Vette, or rather an actor playing his role, featured in a movie about a captain flying a scheduled airline flight diverting his aircraft to guide home a Cessna lost over the vast expanse of the ocean.

# AIR INTER AIRBUS A320
# (Sainte Odile 1992)

### Yet Another A320 Crash

> The following case where an A320 operated by France's domestic
> airline Air Inter crashed into a mountainside partly because it did
> not use a Ground Proximity Warning System has resulted in years
> of legal jousting.
>
> *[Air Inter Flight 148]*

A notable feature of the following incident was that a duo of experienced
captains was flying the aircraft. From a cockpit resources management
(CRM) point of view, this is undesirable as the normal senior vs. junior
relationship breaks down, and corners are sometimes cut as both think they
know everything and do not think they need to be 'bossed.' Despite their
rank, the Air Inter captains making up the duo had little experience of flying
the A320—only 160 and 60 hours respectively.

Air Inter was France's major domestic airline until it merged with Air
France. Unlike British European Airways, which was the 'poor relation'
when it merged with long haul BOAC to form British Airways, the working
conditions and salaries at Air Inter were even more favorable than at Air
France, for Air Inter had for a long times been carrying businesspeople and
affluent passengers on protected routes.

The flight that led to this A320 disaster crash was one such flight, a short
cross-country hop from France's second city, Lyon, to Strasbourg with 90
passengers, four cabin crew and two pilots. It was winter, it was dark, and
although ground visibility was 6 miles (10 kilometers), there were clouds
above 600 ft with the tops some 1,500 ft higher. The Vosges Mountains
were nearby.

The captain flying the aircraft had approval from the tower to make a
straight-in VOR DME approach and landing. Finding he was too high and
going too fast, he asked the controller to be allowed to continue as if landing
but overfly the runway, and on reaching the opposite outer marker, double
back downwind using the ILS until able to turn back again to make a visual
approach to the runway.

However, he was informed that if he did this he would probably be kept
in a holding pattern until the three aircraft waiting to depart had done so.
The A320 captain then decided that landing as they originally intended
(using the VOR DME approach) would be preferable to hanging around in a
holding pattern.

With the approval of the approach controller—who told him to maintain 5000 ft and gave him the required vectors that should have brought him in the vicinity of Andlau and well positioned for a run straight to the airport over relatively low ground—the captain executed the almost 360-degree circuit.

Although there were mountains in the vicinity, and even higher peaks northwest of Andlau, flying at a height of 5,000 ft and with no need to descend steeply there should have been an ample safety margin, even if off course.

According to the radar, after being at 5,000 ft for a minute, the aircraft descended 2,700 ft in the next minute, which was a ridiculous rate of descent in the circumstances.

With no warning, they hit one of Mount La Bloss's ridges at the 2,625 ft (800 m) level. Had they been just a little higher or made a slightly wider turn to actually pass over Andlau, the controlled flight into terrain (CFIT) would not have occurred. Of course, they should have been very much higher at that point.

At the time of impact, the aircraft was unbelievably descending at an angle of 12 degrees and banking at about 18 degrees to the left. It cut a swath through the trees on the pine tree-covered slope, and caught fire. Eight passengers and a cabin attendant survived.

Had the emergency locator beacons been capable of withstanding the fire, another six passengers could have been saved. As it was, survivors had to huddle near a fire at the tail to keep warm.

The cockpit voice recorder (CVR) was recovered intact, while the flight data recorder (FDR) located only a few inches away was too damaged to provide any useful information despite being designed to withstand fires of 1,100°C for 30 minutes.

The official investigation concluded that the pilots had mistakenly entered figures into the Flight Control Unit (FCU) with it set in the 'Heading/Vertical Speed' mode instead of in the 'Track/Flight Path' mode. Thinking they were entering a glide slope of -3.3°, they were actually entering a vertical speed of –3,300 ft/min, which corresponded roughly with the sink rate when they struck the ground. In fact, Airbus had already realized how easy it was to confuse the two modes and was already making modifications.

The pilots received no warning that they were sinking at a alarming rate or that they were about to hit the ground because the Ground Proximity Warning System (GPWS) had been disarmed.

The French weekly magazine *Le Point* is said to have questioned Air Inter on this point, and to have been told that Air Inter's pilots only flew in France and knew the terrain so well they did not need GPWS. Apparently, only five weeks before the crash M. Frantzen, director of the aeronautical training and technical control service, 'enjoined' Air Inter by letter to 'reconnect' these alarm systems, but was 'sent packing' (sic).

The sophisticated GPWS that has prevented many crashes would not only have warned the pilots of the proximity of the terrain, but also of the abnormally high sink rate—an alert that the pilots in the Indian Airlines disaster described above ignored.

In the absence of FDR evidence due to heat damage to the tape, attributing the cause of the crash to the easy confusion over the input mode seems quite plausible, but some people are not convinced the whole truth has been revealed.

On a website called EuroCockpit there is a piece on the affair saying that instead of VOR Bendix + DME TRT as at Air France, Air Inter had a different type of system (VOR + DME-Collins). It also claims that Lufthansa amongst others had forbidden the use of that system for VOR DME approaches six months before the crash, and that Air Inter did likewise after the crash and an incident at Bordeaux.

According to EuroCockpit, it was a problem of hurried certification, and it says it is rumored that the woman elevated to head the Inspection Générale de l'Aviation Civile was previously responsible for VOR DME certification. Also, it is claimed that the records of receiving reports sent by Air Inter staff to Airbus and the BEA regarding problems with the Collins version have disappeared without trace even though there are records of them being sent.

Allegedly, the CVR tape for the St Odile crash showed the pilots were somewhat casual, perhaps because it was two captains together. Macarthur Job suggested the nature of Air Inter's routes with many automatic landings in bad weather may have made them depend too much on the computers in controlling height.

That said, the disarming of the GPWS by Air Inter seems unforgivable. Perhaps they did so because the pilots performing so much low-level flying got tired of so many false alerts. For a long time pilots blocked the introduction of the TCAS collision alert system on similar grounds and said that it just meant an extra thing to think about.

This accident is also notable for the continuing litigation involved, with proceedings taking place even in 2009, some 17 years later.

The Echo Association, founded by the victims' families, commented on the failure of previous efforts:

> Six people have been 'examined' in investigations headed by three
> judges, but experts have failed to determine the exact cause of the
> Airbus A320 crash. It is not so much a fact that no reasons were
> found, but that one court would come to one conclusion for it to be
> rejected by higher court.

# MASKING TAPE BLINDFOLDS 757—PITOT BLOCKED (Lima 1996)

## '$2-per-hour Aircraft Polisher' Brings Down Jet

> An aircraft polisher had failed to remove masking tape he had used to prevent fluid entering the pitot tubes and ports, and the aircraft took off in that condition. Basing its instructions on the incorrect airspeed data it was receiving, the onboard computer seemed to be going crazy, constantly issuing all sorts of warnings.
>
> The pilots finally flew into the sea.
>
> *[Aeroperú Flight 603]*

When the sophisticated computerized Aeroperú 757 hit the sea, bounced 200 ft into the air, inverted, and fell back to drown any surviving occupants, the pilots believed they were at 9,700 ft, as did air traffic control (ATC).

This was despite the GPWS[1] alerting the pilots with the words:

*TOO LOW ... TERRAIN!*

*TOO LOW ... TERRAIN!*

*TOO LOW ... TERRAIN!*

Although it might seem somewhat old-fashioned, pilots rely mostly on their traditional *barometric* altimeter to measure altitude, even though they have a *radio* altimeter that calculates their true height by bouncing a radio wave off the ground or sea underneath.

Besides not behaving wildly when the aircraft goes over a clump of trees, the barometric altimeter has three particular advantages in that it can be set (calibrated) to show:

### 1. Height above mean sea level (QNH)

In the UK referred to as QNH in exchanges with ATC, when they give settings for the altimeter to show this. This is very useful as elevations (heights) given on charts show this. In the case of high buildings or masts, the height above the immediate terrain is added in parentheses to the elevations.

### 2. Height above a specific point of interest

In particular, the height above the airport at which the aircraft is about to land.

In exchanges with ATC, this is referred to as 'height' and called QFE. ATC tells the pilot the setting required for his altimeter to show this.

**3. Height for flight levels (FLs) so all aircraft read from the same hymn sheet. That is to say, aircraft with the same altimeter reading will be exactly at the same height.**

The altimeter is set for the standard pressure of 29.92 inches of mercury regardless of actual conditions. In the US, this applies at heights over 18,000 ft, but can be very much lower in some countries. In the US, apart from in Alaska, there are no peaks over 15,000 ft, so above 18,000 ft, the exact height above ground does not matter. What matters is the height relative to other aircraft, and with them all having the same altimeter calibration one is sure that aircraft assigned to different flight levels[2] (height in hundreds of feet (ht/100)) will truly be on different levels.

Unlike the *barometric* altimeter depending on air pressure, the *radio* altimeter works by bouncing a radio wave off the ground below and is useful for checking the true height of aircraft above ground. Automatic warnings about being too close to the ground depend on this radio altimeter data. However, as the Aeroperú 757 had gone out over the flat sea for the very purpose of avoiding mountains, the pilots would not normally be particularly concerned about the exact height of the 'terrain' below.

**Nightmare**

For the pilots, the flight had been a nightmare from the moment they lifted off on departure. The incorrect data that was making the altimeter and airspeed indicator give erroneous readings was making the aircraft's computers believe the aircraft was flying outside the normal 'envelope.' In consequence, it was issuing a barrage of warnings and setting off a tirade off aural alarms.

Pilots are trained to react to alarms and when these come in rapid succession for no rhyme or reason, and seem unconnected, one can imagine the crew's confusion. For instance, reducing engine power and deploying the air brakes in response to an 'over-speed' alert did not seem to have any effect—at least according to the airspeed indicator, which was not functioning properly.

Sometimes they would get a stick shake—indicating they were about to stall (because of inadequate airspeed)—while being simultaneously warned they were going too fast.

Perhaps out of habit, or because they were too busy coping with the crises and different alarms, or even regressing mentally, the Aeroperú pilots failed to note that, in contrast to the barometric altimeter, the changes in height shown by the radio-altimeter corresponded with what they should have been doing according to their control settings for climbing and descending.

With the incessant warnings and the need to cope with them, it is understandable that the pilots had little time to think. Hardly had they tried to deal with one, when another sounded, and audio alarms are particularly stressful.

To give some idea of the confusion, here is part of the CVR (translated from Spanish), beginning about seven minutes before they hit the water.

Times in square brackets are *elapsed* time in minutes and seconds from takeoff *[00:00]*. The first impact with the water was half an hour later at 30:40 elapsed time.

[22:42] First officer to ATC:

*We have terrain alarm; we have terrain alarm!*

[22:46] Lima ATC:

*Roger, according to the monitor...*

*it indicates flight level 120 (12,000 ft), over the sea, heading northwest course of 300.*

[22:55] First officer to ATC:

*We have terrain alarm and we are supposed to be at 10,000 ft?*

[23:00] Lima ATC:

*According to monitor you have one, zero, five (10,500 ft).*

[23:03] Mechanical voice alert:

*WINDSHEER! WINDSHEER! WINDSHEER!*

[23:06] First officer to ATC:

*We have all computers crazy here...*

[23:07] Mechanical voice alert:

*TOO LOW, TERRAIN!*

[23:07] Captain:

*Shit, we have everything!*

[23:14] Mechanical voice alert:

*WIND SHEAR! WIND SHEAR! WIND SHEAR!*

[23:17] Captain:

*Shit, what the hell have these assholes (Maintenance) done?*

*.............*

[23:47] First officer to ATC:

*We don't have... We have like 370 knots, are we descending now?*

[23:56] Lima ATC:

*It shows the same speed...you have approximately 200 speed.*

[23:56] First officer to ATC:

*Speed of 200?*

[23:58] Lima ATC:

*Speed of 220 over the ground, speed reducing slightly.*

[24:05] Captain:

*Shit! We will stall now...*

[24:07] Mechanical voice alert:

*SINK RATE! SINK RATE! SINK RATE!*
*SINK RATE!*

[Sink rate alarm also sounds]

They managed to avoid stalling and climbed with the barometric altimeters showing over 9,000 ft. They thought they had leveled out at Flight Level 100 (10,000 ft). The flight data recorder (FDR) later showed that (according to the radio-altimeter) they had only climbed to 2,400 ft then re-descended to 1,300 ft and had finally gone no higher than 4,000 ft.

Meanwhile, by noting their different locations with his radar that could independently determine distance and direction (but not height) the air traffic controller had calculated their groundspeed to be 200 knots when the pilots' instruments were showing their airspeed to be 370 knots. To have a difference of that magnitude between groundspeed and airspeed would require a wind over 200 mph. The first officer was surprised, but for some reason it did not immediately make him doubt the over-speed warnings. Perhaps his reaction to them was an understandable automatic reaction to alarms in general.

When unsure of their height, they had gone out over the sea to play it safe. Had they remained over land, they might very well have seen some lights that would have shown how extremely low they were, and anyway over land they would have given more weight to the (accurate) readings shown by their *radio* altimeter.

The controller had informed them that a Boeing 707 taking off from Lima was coming to assist them, and would guide them in. Without waiting, they thought that already being relatively near the airport it would be a good idea to try to lock onto the airport's Instrument Landing System (ILS) glide path, which in normal circumstances would have enabled them to descend safely without relying on their instruments. However, unbeknown to them, they were far too low to pick up the beam.

Unfortunately for the occupants of the Aeroperú 757, civil aviation radar, which is not intended for tracking an enemy trying to sneak in, relies on the transponder in the aircraft to give it its altitude and ID. So when the Aeroperú crew asked ATC to confirm their height, ATC was only repeating what the *barometric* altimeters in the aircraft showed.

Some suggest that this fact was overlooked because all were convinced it was a computer problem. The airline did try to contact the pilots and find out what was happening, but staff there were also led to understand it was a computer problem. Had it been daytime with senior staff at hand, both at the company and at ATC, the pilots might have been better advised. On a sophisticated aircraft with so much run by computer it is too easy to attribute a real problem to the computer as happened when Captain Piché started transferring fuel to the side from which it was leaking and had to glide 80 miles to salvation (page 15).

Some accounts say the pilots were sensibly using their radio altimeter to go back to Lima, but the following cockpit voice recorder (CVR) transcript does not seem to bear this out.

[29:49] Captain:

> *How can it be flying at this speed if we are going down with all the power cut off?*

[29:56] First officer to ATC:

> *Can you tell me the altitude please, because we have the climb that doesn't...*

[29:59] Captain:

> *Nine*

[30:00 ] GPWS:

> *TOO LOW, TERRAIN; TOO LOW, TERRAIN; TOO LOW, TERRAIN*

> *(These warnings continue until aircraft inverts at [30:50].)*

[30:01] ATC Lima:

> *Yes, you keep nine-seven-hundred (9,700) according to presentation, Sir.*

[30:04] First officer to ATC:

> *Nine-seven-hundred?*

[30:09] ATC Lima:

*Yes, correct, what is the indicated altitude on board? Have you any visual reference?*

[30:12] to ATC:

*Nine-seven-hundred, but it indicates 'TOO LOW, TERRRAIN!' ...Are you sure you have us on the radar at 50 miles?*

[30:21] Captain:

*Hey, look...With 370 we have...have...*

*[Presumably, the captain was referring to the airspeed indicated by his instruments.]*

[30:29] First officer:

*Have what? 370 of what?*

[30:36] First officer:

*Do we lower the gear?'*

[30:38] Captain:

*But what do we do with the gear?*
*Don't know...that.*

[30:40] Sound of impact:[30:41] First officer to ATC:

*We are hitting water.*

[30:44] First officer:

*Pull it up.*

[30:48] Captain:

*I have it, I have it!*

[30:50] GPWS:

*... TOO LOW, TERRAIN! ...*

[The ground proximity warning system (GPWS) voice alert ceases because the bottom of the aircraft is no longer facing the sea below.]

[30:55] Captain:

*We are going to invert! (go upside down)*

[30:57]

*WHOOP ... WHOOP ... PU... [Voice alert sounds]*

[30:59] Sound of impact.

End of recording, with barometric altimeters indicating 9,700 ft.

All on board, 61 passengers and 9 crewmembers, lost their lives. The death toll of 70 would have been much higher had the aircraft been full.

The FDR showed the 757 was traveling at 260 knots and descending at an angle of 10 degrees when the left wingtip and left engine pod snagged the water. Ingestion of water no doubt led to failure of that engine. With the other engine already at a low power setting because the pilots *thought* they were flying too fast, their airspeed would have fallen quickly to stalling speed as the aircraft 'bounced' and rose to 200 ft, before inverting and falling back into the sea.

A lawyer made much ado of the suffering the passengers endured in the half-hour preceding the impact with the sea. Though the constant changes in speed and height as the pilots responded to the continuous false alerts must have been truly frightening, they can hardly have expected to fly straight into the sea.

A judge ordered Aeroperú and the '$2-per-hour aircraft polisher' (who had left the masking tape on the pitot probes and static inlets) to pay $29 million to the families of the 70 dead. Another judge had already sentenced the hapless worker to two years in jail.

This incident ultimately led to the closure of the airline.

---

[1] The Ground Proximity Warning System (GPWS) uses the same data as the radio-altimeter, namely a calculation of the height determined by bouncing a radio wave off the ground or sea below.

[2] A flight level (FL) is the height in hundreds of feet when the altimeter is set for the standard mean sea level pressure of 29.92 inches of mercury regardless of conditions. Thus, flight level 200 represents 20,000 ft.

# CHAPTER 13

# MISCELLANEOUS INCIDENTS

## 'RED BARON' THE GERMAN FIGHTER ACE
## (Allied Lines 1918)

### Did He Keep Skills, but Lose Judgment—or Just Not Care?

> The shooting down of Germany's famous fighter ace, Manfred von Richthofen, at the height of his fame in World War I has drawn much attention over the years.
>
> Again, it is the mystery and dispute over *who* actually did shoot him down that gave the story legs. *Why* did he fly so 'out of character' on that occasion?
>
> It has been included in the book as it may have some lessons for us today as regards judgment.

Manfred von Richthofen was born to an aristocratic family in 1892. Enrolled on the insistence of his army officer father in a military academy when only eleven, he hated the discipline, and studied just enough to get by, only gaining respect by winning numerous awards for excelling at a wide range of sports. These sporting achievements demonstrated his verve, good spatial sense and 'good eye'—indeed, his sister said that when they went hunting he had the eye of an eagle. He also had a penchant for risky pranks, such as climbing a church steeple to put a handkerchief on top.

Beginning his military career in the cavalry at a time when barbed wire had reduced the role of cavalry officers to almost mere observers (scouts) and messengers, von Richthofen decided riding atop a more glamorous beast would offer better fighting opportunities, and joined the German Flying Service. Despite some problems with the wind and his clothing, his first flight was for him an exciting experience.

After a stint as an observer in two-seaters during which he apparently shot down an enemy aircraft for which he received no official credit as it crashed behind enemy lines, he began training as a *pilot*. Despite his sporting prowess, he apparently took some time to get the feel of handling an aircraft. Even when sufficiently qualified to fly missions, the aircraft he piloted were again mostly lumbering two-seaters and gave him little chance to score kills.

Only when he inducted into the fighter squadron commanded by the German Ace Oswald Boelcke did he begin his series of kills, always being careful to follow the Dicta Boelcke[1] (eight tactical principles laid down by Boelcke). These included attacking from above and behind, and if possible, with the sun behind you; keeping in mind your line of retreat if over enemy lines; and never breaking off an engagement once it is commenced as in fleeing one would expose one's tail.

After achieving 40 kills, the great Boelcke had a midair collision with a machine flown by one of his own men, which led to his own death but not that of the other pilot. The deaths of several other German aces ensued, leaving von Richthofen to fill much of the vacuum on the heroism front. This he did competently, notching up victory after victory to surpass them all in the total number of kills. The fact that he achieved 21 in the month of April 1917 alone was certainly due to his ability, though the temporary superiority of the German aircraft must have been a facilitating factor.

He became known as the 'Red Baron' when he painted his aircraft red on learning he had downed a famous British ace. His squadron of elite pilots then painted their aircraft partly red to avoid his machine being too conspicuous. Besides being good for their morale, red was supposed to disconcert the enemy gunners—somewhat ironic in that historically English troops had psyched out their enemies with their bright red tunics!

However, on July 6, 1917, perhaps brimming with the extra confidence borne of having 57 victories to his credit, he failed to distance himself from an enemy two-seater bomber some 300 yards (meters) away on the assumption that no good marksman[2] would ever attempt a shot from so far.

Whether a good shot or bad, a shot from the enemy observer-gunner's machine gun glanced off the Baron's head leaving him temporarily blinded and stunned. The Baron's machine, which had been at 13,000 ft (4,000 m), then dropped to 2,660 ft (800 m) before he recovered enough to regain control and land. He later said he could not remember being taken to hospital, where doctors established that the shot had not actually penetrated the brain.

His return to duty after 20 days in hospital and clocking up his 58th victory the very same day might suggest the doctors were wrong in recommending a period of convalescence with no combat flying. In truth, on returning to base that day, the Baron had difficulty landing and had to be helped into bed by his batman.

Over the following months, he 'progressively became depressed and withdrawn.' Many have largely attributed this melancholy to the fact that the head wound had not healed over properly, and bone remained visible. However, quite a stir was recently caused by a paper published in the autumn 2004 edition of *Human Factors and Aerospace Safety* by retired

USAF clinicians, Orme and Hyatt, pointing out how mentally deleterious this head injury would have been had the frontal lobes governing *reasoning* been damaged.

The Baron was, however, much buoyed by the delivery by the designer in person, of a new aircraft virtually tailor-made for him—the new Fokker Dr 1.[3] Said to owe much to the British Sopwith Tri-plane, it had a number of embellishments, including an extra aerofoil between the wheels to provide even more maneuverability. Despite being slower than many opponents' machines with a speed of only 103 mph (166 km/h), its compactness made it a difficult target, while its superior rate of initial climb and sharpness of turn made it able to outmaneuver opponents in dogfights.

Like modern jet fighters, it owed much of its maneuverability to its inherent instability. However, unlike modern fighters, it lacked computerized controls to simulate stability, which meant few pilots could handle it. Yet, in the hands of those that could, such as the Baron and his men, it represented a dangerous predator indeed when first introduced.

Other reasons for von Richthofen continuing to fly combat missions included a sense of duty and the fact that Germany was desperately short of top pilots. No doubt he felt it would seem like 'letting the side down' if he withdrew just on achieving great fame.

Furthermore, his heroic status made it impossible to prevent him from doing so, even though some senior people thought that the loss of such a hero could be bad for German morale and prestige. It is said that his mother finally persuaded the German Kaiser—the one person he would have to obey—to have him taken off combat duties, and that his mission on Sunday, April 21, 1918 was officially to be his last, before going on leave.

The TV documentary *Who Killed The Red Baron?*[4] is recommended viewing for anyone fascinated by von Richthofen's life and final downfall, as it not only gives a really good feel of what it was it was like to be part of the action, but with help from experts and recently discovered documents also seems convincingly to prove *who* actually fired the fatal shot. Though shown on various TV channels in the US and in other countries, one might single out the Nova/WGBH web pages[5] on PBS, to which the following material below partly refers.

## April 21, 1918

As weather conditions improved, nine German tri-planes led by the Red Baron took off at 9:45 from their temporary base. The previous day von Richthofen had shot down two Sopwith Camels and a few days short of his 26th birthday, he had a record 80 kills[6] to his name. Similarly, with the improving weather, five Sopwith Camels took to the air. Novice Canadian Wilfrid May, had been told by his leader, Captain Roy Brown, also a Canadian, to 'observe and not to engage.'

By pure coincidence May and Brown had gone to the same school back in Canada. All the more reason for Brown to take May under his wing and give him some special coaching, which he had done a day or two earlier. Fortuitously, there was also a cozy relationship on the German side, in that another novice, the Baron's nephew, was along for the ride with similar instructions to the ones May had received.

The two groups encountered each other and engaged in combat with the novices holding back. Novice May noticed an apparently vulnerable tri-plane lurking nearby. Unable to resist the temptation, he went in only to see the infamous red markings and realize whom he was up against. He decided to abandon his attempt and in fleeing swooped down very low over his own lines with the Baron in hot pursuit.

Possibly, because the inexperienced May did something abnormal, or wild, the Baron misjudged his speed and fell a little behind. However, the wily Baron fired off several bursts from his machine gun to make May think he was in immediate danger, and the rookie duly zigzagged, thus throwing away the advantage of his aircraft's greater speed. Getting desperate, he dived lower and lower into valleys with both of them just missing a church. When the relentless Baron got close enough to open fire for the kill, his machine gun apparently jammed and May survived his brush with death.

Captain Roy Brown who had been engaged in the main fray broke away to come to the rescue of his protégé and school friend. According to one version, the Baron then broke off the engagement and made for the German lines.

Captain Brown, still some distance behind, got off a burst of gunfire, as subsequently did various gunners on the ground.

Hit by one of these shots, the Baron jerked the stick back causing the tri-plane to commence a loop. Remarkably, he then leveled out and brought the inherently unstable machine safely down to the ground from its already low height. The first soldier on the scene—sent by his officer to arrest the pilot—found the Baron barely alive, and only able to attempt a few words in German before expiring.

The German ace had been killed by a single .303 bullet, which had entered his body several inches below the right armpit and exited from his chest just next to the left nipple. After medical examination, but not a full autopsy, the Allies buried him with full military honors.

Most importantly from the point of view of this book is what led the master tactician to become isolated from his fellow fliers well over enemy lines, fly so low that he would be vulnerable to ground fire, and seemingly be oblivious to the presence of a second enemy aircraft coming down on him from behind?

Arguments about who actually fired the fatal shot have continued for years, and it is perhaps best to look at it from the opposite point of view of who *cannot* have shot him down.

Officially, Captain Brown of the RAF was given the credit, which had the advantage of being good for the morale and prestige of the RAF, even though Captain Roy Brown was Canadian. This was so much better propaganda-wise than a 'lucky' shot from a humble rifleman on the ground. People have said it was a cover-up with pilots and others sworn to secrecy. Interviewed years later, Captain Brown was not at all forthcoming, saying that the official version said *'all that there was to be said.'*

Brown's combat report did not directly claim the 'kill' and one can only assume he had to go along with the version that suited officialdom.

While most of those participating in the burial of the fallen Baron with 'full military honors' were no doubt sincere, from a propaganda point of view such a high-key ceremony was a good way to rub salt in enemy wounds and demonstrate how honorable the Allies were.

The main contenders on the ground for downing the Baron were Australian machine gunners Buie and Evans who were facing the oncoming tri-plane and another Australian, a Sergeant Hopkins firing a Vickers machine gun from a distance of some 600 yards to the right. Though Evans and Buie maintained their claim long afterwards, the fact that they were firing head-on really rules them out as the bullet passed from the Baron's right armpit to the vicinity of his left nipple. This leaves Sergeant Hopkins firing from the right, which fits in with the wound sustained by the Baron. Though some, and even Hopkins himself, have thought the chance of hitting the Baron from so far would be slim, others have maintained that the fact that the .303 bullet was found in the Baron's clothing and not crushed was evidence that it had been fired from a long distance, giving greater credence to it having been fired by Hopkins. Most interestingly, Sergeant Hopkins said he fired on the tri-plane after it had given up chasing May and had turned back towards the enemy lines.

The decisive factor that it could not have been Captain Brown was that the 'improved' .303 bullets used at the time were designed to tumble on passing through human tissue to produce a much more devastating wound. One would have produced a wound impossible to survive for long, and certainly not from the time the shots fired towards him earlier by Captain Brown to the time he was in view of Sergeant Hopkins for the second time and still handling the plane.

In conclusion, Sergeant Hopkins probably was the one who shot the Baron down, though one cannot completely exclude the possibility that a rifleman taking a pot shot was responsible.

The question of how the Baron was defeated has been described here in detail out of historical interest, and because it helps us understand *why*, just as in any other air crash investigation.

According to London's *Daily Telegraph*, Alan Bennett, a Canadian historian and co-author of *The Red Baron's Last Flight*,[7] said that the injury may have affected von Richthofen's judgment but not his flying ability, pointing out that he had shot down two Sopwith Camels within a few minutes the day before. Bennett pointed out that another critical factor was that the prevailing winds had reversed direction and clouds obscured the ground, so German pilots had inadvertently drifted into Allied territory.

In reply, the clinical psychologist, Dr Hyatt mentioned above retorted:

> When you do an accident investigation, you usually find factors built upon each other. That is what happened with the Red Baron.

Dr Hyatt later added:

> The baron was a hunter, and this instinct became unbridled. When he found himself in trouble he could not or would not break off the pursuit to save himself. This rigid behavior is perseveration [sic], associated with *dysfunction involving the frontal lobes.*

Some think Dr Hyatt's invocation of the Baron's frontal lobes to be taking things too far as there was no physical proof of damage to the frontal lobes and detailed knowledge regarding the Baron's head wound was scant.

In the author's view, the reasons for the Baron's uncharacteristic behavior could be more mundane, in that, like the tiger picking out the weakling in a herd, he was pursuing an aircraft piloted by someone he had perhaps identified as an easy kill.

He did not break all the Principles of Combat laid down by Boelcke, one of which was not to break off an engagement, as that would permit the prey to turn on one and attack from behind. He had to continue the pursuit for longer than expected because a split cartridge had permanently jammed his left machine gun and his right machine gun temporarily jammed when he could have downed May earlier on.

Although the Baron's highly maneuverable tri-plane had at one time been a great asset, this was no longer true as the Allies introduced improved machines. Anyway, it had always been slower than the Allies latest machines.

It was to be his last mission—at least for some time—and as an ace, he perhaps did not want to go back to base with his tail between his legs.

Though there are constant references by commentators that he was deep into enemy territory, most of the engagement had taken place in the vicinity of the front line, and only later did he go in some two miles.

Earlier, on a visit to his family, he had mentioned dental trouble but said it was not worth doing anything, implying he did not care.

In general, people such as motorists ease up and become less attentive when nearing the end of a long hard journey. The Baron was coming to the end of many months of combat.

His general physical state was not good and he was no doubt forcing himself and thus more subject to tunnel vision—less able to pay attention to things other than the task in hand.

Even so, he was never fatally defeated in aerial combat. One might add that a commentator has said the Baron was not a particularly good pilot—his successes were largely due to his ability as an expert shooter.

There is a difference between losing one's judgment—losing one's mental ability to make logical decisions—and just not caring due to constant pain from a head wound and 'burn-out' due to too many combat missions. Ironically, some time afterwards, Captain Brown was said to be surviving on brandy and milk before being sent on leave.

---

[1] http://en.wikipedia.org/wiki/Dicta_Boelcke. [English, Dave [2003]. *The Air Up There*, 62. ISBN 0071410368]

[2] One of the Boelcke principles was to get in close before opening fire—firstly so as not to warn them and secondly so as not to use up one's (in those days) very limited supply of ammunition.

[3] http://www.pilotfriend.com/century-of-flight/index.htm

[4] *Who Killed The Red Baron?* NOVA DVD (Zone 1, NTSC) available from Amazon.

[5] http://www.pbs.org/wgbh/nova/redbaron/.
 http://www.pbs.org/wgbh/nova/transcripts/3011_redbaron.html

6 In those days it was thought killing the pilot was more important than downing the aircraft to prevent him fighting another day.

[7] *The Red Baron's Last Flight*, Norman Franks and Alan Bennett. Updated paperback edition published by Grubb Street, 2006.

# USING ENGINES TO CLEAR FOG DOOMS AIRCRAFT (Zurich 1963)

### Braking Overheats Tires

> Without an engineer's knowledge of how systems work, pilots have at times been tempted to experiment or try out their own 'clever' ways to solve a problem. Sometimes it might be as simple as 'I wonder what would happen if we turned that off?'
>
> While obvious with hindsight, the outcomes can be unpredictable, but fatal at the time.
>
> *[Swissair Flight 306]*

In 1963, the pilots of a Swissair Caravelle came up with the bright idea of using their engines to disperse the runway fog when about to take off at 7 a.m. from Zurich Airport. To do this they taxied up and down with the engines at a higher than usual power setting and the brakes half on to hold the aircraft back.

Having 'cleared' a certain amount of fog, the Caravelle duly took off. The pilots, no doubt well pleased with themselves, retracted the gear (undercarriage) not knowing that in doing so they were inserting time bombs into the wings. For, while taxiing around with the brakes half on and the engines at half throttle to clear the fog, the brake disks had heated to abnormal temperatures.

This heat was soon transferred to the wheel rims, also raising their temperature abnormally. However, it was not until the wheels had been retracted after takeoff that the temperature of the tires and hydraulic lines reached critical levels. At that point, the overheated tires exploded and a fire developed inside the wing. All 80 people on board died in the subsequent crash. They included 43 children.

Though this abnormal use of the aircraft was in retrospect most unwise, it did make clear that the temperature of the wheel rims after extended heavy braking only reaches its maximum quite some time after braking has ceased.

Nowadays, even with today's much higher performance brakes, pilots applying heavy braking, such, as in the event of an aborted takeoff, should always allow plenty of time for the wheels and tires to cool down, before making a further attempt to take off.

# ROGUE CONTROLLER DELETES DATA
# (JFK 1979/1980)

## As Soviet Airliner Lands with Soviet Ambassador

> One should not forget that air traffic controllers, like bank staff, are vulnerable or might have their own agendas.
>
> In addition, ATC equipment on the ground could be subject to sabotage. In Japan, some 'activists' managed to find out where the cables linking ground radar facilities passed, and brought down Tokyo's ATC system by cutting them.
>
> In the following case, an air traffic controller allegedly deleted data.

A media piece, whose origin we have been unable to check, dated Thursday, 31 January 1980, and headlined *'FAA Acts to Remove a Controller'* said:

> *The Federal Aviation Administration moved yesterday to dismiss an air-traffic controller for allegedly tampering with radar data and contributing to the 'potential endangerment' of a Soviet airliner being guided to a landing at Kennedy International Airport last January....*
>
> *The announcement of the FAA action said that 'important flight data' on the Soviet plane, a four-jet Ilyushin 62 operated by the airline Aeroflot, had been 'deliberately erased' as the aircraft approached Kennedy ... Among those on board the plane was the Soviet Ambassador to the United States, Anatoly F. Dobrynin.*

There are ways a 'rogue' controller or controllers could put a number of aircraft at the very least in danger, but no more will be said, as the author does not want this to become a terrorists' handbook.

# TEENAGER AT CONTROLS OF AEROFLOT A310 (Russia 1994)

### Failure to Notice Partial Disengagement of Autopilot

> The captain on this flight allowed his teenage son to sit in his seat for a moment. This would not normally have been dangerous as the copilot was at the controls in the other seat. However, the latter had his seat so far back he could not reach the controls when things went wrong.
>
> Full details only became generally available thanks to the diligent research by Macarthur Job and his assistants.
>
> The following distillation is based (with permission) on his account in *Air Disaster* (Vol. 3).
>
> *[Aeroflot Flight 593]*

The Aeroflot A310 was on a regular scheduled flight from Moscow to Hong Kong. The three-man flight crew consisted of Captain Danilov (commander), Captain Kudrinsky who was the reserve commander needed for such a long trip, and Second Pilot Piskarev. In addition, there were 65 passengers and 9 flight attendants. Among the passengers was an off-duty captain.

The presence in the passenger cabin of Captain Kudrinsky's family, and notably his son (El'dar 15) and daughter (Yana 13), would make the trip more memorable than his usual flights. He would be able to relax[1] with them before being called to the cockpit to take over from Captain Danilov who was flying the most difficult sectors out of Moscow—near sensitive areas and where there was always considerable traffic.

When Captain Kudrinsky finally took over from Captain Danilov, with Piskarev still acting as copilot, it seems that the latter—a short man—at some point pushed his seat right back either to relax after his hard work, or to get up for a moment, and left it pushed back.

Just as they were about to pass near the city of Novosibirsk in the middle of Siberia, Makarov (the off-duty captain), brought the two kids to the cockpit, no doubt knowing it would be the last straightforward sector before crossing the frontier into Mongolia.

Vacating his seat, Captain Kudrinsky allowed his daughter to take his place, adjusting the height so she could see out of the windscreen. He told his daughter to hold the controls and adjusted the heading selector on the autopilot slightly, first in one direction and then in the opposite direction. In the girl's gentle hands, the control column duly moved as the autopilot banked slightly to adjust the course to the selected heading. The idea was to let her get the feel of flying the aircraft. Evidently not so enthralled, she soon gave up her seat to her eager elder brother.

El'dar took her place with Makarov filming the event with a video camera.

Instead of being passive like his sister, El'dar, having taken in what his father had said about how the controls worked, asked whether he could move the control wheel. His father said he could, whereupon El'dar sharply turned it 3 to 4 degrees to the left before his father could anticipate his move by turning the autopilot heading-selector as he had done for the young girl. Kudrinsky then returned the selector to NAV (automatic navigation) mode and the aircraft banked the other way to resume its preset track.

By exerting a very positive force on the control column[2], the boy caused the autopilot to disengage in the banking axis. (As already mentioned in the context of the TriStar Everglades crash, manufacturers program autopilots to disengage if a counter[3] force exceeding a certain limit is applied to the control column.)

This meant that a strong boy (with one minute's flying experience and no training) and Piskarev who was short and had his seat so far back he was almost out of reach of the controls were the only people controlling the banking (rolling) of the aircraft.

At the time, the A310 did not have any system (aural or visual) to warn pilots of such an autopilot disconnect, probably because the manufacturer thought it could only happen if a pilot moved the control column sharply, in which case he would know what he had done and would be aware of what was happening. With none of the professional pilots in the cockpit realizing what had happened, El'dar kept pushing the control column (yoke) to the right, perhaps because he was right-handed. In consequence, the aircraft increased its right-hand bank from 15 to 20 degrees in 7 seconds. However, with Kudrinsky chatting to his daughter and with Piskarev thinking his captain had things under control—and anyway assuming the autopilot was doing everything—no one noticed the gradual increase in bank, which would at night only have been evident from the artificial horizon.

With the bank progressively increasing and attaining 45 degrees 40 seconds after Kudrinsky, expecting the aircraft would look after itself, had reset the autopilot to NAV, it was El'dar who realized something odd was happening. He interrupted his father to ask why the aircraft was turning— something he could only have determined from the instruments.

Asked by his father whether it was turning by itself, El'dar said it was, perhaps not realizing the effect of his hand on the control column. The three proper pilots then launched into a discussion as to why the autopilot was making the aircraft turn on its own, and concluded that it must be a holding pattern.

Soon the bank had attained 50 degrees, still without the three pilots realizing anything was amiss.

Pilots, learning to fly on tiny aircraft, know that when an aircraft banks steeply, the amount of lift decreases. In consequence, they increase engine power and raise the nose when doing so to avoid sinking. Likewise, the A310's autopilot increased the engine power and raised the nose in order to maintain its programmed altitude and speed.

It was Makarov, the off-duty captain, no doubt feeling the g-forces on his feet, who noticed something was wrong. No sooner had he uttered a warning than the aircraft, in order to maintain its height, pitched upwards. It then began buffeting—a sure sign it was about to stall.

Kudrinsky called out:

*Hold the control column – hold it!*

Piskarev immediately turned his control column yoke to the left to counter the increasingly precipitous rightwards bank, and would no doubt have succeeded in righting the aircraft had El'dar not also followed his father's instructions—probably intended for Piskarev.

Not knowing what action to take, the boy gamely clutched the yoke, maintaining it firmly in an almost neutral position. This resulted in an unequal battle between the boy ensconced in the perfect position and the ill-placed Piskarev. The latter was only 5 ft 3 in (160 cm) tall, and with his seat right back, his shoulder harness would be keeping him at arm's length from the control column and unable to reach the rudder pedals.

As a result, Piskarev's efforts were insufficient to halt the dangerously increasing bank, which by causing the aircraft to lose lift was making the autopilot raise the nose further to maintain height. Finally, Piskarev must have knowingly overridden the autopilot by pushing the control column sharply forward, thus causing it to disengage completely.

This time there was an aural warning that the autopilot had disengaged. This was followed first by the non-urgent warning that the aircraft had departed from its designated height, and then by the more pressing warning of an imminent stall. With these warnings coming in quick succession and increasing stress levels, all three pilots started shouting conflicting instructions to El'dar.

If the boy had had even minimal flying experience, he might have known instinctively what to do to put the aircraft on a level keel. However, with the general confusion and the situation becoming increasingly scary, there was not much hope. He was probably transfixed.

Meanwhile, the Alpha floor safety function (mentioned in connection with the Habsheim air show Airbus crash) sensed that the aircraft was going into a stall and pushed the nose down by adjusting the tail trim just as

Piskarev was trying to do the same by pushing the control column forward. This put the aircraft into a 40-degree dive that was to last 13 seconds. With the engines still supplying normal cruising thrust, the airspeed continued to build up alarmingly even after the over-speed alarm had sounded.

Piskarev yanked back the control column to pull the aircraft out of its precipitous dive just as Kudrinsky, trying to get back in his seat, was shouting to the boy to *'Get out! Get out!'* The powerful g-forces resulting from the aircraft beginning to level out multiplied the weight of the boy, making it even more difficult for him to clamber out.

With the aircraft leveling out and going into a climb, Piskarev, no doubt concerned by the overspeed warning, called for the engine thrust to be reduced regardless of the fact that he was holding the control column fully back. Why he kept the control column fully back is difficult to comprehend. There have even been suggestions that he was using it to pull himself and his seat forward. Meanwhile, the reduction in g-forces had allowed El'dar to vacate his seat and let his father slip in, albeit with it in the back position, which was not to help matters later.

With full-up elevator and airspeed of only 97 knots, the aircraft slewed to the right, and then slipped into a downward spin to the left. Belatedly Piskarev asked for full throttle, but having the elevators still in the full up position this was not destined to help recovery. As the aircraft reached 200 knots, it went into an uncontrolled spin that was to last for a minute.

With the aircraft in a 20-degree dive and the fully back control column(s) keeping the aircraft in a semi stall, Kudrinsky, now back in his seat, was finally managing to get out of the spin using the rudder.

## So Near Salvation!

They leveled out with only a little over 1,000 ft (350 m) of altitude remaining, which would have been fine had they not at the time been sinking at a rate of 13,870 ft/min (70 m/sec). With insufficient time to arrest their descent, they plunged onto the trees on a snow-covered slope of a 2,000 ft (600 m) hill some 300 nm southwest of the Siberian capital, Novosibirsk.

Rescuers found the fire and explosion impact had destroyed much of the wreckage—not that anyone could have survived the impact anyway.

As in other accidents in this book, a party or sightseeing mood affecting the pilots is very dangerous. Though the captain was wrong to let his children take the controls, he was not the first commercial pilot to have done so. (Nowadays regulations regarding access to the flight deck are more stringent due to the anti-terrorist measures.)

However, it was the disorganization, poor crew resource management (CRM), and a series of errors, coupled with perhaps the poor understanding of the sophisticated systems by pilots more used to seat-of-the-pants flying—actually Kudrinsky did well in bringing the aircraft out of the terrible spin—rather than the presence of the kids that was the real cause of this accident.

So many things could have prevented it, including the obvious one of having an alarm to indicate even partial disengagement of the autopilot. However, with everything now so automatic in today's aircraft, the danger of pilots taking everything for granted and switching off mentally is an increasing problem.

Had it not been for a cockpit video recording taken by the off-duty captain, it would not have been possible to determine exactly what happened, and particularly who did what.

---

[1] In accordance with regulations, medical staff at Moscow checked the pilots' blood alcohol levels and blood pressure before the flight and recorded 'nothing untoward.' The presence of alcohol was not given as a possible contributory factor, though there were suggestions that the captain was drinking with his family. One story said he struggled to get back to the cockpit from the cabin.

[2] Airbus is now famous for now using a sidestick instead of a control column. However, this only began with the 'fly-by-wire' A320.

[3] 'Counter' means counter to what it is trying to do.

# HELIOS 737 FAILS TO PRESSURIZE (Greece 2005)

## Autopilot Takes Unconscious Pilots up and Onwards

> Not realizing they had left the cabin pressurization set to 'manual,' the 737 pilots lost consciousness due to lack of oxygen as the autopilot took them up to cruising height and 'happily on' to their destination.
>
> The pilots of two Greek F-16 fighters dispatched to see what was happening reported to Greek air traffic control (ATC) that the first officer was slumped in his seat and someone was climbing into the captain's seat.
>
> As in a Hollywood movie, the 'someone' was a male flight attendant with just a few hours' flying experience in tiny aircraft. Unfortunately, the ending was not like a Hollywood movie.
>
> *[Helios Airways Flight 522]*

On August 14, 2005, at 9:00 a.m. local time, a Helios Airways Boeing 737-300 took off from Larnaca, Cyprus, for Athens, where it was to make a stopover on its way to Prague. On board were 121 people including the 2 pilots and 4 cabin crew.

As the aircraft climbed through 10,000 ft, the cabin altitude (pressure) wa rning horn sounded. As the same warning sound is also used to indicate a configuration mistake (say failure to extend flaps) at takeoff, the pilots assumed it was merely a false alert. They discussed the problem with their maintenance people at Larnaca, but with some difficulty as the captain was German, the first officer Cypriot and the maintenance engineer possibly English.

On the advice of Maintenance about how to silence the surely irritating horn, the captain left his seat to trip the relevant circuit breaker behind his seat, but due to the extra exertion and lack of oxygen collapsed before he could do so. The last communication received by ATC was 11 minutes after takeoff as the aircraft was passing through 22,000 ft—the height at which lack of oxygen really makes itself felt.

The aircraft continued to climb to its cruising height of 34,000 ft and continued towards Athens as programmed in the Flight Management Control System (FMCS). As it approached their airspace, Greek the traffic controllers were surprised at not being able to communicate, but were initially not too concerned as they had heard about the air-conditioning problem the pilots had mentioned only four minutes after takeoff from Larnaca.

Becoming concerned that some sort of hijacking might be involved, they alerted the Greek Air Force, but told them to hold off, thinking the Helios flight was sorting out its technical problems.

Finally, at 10.55, two Air Force F-16s were scrambled. On intercepting the aircraft, they reported that the first officer was slumped over his seat and that the captain's seat was unoccupied. They then said two people had entered the cockpit wearing oxygen masks. The pilots also noticed that the passengers' oxygen masks had deployed.

The cockpit voice recorder later showed someone with a very labored male voice had made Mayday calls, which the controllers had not picked up, no doubt because the frequency was still set for the point of departure.

The first thing a professional airline pilot taking over control would have done would have been to bring the aircraft down to a height where breathing would have been easier. However, the 'pilot' in question was flight attendant Prodromou, a private pilot with only a few hours experience on a Cessna. Being unfamiliar with the 737 controls, he might well have wanted to seek advice over the radio before performing a maneuver from which he might not be able to recover, and there is evidence he hesitated for a long time.

Greek investigators later said Prodromou (together with a female colleague) had used an emergency oxygen kit, opened the cockpit door using a code, and had managed to fly the plane for ten to twelve minutes before it crashed from lack of fuel.

Post-mortem examinations carried out after the accident showed that many of the passengers were alive when they hit the ground. Of course, unlike the pilots, they had had the benefit of the oxygen masks that deploy automatically, and while these only supply oxygen for a limited time—long enough to allow the pilots to bring an aircraft suffering decompression down to a level where breathing is possible without masks—they would have helped.

The details of what happened on that flight are shown by the following timeline, where the time in hours and minutes is the elapsed time from departure:[1]

[00:00] (09:07 Cyprus time)

Departure from Larnaca for Athens

(Estimated flight time 1:20)

[00:04]

Crew report problems—cabin altitude warning horn sounds at 10,000 ft. As same horn also denotes 'takeoff configuration warning,' crew assumes it is a false alert. At 14,000 ft, cabin oxygen masks deployment lamp (presumably) illuminates in cockpit.

[00:07]

Master Caution sounds at 17,000 ft.

Instruments show an apparent problem with the avionics cooling system—actually due to absence of cooling air.

The German-born captain and Cypriot first officer spend five or more minutes discussing problem—with language difficulties—with English maintenance engineer at their base on Cyprus, who says horn can be silenced by tripping circuit breaker on panel behind captain's seat. Captain leaves his seat, but because of the exertion collapses before being able to trip breaker.

The last contact with the aircraft was as it climbed through 28,900 ft.

[00:11]

Autopilot takes aircraft up to its 34,000 ft cruising height, where it levels out and flies on for *one hour* towards Kea Island.

[01:13]

Aircraft overflies Kea VOR at 34,000 ft; and continues at that height, ready to turn into the Athens Airport Approach. Duly turns, but stays at 34,000 ft, and therefore believing it to be a missed approach flies on before executing a roughly 290-degree turn to bring itself back to the Kea beacon.

[01:31]

Joins Kea holding pattern, making repeated circuits.

[02:17]

While making sixth circuit in the Kea holding pattern, aircraft intercepted by the two Greek F-16 aircraft.

They report:

*Captain not in his seat; first officer slumped over controls; passenger oxygen masks 'dangling.'*

[02:42]

Male seen entering the aircraft's cockpit, sitting in the captain's seat and trying to regain control of the plane.

[02:43]

Left engine flames out due to fuel depletion; aircraft loses height.

[02:47]

> Cockpit voice recorder (CVR) records two Mayday messages transmitted with labored voice. [Not received on the ground as frequency still set to that for departure point (Larnaca).]

[02:53]

> The right engine flames out at an altitude of 7,100 ft.

[02:56] (12:03 local time)

> The aircraft crashes into hilly terrain near the village of Grammatikos about 20 miles northwest of Athens International Airport.

According to early reports, even though the fuel had essentially run out, the flammable brush and grass meant fires smoldered for several hours making many of the bodies difficult to identify. However, the body of a female flight attendant was found in the cockpit area and the blood of a male flight attendant with some general aviation (private pilot) experience was found on the controls.

One slight mystery is that the medical report suggested that some passengers were alive (but no doubt unconscious) when the aircraft hit the ground. This is somewhat surprising in view of the fact that the passengers' emergency oxygen masks only supply oxygen for a limited time.

The final report by the Greek investigators made the following conclusions.

## Direct Causes

1. Non-recognition that the cabin pressurization mode selector was in the MAN (manual) position during performance of the Preflight procedure, Before Start checklist; and After Takeoff checklist.

2. Non-identification of the warnings and the reasons for the activation of the warnings (cabin altitude warning horn, passenger oxygen masks deployment indication, indication, Master Caution), and continuation of the climb.

3. Incapacitation of the flight crew due to hypoxia, resulting in continuation of the flight, non-identification of the warnings and the reasons for the activation of the warnings (cabin altitude warning horn), passenger oxygen masks deployment via the flight management computer and the autopilot, depletion of the fuel and engine flameout, and impact of the aircraft with the ground.

## Latent Causes

1. The operator's deficiencies in organization, quality management and safety culture, documented diachronically as findings in numerous audits.

2. The regulatory authority's diachronic inadequate execution of its oversight responsibilities to ensure the safety of operations of the airlines under its supervision and its inadequate responses to findings of deficiencies documented in numerous audits.

3. Inadequate application of Crew Resource Management (CRM) principles by the flight crew.

4. Ineffectiveness and inadequacy of measures taken by the manufacturer in response to the previous pressurization incidents in this particular type of aircraft, both with regard to modifications to aircraft systems as well as to guidance to the crews.

## Contributing Factors to the Accident

1. Omission of returning the pressurization mode selector to AUTO after unscheduled maintenance on the aircraft.

2. Lack of specific procedures (on an international basis) for cabin crew procedures to address the situation of loss of pressurization, passenger oxygen masks deployment, and continuation of the aircraft ascent (climb).

3. Ineffectiveness of international aviation authorities to enforce implementation of corrective action plans after relevant audits.

The investigators essentially said

*While the maintenance people contributed to the accident by not setting the cabin pressurization mode to automatic, the pilots should not only have picked this up in three separate checks, and should have subsequently realized the nature of the problem, if not from the warning horn, then from the deployment of the passenger cabin oxygen masks and the master caution.*

According to *Flight International,* Helios's lawyers claimed the pilots could not have made such mistakes. However, the non-volatile memory in the pressurization mode unit showed the controls were set to 'manual' during the flight.

The attempts by the flight attendant (in the presence of a female flight attendant) to save the aircraft were not really part of the inquiry. It seems they were only able to gain entry into the cockpit using a code very late on, by which time the oxygen they had was possibly running out, and the fuel certainly was. Had they been able to gain access earlier, and had they been able to communicate by radio for advice on how to fly the aircraft, it might have been a somewhat different story. [It has been argued by some that measures taken since 9/11 to make it impossible to gain access to the flight deck without authorization (from the pilots) could be counterproductive in some circumstances.]

The report criticized the regulatory authorities, saying this was not the first time such a problem had occurred and that those authorities should have insisted the manufacturer did more to prevent such an error remaining undetected.

Founded in 1999, Helios Airways in April 2006 changed its name to A Jet Aviation Limited while continuing operations with its two remaining Boeing 737-800 aircraft.

The fact that without the flight director (FD) took the aircraft up to its cruising height, flew it for an hour towards its destination, brought it into the holding pattern, took it towards the airport, and then returned it to the holding pattern on the assumption that it was a missed approach is a good demonstration of how far automated systems have come.

---

[1] Reference made to *Flight International* (17–23 October, 2006)

# CHAPTER 14

# DECISIONAL ACCIDENTS
# —MILITARY ACTION

## KAL902
## (Kola, Russia 1978)

**Russian Military Shocked at Their Vulnerability**

> Some passengers had noticed that the sun was on the wrong side of the aircraft, but apparently thought the pilots must know what they were doing. Little did they realize they were about to be shot down over the Soviet Union.
>
> *[Korean Airlines Flight 902]*

According to James Oberg,[1] the Korean Airlines 707, en route from Amsterdam to Anchorage (Alaska) on April 20, 1978, for some unknown reason had deviated from its course soon after reaching Iceland. The sweeping deviation to the right was so gradual that it could not have been made manually, and the likely cause was a drift in the inertial navigation system or the inputting of erroneous waypoint coordinates.

Someone in the media attributed the Korean pilots' failure to notice they were on the wrong heading to the fact that they were pre-occupied with something extraneous, such as playing cards. Soon after penetrating Soviet airspace, they found a Russian fighter flying alongside on their right signaling them to land.

Not that it made any difference, as Oberg points out that the ICAO (International Civil Aviation Organization) says the aircraft ordering another to land should fly on the left—perhaps because that is the side on which the captain always sits and he can thus more easily observe the indications of the intercepting fighter. Oberg goes on to say the Korean Airlines captain maintains he lowered his landing gear and flashed his navigation lights to indicate he was going to comply and follow.

Apparently, from the initial size of the 'blip' on their radar, the Russians had first thought it would prove to be a harmless Boeing 747, but when the fighter pilot announced it was a civilian 707 they had their doubts as the same design under the designation RC-135 was used by the Americans for intelligence purposes.

Despite the strongest possible protestations by the Russian fighter pilot—intercepted by the American listening posts—the general in charge ordered that the aircraft be brought down, no doubt on the assumption that the civilian markings were just a trick, for why would a civilian aircraft fly so far into Russian territory? (In his defense, it has to be said that the use of civilian aircraft or civilian-looking aircraft to provoke responses for analysis was not unknown.)

With great reservations, the Russian pilot fired off two missiles, the first of which failed to detonate, while the second exploded in the vicinity of the 707's left wing, damaging the fuselage and killing two passengers.

The Korean pilot initiated a rapid descent to a height where the passengers could breathe without their oxygen masks, as is standard practice. In addition, the passenger cabin would have been getting cold quickly due to the damage to the fuselage. In so doing, he entered low cloud and incidentally became invisible to the fighters who had overshot him. On turning back, they failed to locate him, and unaccompanied he flew for almost an hour looking for somewhere to land, before finally successfully bringing the aircraft down on a frozen lake.

The fact that a possibly hostile aircraft could fly low and undetected over their territory for such a long time came as a great shock to the Russian military. While realizing there had been no intrigue, they feared the Americans might have learnt much from the event, and might exploit that newfound loophole for military purposes.

The passengers were quickly returned, and the crew somewhat later.

---

[1] *Uncovering Soviet Disasters* by James Oberg, Random House, New York, NY, 1988.

# KAL007
# (Sakhalin Island 1983)

**Korean Airlines Again Provokes Paranoid Soviet Defense Forces**

> The event previously described led to a big shake-up in the Soviet air defense system, and recognition that inferior technology was making them vulnerable.
>
> A number of heads rolled; and the climate was such that all involved would do their utmost to ensure another 'rogue'—perhaps a more sinister one—did not get through.
>
> This nervousness, and even the inferior technology, possibly led to a replay with a much less happy conclusion.
>
> *[Korean Airlines Flight 007]*

On September 1, 1983, Korean Airlines Flight KAL007 en route *from* Alaska to Seoul had a similar course deviation as that incurred by KAL902 five years earlier. However, this time, the Boeing 747 had already passed over militarily sensitive areas of eastern Russia and was heading possibly for the even more sensitive area around Vladivostok.

The aircraft was eventually shot down by a Russian fighter just off the northern coast of Japan. All 269 passengers and crew on board the Boeing 747 were to lose their lives.

The US and President Reagan in particular, made much of the fact that the 'Evil Empire' had shot down an innocent airliner. However, some have expressed doubts about what really happened, and books, seemingly enthusiastically researched, have raised all sorts of possibilities, with most of them making the US look devious.

Two TV films were made about the incident, but appeared before more information became available after the opening up of the Soviet Union.

The first, *Shootdown* (1988), starring Angela Lansbury, was essentially about a mother (Lansbury), who had lost a son on the flight, trying to get the truth out of the Russians, and not least the US Government via a kind of deep throat[1] contact.

The second, *Tailspin* (1989) was more of a documentary, using the facts then available.

One positive outcome of the incident was the decision by President Reagan to allow the civilian use of GPS.

President Reagan greatly embarrassed the Soviet leaders by claiming the shooting down of the 'innocent' airliner was an uncivilized act.

297

However, we have now learnt that the Soviet leadership was quite paranoid and thought it quite possible the US might at some point carry out a pre-emptive nuclear strike—and would thus be especially wary of the US getting more information with a 'spy' plane.

Indeed, shortly after this incident a situation developed in which erroneous Soviet satellite detections of US missile launches against the background of an actually harmless NATO 'communication-in-nuclear-war' exercise could have triggered a nuclear exchange (World War III) by mistake.

In addition to the two incidents described in this chapter, family-owned Korean Airlines aircraft were involved in a succession of accidents and incidents. The airline was fast losing international credibility and on the brink of being banned by key countries. A Korean newspaper hack reputedly joked that all the 'female family member' holding the title 'Vice-President Responsible for Safety,' or similar, knew about aircraft was the seat numbers in First Class.

Finally, South Korea's exasperated President ordered a complete shake up of the airline. The authorities gave US airline, Delta, the task of sorting things out with the right to fire those deemed incompetent. Since then, Korean Airlines has regained respectability and seems to be one of the safest.

---

[1] 'Deep throat.' Term derived from the official leaking information to a couple of journalists during the Watergate affair. A highly placed *informant*.

# US WARSHIP DOWNS IRANIAN AIRLINER (Persian Gulf 1988)

## Fabulously Expensive Warship versus Ragtag Gunboats

> A fabulously expensive US warship designed to fight World War III, with a 'gung-ho' captain, found itself larking around with Iranian gunboats, and in the process shot down an Iranian airliner on a scheduled flight.
>
> The loss of the Pan Am 747 over Lockerbie, Scotland, was just *possibly* a consequence of this.
>
> *[Iran Air Flight 655]*

The *Sea of Lies* article in the *Newsweek* edition of July 12, 1992, which is still available online today is one of the best in-depth accounts of what happened, covering the events leading up to the incident, the incident itself, and the cover-up that followed. Rather like the narratives in this book, it is benefits from having been produced long afterwards when much more information was available. It further benefits from being written by a whole group of writers and researchers in collaboration with ABC News Nightline.

Here we just give the basic facts. Anyone really interested in the details should consult that excellent *Newsweek* article, which was used as the basis for much of this account.

### 'Gung-ho' Captain

Much attention has been focused on the gung-ho tendencies of Captain William C. Rogers III, commander of the USS *Vincennes* guided missile cruiser that shot down the Iranian airliner. According to a fellow officer on another ship nearby, he had shown excessive aggressiveness in an earlier action in the area, while others maintained he would take gratuitous risks in order to gain promotion.

Rogers had served on the staff of the Chief of Naval Operations and supposedly had friends in high places. Someone pointed out, 'actual combat action during his dream posting in command of the ultra-sophisticated Aegis cruiser would have been his ticket to Flag rank.'

One officer responsible for his training noted his failure to stick to battle plans.

Captain Rogers was not operating in isolation. He was operating directly under the orders of Fleet Headquarters in Bahrain, and one should point out that the *Vincennes* operated on their time, whereas Iranian time was a confusing 30 minutes ahead of that. (This may have contributed to the confusion when an officer on the *Vincennes* checked the time the Iranian aircraft took off against the published timetable.)

The other key characters (not on the Vincennes)

1. **Captain McKenna was the surface warfare commander in Bahrain.**

2. **Captain Watkins, on Admiral Lee's staff in Bahrain, who at a crucial moment questioned Rogers' location relative to the gunboats and their bearing.**

3. **Rear Admiral Leighton (Snuffy) Smith, commander of Carrier Battle Group 6, was on the aircraft carrier USS *Forrestal* some 200 miles to the southeast. Though he was not in command of Captain Rogers, there were situations in which he could intercede, having dispatched two F-14 fighters and two A-7 attack planes to hold off 50 miles away from the 'engagement' between the *Vincennes* helicopter and some Iranian gunboats.**

4. **Apparently, the Rear Admiral did not intervene at a critical moment because of the well-established Navy principle that the commander on the spot has to make the final decision.**

5. **Mark Collier 25, piloting the *Vincennes'* helicopter, *Ocean Lord*, under the command of Lt Roger Huff, sitting in the co-pilot's seat who followed the Iranian gunboats. He was said to have been unable to resist dropping down to have a closer look at what they were doing, and in consequence had a few shots fired in his direction.**
   **[Captain Rogers was then able to use this as justification for engaging the gunboats, which in fact did not even come within 5,000 yards of the *Vincennes*.]**

6. **Captain David Carlson on the frigate USS *Sides* 19 miles to the east and the captain and officers of the USS *Montgomery*, a somewhat less sophisticated warship compared with the *Vincennes*, which had been allegedly 'pursued' by the gunboats giving the *Vincennes* the original pretext to join in.**

Then there were the officers and crew of the *Vincennes* itself who from all accounts were not all up to the high standard one would expect on such a sophisticated and costly ship—not that that prevented them from getting decorated. (This under-par performance on the part of some may have been partly due to their lack of experience of such situations.)

Key people on the *Vincennes*

1. Commander Guillory, the tactical officer for surface warfare, who had previously been a personnel officer. Rogers had little faith in him, and he was said by colleagues at the time in personnel not to be a computer man, preferring to use pieces of paper stuck on his screen! Although Guillory gave actual orders for the ship's five-inch gun to fire when ready—first at a launch 8,000 yards away! — Rogers had really assumed Guillory's role himself.

2. Petty Officer Andrew Anderson, whose task in the *Vincennes'* Command Information Center (CIC) was to identify any air traffic within range of the ship.

3. Petty Officer John Leach sitting next to Anderson and asked by Anderson for an opinion—cut short by Lt Clay Zocher.

4. Lt Clay Zocher, the petty officer's immediate boss, who according to *Newsweek*, 'had stood on this watch only twice before during General Quarters and had never mastered the computer routines for his console.'

5. Lt Cmdr Scott Lustig, the *Vincennes'* tactical commander for air warfare, who at the crucial moment of deciding whether to fire or not, asked Captain Rogers, 'What do we do?'

6. [Lustig was ultimately awarded the navy's Commendation Medal for 'heroic achievement,' because of his: 'Ability to maintain his poise and confidence under fire enabled him to quickly and precisely complete the firing procedure.']

## The Ship

Conceived in the 1960s at the height of the Cold War, the Aegis class missile cruisers were designed to prevent US naval fleets, including aircraft carriers, getting overwhelmed by an onslaught of missiles. Allegedly, they could simultaneously track as many as 200 missiles or bogies (enemy aircraft) within 300 miles at the same time and at the same time follow what might be threatening the fleet from under the water. Essentially, they were narrow-hulled boats powered by two powerful aircraft engines with a phalanx of computers and monitors below linked to massive arrays of antennas on the superstructure. They could accelerate quickly to high speeds thanks to the powerful engines.

The *Vincennes* was the first Aegis class cruiser to be deployed in a combat situation. However, deploying it in the narrow waters of the Persian Gulf and letting it stray from international waters to engage with Iranian gunboats was like pitting a Ferrari against bumper cars on a fairground and at the same time requiring its occupants to identify foe from friend in the crowd.

The crews of other Navy vessels regarded the crew of the *Vincennes* as arrogant.

A number of US naval vessels were operating in the area ostensibly to protect shipping but covertly to ensure Iraq was not defeated by Iran in the Iran/Iraq War (in which the US was supposedly neutral). The initial reason for including an asset that was as sophisticated and costly as the *Vincennes* was that the Chinese had supposedly supplied the Iranians with a missile that other line ships could not counter.

### The Ship's Combat Information Center (CIC)

This was the nerve center of the ship and somewhat like a computer games arcade, but much better. Here the various personnel would be watching their monitors, with the information they were seeing and annotating being collated by computer to be shown as symbols on two large screens at the front of the room in front of the captain and his two battle commanders.

Officers and personnel in the CIC would wear headphones and communicate over several channels, with left and right ears usually listening to different circuits. Rogers and his key officers in the CIC were all on the same circuit, but unbelievably, according to *Newsweek*, so was half of the ship!

Crewmembers had discovered they could tap into the 'command net' to hear the action over their Sony Walkmans. However, in so doing, they drained power and the volume faded. Whenever it got too low, Lustig had to yell, 'Switch' so everyone could turn to an alternate command circuit. Then the hackers would switch to that channel, too. Besides giving rise to the possibility that vital information could be missed or words misheard, this does not give the impression it was a responsibly run ship. If they had wanted to enable the crew to listen in without compromising their own communications, they surely had the technological wherewithal to do so.

### The Iranian Airliner

Iran Air Flight 655 (IR655, an Airbus 300 with 290 people on board), took off from Bandar Abbas airport in Iran at 09:50 on July 3, 1988 to make the simple 29-minute hop across the Persian Gulf to Bahrain. Allowing 12 or so minutes to start the engines, taxi to the end of the runway and perform the usual checks, it would normally have become airborne at about 09:02.

However, a delay of about 15 minutes due to a passenger having problems at immigration meant it only became airborne at 10:17 Iran time. Senior US officers later disingenuously claimed it took off 27 minutes behind schedule, when in fact it was only 15 minutes, as airliners do not normally actually liftoff at their advertized departure times, which refer to the moment the doors are closed, and they are ready to depart from the gate.

Such a short flight would only involve the aircraft climbing to 14,000 ft, and remaining there for a short while before descending into Bahrain. Furthermore, the route was not only a straight line, but also in a 20-mile-wide commercial airline corridor designated 'Amber 59.'

A pilot flying along the centerline would have had 10 miles leeway on either side, and would not be expecting trouble. On occasions, but not on that day, the control tower would warn civilian aircraft about military action taking place on the sea en route.

## The Ghost Ship

One reason subsequently given to the Senate Armed Services Committee for the *Vincennes'* presence was that 'It had been racing that morning to rescue a Liberian tanker, the *Stoval*.' No such ship appears in any ship registry. In fact the *'Stoval'* was a fictitious ship, created by fake radio messages designed to entice the Iranian gunboats out of their lair, and was a trial run for an American sting operation.

## What Happened?

The more realistic reason for the *Vincennes* being in the area was Rogers' desire to get at the Iranian gunboats that had been trailing a lesser US warship, the USS *Montgomery*. In so doing, he had sent up a helicopter to watch them.

[08:40]

> Captain McKenna in Bahrain returned to his command to find Rogers was 40 miles to the north of where he thought he had told him to stay. Questioned about this, Rogers said he was supporting his helicopter and having difficulties communicating with it.

> When told by McKenna to go back south, Rogers replied with incredulity, *You want me to what?* According to *Newsweek*, McKenna could hear the guffaws in the *Vincennes'* Combat Information Center. Furious, McKenna gives a direct order for the *Vincennes* and the *Montgomery* to come south.

> Obliged to comply, Rogers duly obeyed but left the helicopter watching over the gunboats.

> Mark Collier, the helicopter pilot, followed the gunboats as they retreated northwards, and finally decided to lose height to get a closer look, saying later that he wanted to see how many men were on board and what armament they carried. Evidently, not pleased by this, one of them fired a burst of anti-aircraft fire.

> Collier later described it as 'eight to 10 bursts of light' and 'sparks....just like a big spark' 100 yards from the helicopter.

The occupants decided to 'get out of there,' with the helicopter commander, Lt Roger Huff, sitting in the copilot's seat radioing the *Vincennes*:

> *Trinity Sword. This is Ocean Lord 25. We're taking fire. Executing evasion.*
>
> *[Under the Navy's Rules of Engagement, this allowed Rogers to engage the enemy, even though it had just been one burst of fire, and might have been little more than a warning shot.]*

Ordering 'General Quarters' and 'Full Power,' Rogers reversed course and proceeded northwards at 30 knots.

[9:28]

> Two F-14 fighters and two A-7 attack planes took off from the aircraft carrier USS *Forestall* with orders to hold off 80 miles away from the action—Rear Admiral Leighton Smith on the *Forestall* did not want them shot down by mistake.

[9:39]

> Rogers radioed fleet headquarters in Bahrain, declaring his intention to open fire. Not happy with the situation, they queried his position and the bearing of the gunboats.

Captain Watkins in Bahrain then asked:

> *Are the contacts clearing the area?*
>
> In fact, the gunboats were milling around randomly a long way away, probably thinking they were safe on their own in their own territorial waters and it was not a question of them *'clearing the area.'* Rogers continued to argue in favor of an attack, and although lookouts on the bridge said the boats are milling around used the fact that at one point in time they said a couple were heading in the direction of the *Vincennes* as the 'clincher.' He reported to Bahrain that the gunboats were *'gathering speed and showing hostile intent,'* and that he intended to open fire.

[9:41]

> Admiral Lee finally agreed to Roger's planned attack, just as the *Vincennes* was passing into Iranian waters.
>
> To suggest that the *Vincennes* was under attack when the nearest launch to be shot at was more than 8,000 yards away was ridiculous, and it seemed no one on the *Vincennes* thought that was the case.

[9:45:30]

The Iranian Airbus A300 received takeoff clearance and lifted off a minute later from Bandar Abbas Airport in Iran, some 55 miles to the northeast. Its route southwest to Dubai would take it over the *Vincennes*, which really should have been 40 miles to the south.

Captain Rogers, virtually pushing Guillory his tactical officer for surface warfare aside, set the big consolidated data screen to 16 miles in order to concentrate on the gunboats.

[9:47]

The blip of the Iran Air Flight 655 Airbus A300 climbing out of Bandar Abbas Airport appeared on the *Vincennes* radar, and as a precautionary measure 'tagged' 'Assumed Hostile,' as the airport handled both civilian and military traffic.

Petty Officer Anderson, responsible for identifying any aircraft within range of the *Vincennes*, got the Aegis radar to interrogate the aircraft's transponder using the IFF system, and got a Mode 3 return indicating it was a 'Commair' (commercial airliner). To make sure he scanned the flight schedule for the airport, but somehow missed Flight 655. He was said to have been confused by the half-hour time difference, the four different time zones in the Gulf and not helped by the facts that the lights in the Combat Information Center flickered each time the *Vincennes'* 5-inch gun fired a round at the Iranian gunboats.

Just as he was wondering aloud to the petty officer next to him whether the blip might possibly be an Iranian warplane, he was overheard by his superior, Lt Zocher, who was worrying about an Iranian P-3 patrol proceeding down the coast. Fearing that the two aircraft might be coordinating an attack, he decided to pass the information to his superior, Lt Cmdr Scot Lustig, the *Vincennes'* tactical commander for air warfare.

Instead of getting the two F-16s from the *Forestall* to check it out in the little time available, he ordered Zocher to warn the aircraft it was approaching a US warship.

[9:47]

Captain Rogers was not only engrossed in his battle with the gunboats but making it difficult for others to work, with the ship shuddering and keeling over, as he shouted to the gun crew to load faster and ordered hard right rudder so that his stern gun could bear as well.

As already mentioned, the audio link tying-in the key officers was subject to fading due to the demands of crewmembers listening-in with their Walkmans, and had to be switched repeatedly.

[9:50]

The audio link picked up the words, 'possible Astro' (code word for an F-14 uttered by a never identified person.

Petty Officer Anderson re-interrogated what he thought was the aircraft's transponder but forgot to reset the range and as a result received a reply from the transponder on a military aircraft still on the runway at Bandar Abbas Airport. Naturally, it was Mode 2: military aircraft.

[9:51]

Anderson exclaimed 'possible Astro,' just as Rogers had swung the ship right round for his forward gun to bear again. When it jammed after getting off 11 rounds, he ordered hard rudder, with the result that the ship swung round with books and papers falling off the consoles as the ship keeled over.

With the 'blip' 32 miles away, Lustig said to Rogers:

*What do we do?*

Though it is possible to blame Rogers for creating the predicament by chasing after the gunboats and placing the *Vincennes* where it was, one cannot say he callously shot it down without some cause.

First, in his mind there must have been the case a year earlier of the USS *Stark*, which was struck and almost sunk by two anti-ship missiles launched from a lone Iraqi fighter while its captain had been in the toilet.

The *Vincennes* issued three further warnings:

*Iranian fighter...you are steering into danger and are subject to*
*United States naval defensive measures.*

Rogers could not be certain he was dealing with an enemy warplane. For one thing, it was, at 7,000 ft, somewhat high for an attacking aircraft. In addition, another officer, Lt William Mountford, warned 'possible commair.'

Subsequent playback of the tapes of the Combat Information Center data revealed that Petty Officer Anderson's screen must have shown the aircraft almost at 12,000 ft at 380 knots and still climbing. Yet he and Petty Officer Leach were chanting that it was descending and picking up speed. Anderson was shouting out that the speed was 455 knots, the altitude 7,800 ft and descending.

If Rogers was going to fire he would have to do so before the aircraft narrowed the distance to 10 miles.

[9:54:05]

> With the unsuspecting aircraft 11 miles away, Rogers used the firing key to free-up the SM-2 missiles for firing. The missiles did not launch immediately, as Lt Zocher was so unsettled, he pressed the wrong keys, it is said 23 times. In the end, an experienced petty officer leant over and did it for him.

*****

The crew of the Airbus had not heard any of the warnings issued by the *Vincennes* as all of the four radio bandwidths had been set to ATC (air traffic control) frequencies.

The first of the *Vincennes'* missiles blew the left wing off the Airbus, which fell out of the sky in full view of the shocked crew of the *Montgomery*. Somewhat farther away, the radar operative man on the USS *Sides* was telling its captain he reckoned it had been a civilian airliner.

On the *Vincennes*, the elation at having hit the target gave way to second thoughts as the amount of debris coming down appeared much too great for it to have been an F-14.

*****

As usual, there were many contributing factors. The fact that petty officers Anderson and Leach were saying the aircraft was descending and much lower than it actually was is said to be an example of wish fulfillment, in that one sees what one expects to see.

If one believes, as some quite reasonable people do, that the Lockerbie disaster resulted from this incident, one might go as far as saying that the downing of that Pan Am airliner over Scotland was really the result of top-level promotions in the US Navy having been made in favor of those with friends in high places.

Anyway, as we keep repeating, the causes of accidents are rarely as simple as they first seem.

# CHAPTER 15

# AIRLINERS MORPH INTO FLYING BOMBS

## FAILED PRECURSOR TO 9/11
### (Marseille 1994)

> In 1994, French Special Forces stormed a hijacked Air France airliner that terrorists intended to blow up above the Eiffel Tower. The authorities claimed it was one of the most successful operations of its kind ever.
>
> *[Air France Flight 8969]*

The extremely short timeframe (from start to finish) was one reason why the terrorists' achieved many of their objectives on 9/11 (see next narrative). Contrast that with the extremely long timeframe of this narrative's *failed* attempt to implement a similar, albeit less grandiose, operation seven and a half years earlier.

At 11:15 a.m. on December 24, 1994, Air France flight AF8969, an A300 Airbus, was about to depart for Paris from Algiers Airport, with 220 passengers and 12 crew. As Algeria was in a state of civil war, passengers did not think it untoward that four armed men dressed in sharp blue uniforms with Air Algerie insignia, claiming to be security agents, had come on board to make a final passport check before departure.

That is until there were shouts of '*Allah Akbar*' (God is Great) from the four 'security men,' who, abandoned their passport checks, and staying inside, shut the doors and locked them. Three of them quickly proceeded to the cockpit while the fourth kept the passengers at bay by waving a gun at them. For those at the back of the aircraft it was quite difficult to work out what was going on, and later some even remained unaware that selected passengers had been used as bargaining chips and shot.

Algerian special forces, already on high alert at the airport as the country was in a state of civil war, came to see what was going on, and quickly confirmed the individuals were 'terrorists.' They actually belonged to the Algerian Armed Islamic Group (AIG[1]). It being Christmas Eve, many top French officials were away on vacation and, as usual, Prime Minister

Balladur was at his Alpine chalet in Chamonix where he stayed glued to the phone line for the first day. The French Foreign Minister and Interior Minister were in Paris handling the situation, their roles being to deal with the Algerian authorities and set up a team ready to go into action and overcome the hijackers should that prove necessary.

The hijackers' immediate demand had been the release from house arrest of two leaders of the Islamic Salvation Front (FIS), an Algerian organization banned in Algeria. The hijackers negotiated via the pilots with the Algerian Interior Minister who had rushed to the airport and was using the radio equipment in the control tower.

After an hour or so, the hijackers seemed more intent on going to Paris than seeking the release of the two political leaders. To try and move things along they first shot an Algerian policeman whom they had identified during the passport checks—he was led away asking not to be killed as he had a 'wife and child,' and his body—still quivering—was dumped outside the aircraft. With the Algerian authorities still adamant, the hijackers then killed the commercial attaché at the Embassy of Vietnam in Algeria, who was the only person on board who was neither Algerian nor French—the poor man, thinking he was being released, went back for his coat.

The Algerian authorities had insisted on the release of the elderly, invalids, children and so on. By the end of the second day, Christmas Day, the hijackers had released 63 in all. Their departure probably made it easier for the terrorists to handle things in the aircraft where they had established a strict and oppressive regime, without being rude.

First, they made women and men sit separately and use different toilets. They also ordered the women, including the flight attendants, to cover their faces with whatever material was available, which included cut-up blankets. Then, applying some kind of psychological intimidation, the hijackers instituted a regime whereby they would treat the passengers harshly for 20 minutes, allow them to relax for 20 minutes and then repeat the process. The intention of this 'torture,' as some described it, was probably to keep the passengers off balance.

The authorities had managed to identify the leader of the hijackers and even had his mother brought to the airport to try to persuade him to let the passengers go. This only seemed to provoke him further.

Meanwhile, the French had not been wasting time. Right at the start, they had put their Special Deployment Unit (National Gendarmes Intervention Group or GIGN) on standby. This was an elite police unit trained along military lines for 'intervening' in hijacks and hostage situations. Although they had not been able to get the Algerian authorities to agree to let them 'help,' a team of 40 of these elite commandos set off in an A300 Airbus for Palma de Mallorca in Spanish territory, some 200 miles north of Algiers.

Balladur, the French Prime Minister, had returned to Paris to take overall command, and as the evening of the second day approached the hijackers, who must have been getting tired, realized they were getting nowhere slowly. After threatening to blow up the aircraft, they issued an ultimatum. If the boarding ramp was not pulled back and the plane not allowed to take off before 9:30 p.m., they would kill a hostage every half hour.

Announcing that the first to be shot would be Yannick Beugnet, a cook at the French ambassador's residence in Algiers, they brought him to the flight deck and allowed him to plead for his life over the radio. The cook was then shot and his body thrown onto the tarmac. Balladur was livid at the news, telling the Algerian Prime Minister they would hold him responsible. He then called the Algerian President saying he expected to see the imminent arrival of the aircraft on French soil.

The aircraft took off in the early hours of the next day, December 26, and at 3:30 a.m. landed at Marseille where the hijackers had been told a refueling stop was necessary. There was an element of truth in this, in that much of the fuel initially loaded in Algiers for the flight to Paris had been consumed by the auxiliary power unit (APU) that had been kept running to keep the lights and air-conditioning working. The Special Deployment Unit had taken off from Majorca in their A300 and followed them to Marseille, touching down at an adjacent military base.

In Majorca, the commandos had had time to fully familiarize themselves with the layout of the A300 and prepare. On the ground in Marseille, they went though their routines again. Meanwhile, the Marseille Chief of Police was conducting negotiations with the hijackers, the aim being to wear them down and, if possible, delay any action until dusk, which would be quite early as it was the middle of winter.

The French had received information that the hijackers intended to blow up the aircraft over Paris—something that was given credence by details given by passengers released in Algeria, which demolition experts said indicated the explosives were set to cause the aircraft to explode. This belief was further reinforced by the terrorists demand for 27 tonnes of fuel, when only 10 tonnes would largely suffice. Anyway, the French were determined not to let the aircraft leave Marseille.

At dawn, the hijackers issued an ultimatum, but the negotiators were able not only to extend this but also exploit it by saying some 'servicing' was needed. They sent in commandos in disguise, ostensibly to provide food and water, clean and service the toilets, but in reality to plant snooping devices, identify who was who and where. They noted that the doors were neither blocked nor booby-trapped. As the afternoon wore on with no fuel delivered to the aircraft, the negotiators drew things out by saying that holding a press conference in Marseille would be preferable as the press were there. They even exploited that by having the hijackers move the passengers towards the back of the aircraft, ostensibly to make more room for the press conference, but in fact to make more room for the commandos and to enable them to separate any hijacker in the cockpit—and possibly in charge—from the others.

As 5 p.m. approached, the exhausted hijackers knew things were getting critical for them, and their leader came into the cabin to select a hostage to kill—the youngest member of the cabin crew. However, it seems he was hesitating to put his threat into execution, perhaps out of fear of provoking the French. Instead, in their frustration, they let off some rounds in the direction of the control tower where they knew the scheming negotiators would be. The commandos would eventually have moved in anyway, but their firing of shots at the control tower resulted in Prime Minister Balladur giving the head of the commandos *carte blanche*.

Their plan was to have three teams who would use boarding ramps to access the doors. Two would creep up from the back trying to keep out of sight of the hijackers and open the doors at the back to provide a good escape route for the hostages. The third, led by Major Favier, would have the most difficult role of penetrating the aircraft via the front right door to separate hijackers on the flight deck from their companions.

Despite the commandos having planned and rehearsed the operation so meticulously, they found the height of the ramp they were standing on too high to allow the front door that they had prized ajar to be opened fully. On quickly pulling it back to allow enough space, they almost left a commando dangling between the fuselage and the ramp. Fortunately, he got a good grip on the door and was able to able to hang in there until it was opened successfully. They were faced with a hail of bullets, with one lucky shot from the hijackers hitting a gendarme's gun, setting off the rounds it contained and knocking him backwards down the steps.

As hostages evacuated from the rear doors, the commandos progressively overcame the hijackers, though one held on, firing round after round, for almost 20 minutes. Sharpshooters firing from the control tower were at the beginning unable to get shots in because of the presence of the aircrew. The first officer then slid out of a broken cockpit window, only to injure himself quite seriously on hitting the ground. No hostage was killed—the commandos had flak jackets and the aircrew said the bodies of the hijackers had at times shielded them.

Another reason given for the survival of all the crew was that they had built up a rapport with the hijackers who could so easily have killed them out of spite. Favier, the commando leader, suggested it was a matter of mutual respect. Was it the 'Stockholm syndrome'[2] in reverse?

---

[1] The AIG is an Islamic terrorist group.

[2] Named after a famous case in Stockholm where hostages kept for several days in a bank ended up 'sympathizing' with the hostage takers.

# 9/11—AIRLINERS FLOWN INTO BUILDINGS (US 2001)

Twin Towers Collapsed in Clouds of Dust

The events of September 11, 2001, when four small teams of terrorists hijacked long-haul airliners full of fuel in order to fly them into symbolic buildings in North America, marked America and brought about changes around the world.

Since there were relatively few passengers on board the aircraft it was the 2,700 or more people killed on the ground that made the tragedy so horrible. The total death toll for the occupants *of all four* aircraft hijacked was 265 (or 266), or 246 if one excludes the perpetrators.

*[American Airlines Flight 11]*
*[United Airlines Flight 175]*
*[American Airlines Flight 77]*
*[United Airlines Flight 93]*

On September 11, 2001, 19 terrorists hijacked four aircraft almost fully laden with fuel for long transcontinental flights. They intended to fly them into symbolic US buildings. Hijackers on three of the four aircraft succeeded in doing this.

With so many excellent accounts, documentaries, and movies, covering the events of 9/11, it would be difficult to add usefully to them here. However, the timeline below, presented in tabular form, is perhaps a useful tool for grasping how the overall situation developed. The operation depended largely on timing and 'doing the deeds' before people, and in particular those on the aircraft, realized what was happening. The outcome could have been even worse had airport congestion not delayed the takeoff of the fourth aircraft, enabling the passengers to learn the hijackers' real intentions.

For unknown reasons, the four hijackers on that last flight (UA93 [4]) were rather slow in going into action despite already being behind time due to the 35-minute delay in taking off. When they did finally hijack the aircraft, passengers and cabin crew inevitably started phoning out, only to learn that their aircraft would probably soon become a flying bomb; if they did nothing they were 'goners' anyway.

The following pages show the timeline of the tragic events that shocked America and the world.

Timing was everything.

## Timeline of the Events of 9/11 (Four Aircraft)

| Airline Flight Number [sequence] | American Airlines AA 11 [1] | United Airlines UA 175 [2] | American Airlines AA 77 [3] | United Airlines UA 93 [4] | Total Death Toll |
|---|---|---|---|---|---|
| Aircraft type | Boeing 767 ER | Boeing 767 | Boeing 757 | Boeing 757 | |
| Departing | Boston | Boston | Dulles Washington | Newark New York | |
| Destination | Los Angeles | Los Angeles | Los Angeles | San Francisco | |
| Passengers | 76 | 51 | 53 | 33 | 213 |
| Crew | 11 | 9 | 6 | 7 | 33 |
| Hijackers | 5 | 5 | 5 | 4 | 19 |
| Total deaths [ - hijackers] | 92 | 65 | 64 | 44 | 265 [246] |
| Actual takeoff | 07:59 | 08:14 | 08:20 | 08:42 | |
| Delay in taking off | | Approx. 10 min. | Approx 10 min. | Approx. **35 min.** | |
| Pilots alerted of danger | | | | 9:00 a.m. UA issues system-wide warning of 'cockpit intrusion.' Flight 93 replies 'Confirmed.' | |
| Hijacked | 08:14 | 08:42 | 08:52 | 09:10-09:20 | |
| Hijack suspected | 08:20 | Immediately | 09:05 | 9:28 | |
| Sounds heard by ATC due to radio mike switch being left on | 'We have some planes. Just stay quiet and you will be OK.' | | | Sounds of scuffling/ Arabic voices | |
| NORAD informed by FAA | 08:40 | 08:43 | 09:24? | No available data from NORAD (ongoing exchanges) | |
| ATC certain | 08:25 | 08:52 | 08:56 | 09:32 | |

| Time of impact | 08:46 | 09:03 | 09:37 | 10:03 or 10:06 (disputed) | |
|---|---|---|---|---|---|
| Level | 95th-103rd floors ------------ | 80th floor ------------ | Ground Level -------------- | Crash into terrain -------------- | |
| Location | N. Tower World Trade Center ------------ | S. Tower World Trade Center ------------ | Pentagon -------------- | Open country --------------- | |
| Effect | Catches fire; tower collapses on itself at 10:29 | Catches fire; tower collapses on itself at 09:59 | 5-storey section collapses | (Passengers confronted hijackers) | |
| Ground fatalities | **2,793** including woman who died months afterwards due to inhalation of cement, glass, lead and asbestos dust while fleeing the scene.* | | 125 | 0 | |

|  | **Other ATC-related Events** | | |
|---|---|---|---|
| **Between 09:03 and 09:07** | **FAA's New York & Boston Regional Centers stop takeoffs and landings** | **NY Port Authority closes Newark Airport** | |
| **09:25** | **FAA National Command Center STOPS ALL US TAKEOFFS** | | |
| **09:45** | **FAA orders all 4,500+** aircraft still airborne over the US to land.**  **Orders those that have not yet reached US territory to turn back or land at non-US alternates.**  ** Under instrument flight rules | | |

* The pernicious dust clouds may add hundreds of deaths to this 2,793 death toll as an increasing number of cases of cancer and other medical problems are now beginning to be found amongst those who so heroically took part in the rescue and clean-up.

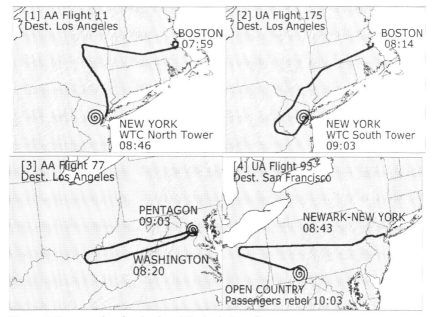

Figure 8  Routes taken by the four hijacked aircraft.

(Based on Official 9/11 Report)

## Outline of Events

The movie *United 93*, about the passengers in the last of the four aircraft to be hijacked who rebelled after learning by phone what had happened to the other hijacked aircraft, is based on the FAA's Herndon Command Center, which supervises ATC throughout the United States.

Its Operations Director, Ben Sliney, had an overall view of the unfolding situation, which he faced on his first day in the job, having returned to the agency after a period in private law practice.

He has very cogently explained how difficult it was to assess what the hijackers were doing and which aircraft had been hijacked, or whether there might not be many more with some coming in from overseas.

In an interview with Jeremy Vine on the UK's BBC Radio 2 program to promote the above movie in which he played himself, Sliney said he heard about the hijacking of an airliner just before attending a meeting. He had not been unduly concerned as there were well-tried protocols for dealing with hijacks, and hijacks took time to play out and usually ended with no loss of life or serious consequences. Interestingly, they thought September was an odd time of the year for a hijack.

In its role of overseeing air traffic throughout the United States, the FAA's Command Center at Herndon does not communicate with aircraft directly. However, it does receive all the necessary data relating to aircraft movements, weather patterns, delays and problems, and special situations such as military activity and the need to clear airspace for Air Force One— the US President's aircraft. It then gives instructions to ATC centers and other ATC facilities all over the USA. It also communicates with North American Aerospace Defense Command (NORAD) responsible for defending North American aerospace.

While not handling individual aircraft, its monitors do show the situation of air traffic throughout the country. If pilots enter the squawk code for a hijack code into their transponder, this would instantly show up on its screens as well as on those of the handling ATC. It would also be shown on those at NORAD, which meant that in the days when the controls for transponders were more primitive, pilots had to be careful not to mistakenly squawk the hijack code and attract the attention of a couple of fighters.

However, none of the four aircraft hijacked that day squawked that code, and as a result the controllers in direct contact were the only ones able to progressively deduct that a given aircraft had been hijacked (from the fact that it was not replying or obeying instructions, was changing course or height unduly, or had its transponder switched off). In some cases, controllers heard snippets of conversation in a foreign language, shouts, or in the case of the first aircraft to be hijacked, an announcement destined for the passengers—but which was transmitted because either one of the pilots keyed the radio mike, or a hijacker did so by mistake, saying:

*We have some planes; just stay quiet and you will be OK.*

In every case, the transponders were ultimately switched off, making it difficult to even be sure which aircraft was involved as the controllers could just see the radar echo without the Flight Number and height on their primary radar.

Thus the FAA Command Center and Operations Manager, Sliney, only belatedly became aware of the gravity of the situation. Sliney said it was only when he saw CNN coverage of the burning North Tower of the World Trade Center with most people assuming it had been struck by a light aircraft that he realized from the size of the hole and the amount of fire that it must have been a big jet and possibly flight AA11 [1].

Indeed, it was only when the second aircraft hit the South Tower while everyone was watching the burning North Tower on CNN that the FAA Command could grasp the likely implications of any other hijackings that day. They exchanged information with NORAD, and at times were frustrated that the military liaison man could not seem to put them in the loop.

However, in the BBC 2 interview, Sliney expressed sympathy for the military in view of the constraints under which they must have been operating. Who could order the shooting down of a civilian airliner and an American one at that?

The first two aircraft struck the twin towers of the World Trade Center in almost perfect fashion—from the hijackers' point of view.

However, the third aircraft, having taken off from Washington's Dulles International Airport not far from the Pentagon, was later seen heading for it, with its wings level as if the pilot knew what he was doing.

Some have said it was a great feat of airmanship for a novice to have hit the Pentagon at almost ground level with the maneuver simulating a perfect landing. However, damage and the effect of the inevitable fire would surely have been much more significant had he been able to bring the aircraft down in the hollow at the center of the five-sided low-aspect construction, and one wonders whether that had not been the intention and the piloting had not been so wonderful after all.

It is thought that the fourth aircraft was heading for either the White House or more likely the massive Capitol Building perched like a wedding cake at the end of the two-mile National Mall, making it an easy target and as symbolic as the World Trade Center in New York City. However, the 35-minute takeoff delay due to congestion at Newark Airport coupled with the long time the hijackers for some reason took to take over the aircraft meant that passengers and cabin crew would learn their likely fate by phone and not be so amenable.

From the phone and other evidence, and as shown in the film *Flight 93*, the passengers decided to take on the hijackers. They did so, and very likely managed to penetrate the cockpit, breaking down the door with a food cart from the galley. Confusion apparently reigned and the aircraft flew into the ground.

Some say the hijackers crashed it on purpose. Others have maintained a fighter shot it down just when the heroic passengers had gained control—a story that would not make for pleasant reading. Much material is available on the Internet for anyone interested in exploring the matter further, although as mentioned in the Acknowledgements at the beginning of this book, one can waste a lot of time going down the conspiratorial alley without coming to any definite conclusions.

### Hijackers' Modus Operandi

Each of the four hijacker groups included one or more members who had learnt how to fly at various flying schools for light aircraft. Their instructors had been surprised that learning how to land did not seem to interest them. Using manuals for the airliners concerned, namely the Boeing 757 and 767, and no doubt PC flight simulation programs, they had acquired the necessary flying skills for their task.

Although some of their number were stopped and searched at the airport security checks, they were allowed to board. It seems they largely depended on bluff—having a member go into the toilet and come out wearing something harmless made to look like a bomb that could be detonated at any moment if the passengers and cabin crew did not comply—and having other items including pepper spray that could be used to subdue or kill. The fact that there were relatively few passengers on board the aircraft made the passengers easier to control, as it was possible to herd them into the rear of the aircraft, away from the events and the murdered aircrew at the front.

## Hijack Protocols

Aircrew, cabin crew, and even passengers had learnt that the way to deal with a hijacking was to at least initially comply with the hijackers' demands, and in most cases this had worked well, with the authorities able to wear the hijackers down with endless negotiations on the ground. Normally, special forces would only quickly storm the aircraft if the hijackers commenced systematically murdering the occupants.

The pilots of the last aircraft to be hijacked did receive a warning about 'cockpit incursion,' but unless they were aware that the 'protocols had changed' and what the likely consequences would be, they would have let the hijackers in, for example if they threatened to kill a flight attendant unless they opened the flight deck door.

Nowadays the protocols are different. Cockpit doors are reinforced, and are not opened regardless of any threats made. Passengers are screened more carefully, with flights from abroad required to give details of passengers and the aircraft turned back or required to land at an isolated airfield if anyone suspicious is on board. Passengers and their luggage are checked with much greater attention. Very often an armed air marshal will be on board. How easily the order to shoot down an airliner will be given is still subject to some doubt. However, with passengers and pilots aware that compliance with the hijackers' instructions is unlikely to save them, it will be virtually impossible for hijackers to take over aircraft as easily.

## The Planners

The events of 9/11 did not represent original thinking in that there had already been the scheme to use an airliner as a flying bomb against the Eiffel Tower and the thwarted plan to blow up several US airliners simultaneously over the Pacific. The training of at least one member of each hijacking team to actually fly the aircraft well enough to hit an albeit easy-to-find target was possibly novel as there was no mention of it as far as the author is aware in connection with the Eiffel Tower case just described.

Probably the biggest issue for the planners was how many teams could be prepared before the sheer number risked jeopardizing the entire messianic mission through someone being caught due to bad luck, an error, or loose talk. The choice of early morning flights less subject to delay and with relatively few people on board greatly increased the chances of success. Indeed, it was the terrorists in the delayed aircraft that failed in their mission. As mentioned in the previous narrative, the short timeframe was the key to success or failure.

## Conspiracy Theories

Perhaps partly because the US administration had seemed to benefit from 9/11, some conspiracy theorists have maintained the operation was carried out with the administration's connivance or even at its instigation. They claimed that genuine terrorists would surely have flown straight to their targets in order to reach them before the authorities realized what was happening. To most people the opposite would seem to be true, since the hijackers would surely have needed time to get the feel of the controls of an aircraft they were presumably flying for the first time before attempting delicate maneuvers. In addition, they could hardly start moving around the aircraft or go to the toilets to prepare for the hijacking while the seat belt signs were still illuminated.

Conspiracy theorists also note Flight AA11 passed over the nuclear power stations at Indian Point only 24 miles north of New York City. A strike there could have caused a release of radiation leading to perhaps 20 million deaths, so why didn't the hijackers aim for that much 'better' target?

## A One-off?

With the airport checks, reinforced cockpit doors, new protocols and, in particular, the knowledge by both crew and passenger as to a hijacker's possible intentions, it is unlikely that 9/11 will be repeated. One has to say the perpetrators were very lucky to have pulled it off almost as intended. Had it not been for the delay in taking off allowing passengers on Flight 93 to learn by phone what was happening, the perpetrators might have achieved all their goals.

Whether intended or not, the great loss of life gave the US administration a blank check to use on the international stage, making the instigators initially the losers. That said, it is difficult for people outside the US to realize just how much this event traumatized the country, not only in terms of loss of life but also by seeming to be a lance pointed at its commercial and political heart.

Had the passengers on the fourth airliner heading for Washington DC not gallantly confronted the hijackers, this would have been even truer. For the target of that fourth airliner was probably the Capitol building, the legislature, standing majestically at the far end of the long wide Washington Mall, which would have provided an ideal approach path and made it a far easier target than the White House, or even the twin-towers of the World Trade Center in New York.

## CHAPTER 16

# QUESTIONS & ANSWERS

### Is Blame Dangerous?

The philosophy in the aviation community used to be that indulging in the blame game made finding the underlying causes of an accident more difficult. With the financial stakes nowadays so high, tremendous pressure is being exerted on accident investigators by all the parties—airline, aircraft manufacturer, engine maker, airport, air traffic control (ATC) and not least the pilots and their unions—with each putting their own spin on the event.

As mentioned on page 221, aviation lawyer Healy-Pratt has said to the author that all investigations are somewhat political. One can see his point, especially in cases where the cause is not obvious and where the investigators may have the future of one of their country's key industries in their hands.

In addition, there are some countries, such as Japan, where the cultural impetus to identify someone responsible is so strong that the police are in the front line with the aircraft treated as a crime scene.

In France, there seems to be a conflict between the judicial side and Aviation Safety Board side of investigations, with the one impeding the other. In the US, if the FBI suspect an air crash may have been due to a bomb or terrorist sabotage, such as was initially the case in the TWA-800 disaster, their investigation takes preference, with the danger that they will make the subsequent work by the NTSB more difficult.

Another major problem inherent in today's litigation culture, where lawyers seek punitive damages on the grounds that the manufacturer or the airline failed to rectify or publicize a problem of which they were *aware*, is that organizations may resort to shredding paper trails or nowadays deleting the electronic trail of emails and computer files. They may even resort to holding informal meetings with no notes taken. Admittedly, even with the most comprehensive notes, determining the non-verbal language that actually swayed a meeting is difficult enough anyway.

While in their internal communications, airframers may be tempted to destroy any evidence indicating that they failed to take action regarding a safety issue of which they were aware, in their external documentation, they defensively mention possible problems, however unlikely, to show in court that they have duly warned users. This makes it more difficult for pilots to find what is essential in manuals and the like.

## Air Accident Investigations
## (No Role for Victims' Families)

The primary aim of air accident investigations has been to find the cause or causes so that similar accidents could be avoided in the future, rather than to attach blame, which as mentioned above would increase the likelihood of people being less than frank. Thus the passengers (or their next of kin), having no role in the operation or design of the aircraft, do not come into the equation. They therefore have no standing in the actual inquiry other than as witnesses, assuming they are still able to speak.

The general rules regarding the compensation paid for victims used to be set by the Montreal Convention, which states that an airline can only be taken to court in the country the aircraft took off or landed in. It does have one advantage for the victims in that they can receive a modicum of compensation of up to (100,000 SDR (Special Drawing Rights)), which is roughly equivalent to US$150,000, without having to prove the airline was at fault.

This is much less than they might receive in some courts and especially in the US where they *might* be able to obtain punitive damages. Thus, lawyers will often try to put the blame on a piece of equipment made in the US, which is not so difficult as many items used in airliners are from there. In a recent (2011) debate on the subject at the British Royal Aeronautical Society, a speaker made the point that not only was it ridiculous to apply US levels of compensation to those in less developed countries, but potentially harmful. He cited the case of a woman in a South American country murdered by her family wanting the unbelievable (to them) sum of money she had received in compensation.

Paradoxically, in demanding additional compensation for the anguish passengers suffer in the expectation of death, lawyers are creating a situation whereby damages might well be less if the pilot of a stricken aircraft were to let it crash right away rather than engaging in a long struggle to save it. Even in the US, getting compensation for this aspect of a crash is problematic as it depends on the State in which the case is heard.

In the light of (or shadow of) the Air France AF447 disaster, the European Union is considering a review of the regulations governing air accident investigations and the question of factoring in the families.

## The Insurers

It is usually the insurers who, under pressure from the lawyers for the various parties, determine the settlement. Very often, they will want to reach an early settlement rather than spend a fortune fighting in the courts. Indeed, with just a few large insurers and reinsurers operating in this specialized field, it could happen that the insurers, not forgetting the reinsurers, could find themselves representing more than one party in a dispute and be fighting themselves. In theory, there should be Chinese walls—not so easily achieved in practice.

Perhaps more so than lawyers, insurers have the power to do good. Though an airline seen as a bad risk will pay juicy premiums, repeated claims would squeeze the fruit dry. The insurers therefore will put tremendous pressure (to improve) on airlines involved in a string of accidents by either raising premiums to unsupportable levels or threatening not to insure them at all. While it was said earlier in this book that it was the exasperated Korean President that forced the privately owned Korean Airlines to reinvent itself safety-wise with the help of the US airline Delta, the insurers also played a key role in pushing this through. Now the airline seems to be one of the safest. Admittedly, the airline may not have had the powerful unions and employment laws making such a proposition so difficult elsewhere.

While the airlines and manufacturers have their reputation and eventually their future insurance premiums at stake in the event of a disaster, the insurers have their money at stake. With the intertwining interests and the fact that the money may largely be coming from the same pot regardless of the agreement made in collaboration, or otherwise, with the lawyers, things may not always be what they appear to be, with it unclear who is acting for whom.

## Is Confidential Reporting the Solution?

In view of the difficulty of getting people to talk in the case of actual accidents—they might even be dead—increasing emphasis is being put on getting pilots and maintenance staff to talk about 'close shaves' and mistakes that do not have consequences leading to litigation. In getting pilots to fearlessly report incidents, there is a tricky line to draw, as the pilot may really need firing.

The British introduced the CHIRP (Confidential Human Factors Incident Reporting) system whereby professional pilots and ATC staff may report in confidence incidents arising from human errors (by captains in particular) for analysis by the RAF Institute of Aviation Medicine at Farnborough. Other countries have similar systems.

After World War II, there was a great shortage of civilian airline pilots in the UK and a number of ex-RAF officers were catapulted straight into captains' positions in British Overseas Airways Corporation and British European Airways. With no experience of working as a team member in an airline, some were very domineering while not being the most able. One retired Concorde captain told the author they would not be acceptable these days.

## Human Factor: Most Difficult to Determine

In their excellent book, *A Human Error Approach to Aviation Accident Analysis*,[1] Douglas Wiegmann and Scott Shappell point out that air crash investigators have a panoply of tools allowing them to definitively determine the state or setting of a piece of equipment at the time of an accident. However, other than tests for alcohol or drug levels, they have only poor tools for establishing the mental state of the humans involved.

For instance, investigators can even tell whether an indicator light was on or off at the time of a crash simply by how much the bulb filament stretched on impact. Contrast that with their inability *in the absence of cockpit video recorders* to tell whether the pilot was asleep or more pertinently committing suicide!

## Proactive Analysis—Data Mining

While lessons still have to be learnt from accident investigations, some say[2] the 'the low-hanging fruit' has been picked, and instead of reacting to the very occasional accident, the emphasis should be on a proactive approach based on data mining. This means data not related to tragic events or even to any obvious anomaly should be evaluated.

This data would come from voluntary safety programs, such as the Flight Operations Quality Assurance (FOQA) program, which gathers engineering data during flights that is subsequently used by analysts to 'discover' lurking problems or analyze what happened in an incident without naming names. De-identified summaries are provided to the FAA in return for immunity against prosecution. Another program is the Aviation Safety Action Partnership (ASAP), which provides narrative data regarding crews' actions and even thoughts.

The big problem is finding ways to make the data meaningful and pick out things that are significant from a safety point of view, and in this respect, software is proving increasingly helpful. It is said that in the old days a lot of safety information left an airline when key people retired, but now computers with their sophisticated databases enable details of incidents to be retained and more importantly easily retrieved.

One should not forget that pilots have customarily garnered useful information from de-identified reports of difficulties encountered by pilots of their own airline.

## The Main Academic Accident Models

Air crashes are high up in people's minds on account of the drama, the innate fear of falling, the seemingly utter hopelessness of the situation, and the fact that air travel is an integral part of our daily lives. However, the victims of an air disaster are usually limited to the occupants of the aircraft involved and not so significant in the great scheme of things. As a result, much of the exciting academic work has originated in domains where an accident could have untold consequences, notably in the nuclear power industry or in military standoffs where nuclear missiles might be launched accidentally. The focus in those cases has been placed on determining the likelihood, or hopefully improbability, of such an accident occurring, and whether, for instance, nuclear power plants should be built in the first place.

Yale sociologist Charles Perrow's *Normal Accidents: Living with High-Risk Technologies*,[3] published in book form in 1984, scarily suggests that accidents are inherent in complex systems and that it is sometimes the extra complexity introduced by the incorporation of various safety and backup systems that may well bring about the accidents they are meant to avoid. (The Chernobyl nuclear power station disaster came about in the course of testing safety systems.) In fact, the term *normal accident* is another way of saying *system accident.*

Professor Reason has proposed the so-called 'Swiss Cheese' accident model, which is said to have revolutionized the approach to accident investigations in that it makes investigators look at the deeper organizational causes.

On a simpler level, one can say accidents are rather like chemical compounds, in that they are made up of several different elements. Take any one away and they cease to exist. As pointed out in a study made by Boeing many years ago, accidents are usually associated with several missed opportunities to prevent them. Unfortunately, much of this book is concerned with lessons learnt from the misfortune of others—lessons that would have been unnecessary had there been a more proactive attitude or had corrective action not been deferred for one reason or another.

'Collateral' damage arising from a failure that was not in itself fatal to the aircraft has figured in a number of disasters.

With so many people involved in designing an airliner, how was it that obvious preventive measures—such as having holes (vents) in cabin floors to relieve any air pressure differential if a cargo hold door failed—were not introduced prior to the terrible Paris DC-10 disaster thus caused?

## Effect of the Cultural Framework

By cultural framework, we mean the way people in a society are brought up or are expected to behave, and the way that society functions or sometimes malfunctions.

Some accidents described in this book have been partly attributed to the double-whammy of having pilots that are both ex-military and brought up in Asian cultures, where questioning seniors can only be done in the most oblique way, and for which there is no time in a crisis. (That is not to criticize ex-military pilots per se. Some claim they are better able to handle crises.)

Recently, with so many studying abroad and so many lessons learnt by airlines regarding selection, training and management, generalizations as to how pilots from a given culture react to authority and so on are probably less and less valid.

## What Factors should be Considered Pertinent to a Crash?

Many accidents would not have happened if some extraneous factor had not been associated with them. Lawyers or the courts focus on events where they hope to prove someone is at fault and therefore can be sued or prosecuted, though the accident would equally not have happened if any number of other things had or had not occurred.

A good example is the supersonic Concorde crash in Paris where one of the poorly designed tires fragmented after running (by a rather freak coincidence) over a strip of titanium lying on the runway. The French prosecutors targeted Continental Airlines as the strip had fallen off one of their airliners where a minor repair had been made using titanium when it should have been aluminum.

However, one could equally say the accident would not have happened had the Concorde taken off more safely into the wind, rather than downwind, as the ground speed would have been lower and it probably would not have hit the aluminum strip anyway, or have hit it at a less vulnerable time. In turn, one could say the captain took off downwind to save time and, more importantly fuel, as the aircraft was operating at the extreme limit of its range, something for which Air France was responsible. Should the company have operated it with fewer passengers and less luggage?

Other examples include a case where the pilot was alleged to have been tired because of his wife's insistence that he get up in the night before the flight to look after the baby. We are verging on the ridiculous, but the question of how far we should go in seeking causes remains.

## Marginal Pilots

When many US commercial pilots came from the military, there was the great advantage that the weaker ones had been weeded out—sometimes ruthlessly. In the accidents described in this book as well as others, one can see with hindsight that some of the pilots reacting inappropriately and had already shown themselves to be marginal. In some cases, instructors have said they would *eventually* make good pilots with the right support.

For many reasons, including the money invested in their training, airlines do not dismiss pilots easily. If they fail check rides and so on, they are usually given remedial training. In the piece on the Colgan Air turboprop crash, we mentioned that the NTSB proposed that the FAA set a maximum number of times pilots can retake failed tests and check rides. However, the FAA thought this too arbitrary and impractical.

## Favoritism, Corruption, Backhanders

Airlines can shunt truly incompetent pilots who fail checks to management positions, but be saddled with marginal pilots, who stay at the airline for their whole working life. Like massive supertankers, airlines take time to alter course.

In countries where the role of sponsors and connections is still notorious, it is probably not so much in the area of the selection of pilots as in the area of their promotion and the management of the airline that there lies a major problem. In addition, bribes can influence the purchasing of aircraft and equipment to the detriment of the airline; though this is not always so—in one case, they were beneficial in that they resulted in an airline not buying the DC-10 that was potentially dangerous at the time.

## Engineering Ethics—A Higher Duty?

Moving away from untoward actions taken for naked personal gain, there are the pressures that cogs in an organization are under, forcing them to act for the benefit of the institution perhaps against their engineering judgment.

Do engineers, as professionals like doctors, have a 'higher duty' meaning that they should publicize any instances where they feel passengers' lives are being put at risk by poor design and other shortcomings obvious to them but not the nonprofessional? On the other hand, one has heard of engineers so fastidious that no aircraft made by their company would ever fly if they had their way!

There are two detailed books covering such cases, *THE DC-10 CASE—A Study in Applied Ethics, Technology, and Society* by John Fielder and Douglas Birsch[4] and *The Challenger Launch Decision—Risky Technology, Culture, and Deviance at NASA* by sociologist Diane Vaughan.[5] The Challenger launch decision at one time was seen as a simple case of a fatal decision being made *with a key engineer not being listened to and a key manager being told to take off his engineer's hat and put on his management hat.* In her extremely detailed book, Diane Vaughn suggests the situation was more complicated than appeared, and the cause was the acceptance of *deviations* over a long period. It is impossible to do justice to the two books here in a paragraph or two. They both would make fascinating reading for administrators and managers.

## Whistleblowers

Whistleblowers have saved lives, sometimes by highlighting problems after the event, but rarely are they thanked or protected properly. Shunned by colleagues and management, they often end up in unfortunate circumstances. The lot of those in the FBI's 'witness protection programs' is usually a better one. For example, the engineer (working at NASA contractor Thiokol) mentioned above in the context of the *Challenger*

*Launch Decision* fell out with his colleagues and his life thereafter could hardly be said to have been a happy one.

Besides being a thankless task, successful whistle blowing may require Machiavellian skills and nerve not typical of the 'modest-honest-Joe' engineer.

Especially, if time is short, he or she may have to involve legislators or even a president or prime minister—not an easy feat. Even then, the whistleblower's efforts may come to naught. Again, the potential whistleblower has to weigh up whether on gaining access, he or she can convince those with influence of the exactitude of his or her claim.

## A 'Just' Culture—the Nimrod Report
## (Applicable to all Organizations)

The 500+ page Haddon-Cave *Nimrod Report* into the 2006 conflagration during midair refueling over Afghanistan of the Royal Air Force Nimrod 'spy plane' (unbelievably based on the first jetliner, the Comet) looks at safety from the organizational point of view.

Recommended reading for administrators and others responsible for safety, it makes many points including the following, and even those are headings with their own sub-points and detailed clarifications:

1. Danger of assumptions

2. Danger of not defining and identifying duty holders who are accountable and who:

   a. Know who they are and what their roles and responsibilities are (and everyone else does too)

   b. Who have the help and resources to carry out their duties

   c. Who are accountable for their actions and omissions

3. Avoid change for change's sake as this distracts people

4. Safety is really all about management and leadership

5. Avoid the *comfort blankets* of complexity, compliance and consensus

6. Beware of *plain sailing*—where things seem ok superficially but underneath there are myriad problems, errors, and deviations that must be reported as they are often the precursor to a major disaster

7. It is important to understand accident theory such as expounded by James Reason, Charles Perrow, Scott Sagan, Diane Vaughan, and Karl Weick

8. Outsourcing in particular must be carefully managed with clearly defined responsibilities, and care taken to see the core organization is not laid bare with insufficient technical talent to monitor and question

9. Principles are sacred; not rules. The four key ones being:

   a. Leadership from the top

   b. Independence

   c. People (not paper)

   d. Simplicity

10. Culture (the four cultures mentioned in work done by NASA)

   a. A Reporting Culture (climate where people readily report problems, errors, and near misses)

   b. A Just Culture where reporting safety-related information is encouraged and where everyone is aware of what is acceptable and unacceptable behavior

   c. A Flexible Culture that can adapt to changing circumstances while maintaining its focus on safety

   d. A Learning Culture where the right conclusions are drawn from safety information with the corollary that there must be the will to implement major safety reform

   Haddon-Cave would add a fifth culture that is a Questioning Culture.

In commenting on his report, Haddon-Cave pointed out that a *Just Culture* is one that strikes a sensible balance between a *blame culture* and a *blame-free culture*. To achieve this, a good degree of *trust* must prevail in the organization.

Elsewhere in this book, we have said that airlines are like supertankers in that changing their course is no easy matter—for, attitudes and proficiencies of staff depend on hiring practices or malpractices prevalent years before. This applies not least to the military, and one has to bear in mind that the qualities that enable someone to rise in an organization may not be those needed to ensure safety.

Of particular interest were Haddon-Cave's comments regarding Item 2 (the importance of identifying duty holders who are accountable). He noted that many who rise to a position of responsibility (i.e. Duty holder)—whether in an airline, in an air force, or even in local government—cleverly obfuscate by delegating so they themselves can never be held responsible.

## Regulatory Framework

Aviation is perhaps the most regulated activity in the world and this is especially true in the USA. This has brought great benefits as regards safety. Nothing is made, or happens, without approval—at least in theory.

In the USA, the two key bodies concerned with aviation matters are:

### (1) The Federal Aviation Administration (FAA), responsible for supervising and regulating

It represents not only the public interest but also that of the industry, in other words the airlines and the manufacturers. Some maintain this conflict of interest on the part of the FAA was a major factor in the DC-10 disasters.

Many other countries have a free ride on the back of the FAA, though as a major aircraft manufacturing country, the US gets its money back in other ways, notably via the aircraft certified. Europe now has the European Aviation Safety Agency (EASA) with a role similar to that of the FAA.

### (2) The National Transportation Safety Board  (NTSB), responsible for investigating accidents

The NTSB can only make recommendations; their execution depends on the FAA .

## Cost Benefit/Your Life = $2,700,000?

Where the FAA has to decide whether to make a given safety improvement mandatory, the question of cost-benefit comes to the fore. Various formulae are used to calculate the value of a life, not only in terms of lost earnings power but also in terms of the loss to society and family. One figure quoted for the US is US$2.7 million. The FAA has to look at the number of lives a given measure is likely to save, the cost of incorporating it in all the aircraft and so on, and so on.

## Comparing Risk of Flying and Driving (Statistics)

Crude statistical comparisons showing flying to be much safer than driving may often exaggerate the relative safety of the former. The reason is that when traveling by motor vehicle, the risk may differ greatly[6] depending on the ability, intelligence, experience, age, temperament and not least substance-intake-status of the driver. On the other hand, pilots are a carefully selected and evenly capable group, with little chance that pilots would *both* be inebriated.

Therefore, *if* as mentioned on a Boeing 'advice for travelers' website,[7] the average risk makes flying twenty times safer than driving, then for passengers in the safest cars with the safest drivers (possibly readers of this book!), flying may only be say 5 or 10 times safer. That is to say, safer than safe.

For others, the risk of driving might well be 40, 50, 100, or even 3,000 times greater than the risk of flying, assuming the individual in question does not spoil the argument by getting drunk at airport and fall to his or her death on boarding the aircraft or on disembarking.

## Do Accident Rates for an Aircraft Depend on Customers? (Statistics)

Some weeks after the mysterious crash of an Airbus 330 flying from Rio de Janeiro to Paris, a British newspaper had the headline *Another Airbus crashes!*

This gave the impression Airbuses were inherently unsafe. In fact, it referred to an accident involving an old aircraft and different model that a couple of years previously had been found to be so faulty that it was not allowed to fly in European airspace. In addition, the accident the headline referred to occurred in Africa, where safety standards are known to be generally lower than elsewhere.

In discussing Qantas' enviable statistical safety record we have pointed out that the type of route flown surely affects accident rates and that an airline flying long legs to good airports is likely to have fewer accidents.

Interestingly, no one seems to have applied this logic to how the nature of a maker's customers can affect the number of crashes their aircraft suffer. It is possible that Airbus sells more aircraft than Boeing to airlines in countries with poor facilities and poor administrative oversight and that this is reflected in the accident statistics. Some of the early Airbus crashes were attributed to the fact that the crews, from less advanced countries, were not up to handling such sophisticated aircraft.

However, as pointed out recently by *Flight International*, one should be careful about making about generalizing according to country or continent as such arguments can work both ways—Air France's record is not perfect either. It is just mentioned here as an avenue worth exploring.

## Unforeseen Consequences of Good Intentions

On the face of it, it would seem sensible to endorse proposals to oblige parents intending to fly with a baby to purchase a seat in addition to their own so their offspring can sit in a properly affixed and obviously safer baby seat.

While new parents would not generally be at the extreme end of the risk spectrum (learner-drivers, substance-takers and daredevils), they might well be at the 40 times mark since they would probably be young and inexperienced drivers and not able to afford the safest cars. Thus, any well-meaning legislation that might make parents drive rather than fly could expose them and their baby to far greater risk. A further statistical argument against doing so is that in the very few air crashes that do occur, the extra baby seat would not always be the panacea it is purported to be.

An example in another area where good intentions may have similar undesired results is the railways, where imposing crippling safety regulations on minor branch lines has resulted in their closure, thereby forcing the passengers onto the roads where many more are killed.

## Checklists[8] and Flight Manuals

At a time when movies were portraying airline pilots as heroes and consummate lovers, a shrewd kindergarten headmistress pointed out to the author that much of what they were doing was simplicity in the extreme.

'Imagine them,' she said, 'just about to go to bed, in slippers and without their natty uniforms, running through the following checklist with their wives:

> Central Heating: *Off;* Cat: *Back In;* Front Door: *Double-Locked;* Kitchen Door: *Locked and Bolted.'*

Leaving subsequent checklists to the imagination, the headmistress did have a valid point, in that many of a pilot's tasks are not mentally demanding.

However, in *Commercial Aviation Safety*,[9] Alexander Wells says:

> *It is ironic that with all of the sophisticated and costly devices on board an aircraft and those supporting the aircraft through the air traffic control system (ATC), the most important guardian of the safety of the plane and its occupants is a single piece of paper, the checklist.*

> *It is the linchpin of aviation operations, not only for pilots in the cockpit, but also for those who are making and maintaining the aircraft.*

Checklists are great if gone through properly as is usually the case for pilots, but in manufacturing and maintenance, tasks jobs may be signed off cursorily. An instance of this is the crash of the DC-10 outside Paris, where McDonnell Douglas, or its subcontractor, signed off on modifications to the door locking mechanism that had not been done, and in consequence had to pay a considerable sum in damages. However, no one could determine what really happened as the employees concerned maintained they could not remember and would say nothing that might incriminate them.

While not a primary guardian of safety, the flight manual for a given aircraft can also be a life-safer in the case of something unusual happening, as well as preventing the pilots trying to do something inadvisable. Much of the information is based on flight tests prior to the aircraft entering service, with modifications as more lessons are learned. It tells the pilots what to do in every conceivable situation with emphasis on what to do in situations where the instruments show something out of the ordinary. The layout of the manual is important, as pilots have to thumb through it in an emergency. There have been emergencies where the pilots have not been able to find the relevant section because the key word they were looking for had been omitted from the index or their problem was dealt with under an unexpected heading.

## Crew Resource Management (CRM)

Some readers may share the author's view that a significant number of the tragedies described might have been avoided had the 'junior person'—not meant in a derogatory sense—either on the flight deck or back in the organization been listened to, or rather had they had enough persona to convince others of their views. Two notable instances would be:

1. KLM Flight Engineer Schreuder using the words, 'Did he not clear the runway then?' just before the worst-ever multi-aircraft disaster at Tenerife.

2. First Officer Molin (said to have fatally overused the rudder when caught up in wake turbulence from a Japan Airlines 747 ahead) asking his captain before takeoff, 'Are you happy with that distance?' rather than making it clear he thought they should wait to allow more distance between the two aircraft.

Parallels have been drawn with the medical profession, in that pilots or doctors work best as a team with every individual able to contribute fearlessly, and not as a group of yes-men under a Godlike airline captain or domineering medical consultant. However, one needs to be a little careful in drawing too close a parallel between medicine and aviation, as aircrew are generally an evenly competent group, whereas in medicine there is an enormous gulf between the ability of the best and worst doctors.

The airlines themselves have been very conscious of the need for teamwork with proper delegation of duties, and particularly so since the formal introduction of Cockpit (now Crew) Resource Management (CRM) by United Airlines following the fuel depletion disaster at Portland in 1978.

## NTSB Wish List (Most Wanted!)

Somewhat along the lines of the 'Most Wanted' felons list, the US National Transport Safety Board has a wish list of the things they think would most contribute to airline safety.

Here are perhaps the three most notable items on the list:

1. Stop runway incursions/ground collisions of aircraft:

   a. By giving warnings of probable collisions or incursions directly to flight crews in the cockpit.

2. Improve audio and data recorders and require video recorders:

   a. By requiring that cockpit voice recorders (CVRs) retain at least two hours of audio.

b. By requiring back-up power sources so cockpit voice recorders collect an extra 10 minutes of data when an aircraft's main power fails.

c. By inspecting and maintaining data recorders yearly to make sure they operate properly.

d. By installing video recorders in cockpits to give investigators more information to solve complex accidents.

3. Reduce accidents and incidents caused by human fatigue:

a. By setting working hour limits for flight crews and aviation mechanics based on fatigue research, circadian rhythms, and sleep and rest requirements.

As explained, the NTSB can only make recommendations, and it is up to the FAA to put them into effect.

Video cameras on the flight deck monitoring the pilots' information displays as well as the pilots' actions would increase the likelihood of accident inquiries arriving at the correct conclusions. Pilots have long resisted this—but one has only to remember their stance on the installation of CVRs that have helped resolve the causes of so many fatal crashes.

Video cameras are getting so small (light) and efficient, not to say cheap, that they could be used to monitor control surfaces, such as the rudder, with the advantage of giving a continuous 'picture' unlike data recorders, which only sample the angle at intervals.

Video cameras could be used to gather information about the way pilots study their instruments—it is said that people tend to look up to the right when analyzing a complex problem. Cameras could also be used to warn pilots if both fall asleep!

## Safest Seat

Some readers of the first galleys of this book insisted on the inclusion of conclusions regarding the safest seat.

As the nature of accidents and their incidence has changed so much over the 50 or so years covered, one cannot extrapolate. In the early years, controlled flight into terrain (CFIT) accidents were frequent, but with better navigation tools, even combining GPS with a database showing the height of the terrain ahead, these accidents—in which sitting in the tail section often offered the best chance of survival—are few and far between.

Now, in general, sitting as near as possible to an exit (at least within five or six rows) is the best choice, as is an aisle seat, which besides allowing you to walk around and avoid deep vein thrombosis, lessens the chance of you being hemmed in. Having cotton clothes covering arms and legs, and avoiding nylon panties[10] that are liable to melt and produce severe burns as you go down the emergency chute is advisable. Sensible shoes (high heels not only make getting around more difficult but also could tear the chute (page 165)) are also a good idea.

Analysis of various air disasters has shown that survival can greatly depend on one's sheer determination to survive. Even a few seconds' hesitation can be fatal, and in this regard counting the rows to the exit can gain valuable time in exiting if the aircraft has filled with smoke.

## More and More Accidents Survivable (Airbags)

Improvements in equipment and computerization are making devastating mid-air collisions and unforgiving controlled flight into terrain accidents increasingly rare, and hence accidents such as runway overruns now figure relatively more often. Fortunately, in many such incidents the percentage of survivors is getting higher and higher, with it often being 100%. This is partly due to better equipment and the attention paid to the means of evacuation and the design of seats, though passengers bent on bringing their hand baggage with them remains a major problem.

The FAA would like future aircraft seats to be able to withstand much greater forces than the norms applied today, which were set many years ago when there were much fewer obese people, but is meeting resistance from the airlines because strengthening cabin floors would incur weight penalties. Greater space between the passenger and the seat in front would give a safer environment, but would mean fewer passengers could be carried. Instead, it seems the problem is being partly resolved by introducing airbags on the latest aircraft. (Some airlines are already using these in First and Business Class, not because those passengers are more valuable, but because the spacious layout of the seats means there are more situations where the passenger could bang against something.)

Unlike the airbags used in automobiles that com e out towards the passenger, airline airbags are usually incorporated in the seatbelt and go outwards from the passenger. This lessens the possibility of injury, and means they are suitable for anyone other than babies and tots.

## Miracle Landings

Strictly speaking, one should define a miracle landing as one where the pilots land the aircraft safely, or with some survivors, *against all odds*. In practice, the *apparent* precariousness of the situation and not the true difficulty of resolving it means others are viewed as miracle landings as well. Some true miracles are not mentioned at all. These would include cases where great feats of airmanship were required to bring an aircraft down in the presence of gusting crosswinds or windshear, with the whole incident perhaps lasting no more than a few seconds and the passengers being none the wiser.

There have been scary TV programs showing emergency landings being made with, for example, no landing gear down or with the gear only down on one side. These are very dramatic partly because cameramen had time to get ready while the aircraft was burning up fuel to make the landing safer. However, they were not against all odds as such landings are not so rare and mostly depend on the pilot touching down precisely and keeping the wings level as long as possible lest a wing or engine snag the ground causing the aircraft to spin around and perhaps break up. That is not to say the incidents were not very scary, there always being the chance that things could go horribly wrong.

Though making comparisons is rather invidious, the following order might be appropriate as regards the most miraculous and well known:

1. Captain Haynes' landing (page 125), thanks in very large measure to the help of deadheading Captain Dennis Fitch at the throttles, of the uncontrollable DC-10 at Sioux City using engine power alone was an exceptional feat, that despite many attempts could not be achieved on the simulator.

2. Captain Piché's (page 15) 80-mile glide culminating in an all-or-nothing touchdown at a US military base on a mid-Atlantic island was a very great achievement. However, Piché blotted his copybook by transferring fuel to feed an engine whose fuel feed line was damaged, thus contributing to the critical situation in the first place.

3. Captain Bob Pearson's (page 35) 'Gimli Glider' feat in Canada where his experience gained on gliders enabled him to lose speed and height to touchdown safely on a small landing strip after running out of fuel. However, he should perhaps have picked up on the fuel calculation error that partly led to the fuel running out.

4. Captain Leul Abate's (page 13) ditching of his Ethiopian 767 off a beach in the Comoros after it had run out of fuel as he fought off hijackers with one hand . Furthermore, lack of electrical power for the computers made the aircraft difficult to handle. Incidentally, he had been hijacked twice before.

5. Captain Sullenberger's (page 19) 'perfect' ditching of his Airbus in New York's Hudson River after its engines ingested Canadian geese just after takeoff. It was a great achievement based on good judgment in deciding to ditch in the river and not least on switching on the Auxiliary Power Unit (APU) to provide electricity for the aircraft's computers thus enabling him to fly the aircraft optimally. However, it was not against all odds in that such an ideal—water temperature apart—ditching site was at hand.

6. Captain Moody's (page 9) successful landing of his Boeing 747 after all four engines had flamed out (stopped) on entering a cloud of volcanic ash most certainly seemed a miracle to the passengers. It must have been terrifying for all concerned, and is particularly notable for the theatrical style with which the captain reassured the passengers, and no doubt his colleagues as well.

We have not included:

1. The skilful landing of the virtually uncontrollable DHL Airbus freighter (page 131) after being struck by a shoulder-launched missile at Baghdad, as it did not have the same degree of drama in terms of the number of passengers and publicity.

2. Cases where captains brought their stricken aircraft down safely with various systems, such as hydraulics, not working.

3. Cases where there were structural problems, such the landing of the Aloha 737 (page 231) with the cabin roof missing and the aircraft held together merely by the rails along the cabin floor used for attaching the seats.

As seen in the case of the BA 777 fuel icing incident (page 52) where the engines failed to spool up on late final approach to London's Heathrow airport, a few yards can make the difference between a miracle landing and a calamity, no matter how capable the pilots. Had the BA 777 been a little further back when power was required and not forthcoming, the captain's savvy adjustment of the flap setting would not have sufficed to enable it to make it over the over the highway and onto the grass beyond airport perimeter fence.

[Though we have only cited the captains' names in our main numbered list, one should not forget the vital roles played by others on the flight deck in those events.]

### 'Hero' and 'Fighting to Save the Aircraft'

We have to accept the media's tendency (for want of a better word) to label pilots heroes when the qualities that save a situation are usually competence and clear thinking. Granted some pilots may have to force themselves to stay calm and collected as Captain Sullenberger frankly admitted in an interview following the ditching of his aircraft in the Hudson River.

Rather than quibble over the use of the word hero, one should have more qualms about the phrase 'the pilot was fighting desperately to save the aircraft,' often used immediately after a crash when the press has little hard information and where many if not all the occupants have died. On occasion, it has later transpired those desperate actions were what that caused the crash.

Where crew—and not least cabin crew—have demonstrated great and often unsung classic heroism has often been after incidents when staying behind at great risk to themselves to help others escape from burning smoke-filled aircraft.

## Automation Blunts Pilots' Flying Skills

Flying had seemed to be getting safer and safer, with not so long ago as many as four years going by without a major accident involving a US carrier, and other major Western carriers suffering hardly any either. However, more recently there has been a series of incidents and accidents attributed to the fact that with computers able to fly aircraft more perfectly than humans, and hence more reliance being placed on them, many pilots are forgetting the basic flying skills, and are unprepared for certain rare situations where the computer cannot help.

Since the Air France 447 and Colgan Air 3407 disasters, the airlines and the regulatory authorities have made particular efforts to rectify this by improving training and manuals.

## Deceptive Cessation of Warnings (False Positive)

As mentioned, Professor Ladkin said the Kegworth air disaster where the pilots shut down the good engine by mistake was the only case he knew then of a false positive figured in a disaster. (See page 144.)

However, there have been notable cases where the cessation of warnings has not meant they no longer applied. Most notable are:

1. The AF447 crash, where the stall warnings stopped sounding when the airspeed fell to what the computer programming considered to be an absurd value, perhaps resulting in the captain not realizing what was happening when he returned to the flight deck. This was programmed to prevent them sounding when on the ground, for example.

2. The cessation of the fire and smoke alert when a Saudia L1011 was returning to Riyadh with an onboard fire, perhaps leading the captain to believe the situation was less serious than it was. In fact, the alarms stopped because the fire was so intense it had burnt through the sensors!

## Fatigue and Flight Time Limitations (FTL)

Fatigue, important to unions, is currently a topic of great concern. Many airlines think it better to allow one of the pilots to have a nap, but for no longer than for 40 minutes, since longer results in a deep sleep from which it takes much longer to recover fully. In January 2011, an Air Canada first officer on a flight from Toronto to Zurich slept for 75 minutes, and on waking up mistook the planet Venus for an oncoming aircraft and pushed the aircraft into dive to avert it. As a result, a few passengers without seatbelts attached and a flight attendant in a toilet received minor injuries.

On the other hand, having both pilots falling asleep on autopilot, as is sometimes the case, is far less serious than the driver of a motor vehicle falling asleep. The greatest danger is lack of sleep impairing cognitive ability and reasoning when needed—sometimes in an emergency, or the lead up to an emergency, as was perhaps the case in the Colgan Air crash (see page 185).

### Pilots' Unions Contribution to Safety—Cockpit Video Recorders

In the UK pilots' unions once opposed the introduction of cockpit voice recorders (CVRs), even though they had been made mandatory in Australia, and then in the US. It was only after the 1970 Trident crash near London's Heathrow Airport (see page 167) where the captain had a heart attack and investigators could not work out who did what, that the British Government faced down the unions and mandated their use.

Today, cockpit video (image) recorders are high on the NTSB wish list. Referring to the 2009 Air France AF447 crash into the South Atlantic, one aviation commentator has said it is crazy that a humble pizza restaurant kitchen can have them, but not a sophisticated airliner cockpit, where they would be of much greater value. Will the unions finally accept them? A number of individual pilots seem to have no objection, saying they would not make much difference since they are already closely monitored.

The main French pilots' union has objected to the publication of the CVR recordings in the case of the AF447 crash, saying it infringes the pilots' privacy. In fact, it was the reason the BEA (the French investigators) gave for initially omitting the part where the pilots finally said something showing they realized they were going to crash. It was only published after having been leaked, leading to accusations from the families of the victims that there had been a cover up. What else were they hiding?

That aside, pilots' unions can contribute greatly to safety, which of course is in their members' interest. BALPA (the main UK pilots' union), for example, is now tackling the issue in a highly professional manner, with a dedicated team working with true experts, academic and otherwise.[11] They point out that the team will benefit from the vast experience of their members over the years, while being uniquely placed to get them to accept their conclusions.

### 'Accidentology'

The French have the excellent word *accidentology* (Accidentologie) for the study of accidents. Unfortunately, it does not sound right in English, though people could no doubt quickly get used to it.

We need such a portmanteau word to do justice to this fascinating subject, demanding expertise in domains ranging from psychology and sociology on the one hand to mathematics and engineering on the other. In fact, psychologists and sociologists have done much of the outstanding academic work on accidents with many famous ones having started out working on safety in the field of nuclear energy where the effects of accidents could be truly horrendous for the many, rather than devastating for the few as in most air accidents.

As made clear by one of their number, psychology professor James Reason, the *underlying* causes of accidents are rarely as simple as they first appear.

[1] Wiegmann, D. A. & Shappell, S. A. *A Human Error Approach to Aviation Accident Analysis*, Ashgate Publishing. UK (September 2003).

[2] Marion Blakey, FAA. See article by John Croft, *Flight International*, 9–15 January 2007, pp 26–28.

[3] Charles Perrow, *Normal Accidents: Living with High-Risk Technologies*, New York: Basic Books, 1984. Paperback reprint, Princeton, N.J.: Princeton University Press, 1999, ISBN 0-691-00412-9

[4] John H. Fielder & Douglas Birsch, *The DC-10 Case—A Study in Applied Ethics, Technology, and Society* (State University of New York Press), July 1992.

[5] Diane Vaughan, *Challenger Launch Decision—Risky Technology, Culture, and Deviance at NASA*, University of Chicago Press, April 1997.

[6] Leonard Evans, Michael C. Frick and Richard C. Schwing, *Is It Safer to Fly or Drive?*, Risk Analysis 10(2):239-246, 1990, quoted by Professor Peter B. Ladkin in '*To Drive or To Fly - Is That Really The Question?*' Peter B. Ladkin 24 July 1997.

[7] With accidents for the major airlines becoming such a rarity, the figure of 20 times *safer* than driving may be very much on the low side.

[8] Interestingly, only recently, a survey has shown that use of checklists and aviation safety techniques, often scoffed at by surgeons, considerably lessens the incidence of mistakes in the operating theater.

[9] Alexander T. Wells, *Commercial Aviation Safety* (McGraw-Hill), 2004. Comprehensive book covering the nuts and bolts of aviation safety.

[10] The danger of nylon panties melting due to friction with the escape chute and causing burns was mentioned by the late Professor Helen Muir to bring some levity to a TV chat show discussing a new book on aircraft safety.
Helen Muir made a great contribution in the area of aviation safety and notably the evacuation of aircraft. She was Director of the Cranfield Institute for Safety, Risk and Reliability, as well as being the Head of the Department of Human Factors and Professor of Aerospace Psychology at the UK's Cranfield University.

[11] Team led by Dr. Robert Hunter. The *BALPA Safety Plan* is 'An on-going assessment of the latent risks, together with BALPA's plans to mitigate them. It covers sensitive areas such as pilot error (actual and apparent), regulatory issues, commercial forces, training, security, pilot cognition and other human factors issues.'

# INDEX

Made in the USA
Lexington, KY
25 October 2012